■ The Wisconsin State Constitution

The Oxford Commentaries on the State Constitutions of the United States
Lawrence Friedman, Series Editor

Lawrence Friedman, Professor of Law at New England Law | Boston, serves as General Editor for this series, which in its entirety will cover the constitutions of each of the fifty states and Puerto Rico. Each volume of *The Oxford Commentaries on the State Constitutions of the United States* contains a historical overview of the state's constitutional development, plus a section-by-section analysis of the state's current constitution. In addition, each volume contains the text of the state's constitution, a bibliographic essay, a table of cases, and an index. This series provides essential reference tools for academics and students investigating state constitutional development and constitutional law, as well as lawyers and judges seeking a guide to understanding the particular provisions of a state's constitution.

The Wisconsin State Constitution

Second Edition

Jack Stark and
Steve Miller

Foreword by Shirley S. Abrahamson

THE OXFORD COMMENTARIES ON THE STATE
CONSTITUTIONS OF THE UNITED STATES
Lawrence Friedman, Series Editor

OXFORD
UNIVERSITY PRESS

OXFORD
UNIVERSITY PRESS

Oxford University Press is a department of the University of Oxford. It furthers the University's objective of excellence in research, scholarship, and education by publishing worldwide. Oxford is a registered trademark of Oxford University Press in the UK and certain other countries.

Published in the United States of America by Oxford University Press
198 Madison Avenue, New York, NY 10016, United States of America.

Library of Congress Cataloging-in-Publication Data

Names: Stark, Jack, 1939– author. | Miller, Steve (Stephen R.), 1950– author. | Abrahamson, Shirley Schlanger, 1933–, writer of foreword. | Wisconsin. Constitution.
Title: The Wisconsin state constitution / Jack Stark and Steve Miller; foreword by Shirley S. Abrahamson; Lawrence Friedman, series editor.
Description: Second edition. | New York, New York : Oxford University Press, Inc., 2019. | Series: The Oxford commentaries on the state constitutions of the United States | Includes bibliographical references and index.
Identifiers: LCCN 2019017355 | ISBN 9780190927714 (hardback)
Subjects: LCSH: Constitutions—Wisconsin. | Constitutional law—Wisconsin. | Constitutional history—Wisconsin. | BISAC: LAW / Constitutional. | LAW / Legal History. | LAW / Administrative Law & Regulatory Practice.
Classification: LCC KFW2801 1848.A6 S728 2019 | DDC 342.77502—dc23
LC record available at https://lccn.loc.gov/2019017355

Printed by Bridgeport National Bindery, Inc., United States of America

Note to Readers

This publication is designed to provide accurate and authoritative information in regard to the subject matter covered. It is based upon sources believed to be accurate and reliable and is intended to be current as of the time it was written. It is sold with the understanding that the publisher is not engaged in rendering legal, accounting, or other professional services. If legal advice or other expert assistance is required, the services of a competent professional person should be sought. Also, to confirm that the information has not been affected or changed by recent developments, traditional legal research techniques should be used, including checking primary sources where appropriate.

(Based on the Declaration of Principles jointly adopted by a Committee of the American Bar Association and a Committee of Publishers and Associations.)

You may order this or any other Oxford University Press publication
by visiting the Oxford University Press website at www.oup.com.

For Faye and Jeremy
—*Jack Stark*

For Gay
—*Steve Miller*

"Much confusion in public affairs would be prevented by more study of the fundamental law and a better appreciation of what it means and of [the] importance of fidelity thereto. It is as necessary now, if not more so, to the general welfare, both in respect to the people of the present and those who will come after us, as it ever was."
—*Justice Roujet Marshall, State ex rel. Owen v. Donald, 1915*

■ CONTENTS

Article VII: Judiciary

It is difficult today to escape the focus in American political discourse on the U.S. Constitution and the Supreme Court's interpretations of it. But it is worth remembering that the U.S. Constitution did not emerge fully formed from the head of James Madison in 1787. Before the United States, there were the states— and state constitutions. As noted by G. Alan Tarr, the first Series Editor of *The Oxford Commentaries on the State Constitutions of the United States,* in his Series Foreword, the original state constitutions reflected a variety of approaches to democratic self-rule, experiments in governance that inspired audiences both across the Atlantic and closer to home.

Indeed, despite the misgivings about the state of the states entertained by some of the delegates gathered at the Constitutional Convention, they found in the existing state constitutions much to admire, from the Virginia Constitution's Declaration of Rights to the bicameral legislative scheme embraced by John Adams's Massachusetts Constitution of 1780. Which is not to slight the audacity of the U.S. Constitution, with its grant of limited powers of national scope to the federal government and preservation of state rule in virtually all other aspects of the lives of citizens. The Framers, as Supreme Court Justice Anthony Kennedy observed in *U.S. Term Limits v. Thornton* (1995), had in effect "split the atom of sovereignty."

And the U.S. Constitution, as interpreted by Chief Justice John Marshall's Supreme Court, provided the young republic the national governmental structure it needed to thrive. The outcome of the Civil War validated the preeminence of the federal government in our constitutional scheme, and the subsequent ratification of the Fourteenth Amendment anticipated the U.S. Constitution's eclipse of its state counterparts. For the Fourteenth Amendment's commitments to due process and equal protection in the face of state action became, in the middle decades of the twentieth century, the vessels by which the judiciary federalized the protection of individual rights and liberties as against the states.

The Supreme Court's extension of the Fourteenth Amendment's reach followed a period of change in the nature of state constitutions themselves, as popular movements succeeded in revising state charters to allow for varying opportunities for direct democratic lawmaking. One result was an increase in state constitutional provisions that resembled more closely legislative enactments than the core, foundational principles typically associated with constitutions. And so, as the decades passed, the utility of state constitutions as constitutions increasingly suffered by comparison to the U.S. Constitution—if not in terms of authority, for these documents still controlled the organization of state governments and served as the primary means by which those governments regulated their citizens, at least in terms of respect.

Just as changes to the federal judiciary's approach to the Fourteenth Amendment ushered in a new era of restrictions on the police power of states, with *Brown v. Board of Education* (1954) perhaps the most famous example, lawyerly and judicial interest in state constitutions was awakened when, in the 1970s, the U.S. Supreme Court signaled the beginning of its retreat from federal rights enforcement, a development playing out to this day. From this retreat was born the phenomenon called the "new judicial federalism," as individual rights advocates began to look to the protections contained in state constitutions as the basis for challenging state action. In state constitutions, moreover, lay what Alan Tarr referred to as "an unsuspected richness"—not just provisions that parallel those in the Bill of Rights, but constitutional guarantees regarding such matters as privacy and equality that have no federal counterpart. And rather than the exclusively negative orientation of federal constitutional protections, which forbid state action exceeding certain limits, state constitutions contain positive protections which appear to demand such action in respect to a range of interests, from the adequacy of educational standards to environmental protection.

And so, notwithstanding the predominance of the U.S. Constitution in American public discourse, state constitutions continue to play a vital and important role in the daily lives of citizens. The federal judicial retreat from rights-enforcement through the Fourteenth Amendment has led not just to the revitalization of state constitutional individual rights protections, but to fewer federal constitutional restraints on the ability of state governments to be the laboratories of American democracy to which Supreme Court Justice Louis Brandeis famously referred in *New State Ice Co. v. Liebmann* (1932). And the content of state constitutions continues to be a source of energetic debate among citizens, whether through efforts to codify in the state's charter a symbolic resistance to federal encroachment or to constitutionalize, through the initiative process, policy positions that legislatures would otherwise reject.

Operating in the shadow cast by the U.S. Constitution, state constitutions and the state court decisions interpreting them remain critical sources of governmental authority and restraint. It has been the goal of *The Oxford Commentaries on the State Constitutions of the United States* to illuminate these constitutions for a wide audience—to explain the unique history of each state constitution and explore, in an accessible way, what the various provisions of the American state constitutions in their great variety mean and how they have been interpreted and applied over time. Each book in the series—many now in their second or third editions—provides, in addition to a history of and commentaries on the provisions of each state's constitution, a bibliography of materials related to the constitution as well as a table of notable cases and a topical index. The series aims, in short, to present to lawyers, scholars, and students the most relevant and comprehensive guides to all the other United States constitutions.

Lawrence Friedman
Series Editor

■ FOREWORD

When the first edition of this book was published, Wisconsin was preparing to celebrate the 150th anniversary of its statehood in 1998. In 2018, we are now 170 years from the adoption of the Wisconsin constitution and the state's admission to the union in 1848.

The years since the first edition was published have seen many changes to the Wisconsin constitution. The people of the state have voted to amend the constitution over a dozen times since 1998 to address subjects as varied as gambling, guns, marriage, and transportation, to name but a few.

Like the first edition, this book is a valuable resource for those who seek the basic documents, cases, and historical material on Wisconsin state constitutional law. Steve Miller has maintained the original volume's comprehensiveness, convenience, and accessibility while adding discussion and analysis of the significant developments of the past twenty-two years.

As Part One's discussion of history notes, the concept of "new judicial federalism" emerged in the 1980s—the idea that state courts should look to their own state constitutions to protect individual liberties, in addition to the U.S. Constitution. At the time the first edition was published, the idea was largely academic. In the years that followed, however, many states began to look to their own constitutions for greater protections than those afforded by the U.S. Supreme Court's interpretations of the federal Constitution. Miller details the Wisconsin Supreme Court's embrace of the Wisconsin constitution during the first decade of the twenty-first century, as well as its subsequent return to interpreting it primarily in lockstep with the U.S. Constitution.

Many other state supreme courts have continued to place their own constitutions at the forefront of their decision-making. Witness, for example, the Pennsylvania Supreme Court's reliance on the Free and Equal Elections Clause of the Pennsylvania constitution in striking down the state legislature's partisan formation of legislative districts, commonly known as gerrymandering.[1] State legislative districting, which may raise both state and federal constitutional issues, has become a hot-button subject in recent years, as evidenced by cases pending in both federal and state courts. In the coming decades, we can expect to see this and other new and old state constitutional questions presented to the federal and state courts. State constitutional law will grow and take on increasing importance.

---

[1] *League of Women Voters v. Commonwealth*, No. 159MM2017, slip op. at 2 (Feb. 7, 2018).

I conclude, as I did in the foreword to the first edition, by reminding the reader of the words of Wisconsin Supreme Court Justice Abram D. Smith, who wrote in 1856 of his obligations under the Wisconsin constitution:

> In view of the obligations imposed upon me, or rather voluntarily assumed by me, when I gave my assent to our present form of state government, and more especially, in my present position, I have felt bound to sustain that fundamental law—the constitution of the state, according to its true intent and meaning. That is the great charter of our rights, to which the humblest may at all times appeal, and to which the highest must at all times submit.
>
> Let us then look to that constitution, adopted by the people of Wisconsin, and endeavor to ascertain its true intent and meaning. . . .
>
> The people then made this constitution, and adopted it as their primary law. The people of other states made for themselves respectively, constitutions which are construed by their own appropriate functionaries. Let them construe theirs— let us construe, and stand by ours.[2]

Shirley S. Abrahamson
Justice, Wisconsin Supreme Court

---

[2] *Attorney General ex rel. Bashford v. Barstow,* 4 Wis. 567 (1856) (Smith, J., concurring).

PART ONE

The History of the Wisconsin Constitution

Like all state constitutions, Wisconsin's interacts with the society and the people to whom it applies. By providing the basic framework within which the legislature and the governor enact laws and within which the courts adjudicate, the constitution, of course, profoundly affects the state's legal system. In turn, that legal system produces statutes and legal decisions that significantly affect the people's behavior by specifying the actions that they may take, are required to take, or are forbidden to take. That is, the constitution influences the lives of the state's residents. Conversely, Wisconsin's society and people have affected the constitution. The people most obviously and definitively do so by voting on proposed constitutional amendments: the final step in amending the constitution. The people also elect the legislators who propose and deliberate on constitutional amendments; two consecutive legislatures must pass a proposed amendment to advance it to a vote on ratification. Also, the people elect the judges and justices (except those appointed to fill vacancies) who interpret the constitution and determine whether statutes are constitutional. In addition, the state's political culture and predominate values subtly and almost imperceptibly have influenced the constitution's development and, through judicial interpretations, its meaning. Just as those two evanescent entities—that culture and those values—make life in Wisconsin different from life in other states, they make the Wisconsin constitution different, not only in trivial details but also more basically, from other states' constitutions.

The preceding analysis probably does not startle anyone or provoke disbelief. We intended to do neither but to justify a very brief description of Wisconsin's uniqueness. Except for its literature, perhaps nothing more clearly illuminates a state's distinctiveness than does its legal history. For decades Wisconsin has had a reputation for good government, a government that demonstrates more concern for the public weal than do those of some other states. To a large extent that reputation persists because Wisconsin has repeatedly led in enacting legislation and in propounding legal doctrines that most other jurisdictions have later accepted as rational and equitable. For example, Justice William O. Douglas, speaking in Milwaukee during the revolution in federal constitutional law that the Warren Court caused, responded to an introduction that pointed out that Court's stalwart protection of individual liberties by remarking, "[w]e are just trying to catch up with the Wisconsin Supreme Court. We are almost at the point where it was thirty years ago." As to legislation, Wisconsin enacted this nation's first workable income tax and the first workers' compensation law that withstood a legal challenge, and the Wisconsin legislature was ahead of its time in creating a central administrative agency for the state government, in creating an Industrial Commission, in ensuring safer work places, in creating a highway commission, in creating a state life insurance plan, and in protecting the environment. All of those accomplishments were completed in just six months by the 1911 legislature, the most remarkable in Wisconsin's history.

Two important direct causes of Wisconsin's political culture deserve recognition. One is the Progressives, the creators and adherents of a political movement that Robert M. La Follette best exemplifies. At first, they formed a faction within the Republican Party; later, after disagreements among Progressives became more virulent and, as a result, the group's power waned, its members revitalized it, albeit in an attenuated form, as the Progressive Party. La Follette adopted such goals as overcoming the alliance between party bosses and those who represented economic power and treating more equitably, and clearing the way for progress by, common people.

The other important cause of Wisconsin's uniqueness is the Wisconsin Idea: the belief that the University of Wisconsin should serve the state. The university's service to the state government has taken the forms of faculty members and administrators serving in office, giving advice about public policy issues, providing information and exercising technical skill. Its service to the citizenry has taken the forms of offering outreach programs and of providing research on problems that are important to the state. The university's service to the state government has been a crucial component of the state's political culture. Exemplars of the Wisconsin Idea and leading Progressives worked together to create many of the public policy innovations that Wisconsin can claim. For example, University of Wisconsin professors, most notably the economist John R. Commons, and the Progressives, who at the time controlled state government, deserve much of the credit for the 1911 legislature's splendid achievements. Both the Progressives and the Wisconsin Idea directly affected the state's constitution less than they did the state's statutory law, but we will see some of their direct influences. In addition, the tone they set indirectly affected the constitution. The Progressives' concern for the rights of common people, which probably influenced courts to interpret expansively the individual rights that Article I grants, and the tenacity with which the advocates of the Wisconsin Idea worked on social and economic problems, which probably indirectly influenced the frequent changes to the parts of the constitution that deal with those topics, are examples of this influence.

Although the Progressives have long since left the Wisconsin political scene and although the Wisconsin Idea has faded as faculty members and administrators at the University of Wisconsin–Madison have become more interested in national and international issues and problems and less interested in issues and problems that are specific to Wisconsin, these two influences continue to have an important and general effect on Wisconsin law and specifically on the constitution. That effect is not to be found in the political strain in recent Wisconsin legal history. The Progressives' positions on issues no longer dominate. In fact, as we shall see, Wisconsin courts, in interpreting constitutional provisions that were ratified because of the Progressives' efforts or were the basis of some of their legislation, negated their efforts. An example is *State ex rel. Owen v. Donald* (1915), in which the Supreme Court held the Progressives' comprehensive forestry act unconstitutional. Other examples include the holdings in cases on the internal improvements clause (Art. VIII, Sec. 10), the right to navigation (Art. IX, Sec. 1), and the public purpose doctrine, which is not explicitly stated in the constitution. In those cases, which are discussed in Part Two, courts interpreted more loosely the impediments to economic development that those sections and that doctrine presented. The Progressives would have been more pleased with the opposite result.

The enduring legacy of the Progressives and of the proponents and practitioners of the Wisconsin Idea is the spirit of innovation. That spirit is easier to discern in Wisconsin's statutory law, but it is also present in the state's constitutional law. For example, two Wisconsin Supreme Court justices, Nathan Heffernan and Shirley Abrahamson, each of whom later became a chief justice, were among the earliest advocates of the "new judicial federalism." That advocacy is a particularly useful example of innovation in the law because it demonstrates that the constitution itself can be a source of new ideas and approaches. Like all other constitutions, the Wisconsin constitution is framed in general terms. Judges accordingly can interpret its provisions in different ways. Some interpretations of provisions in Article I have merely echoed federal courts' interpretations of similar or identical provisions in the federal Constitution, but other interpretations have established a Wisconsin position that is distinct from the federal position. Moreover, the constitution can of course also be amended to accommodate changing conditions. In other words, although the approach of the new judicial federalists has not always prevailed, they have performed a vital service by calling attention to the fact that the constitution offers opportunities for innovation, a practice that is very much in the Wisconsin grain. Because of those opportunities and because the constitution both affects and reflects life in this state, it is important for all Wisconsinites, not only lawyers and judges, to know the document. This book's epigraph provides a useful reminder of the importance of knowing the constitution, regardless of the use to which one puts that knowledge. Ironically, that epigraph is a quotation from the opinion in *State ex rel. Owen v. Donald* (1915); it appears in the midst of a lengthy opinion by Justice Roujet Marshall in which the court invalidated the Progressives' forestry program.

■ THE CONSTITUTIONAL CONVENTIONS: BUILDING A STATE

The story of Wisconsin's constitution begins with a failed attempt: a document that the voters of the territory refused to ratify on April 6, 1847. Examining it briefly will identify some of the political forces at work in the geographical area that was soon to become the state of Wisconsin, and it will shed light on the constitution that the voters shortly thereafter did ratify. The federal government in 1846 had given the territory the authority to draft a constitution. If a convention drafted a constitution, if the voters ratified that constitution, and if Congress approved it, Wisconsin would become a state. The first constitutional convention began its deliberations in October 1846 and concluded them in December of that year. Only nine of the delegates were members of the territorial legislature, although many of them achieved political prominence after the convention. Their political inexperience, as well as the forceful and aggressive personalities of Edward Ryan and Moses and Marshall Strong and the machinations of James Doty, led to a tumultuous convention. Of the delegates 103 were Democrats, eighteen were Whigs, and three were independents. One might expect one party's dominance to temper the proceedings' heat. The huge Democratic majority, however, did not result in a unified purpose. The Democrats ranged all over the political spectrum. Many admired Andrew Jackson or could be considered reformers for other reasons, but others adhered to conservative positions. Moreover, many of the delegates strongly supported the interests, as they perceived them, of their sections of the state. At that time, the central and northern parts of the state were sparsely populated, so they provided few delegates. Most of the delegates represented either the southwest or the area near Lake Michigan. Persons who had emigrated from the border states and the South predominated in the southwest, and agriculture and mining drove its economy. Persons who had emigrated from New York and New England predominated along the lakeshore, and its economy included an important commercial sector.

The voters rejected the 1846 constitution 20,233 to 14,119 (roughly 59 percent to 41 percent). Three provisions inspired passionate disagreement at the convention and were probably the main reasons why the voters, despite their desire for statehood, voted down the constitution. The delegates borrowed two of them from Texas' constitution. By a vote of 68 to 27, they included a provision that prohibited creditors from seizing a debtor's home and land, up to a combined value of $1,000, a provision commonly denominated the homestead exemption. By a vote of 58 to 37, the delegates included a provision that gave women the right to control their property and exempted their property from seizure for their husbands' debts. The latter provision ran counter to the almost universal belief at the time that husbands owned their wives' property. Both provisions would have facilitated the advancement of persons who had little power by shielding them from more powerful persons.

The third controversial provision, and the one that was perhaps most responsible for the negative vote on ratification, was the banking article. On the day following his appointment to the chair of the Committee on Banks and Banking, Edward Ryan brought before the convention an article that would have prohibited banking. He had written it and had attained the approval of the other Democrats on his committee, although he had not shown it to the Whig member. The convention amended Ryan's draft of the article, but the revision allowed only private banking and virtually precluded out-of-state banks from operating in Wisconsin by forbidding the circulation of out-of-state bank notes in denominations less than $20. Ryan's position reflected the reality of the time that every bank chartered by the territorial government had plummeted into insolvency and that the only banking activity conducted by any Wisconsin concern was a sham. Although it had no banking charter, the Milwaukee Marine and Insurance Company issued commercial paper that looked and functioned like bank notes. Ryan vigorously defended farmers and laborers and implacably opposed organized capital. The Democrats at the convention who remembered and supported Andrew Jackson's war against the National Bank eagerly abetted Ryan's war against banks. Ryan narrowly prevailed and then fought off, on a tie vote, a motion to reconsider.

The 1846 convention grappled with four major divisive issues—anti-banking laws, voting rights for free black males, married women's property rights, and the homestead exemption—that led to its unhappy reception and ultimate demise at the ballot box. After the 1846 constitution failed, the 1848 constitution took a wiser approach—it delegated these difficult issues to the legislature. Due to the diverse nature of the state's population in the 1840s and the strong desire for statehood, the constitution took a more inclusive approach to suffrage, allowing the legislature to decide who could vote.

Cognizant of the advantages of statehood, the legislature and governor soon began the process that led to a second constitutional convention. It began work on December 15, 1847, and finished on February 1, 1848. In the brief interlude between the two constitutional conventions the world changed. One of the second convention's delegates, George Lakin, observed, "this has been regarded as an age of reform, and properly so." Within a few months, events sweeping across Europe would make it an age of revolution. Nevertheless, the rejected constitution was more of a reform document than the second, accepted constitution. By this later time, too, the support for President James K. Polk, a Democrat, had waned for several reasons, among them his advocacy of the Mexican War and his opposition to certain kinds of internal improvements. Wisconsin had recently sent John Tweedy, a Whig, to Washington to represent it. The Democratic Party's declining fortunes were reflected in the convention delegates' party allegiances. Those delegates included forty-six Democrats and twenty-three Whigs. The declining majority of the Democrats caused them to become more conciliatory—and, having fewer delegates, they had fewer factions.

Only six members of the first convention returned for the second, and they did not include the three assertive delegates who caused much of the first convention's tumult. The youth of the delegates surprises one, although it may have mirrored the population's. Twelve members were younger than thirty, thirty-two were in their thirties, and only two were older than fifty. Other factors balanced this youth. Nineteen attorneys, including Charles Dunn, the chief justice of the territory's supreme court and an influential delegate, contributed legal knowledge. The delegates were well educated compared to other residents of the territory; fourteen had attended colleges and twelve others had attended academies. Several of the delegates went on to successful careers. James Lewis and Louis Harvey became governors of Wisconsin, and Harrison Reed became governor of Florida. Edward Whiton and Orsamus Cole became chief justices of the Wisconsin Supreme Court. Rufus King became a distinguished newspaper editor, the commander of Wisconsin's Iron Brigade during the Civil War, and minister to the Papal State. The thoughtful arguments during the convention's meetings demonstrate its members' intellectual talents.

The convention's procedures helped ensure rational deliberation. A rule prohibited a debate and a vote on any measure on the same day. The delegates appointed only six committees, rather than the twenty-two of the 1846 convention, and the convention as a whole returned to the appropriate committee any issue on which it could not reach agreement. The other delegates resisted Byron Kilbourn's attempt to make only minor revisions in the 1846 constitution (and attach a pro-banking article that he had drafted). They chose instead to start afresh and to proceed with appropriate deliberation. The convention's decorum, even on controversial issues, greatly exceeded that of the first convention. One exception, surprisingly, was the debate on choosing a printer for the convention's documents. At the time, printers allied with political parties, so printing contracts generated political patronage. This issue consumed a substantial portion of the first few days and appeared briefly later. Debate on it does not rank among the convention's finer hours. Despite that lapse, the record of the convention's debates probably impresses most readers of it.

The delegates knew full well that the banking, homestead exemption, and married women's property rights provisions doomed the first constitution to defeat and that, therefore, they had to rationally resolve or avoid those issues. Opinions on banking varied widely. At one end of the spectrum was Warren Chase, a follower of François-Marie Fourier, a French social theorist who believed that society should be organized into communal agricultural associations. Chase, who had been a member of such an association, thought that banking was akin to theft and opposed all forms of it. Other delegates would accept banking under various kinds of controls. At the spectrum's other end, Byron Kilbourn believed that banking would benefit all persons. The delegates also disagreed on the amount of detail to include in the banking provision, and on what should be left for legislation. After rejecting a long skein of banking provisions, the convention finally left the matter to the legislature, with the protection of two referenda: one about whether banking should be allowed in the state and the other, to be conducted if the first passed, about whether the resulting banking legislation was acceptable. The banking provision specified that the legislation could be general or could grant individual charters to banks, a question about which the delegates disagreed. The first referendum passed; a general banking law, which created fairly rigorous safeguards, was enacted in 1852, and the voters approved that law.

Morgan Martin, the president of the convention, advanced an article that would exempt from seizure by creditors property that widows acquired upon their husbands' death, but the convention decided entirely to avoid the married women's property issue. The constitution contains nothing on that subject. Future legislatures would be free to do whatever they chose, including nothing, to protect married women's property rights. In 1850, a law was enacted to give women separate rights to the property that they owned at their marriage and to the property that was conveyed to them later, and to allow them to receive and convey property without their husbands' consent (Chapter 44, Laws of 1850).

The convention finessed the homestead exemption issue. After considerable argument about whether they should include such an exemption and, if they did so, about the kinds and monetary value of property that they should protect, the delegates agreed to address—not very forcefully—that subject in Article I, the bill of rights. That provision remains to this day, and its language now seems quaint. It reads: "[t]he privilege of the debtor to enjoy the necessary comforts of life shall be recognized by wholesome laws, exempting a reasonable amount of property from seizure or sale for the payment of any debt or liability hereafter contracted" (Art. I, Sec. 17). The convention thus also left the issue of protecting debtors in the legislature's hands, although it signaled that it expected some action on that subject. The legislature complied, enacting an exemption law in 1849.

Although the 1846 constitution would have instituted more reforms than the 1848 version, in one respect the latter, ratified constitution went slightly further. During the 1846 convention some delegates wished to allow African-Americans to vote. Adhering to the wishes of their constituents, delegates from the southwest corner of the state vigorously opposed this policy and occasionally spoke astringently about the persons whose suffrage was at issue. The 1846 convention agreed to submit to the voters a separate article allowing African-Americans to vote. Only about 34 percent supported it. The issue arose again during the 1848 convention. Although at that time a higher percentage of the delegates supported it, the convention rejected a motion to include a provision that explicitly allowed African-Americans to vote. In its place the delegates included a section—the former Article III, Section 4—which gave African-Americans the same suffrage rights as others, if the voters approved. The slight progress consisted of placing the article in the constitution, although the contingency of approval by the voters remained.

Two qualities of the ratified constitution deserve recognition. First, it created a constricted government. It limited the governor's term to two years (one delegate wanted to make it one year) and gave the governor only a few powers. It granted some powers to the legislature but constrained that body by mandating referenda for banking legislation and stating that the laws on exemptions for debtors must be wholesome, allowing a legal challenge on that ground to any exemption laws, and adding other limitations. As we shall see in the analysis of the constitution's preamble, the delegates concentrated on protecting the rights of individuals much more than on establishing an effective and powerful government. The delegates did not discuss this philosophical issue at any length, so one can only speculate on their motives. One might have been the desire to avoid another unfavorable vote on ratification. Another might have been making less likely the corruption and ineptness that some legislatures at that time exhibited. Many delegates had spent part of their adulthood in other states and knew firsthand the ways in which legislatures might perform.

The other salient quality of the ratified constitution is its generality. On this point the delegates did speak fairly often, stating that constitutions should enunciate general principles and leave details to legislation. Occasionally they made these statements in the hope that the legislature would resolve an issue more satisfactorily than would the constitutional convention, but the delegates seem mainly for philosophical reasons to have drawn this distinction between the functions of constitutions and statutes. The constitution's drafters underscored their belief in that distinction by peppering the document with phrases like "as the legislature shall determine" and "as provided by law." Those phrases signal that the legislature must fill in the details. This generality has reduced the need to undergo the cumbersome process of amending the constitution when one of its provisions becomes dated or obviously bad public policy. A fairly large number of amendments have been ratified, but the constitution's basic shape has changed little. This generality also makes the legislature accountable to the electorate; whereas, a very specific constitution would have allowed legislators to argue credibly that the constitution had tied their hands. In short, on this matter the delegates chose wisely.

The constitution's generality, along with its rationality and its congruence with the state's political culture, made it appealing to the voters and has allowed it to endure. The voters ratified it 16,759 to 6,384 (72 percent to 28 percent) on March 13, 1848, and Wisconsin was at last on its way to statehood. Unlike most states, Wisconsin has never jettisoned its constitution and replaced it with another. Its constitution is the sixth oldest state constitution. Accordingly, its history after ratification consists of legal opinions that interpreted it and of amendments. Under Article XII, Section 1 the constitution may be amended by the legislature passing an identical joint resolution during two consecutive sessions, which the voters must then ratify. The joint resolution that is before the second legislature includes the question that the voters will consider. Despite the rigor of these requirements, the constitution, after the April 2015 election, had been amended 145 times, reflecting an average of a little more than one per section and of nearly once per year. Before 1910, fewer than ten amendments per decade were ratified. During the next two decades, the number rose to fifteen per decade, partly because of the Progressives' activism. During the 1930s, 1940s, and 1950s, the number declined to ten or fewer per decade. During the 1960s, due in large part to amendments to sections about the powers of local units of government, the rate of amending increased nearly fivefold. That rate remained high during the 1970s, mainly because of amendments to the article on the judiciary, and during the 1980s, when many of the amendments were technical. Amendments have ranged from, on the one hand, stylistic changes and deletions of obsolete provisions to, on the other hand, changes that made possible major legislation or significantly altered the state government's framework. The following material explains the more important amendments and a few court decisions that have implications beyond merely interpreting particular constitutional provisions.

■ EARLY STATEHOOD: SENSATIONAL CASES, SOME CONFUSION

After deciding a few routine cases, most of them involving property rights, the new Wisconsin Supreme Court decided two cases in which it had to interpret the constitution, and it used a different approach in each. In the first case, *State ex rel. Dunning v. Giles* (1849), a candidate for sheriff sought a writ of mandamus (an order requiring a public official to perform an act) so that his election would be certified. He had received the second highest number of votes, but he argued that a territorial law forbade sheriffs from serving two consecutive terms, that Article XIV, Section 2 specified that territorial laws that were "not repugnant to this constitution" were still in effect and, therefore, that the person who received the most votes—the incumbent—could not take office. The court responded that the territorial law, in an unspecified way, was repugnant to the constitution. In short, the court decided the case by, very generally, determining the intent of the relevant constitutional provision. In so doing, the courts affirmed an important principle: that the constitution was "the work of the people—of the whole people—in which all had an equal and common interest and right, and to which all owed a common duty and allegiance."

Soon afterward, in *State ex rel. Bond v. French* (1849), the court more directly and extensively interpreted the constitution. Judge Alexander W. Stow (at that time members of the supreme court were called judges, not justices) stated the court would approach the constitution as it did statutes. He proceeded to read the constitutional provision literally. Thus, after two constitutional cases there were two methods of interpretation: one based on determining, in a very general way, the relevant constitutional provision's intent, the other based on literally reading the constitution's relevant portion. Later courts used both techniques, as well as others, and recently they have combined those techniques with examination of the first laws that were enacted after the relevant provision became part of the constitution.

French concerned an attempt by an elected probate judge to obtain a court order ousting the incumbent, who had been elected while Wisconsin was a territory and who refused to turn over the office. The incumbent's arguments included an assertion that the election law enacted soon after Wisconsin became a state and applied to the election of the plaintiff was unconstitutional. The court had no trouble with that argument. The constitution, in Article XIII, Section 1, made a broad statement, which established the date of general elections, and the statute in question supplied the details, such as the offices that would be filled at that election. "Judges of probate" appeared in the statute's list, so the statute did not conflict with the constitution. The reasoning was obvious; the case's importance—in addition to its status as the first rigorous Wisconsin constitutional case and the theory of constitutional interpretation that the court used in it—lies in an assumption that the court made. Unlike Chief Justice John Marshall of the U.S. Supreme Court in *Marbury v. Madison* (1803), Judge Stow assumed that the court had the authority to rule on the constitutionality of statutes; he did not argue that it did. By 1849 both the federal courts and the state courts had been regularly doing so for decades.

The courts' plenary judicial power, as set forth in Article VII, Section 2, was important as the basis not only of its authority to declare statutes unconstitutional but its authority to resist an attempt by another branch of government to diminish the courts' power. *State ex rel. Resley and others v. Farwell, Gov., etc.* (1852), a case brought against the governor to obtain stock certificates that, under a statute, the plaintiffs had the right to receive, illustrates the courts' power. The court's reasoning was sophisticated: it first distinguished between the office of governor and the person who occupied that office. While the courts could not erode the office's power, they did have jurisdiction over the persons who occupied the office and had the authority to determine the legality and constitutionality of their actions. The court reasoned that the debts of a person did not become uncollectible when he or she became governor because the courts had no authority to enforce those debts. It followed that a court could scrutinize the governor's actions while he or she held office. The court also distinguished between English monarchs, who "could do no wrong," and the Wisconsin governor, who was not above the law. In this way, Wisconsin courts asserted jurisdiction over governors regarding actions that were beyond the authority of their office.

Although the Wisconsin Supreme Court had rationally drawn the line between its constitutional authority and that of the governor, it soon acted irrationally in drawing the line between the authority that the state constitution gave it and the authority of the federal legal system. Sherman Booth, who had been arrested for freeing fugitive slaves from prison, sought a writ of habeas corpus (essentially, a judicial determination as to whether he was being legally held in custody). The Wisconsin court, in *In re Sherman Booth* (1854), determined not only that it had the authority to issue the writ, even though Booth was a federal prisoner, but that the federal Fugitive Slave Law was unconstitutional because it did not grant slaves a jury trial and because commissioners, not judges, determined whether a slave was to be returned to his or her owner. The court added that the federal government had only the powers that the states granted it. This states-rights argument and its corollary, that states could nullify federal laws and the actions of the federal legal system, were familiar at the time because Southerners were asserting them, usually for purposes very different from the reasons why the Wisconsin court asserted them. Meanwhile, a federal grand jury was considering an indictment (a request to determine whether the actions charged, if proved, would result in a conviction for a crime) against Booth. The jury determined that he should be brought to trial. This time the Wisconsin Supreme Court would not grant a writ of habeas corpus. *Ex parte Booth* (1854). A federal court then convicted Booth, but the Wisconsin court issued a second writ of habeas corpus and released him. *In re Booth & Ryecraft* (1855). Finally, the U.S. Supreme Court claimed its proper dominance over state courts by convicting Booth and a coparticipant. *Abelman v. Booth* (1859); *United States v. Roth* (1859).

The court decided another case involving the relationship between the courts and the governor, *The Attorney General ex rel. Bashford v. Barstow* (1856), a few years later. William Barstow, a Democrat, was elected governor in 1853. His administration was marred by controversy, even to the point of charges of corruption being leveled against him by some of his fellow Democrats. He nevertheless sought re-election in 1855, running against Coles Bashford of the new Republican Party. The Board of Canvassers (the body that was responsible for counting votes and declaring winners of elections) reported that Barstow had won by 157 votes, but suspicions about that election arose almost immediately. Bashford initiated litigation to overturn the result, and Barstow responded by staying in the capitol and releasing a statement that implied his willingness to resist with arms any attempt to oust him. Barstow's counsel asserted that the Wisconsin Supreme Court lacked jurisdiction to decide the case, mainly because it presented a political question, which ought to be beyond the court's reach. The court answered by pointing out that the constitution vested the executive power in a governor, not in a particular person, and that it vested the judicial power in the courts. Therefore, it determined, courts had the power to resolve legal disputes, even those that involve governors, thereby protecting its authority. The court proceeded to conclude that some of the election results were fraudulent and that Bashford was the governor.

The court was less decisive in its early tax cases. The first attempts to interpret the uniformity clause of the constitution, Article VIII, Section 1, requiring uniform taxation, illustrate the difficulty that the Wisconsin Supreme Court had in establishing an approach to the constitutional review of statutes. In the first reported case on that clause, *Knowlton v. Board of Supervisors* (1859), the court held unconstitutional a provision in the City of Janesville's charter, which was in the statutes because of the practice at the time of granting municipal charters by statute. That provision limited the property taxes imposed on agricultural land in the city. The constitution's framers designed the uniformity clause to preclude exactly such preferential treatment of taxpayers. The dissent argued that an earlier, unreported case, *Milwaukee & Mississippi Railroad v. Waukesha* (1855), ought to have been followed. Because unreported cases are not viewed as precedential, the dissent appended a memorandum that purported to summarize the case. In the earlier case, according to the memorandum, the court had held that uniformity within a class would satisfy the clause. That holding would have eviscerated the uniformity clause by allowing the creation of innumerable classes of property, allowing various kinds of preferential taxation. Several confusing and not particularly logical uniformity clause cases, some of which followed *Milwaukee & Mississippi Railroad v. Waukesha*, ensued.

Later another railroad taxation case, *State v. Chicago & Northwestern Railway* (1906), reached the court. The plaintiff attacked a gross earnings tax on railroads' income. In the *Mississippi Railroad* case, the court had not only held that creating classes of property and maintaining uniformity within each of them was enough to pass constitutional muster, it distinguished between the gross receipts tax, which it called consideration that the railroads paid for their property tax exemption, and the property tax itself. The later court followed up on that second point, distinguishing between the gross earnings tax and the property tax, which it held was regulated by the uniformity clause. Thus, the court made possible strict interpretation of the uniformity of taxation requirement regarding the property tax while allowing for differential treatment regarding other taxes, thereby eliminating the muddle created by the failure to report a case, the simultaneous existence of two contrasting views of the uniformity clause's requirements, and the illogical opinions in which the court tried to deal with the first two problems. It had taken fifty-one years for the court to determine authoritatively that uniformity of taxation meant true uniformity, and that it applied only to property taxation.

A few years after *Knowlton*, in 1860, the court decided *Bull v. Conroe*, which involved a law created in response to the constitutional imperative to enact "wholesome laws" to exempt property from creditors' judgments. Writing for the court, Chief Justice Luther Dixon, one of Wisconsin's more eminent chiefs, addressed two issues that helped to establish the supreme court's role in constitutional interpretation. The case concerned a debtor who had lost his homestead exemption because the law on that subject granted the exemption for a certain number of acres of agricultural land and because a later law extended the City of Racine's boundaries to include his farm, making it nonagricultural.

Like Judge Stow in *French*, Chief Justice Dixon assumed that his court could rule on a statute's constitutionality. Dixon went a step further, because one constitutional provision at issue in this case was a directive to the legislature to enact a certain kind of law. Dixon assumed that a court could rule on the constitutionality of those laws, too, despite their specific underpinnings in the constitution. That is, just as the court, in the two cases that involved governors, had protected its own power against encroachment by the executive branch of government, the court in this case protected its own power against encroachment by the legislative branch. In fact, Dixon asserted that the court had a right to strike down a homestead exemption law that it considered unconstitutional. As we shall see, courts later did strike down such a law.

In *Bull*, Dixon also explicitly established the principle that none of the provisions of the constitution overrode any of the others. The constitutional directive about homestead exemption laws did not diminish the legislature's power to establish municipal boundaries by statute, a power rooted in the constitution. That is, the constitutional directive to enact "wholesome" exemption laws did not justify diminishing another constitutional provision's effect. Rather, the duty to enact such exemption laws and the power to create municipalities were to be harmonized. Dixon did not specify the constitutional provision establishing the former power, but the relevant provision is the grant of power to form corporations, including municipal corporations, made by Article XI, Section 1. The power to exempt agricultural property derived from Article I, Section 17, the provision about the exemption from creditors' judgments. As we shall see, later courts accepted the principle that "all parts of the constitution are equally binding and imperative."

Shortly after ratification of the constitution, the legislature, using the power granted to it by Article III, Section 4, enacted a law extending the right to vote to African-Americans and submitted the issue to the voters. The vote in the

1849 referendum was 5,265 to 4,075 in favor of the extension. However, the number of affirmative votes was fewer than half of the votes that were cast on all issues at the election, so the Board of Canvassers ruled that the referendum had failed. The issue also failed in referenda in 1857 and 1861, although 46 percent of the voters favored it in the later referendum. Nevertheless, in 1865 an African-American tried to register to vote. After he was refused, he litigated, arguing that the reference in Article III, Section 4 to a majority of the votes "cast at such election" meant the majority of the votes cast on the suffrage issue, not the majority of all votes cast in the election at which the voters considered that issue. The court in *Gillespie v. Palmer* (1866) agreed, holding that African-Americans had had the right to vote since the 1849 referendum.

Only one Wisconsin judge, circuit court judge Levi Hubbell, has been impeached under Article VII, Section 1. During the middle of the nineteenth century the Democratic Party in Wisconsin splintered into three hostile factions. Hubbell's prominence in one faction was one cause of the impeachment. When the process began, in 1853, Democrats controlled both houses of the legislature, and the attorneys for and against Hubbell were Democrats. However, the impeachment was also justified because of a number of Hubbell's highly questionable actions, most of which he undertook for money. The last straw was a remark he made during a murder trial at which he presided. The defendant had confessed his guilt to his attorney, who told the other attorneys in the case and Hubbell. Because the attorney-client privilege protected conversations between lawyers and clients, the confession could not be used as evidence. After the jury acquitted the defendant, Hubbell asked the foreman if that indeed was their verdict. When the foreman confirmed that it was, Hubbell replied, "All I have to say is, if this is so, may God have mercy on your consciences!" Not surprisingly, the members of the jury, and others, were incensed.

At that point, Edward G. Ryan, one of Hubbell's political enemies, pressed for his removal by address under Article VII, Section 13, but the Wisconsin assembly proceeded to impeach Hubbell. Although a significant number of senators voted for some of the articles, Ryan, the prosecutor, could not convince the required two-thirds on any one article. Hubbell thus avoided removal from office, although the proceedings badly bruised him. He did not substantially reform his behavior. In 1871, President Ulysses S. Grant appointed him U.S. Attorney for the eastern district of Wisconsin. In 1875, he was suspended from that office because of his association with the Whiskey Ring: a group of distillers, operating in Milwaukee and elsewhere, which conspired to evade, or to obtain for themselves, the taxes that were due on their whiskey.

A few years after Judge Levi Hubbell brought a measure of shame to the judiciary, a Wisconsin Supreme Court justice took a position well ahead of his time. In 1859, an attorney who had been appointed by a circuit court to defend an indigent in a criminal case and had not been paid sued the county in which the trial took place. On appeal to the state supreme court in *Carpenter & Sprague v. Dane*

County (1859), the county argued that the statutes and the constitution did not require payment. Justice Orsamus Cole noted that Article I, Section 7 gave an accused person certain rights, and continued:

> is the right to meet witnesses face to face, and to have compulsory process to compel the attendance of unwilling witnesses, more important, or more valuable to a person in jeopardy of life or liberty, than the privilege of having the benefit of the talents and assistance of counsel in examining the witnesses, or making his defense before the jury? And would it not be a little like mockery to secure to a pauper these solemn constitutional guaranties for a fair and full trial of the matters with which he was charged, and yet say to him when on trial, that he must employ his own counsel, who could alone render these guaranties of any real permanent value to him[?]

Justice Cole upheld the circuit court judge, who had ordered the county to pay the attorney. The Wisconsin Supreme Court decided this case 104 years before the U.S. Supreme Court granted the same right to indigent defendants in *Gideon v. Wainwright* (1963).

The voters ratified the first significant constitutional amendment in 1871. It created Article IV, Section 31, prohibiting special or private laws (laws that apply very narrowly) on nine specified subjects. The list of subjects provides some clues about the motives of the new section's proponents. First on the list is changing persons' names. Its appearance on the list suggests that its supporters advanced it partly to save the legislature's time by delegating to a governmental official the power to effect a change that had minimal consequences. In fact, the legislature before 1871 passed many bills on subjects mentioned in the new section. Another item on the list is the assessment or collection of taxes and extending the time for collecting them. One can imagine requests by constituents for tax relief in the form of special laws. Those requests would make it necessary for a legislator to choose between an awkward refusal or an acceptance that smacked of corruption, unless he or she could think of a way to finesse the matter or dissuade the requester. Interestingly, the list of topics has changed very little.

▪ THE PROGRESSIVES AND THEIR PRECURSORS: ATTEMPTS TO BUILD A MORE JUST STATE

The next landmark constitutional case occurred in the context of the Granger movement. For a brief time span during the 1870s, the members of this movement, most of whom were farmers of moderate means, used political pressure and tight alliances to strengthen their hand against powerful economic entities that they considered to be their enemies. For example, they fought fiercely for laws that would regulate the railroads, particularly their rates, which the Grangers thought were confiscatory. On that issue, they succeeded in Wisconsin. In 1874, the legislature enacted the "Potter Law," which created rate limits, established a railroad commission and authorized it to examine the railroads' finances and to reduce freight rates, and provided for criminal prosecution of railroads that violated the rate limits that the commission set. The railroads ignored the law. Governor Williams R. Taylor was determined to fight back. Meanwhile, Luther Dixon had resigned as Chief Justice, so Taylor sought a replacement who would be inclined to regulate the railroads. He chose Edward Ryan. Litigation ensued.

Writing for the court in *Attorney General v. Railroad Companies* (1874), Ryan had first to demonstrate that the court had the authority to issue the injunction that the state sought to compel the railroad companies to obey the Potter Law. Article VII, Section 3(2) granted to the supreme court the authority to issue certain writs. All but one of those writs existed in English common law (see the commentary on Article XIV, Section 13) and had traditionally been prerogative, meaning the court had jurisdiction to issue them even if that was the only action in the case. The exception in the list was injunctions. The railroad companies argued that injunctions never had been prerogative but had been allowed only along with a judgment. In response, Ryan advanced two arguments. He invoked the rule of constitutional and statutory interpretation that items in a list are to be interpreted so that they all belonged to the same category. Specifically, if injunctions were included in a list of which all of the other items were prerogative writs, they, too, were prerogative. He also argued that the framers of the constitution intended that the writs "make this court a supreme judicial tribunal over the whole state; a court of first resort on all judicial questions affecting the sovereignty of the state, its franchises or prerogatives, or the liberties of the people." Thus, Ryan expansively interpreted the court's constitutional power to issue writs and thereby to enforce its decisions. Later, this provision of the constitution was amended to grant the court the authority to issue "all writs."

Ryan's opinion also augmented the court's power by limiting the application of the constitutional prohibition against impairing contracts (Art. I, Sec. 12). This move required him to confront the U.S. Supreme Court's decision in *Dartmouth College v. Woodward* (1819), in which the court held the federal prohibition against impairing contracts in the U.S. Constitution applied to corporate charters. The railroad companies argued that the same reasoning should apply under the state constitution, and the court should hold that limits on rates impaired the companies' charters by diminishing the power that those charters granted. A speech Ryan had delivered at the University of Wisconsin Law School the previous year foretold the result. He told his audience that "[t]he question will arise, and arise in your day, though perhaps not fully in mine, which shall rule—wealth or man; which shall lead—money or intellect; who shall fill public stations—educated and patriotic free men, or the feudal serfs of corporate capital."[1] Ryan's opinion made the same point in more

---

[1] A recent high school graduate, Robert M. La Follette, listened enthralled as the speech marked out his future political career.

measured language: "such aggregations of capital and power, outside of public control, are dangerous to public and private right." He pointed out that the flimsy impediments available under the common law could not stop economic juggernauts, and noted that the federal Constitution's prohibition against impairing contracts was written before the immense aggregation of corporate power and that therefore the cases interpreting it were irrelevant. He held that the contract clause of the Wisconsin constitution did not prevent the state from regulating corporations and that the authority under Article XI, Section 1 to grant corporate charters implied the right to amend them, which, in effect, the Potter Law had.

The Potter Law was soon repealed because conservative Republicans, who were favorably disposed to the railroads, regained control of the legislature and the governorship from reformers. After the repeal, the railroads went about their business in much the same way as they had before *Attorney General v. Railroad Companies*. For some time, the Wisconsin Supreme Court rarely used its injunctive power in a prerogative manner. However, in 1901 Robert M. La Follette became governor with the intention to exercise greater control over railroads and to tax them more severely. He and his fellow Progressives achieved both goals, and in general reined in corporate power, aided by the decision in *Attorney General v. Railroad Companies* (1874). Moreover, that decision made it easier for governmental officials who succeeded the Progressives to regulate businesses in the state.

Also in 1874, the voters ratified a constitutional amendment that limited the debt of counties, cities, towns, villages, school districts, and other municipal corporations to 5 percent of the value of their taxable property (Art. XI, Sec. 3) and specified that if one of those units of government incurred debt, it must impose a direct tax (a property tax) sufficient to retire the debt within twenty years. That section's original version had required only that the legislature restrict the borrowing of cities and villages. Courts had held that municipalities could borrow for non-municipal purposes, see, e.g., *Bushnell v. Town of Beloit* (1860), and specifically, that they could incur debt to subsidize railroads, see, e.g., *Rogan v. City of Watertown* (1872). During this era many local officials, convinced that their constituents' future well-being depended on their access to railroad transportation, approached the legislature for permission to incur municipal debt to subsidize railroads, as well as for other purposes. In considering this amendment, several legislators were no doubt motivated by animosity toward railroads. Municipal borrowing also caused concern. Moreover, between 1865 and 1869, 120 special laws authorizing municipal debt were enacted. Although loath to deny requests for individual authorizations to borrow, legislators recognized that borrowing had careened out of control, so they passed the joint resolution that limited municipal debt. That took them out of the business of abetting local officials who borrowed recklessly. Requiring imposition of a property tax to fund municipal debt deterred profligacy and protected creditors. This section of the constitution has frequently been amended, but its purpose of forcing fiscal prudence on local officials has remained constant.

Having improved municipal finance, the legislature turned to state finance. During 1908, the voters ratified an amendment to Article VIII, Section 1, which authorized taxation of incomes, privileges, and occupations. When they decreed that taxation is to be uniform, the framers of the constitution thought only of the property tax. At that time, it was, and until 1911 it was to be, the only tax imposed in Wisconsin. For that reason, most persons in Wisconsin who had an opinion about it thought that no other tax could be imposed unless the constitution was amended. However, because of a misreading of a precedent, the amendment may not have been necessary. The subject of *State ex rel. Brown County v. Myers* (1881) was property tax equalization (a higher official's adjustment of the values that a local assessor had established during the property tax process). The court remarked that "this whole matter is within the control of the legislature." The meaning of "this whole matter" is not completely clear, but its most plausible interpretation is equalization. Twenty years later, however, the court in *State ex rel. Ellis v. Thorne* (1901) understood the phrase to refer to taxation. Citing the previous case, it held that "the legislature has plenary power over the whole subject of taxation within constitutional limitations." In six later cases the court accepted *Ellis: State ex rel. Hessey v. Daniels* (1910); *Milwaukee County v. Dorsen* (1932); *State ex rel. Thomson v. Giessel* (1953); *City of Plymouth v. Elsner* (1965); *City of West Allis v. Milwaukee County* (1969); and *Thompson v. Kenosha County* (1974). Later, the court would hold that the legislature has "wide latitude," not "plenary power," in taxation. *WKBH Television, Inc. v. Dep't. of Revenue* (1977). By upholding the legislature's power over taxation, this line of cases validates the Wisconsin taxes that are not among the types specified by Article VIII, Section 1.

The 1908 amendment allowing income, privilege, and occupational taxes illustrates the effects of governmental administration and a changing economy on a state constitution. Because the property tax depends on assessing the value of property, it is difficult to administer, invites corruption (of which there were many examples in the nineteenth century), and generates many complaints about inequity. Also, owners of personal property, especially intangible personal property, can conceal it from assessors. The property tax suits a society composed mainly of farmers, shopkeepers, and artisans because in such a society the value of a person's property correlates reasonably well with the person's income. It does not suit a society in which other means of producing income dominate. One historian has argued that the supporters of an income tax were part of a long tradition of promoting tax policy that would favor farmers at the expense of others.[2] Examination of the legislature's voting on the income tax bill, of the

---

[2] David P. Thelen, *The New Citizenship: Origins of Progressivism in Wisconsin 1885–1900* (Columbia: University of Missouri Press, 1972).

shift in the tax burden after that bill became law, and of other historical evidence, casts doubt on that interpretation.[3] Rather, the supporters of that tax seem to have desired mainly to establish a more equitable system of taxation.

Two years after approving the income tax amendment, the voters approved an amendment authorizing a state property tax to raise funds for forestry and water conservation. That amendment illustrates several causes of a constitution's development: influential individuals, national movements, and physical changes in the state. It also illustrates the need to use the required procedures to amend the constitution. At that time, Charles Van Hise was the president of the University of Wisconsin. A geologist, he had done fieldwork in northern Wisconsin and in the process had noticed that the sudden deforestation caused by predatory logging had deprived the region of a valuable resource and threatened its watersheds. Van Hise had been a friend of Robert La Follette when they were undergraduate students at the University of Wisconsin, and their continued friendship and community of interests were major reasons for the vitality of the Wisconsin Idea during the first decade of the twentieth century. As the president of the Department of State Forestry and the chairperson of the Conservation Commission, Van Hise vigorously supported efforts to preserve existing timber and water resources and to reforestate. His efforts led to the 1910 constitutional amendment.

The forestry and water conservation amendment made possible a comprehensive forestry law, which was one of the main achievements of the 1911 legislature, and, due to a legal challenge to that act, resulted in a significant constitutional case, *State ex rel. Owen v. Donald* (1915). The secretary of state, skeptical about the law's constitutionality, had refused to audit (approve) a payment on a land contract through which the state was acquiring property for its forestry program. In an extremely lengthy opinion, Justice Roujet Marshall made it clear that constitutional amendments are invalid unless the procedures set forth in the constitution for accomplishing them are meticulously followed. He also interpreted many constitutional provisions very restrictively to limit the state government's authority to enact innovative programs. This case thus restrained the Progressives' activist tendencies. As to the procedural issue and the validity of the constitutional amendment upon which the forestry law rested, the legislature had properly taken the first step toward amending the constitution by passing a joint resolution, but, rather than passing an identical joint resolution during the next session, as Article XII, Section 1 required, it had prematurely submitted the question to the voters. A few years earlier, discovering that the second joint resolution on the income tax amendment differed slightly from the first joint resolution on that subject, it prudently had reinitiated the amendment process, but this time it was not so careful. Although Wisconsin courts, seeing

---

[3] John Stark, "The Establishment of Wisconsin's Income Tax," *Wisconsin Magazine of History* 71, no.1 (Autumn 1987), 27–45.

such matters as political questions have consistently declined to enforce legislative rules of procedure, see, e.g., *State ex rel. La Follette v. Stitt* (1983), Marshall believed that the procedural rules that the constitution established were mandatory, and his position has prevailed.

As to the substantive provisions of the forestry law, Justice Marshall adduced a host of reasons to find them unconstitutional. One was the debt limits in Article VIII, Sections 4 and 9. Another was the prohibition against the state incurring debt for works of internal improvement. One might question Marshall's analysis on this point, because "works of internal improvement" usually refers to building projects, not to the type of work that would be done under the law in question. He also seems to have overreached in ruling that the forestation and water conservation projects served no public purpose and that the act violated the prohibition against special acts for the collection of taxes in Article IV, Section 31 (he ignored the fact that the tax applied across the state, not to a limited number of taxpayers). He also held that the act violated several other constitutional provisions. It is very unlikely that any other judicial opinion in the state's history has invalidated a law on so many constitutional grounds, and many of his substantive objections to the statute may be regarded anomalies.

It follows that, after *Owen*, Wisconsin still had problems with forestry and water conservation. During the administrations of Governors Francis McGovern (1911–1915) and Emanuel Philipp (1915–1921), the state made minimal progress in enacting legislation in these two. Meanwhile the problems became more acute. In 1809, shortly before logging began in the area that was to become Wisconsin, about 30 million acres of forests existed there. By 1923 fewer than 2 million acres of forests remained. In 1910 Wisconsin led the nation in proceeds from logging, but in 1920 it ranked only seventh. As it had when it first recognized these problems, during the 1921–1922 session the legislature enacted a joint resolution to amend the constitution so that it could pass the needed laws. That amendment allowed appropriations, up to an amount equal to 0.2 mills multiplied by the value of the taxable property in the state, for forestation. This time the legislature carefully followed the prescribed procedure for amending the constitution, and the voters, in 1924, approved the amendment.

Three years later the voters approved a related amendment to the uniformity clause, Article VIII, Section 1, that allowed forest land to be taxed differently from the taxation of other kinds of land. Based on the former amendment, the state imposed a property tax of 0.2 mills for forestry purposes. That tax revenue made possible a substantial forestry program. Based upon the latter amendment, the state enacted a forest cropland act, which authorized contracts between property owners who promised to hold land solely for growing timber and the state, in exchange for a property tax exemption for that land. That act preserved some of the state's forests, although the constitutional amendment that made possible its enactment created the first exception to the principle of uniform property taxation. Attenuating that principle allowed statutory responses to changing economic conditions, but it also allowed special interest groups to gain tax advantages.

■ BETWEEN THE WORLD WARS: ADJUSTING QUANTUMS OF POWER

In the same election, November 1924, at which voters approved the constitutional amendment authorizing appropriations for forestry, they ratified an amendment to Article XI, Section 3(1) to grant cities and villages the power, within limits, to manage their affairs. That section's former version had given the legislature both the duty and the power to restrict those local governments' conduct of their financial affairs. The amendment allowed cities and villages to determine their own affairs, subject only to the constitution and to acts of statewide concern that affect every city and village uniformly. This amendment, like the amendment forbidding special laws on certain enumerated subjects, relieved the legislature of a burden; it no longer had to determine policy, to a large extent, for cities and villages, and accordingly could concentrate on determining policy for the whole state. The amendment also reflects the demographic changes in the state. In 1850, two years after the constitution was ratified and Wisconsin became a state, 9.4 percent of the population was urban. In 1930, 52.9 percent of the population was urban. In fact, the percentage probably passed 50 percent at about the time that the voters ratified the home rule amendment. This increasing urbanization made it inappropriate for the state to continue to regulate closely the affairs of cities and villages.

The 1927 amendment to Article VIII, Section 1 that allowed nonuniform taxation of forest land also allowed nonuniform taxation of minerals. Before the state of Wisconsin was formed, mining was conducted in the area. The lead mines in the southwestern sector of the state prospered briefly, and many emigrants came to that area to work in them. The miner on the state seal and the nickname of the state's citizens (and the University of Wisconsin–Madison's sports teams), the badgers (a digging animal), reflect this mining heritage. It is difficult to tax minerals and mining land fairly, because tax assessors cannot see unmined minerals and thus cannot rationally value them. One attempt to tax mining companies was an 1877 law that directed mineral land to be assessed by valuing the land and buildings on it and then adding the value of minerals that had been extracted during the previous year. That method deviated from the assessment of other property and probably violated the uniformity clause, Article VIII, Section 1. At least the persons who produced the 1878 revision of the statutes thought so, for they did not include it in the new statutes. The Progressives, being concerned with equitable taxation, sought a fair way to tax the mining industry. Governor McGovern, in 1911, reminded the legislature that property tax assessors could not see unmined minerals and added that, shortly after minerals were extracted, mining companies shipped them out of state, thereby usually escaping taxation. He proposed a severance tax (a tax based on the value or amount of minerals that were extracted). Finally, others recognized the wisdom of his position and, because that method of taxation was thought to violate the uniformity clause, an amendment to that clause was proposed. That amendment was passed twice by the legislature and ratified by the voters.

In 1930, the voters ratified the most controversial amendment to the constitution. Before that year Article V, Section 10 had given the governor the authority to veto bills in their entirety. The amendment expanded the governor's power by allowing him or her to veto appropriation bills "in whole or in part." Shortly before the vote on ratification, the amendment's drafter, Edwin Witte, the Chief of the Legislative Reference Bureau, wrote that the amendment did not allow the governor to "reduce items, but only to veto them entirely." Witte also referred throughout his memorandum to "items," rather than to "parts." He seems to have thought that the terms were synonyms, and he had used "item" in earlier drafts of the amendment. The first supreme court opinion on the amendment's effect, *State ex rel. Wisconsin Tel. Co. v. Henry* (1935), nevertheless ignored Witte's statement of intent and turned to a dictionary for a definition of "part." The court interpreted the word to mean a portion and went on to conclude that the use of "part," which no other state constitution except New Jersey's uses to identify the proper object of gubernatorial vetoes, allowed the governor to "join and enact separable pieces of legislation in an appropriation bill," if a "complete, entire, and workable law" remained after the veto.

Wisconsin governors have vetoed words, letters (until a 1990 constitutional amendment forbade that tactic), and digits in appropriation bills. As the court approved such veto practices, governors became more inventive. The only successful challenger of a veto convinced the court that the bill in question was not an appropriation bill and therefore could not be vetoed, not that the veto itself was unconstitutional. *State ex rel. Finnegan v. Dammann* (1936). In a later case the supreme court correctly noted that Wisconsin has "the most liberal and elastic constitutional provision—adopted almost 60 years ago—regarding the governor's partial veto authority over appropriation bills." *State ex rel. Wis. Senate v. Thompson* (1988). This amendment, as it has been interpreted, has significantly shifted power from the legislative branch to the executive branch. The shift rests ultimately on the use of "part" rather than "item," a change that the drafter thought was merely stylistic. An amendment to Article V, Section 10, ratified in 2008, helped to re-establish some of the balance of power between the governor and the legislature.

A long battle for women's suffrage culminated in ratification of an amendment in 1934. Warren Chase, as well as a few other delegates, had advocated women's suffrage at the two state constitutional conventions, but they had little support. Beginning in 1869 the Wisconsin Women's Suffrage Association took up the cause. That organization's only notable success, adoption, by referendum, in 1886 of a law allowing women to vote at school elections, proved to be fleeting.

The supreme court in *Brown v. Phillips* (1888) held that that right applied only if there were separate ballots for school elections, which the legislature refused to authorize. After that case, the advocates of women's suffrage adopted a gradualist strategy, and the Wisconsin Federation of Women's Clubs assumed leadership of the movement. Robert La Follette and the Progressives enacted a law that authorized separate ballots for school elections. However, even support by some Progressives did not suffice to prevail in a referendum in 1912 that would have given women the right to vote in all elections. Indeed, the ratification in 1919 of the amendment to the U.S. Constitution that allowed women to vote in national elections did not lead to Wisconsin enacting a law that extended women's suffrage to state elections. In 1919, the legislature narrowly defeated a bill to do so. Although Wisconsin has an impressive record of preceding other states in adopting progressive reforms, it does not include women's suffrage.

▪ THE POSTWAR ERA: THE FAMILIAR ISSUES OF TAXES AND MUNICIPALITIES, THE NEW ISSUES OF RELIGION AND GAMBLING

A 1949 amendment to the constitution clearly illustrates the effect of the nation's history on that document. Soon after the conclusion of World War II, the state rushed to enact legislation that would benefit veterans of that war, including the creation of a veterans' housing program. However, the supreme court held in *State ex rel. Martin v. Giessel* (1948) that the program violated the internal improvements provision, Article VIII, Section 10, of the constitution. In response, the legislature began the process of amending the constitution. Its efforts bore fruit when the voters ratified the amendment. This amendment is also notable because of the legislature's attempt to control later judicial interpretations of it. The amendment's brevity and generality (it added "or the acquisition, improvement or construction of veterans' housing" to the list of permissible types of internal improvements) left considerable room for interpretation. For example, it was not clear whether only veterans could occupy the housing. The legislature, therefore, took the unusual steps of preparing a statement of its intent, having that statement read to each house before the vote, and ensuring that it was disseminated widely by means of newspapers and the radio. This strategy made sense because at that time Wisconsin courts sometimes examined the intent of the framers of the provision that was at issue in interpreting the constitution. The legislature also could have included the substance of the intent statement in the constitution, but that would have run counter to the accepted practice of inserting only general principles in that document and leaving details to legislation.

A 1954 amendment on redistricting the legislature had both an unusual origin and an unusual outcome. A 1910 amendment mandated redistricting during the first legislative session after each federal census. The legislature had failed to do so in any substantial way after both the 1930 and 1940 censuses. Determined to right this wrong, shortly after the 1950 census the legislature formed a Legislative Council committee on the subject and appointed Chief Justice Marvin B. Rosenberry as its chair. The committee, in addition to proposing a plan, recommended that the legislature pass a joint resolution leading to an amendment of the constitution to allow area, as well as population, to be a factor in redistricting. By this time, the state's urbanization was proceeding apace. The 1950 census revealed that 57.9 percent of the population was urban. Moreover, the population was becoming more concentrated. The southeast and the area running from the southern shore of Lake Winnebago, at Fond du Lac, along that lake's western shore and down the Fox River Valley to Green Bay were fairly densely populated; other areas of the state, particularly in the north, were sparsely populated. The inhabitants of the sparsely populated regions felt overpowered and underrepresented. The legislature passed several joint resolutions. It twice passed one that would allow both houses of the legislature to be redistricted based on both factors, but in November 1952 the voters rejected it. The legislature responded by passing for a second time another of the joint resolutions, which would allow only the state senate to be redistricted based on both area and population. The voters approved that proposal, and the legislature enacted a plan that weighted the redistricting: 30 percent on the basis of area and 70 percent on the basis of population.

Litigation attacking both the constitutional amendment and the redistricting plan soon followed. In *State ex rel. Thomson v. Zimmerman* (1953), the court held that, in addition to its main purpose of allowing redistricting partly based on area, the amendment had three other effects: deleting the prohibition against voting by untaxed Indians and military personnel, discontinuing the requirement that senate district lines be bounded by town, ward, or village lines, and discontinuing the requirement that each assembly district must be entirely within one senate district. Because four issues were offered to the voters, the court held, they should have been offered as four amendments, so the effort was invalid. The court also held that the summary that was submitted to the voters with the amendment inaccurately stated one of the amendment's details. Article XII, Section 1 requires separate questions for separate issues but does not require summaries. In light of the contemporaneous U.S. Supreme Court's decision that districts significantly unequal in population violated the Equal Protection Clause of the U.S. Constitution, one would expect that the redistricting act based on the amendment would also have been struck down on that ground. However, because it invalidated the amendment on procedural grounds, the court did not reach the constitutionality of the proposal.

The next amendment to the constitution, which authorized nonuniform taxation of certain kinds of personal property, resulted from the long-standing discontent with the taxation of that property. As we have seen, that discontent was one reason the amendment authorizing the income tax was ratified and one reason that tax was enacted. During the late 1950s, owners of livestock, merchants' inventory, and manufacturers' stock and finished products paid 97 percent of the taxes on personal property, and the taxes on personal property accounted for 18 percent, about $68 million, of all property taxes. During that decade, business and industrial interests, aided by the state Division of Industrial Development and a few business professors at the University of Wisconsin, vigorously opposed that tax. They argued that the tax unreasonably burdened Wisconsin businesses and advocated imposing a sales tax to reimburse local units of government for the revenue loss that a tax exemption for personal property would cause. A Legislative Council committee studied the tax on personal property, and during 1959, Governor Gaylord A. Nelson announced his support for legislation that would gradually eliminate the personal property tax. Shortly thereafter, a study committee appointed by the governor assailed the personal property tax.

The next major amendment altered the uniformity clause, Article VIII, Section 1, to regulate uniform taxation of the four kinds of personal property that were at issue. Immediately exempting that property would have been constitutional under the uniformity clause prior to the amendment, but an immediate exemption would shift the property tax burden so suddenly and dramatically that the legislature and governor wished to arrive at the exemption in stages, and the case law on the uniformity clause indicated that all property must be either fully exempt or fully taxed. The law that was enacted after the amendment was ratified in 1960 allowed owners of personal property to pay only half of the taxes that would otherwise have been due on it. The law also required the state to pay to taxing jurisdictions $55 million. That payment was thought to be a reimbursement for lost taxes. However, money being fungible, exact reimbursements are impossible, and, because the money went to taxing jurisdictions, some of it benefited the owners of the partially exempt property. The state imposed a 3 percent sales tax on ten kinds of goods and four kinds of services to generate the revenue for the payments to property-taxing jurisdictions.

That amendment led to another that the voters ratified two years later, in 1963. The legislation that was enacted in the wake of the personal property tax amendment not only shifted the property tax burden, it also reduced the property tax base. The latter result did not necessarily reduce property tax revenue, because local officials could increase rates to compensate for the reduction of the base. However, the local debt limit in Article XI, Section 3 was expressed in terms of the property tax base of the unit of government that wished to borrow. Thus, the personal property tax amendment indirectly lowered the debt limit, which particularly harmed manufacturing and commercial centers. Its effects were most acute in Milwaukee, the state's largest city. Moreover, the financial relationship between the City of Milwaukee and the Milwaukee Public Schools, which was unique in the state, exacerbated the problem. The school district notified the city of the amount of property tax revenue that it needed, both for operating expenses and to fund its debt for capital expenses, and the city then levied the necessary taxes and turned over the revenue to the school district. As a result, the school district's debt was combined with the city's, and the total had to be less than the debt limit that the constitution established. As the district's enrollment grew, necessitating more capital expenditures, and the city's tax base eroded, due to the personal property tax exemption and other causes, the city had great difficulty staying within the debt limit.

The legislature soon perceived this difficulty and began the process of amending Article XI, Section 3. The relief for Milwaukee consisted of adding a provision that increased by 10 percent the debt limit for cities that issued bonds for school purposes, the new allowance applying only to school bonds, and the city's own debt limit remaining at 5 percent. Thus, the city could use the full 5 percent limit for its own debt. The same amendment also clarified this section, which had become unwieldy. Finally, this amendment made the measure of the property value for the debt limit equalized value (the value that the Department of Revenue determined) rather than assessed value (the value that local assessors determined). Although the quality of local assessments had improved, they were still inaccurate enough to make that change wise.

Article IV, Section 24 remained unchanged until 1965. In its original version, it bluntly prohibited lotteries. "Lottery" may seem to be a synonym of "raffle," but some laws that were enacted shortly after 1848 suggest that during that era the legislature thought that the term had a broader meaning. By 1965, both the state supreme court and the attorney general were defining the term to mean any scheme that involved consideration, chance, and a prize. For example, the state supreme court had held unconstitutional a statute specifying that merely listening to a radio program or listening to and watching a television program were not consideration. Therefore, despite the statutory exception, a scheme that involved those activities was a lottery and illegal. In other words, the court held that those activities, notwithstanding the statute, were consideration, that the scheme of which they were a part was therefore a lottery, and that participating in the game shows that were beginning to become popular during that time violated the constitution. *State v. Laven* (1955) and other cases made it necessary to amend the constitution if certain kinds of gambling were to be allowed. The amendment that was designed to do so specified that, in determining whether a lottery was being conducted, consideration did not include the activities that were at issue in *Laven*, filling out a coupon or entry blank or visiting a mercantile establishment or other place. Authorizing those innocuous activities probably did little harm, but it also codified the broader definition of "lottery" as that word is used in the constitution, and it began the changes in this section of the constitution. In other words, the first steps had been taken on a road that became increasingly controversial—particularly when a state lottery was authorized and that step in turn authorized Indian gaming.

In 1964, Governor John W. Reynolds' Commission on Constitutional Revision recommended amending the constitution to lengthen the term of state constitutional officers to four years. That was done in 1967, see Article V, Sections 1m and 1n; Article VI, Sections 1m, 1n, and 1p. Also at that time Article V, Section 3 was amended to provide that a candidate for governor must run on a slate with a candidate for lieutenant governor. One can see the significance of these changes by placing them in historical context. The amendment was ratified near the middle of an era during which both the executive and legislative branches increased their strength. The Department of Administration, which performs several functions including policy research for the executive branch of government, was formed in 1959. Two years later, the legislature created a committee to determine its own staffing needs. In 1964, a policy analyst was assigned to each party caucus in each house. The committee also recommended that the legislature hire fiscal experts, which it did when it formed the Legislative Fiscal Bureau. Shortly thereafter the Legislative Council was given permanent staff members, and the Legislative Reference Bureau, which drafts legislation and performs research, increased the number of its employees. Soon thereafter a well-staffed legislature, the members of which were moving toward full-time status, was balanced against a well-staffed executive branch that was headed by a governor whose tenure was long enough for him or her to grasp state government's intricacies. In this way, the nature of state government changed radically.

Since its ratification, Wisconsin's constitution has contained a provision that resembles the U.S. Constitution's prohibition, in the First Amendment, of the establishment of religion—Article I, Section 18. The Wisconsin version reads: "nor shall any money be drawn from the treasury for the benefit of religious societies, or religious or theological seminaries." The Wisconsin Supreme Court has interpreted that provision much more rigorously than the U.S. Supreme Court has interpreted the Establishment Clause. That rigor derives in large part from an early decision involving the transportation of children to a parochial school. The Wisconsin court has ruled that the key issue in such a case is identifying the expenditure's beneficiary. If it is the child, the constitutional prohibition is not violated; if it is the school, the opposite result obtains. The leading case, *State ex rel. Van Straten v. Milquet* (1923), arose when a school bus driver sued for his wages for transporting children to a parochial school after the local public school was closed. The court held that payment of those wages would violate Article I, Section 18. To allow the state to pay part of the cost, by providing school aid, of transportation of children to parochial schools it would be necessary to amend the constitution—which happened in 1967, with the adoption of Article I, Section 23.

In 1969, the voters ratified one of the longer and more complex of the constitutional amendments that the legislature has submitted to them. The original version of Article VIII, Section 7 had prohibited the state from contracting debt except to repel invasion, suppress insurrection, or defend the state during a war. Those events being rare, one might wonder whether the state operated on a cash-and-carry basis for 119 years. The amendment itself, by referring to such entities as the Wisconsin State Agencies Building Corporation, indicates the answer. The state had created several dummy corporations that, because they were not part of state government, evaded the prohibition on incurring debt for ordinary state purposes. The amendment made such corporations unnecessary and imposed limits on the state's assumption of debt. One limit was a dollar amount based upon the value of taxable property in the state, which was odd because the tiny state property tax funded only reforestation expenses. The state also pledged its "full faith, credit and taxing power" to the payment of debt incurred under that section. Strengthening the security for state bonds, the proceeds of which were to be used to retire the state debt, facilitated their sale. The amendment also required the legislature to state the public purposes for which debt was to be incurred. That portion of the new section explicitly recognized the public purpose doctrine, which before that time had been somewhat unconvincingly deduced from other constitutional provisions.

The changes that have been made to Article IV, Section 23 illustrate a gradual and rational evolution of a constitutional provision. Those changes culminated in an amendment ratified in 1972, which allowed the legislature to establish more than one system of county government. The section's original version required one system of county government, which had to be as nearly uniform as practicable. Eventually, as counties became more populous and diverse and their functions more numerous, uniformity became less desirable. In 1950, Attorney General Thomas E. Fairchild and Charles P. Seibold, in an article calling for an extensive revision of the constitution, advocated allowing "optional forms" of county government from among which voters could choose.[4] They argued this would allow for flexibility and reduce the confusion between the respective powers of counties and municipalities. To be more precise, cities and villages already had home rule power. If counties, which overlapped those units of governments, also were given home rule powers, chaos would result. A 1962 amendment made the first breach in the uniformity requirement by authorizing counties that had a population of at least 100,000 (at that time there were nine) to elect a county executive. Nine years later this right was extended to all counties. The Task Force on Local Government Finance and Organization (the Tarr Task Force) recommended amending the constitution to allow alternative systems of county government in 1969, and the legislature soon embarked on the process of effecting that recommendation.

The issue of released time from school for religious instruction has been alive in Wisconsin for more than seventy years. As we have seen, the supreme court, in *Milquet*, held that expending money for religious purposes (in that case, for

---

[4] Thomas E. Fairchild and Charles P. Seibold, "Constitutional Revision in Wisconsin," *Wisconsin Law Review* (1950): 201–235.

transportation of children to parochial schools) violated Article I, Section 18. Three years later, the attorney general, recognizing the seriousness with which Wisconsin courts took the state's equivalent of the U.S. Constitution's prohibition against the establishment of religion, opined that a school would violate that section and Article X, Section 3 if it passed out forms to its pupils to take home so that their parents could request one hour of released time each week for their child's religious instruction. However, by about 1970 forty-seven states allowed released time for religious instruction, and advocates of religion pressed for Wisconsin to do the same. They succeeded; in 1972, Article I, Section 24, allowing released time, was added to the constitution. Of course, the very need for that amendment reinforced the courts' absolutist understanding of Article I, Section 18 and Article X, Section 3.

By 1970, agriculture in the state had become less viable financially, partly because of the property taxes that farmers owed. A statute required that all property be valued at its fair market value. Farms near growing cities could be sold to developers at high prices, so they were assessed at those values. As farmers sold their land to developers, the amount of land devoted to farming decreased. The uniformity clause, Article VIII, Section 1, blocked the way to some possible kinds of relief. Proponents of changing the method of assessing agricultural land advocated amending that provision to allow agricultural land to be taxed differently than other kinds of land. They argued for the change not as a tax break for farmers but as a deterrent to urban sprawl. In 1974, the voters narrowly (353,377 to 340,518) ratified an amendment that allowed agricultural land and undeveloped land to be taxed differently from other kinds of land. Shortly after that amendment was ratified, Richard Barrows pointed out some options for reducing the taxes on agricultural land that the amendment made possible.[5] Barrows, a University of Wisconsin professor, was working in the tradition of the Wisconsin Idea by offering advice on questions of public policy. The first result of that amendment was the 1977 farmland preservation law, which created an income tax credit for farmers whose land was subject either to exclusive agricultural zoning or to an agreement between the owner and the state that would prevent nonagricultural uses of it. The credit was calculated by means of an ingenious formula that had income and property tax factors and resulted in higher credits for land that was more difficult to convert to nonagricultural uses.

At about the same time, the prohibition against gambling was further eroded, again to allow relatively innocent behavior. In 1973, voters ratified an amendment to Article IV, Section 24 allowing bingo, and in 1977, they ratified an amendment to the same section allowing raffles. Both amendments allowed those forms of gambling only if a religious, charitable, service, fraternal, veterans', or other tax-exempt organization conducted them. The supreme court in

---

[5] Richard Barrows, "Lower Taxes for Farmland and Open Spaces?" (Madison, Wisconsin: University of Wisconsin-Extension, 1974).

State ex rel. Trampe v. Multerer (1940) had been unwilling to read into the constitutional provision an exception for gambling that raised revenue for a charitable organization, and the attorney general had agreed with that position. See 38 Op. Att'y Gen. 303 (1949). One suspects that charitable organizations conducted raffles and bingo long before the constitution authorized those games. In this instance, constitutional changes probably followed, rather than preceded, behavioral changes. Like the amendment specifying that listening to a radio program and watching and listening to a television program are not consideration in determining whether those activities are part of a gambling scheme, the bingo amendment reflected the belief that "lottery" in Article IV, Section 24 meant more than a raffle.

■ THE LATE TWENTIETH CENTURY: THE POWER OF THE COURTS AND THE GOVERNOR, MORE ATTENTION TO GAMBLING

By about 1970 the supreme court's workload had become intolerable. In fact, as early as 1954 Chief Justice Hallows called attention to the need for court reorganization.[6] Between 1962 and 1972 the number of cases that the court annually disposed of increased from 291 to 431, and the number of its undecided cases at the end of the year increased from 40 to 335. At the end of the 1973–1974 term, the court carried over into the next term 383 cases: almost a year's work. Nearly all of the justices who sat on the court at the time recall rushing to complete the opinions assigned to them and having little time to write concurrences or dissents, to participate in consideration of cases in which another justice took the lead, to comment on the opinions of other justices, or to perform superintending duties. The *Wisconsin Bar Bulletin* published a series of articles during 1971 on the supreme court's perilous state. Efforts to determine the problem's exact nature and seriousness and to propose solutions soon began. Governor Patrick J. Lucey appointed a Citizens Study Committee on Judicial Organization, which issued a report in January 1973, as did the Legislative Council's study committee. The supreme court commissioned a study by the National Center for State Courts, which presented its findings in December 1975. There was broad agreement on the need to act and on the general outline of the needed action.

Several constitutional amendments were required before the desired policy changes could be statutorily implemented. In 1977, the voters decisively approved many changes. The most important created a court of appeals. After ratification of these amendments and the enactment of implementing statutes, the supreme court could exercise original jurisdiction and discretion in reviewing courts of appeals and better control its workload. As a result, its caseload dropped and in

---

[6] E. Harold Hallows and J. R. DeWitt, "The Need for Court Organization," *Wisconsin Law Review* (1954): 376.

turn the number of concurring and dissenting opinions increased. The justices reported that they could return to deliberating and deciding cases collegially, rather than assigning one justice to supervise each case. The amendments also added administrative duties to the court's superintending duties and named the chief justice as the administrative head of the judicial system.

In 1977, U.S. Supreme Court justice William Brennan wrote an article for the *Harvard Law Review* calling for a change in the way that state supreme courts interpret state constitutions.[7] In the wake of the U.S. Supreme Court's turn away from an emphasis on the protection of individual rights and liberties in the 1970s, Brennan urged state courts to do so under their state constitutions, even when the wording of the constitutional provisions was identical and the federal interpretation less protective. Brennan's article announced what has come to be known as the "new judicial federalism."

In public speeches, Justice Nathan S. Heffernan and Justice Shirley S. Abrahamson echoed Brennan's theme. Heffernan, who became chief justice in 1983, expressed the idea in a speech to the Madison Literary Club that year. He traced the changes in the relationships between the U.S. and Wisconsin constitutions, noting that, primarily because of the dramatic contrast between the preambles, Wisconsin's courts recognized, long before the U.S. Supreme Court did, that citizens had certain rights that the government could not abridge. Although during the years when Earl Warren was the chief justice of the U.S. Supreme Court and that Court was expanding individual liberties, state supreme courts, including Wisconsin's, depended on the federal courts to protect individual liberties and relied less on their states' constitutions, that changed when Warren Burger became chief justice of the U.S. Supreme Court. State supreme courts at that time renewed their interest in their own constitutions. In 1983, the *Wisconsin Law Review* published a comment that amplified and provided further support to Justice Heffernan's arguments.[8] In 1985, Justice Shirley Abrahamson, who became the chief justice of the Wisconsin Supreme Court in August 1996, delivered an address on this subject to the Conference on the Emergence of State Constitutional Law. The *Texas Law Review* published a revised version of that address.[9] Therein, she explained many possible uses by state supreme courts of their own constitutions. Like Justice Heffernan before her, she advocated that state supreme courts more frequently turn to their state's constitutions. The commentary that follows, particularly on Article I, will indicate some of the differences between the state constitution and the federal Constitution and

---

[7] William J. Brennan, Jr., "State Constitutions and the Protection of Individual Rights," *Harvard Law Review* 90 (1977): 489.

[8] Junaid H. Chida, "Rediscovering the Wisconsin Constitution: Presentation of Constitutional Questions in State Courts," *Wisconsin Law Review* (1983): 483.

[9] Shirley Abrahamson, "Criminal Law and State Constitutions: The Emergence of State Constitutional Law," *Texas Law Review* 63 (1985): 1141–1183.

some of the results of Justice Abrahamson and Justice Heffernan's recourse to the Wisconsin constitution rather than to the more conservative federal cases interpreting the U.S. Constitution. More recently the court has jettisoned some of its distinctive interpretations of its constitution and adopted the U.S. Supreme Court's interpretation of analogous provisions in the U.S. Constitution.

Eroding the prohibition against gambling by authorizing radio and television games and certain bingo games and raffles led, predictably, to demands for further erosion. The state reached a turning point in 1987, when the legislature offered two amendments to the voters. Prospective owners of dog tracks were the main proponents of Article IV, Section 24(5), which authorized pari-mutuel betting. They argued that other states were rushing to legalize gambling and that tracks would increase tourism, provide entertainment, and create jobs. Soon after the voters ratified the amendment, promoters built a handful of dog tracks in the state. The other amendment, which created Article IV, Section 24(6), authorized a state lottery and required that the net proceeds be used for property tax relief. In that amendment "lottery" was probably intended to have its ordinary-language meaning. That tax relief, along with the possibility of large winnings, convinced a majority of the voters to support the amendment. Despite, or perhaps because of, these expansions of legal gambling, lobbyists and citizens have continued to pressure the legislature for further expansion by means of legislation, some of which would not have been clearly constitutional, or by means of additional constitutional amendments.

Since the ratification in 1930 of the amendment to Article V, Section 10 that expanded their veto power, Wisconsin governors have frequently used the veto. After it became clear that the courts interpreted the power very broadly, governors were tempted to push it a bit further. In 1971, a governor vetoed letters in words and digits in numbers, and the court found those acts to be within a governor's powers. Later governors became even more adventurous. One vetoed most of a paragraph to change the period for which juveniles may be detained and wrote in lower numbers to replace amounts that had been appropriated. The transfer of power from the legislature to the governor that the veto power effected had become, particularly when one party controlled both houses of the legislature and the governor was of the other party. Then the governor could use the veto power to tinker with bills, even reversing the effect of some of their provisions, and, because it takes a two-thirds vote of both houses of the legislature to override a veto, if the governor's party held one-third plus one seat in either house and the members of his party voted as a bloc, the veto would stand. Because Wisconsin's biennial budget bills are replete with policy provisions and enormously long, they offer a myriad of possibilities for creative vetoes.

By the late 1980s, some members of the public and many Democratic legislators—at the time, their party controlled both houses of the legislature but not the governor's office—thought that the veto power had to be restricted. A veto could not stop the legislators from amending the constitution to accomplish their purpose, because the first two steps in that process are passage of two identical joint resolutions, which can be done without the governor's approval. However, limiting the veto power presented a thorny technical problem: the supreme court had repeatedly drawn a distinction between Wisconsin's partial veto and other states' item veto. The legislature, therefore, could have tried to replace "in part" in Article V, Section 10 with an expression that would signify that the governor had an item veto. The court would probably respond by interpreting the amendment so that the veto power became narrower, but no one could predict the court's reaction to that gambit, or the kinds of vetoes that would be unconstitutional, and the proponents of such an amendment would have difficulty explaining its effects to the voters. Justice Connor T. Hansen, dissenting in *State ex rel. Kleczka v. Conta* (1978), suggested allowing only vetoes that removed a portion of a bill that could have been enacted separately. The legislature also could have specified either permissible or impermissible vetoes, but it would have had difficulty phrasing those limits. Instead, the legislature chose to offer to the electorate an amendment that forbade vetoes that created a new word by rejecting letters in the words of the bill. The voters ratified this minor diminution of the governor's veto power in 1990. Then, in 2005, the people approved an amendment that prohibited the governor from creating a new sentence by combining parts of two sentences in the enrolled bill.

By the early 1990s, several Indian gaming establishments, some of them highly successful, operated in Wisconsin. Their legality derived from the Indian Gaming Regulatory Act, which specifies three classes of gaming. Class I consists of social gaming, which, in regard to Indians, states could neither prohibit nor regulate. Class II consists of such gaming as low-stakes bingo, which Indians could conduct if the state allowed anyone to conduct it. Class III consists of such large-scale operations as casinos and animal racing. If the state did not prohibit a type of Class III gaming, it was required to negotiate a compact with any tribe that wished to conduct that type of gaming. However, the U.S. Supreme Court had ruled in *Seminole Tribe of Florida v. Florida* (1996) that a tribe could not sue a state to compel negotiation of a gaming compact. At the time, Wisconsin did not actually prohibit any forms of gaming, despite the apparent prohibition in Article IV, Section 24. The reason for this is that the 1987 amendment to that section authorized a state "lottery," and, as has been discussed, Wisconsin courts have interpreted that word broadly to include all forms of gambling.

In 1993, the voters ratified several changes to Article IV, Section 24. One change replaced "lottery" with "gambling" in subsection (1) to nullify the argument that "lottery" had a narrow meaning so that the subsection merely prohibited raffles, with the specified exceptions. Another change described in substantial detail the kind of lotteries that the state may conduct: its purpose was to nullify the argument that the state permitted itself to run all kinds of gambling and thus was required to negotiate compacts with Indians so that they could run any kind of gambling that they liked. Another amendment inserted into the constitution a long list of games that the state could not operate under its authority to operate a lottery. The confusion that this section has caused becomes obvious when one sees the number of, and the multitudinous detail of, the changes that were needed to arrive at the desired result. The ultimate effect of these changes will become clear only after litigation.

■ INTO THE TWENTY-FIRST CENTURY AND IDEOLOGICAL CHANGE

As in many states, the twenty-first century brought a broad ideological change to Wisconsin politics, which in turn affected the state's constitutional law. If 1911 was the miracle year, when Wisconsin led the nation with progressive legislation, 2011 was the bookend to that era and clearly reflected the change.

An undercurrent in the development of the United States, existing since the American Revolution, is the issue of assimilation or merger of a broad variety of cultures into a single American culture, and similarly, a single Wisconsin culture. This undercurrent is evident in the state constitution, the constitutional amendments proposed by the legislature, and the court's decisions relating to them. However, in the new century, the prevailing ideology has shifted from favoring assimilation to disfavoring it. Rather than foster assimilation of diverse populations, the government has encouraged sectarian schools and division in the general population. Changes in the educational system provide the prime example.

Other themes in constitutional law illustrate the ideological change, which reveals itself in political and legal issues. Part of the controversy relates to the "new judicial federalism," which was addressed previously in the discussion of late twentieth-century developments. In 1983, in *Michigan v. Long*, the U.S. Supreme Court held that state supreme courts, when considering a state constitutional provision that is the same as one in the U.S. Constitution, may make clear that a decision rests on "adequate and independent" state constitutional grounds, which federal courts will not review. The "adequate and independent ground" principle gave state courts the freedom to expand personal rights beyond the holdings of the federal courts, but when state courts exercise this authority, it can generate controversy. Some of the opposition to the new judicial federalism is based on "textualism," which teaches that the court should look only to the plain meaning of the words used in the constitution, and only when those words are ambiguous should the court refer to other sources for the meaning. Textualism opposes the court's regular three-part practice of looking at the intent of those who drafted the constitution, the first act of the legislature regarding the section in question, and other historical sources. Textualism is generally seen as a politically conservative approach to constitutional interpretation. A related belief is that the new judicial federalism is really disguised policymaking that should be left to the legislature and the governor while the judges (especially elected judges) should observe judicial restraint, follow precedent, and avoid political questions. Conservative jurists advance the proposition that state court decisions are political because they vary from U.S. Supreme Court decisions on the identical issue, but they often fail to acknowledge the political and policymaking nature of federal court decisions.

Five Wisconsin supreme court decisions from 2005 set the stage for a debate on these perspectives, and led to a major shift in the court's approach to constitutional interpretation: *Ferdon v. Wisconsin Patients Comp. Fund, Thomas v. Mallett, State v. Knapp, State v. Dubose*, and *In re Jerrell C.J.*

In *Ferdon*, the court held that a statute that capped damage awards in medical malpractice cases violated the equal protection clause of the Wisconsin constitution because severely injured persons could only recover part of their damages but less injured persons could recover fully. Purporting to apply a more intense rational-basis scrutiny, the court held that the statutory caps had only a speculative relationship to the primary legislative objective of improving healthcare in Wisconsin and declared the statute unconstitutional. The court overruled *Ferdon* in *Mayo v. Wisconsin Patients Comp. Fund* (2018), holding the earlier case a usurpation of the legislature's policymaking authority and concluding that statutory caps on non-economic damages do not violate equal protection.

In *Thomas v. Mallett*, a child who suffered lead poisoning sued seven paint pigment makers under the "risk contribution theory." The court held that although the child could not identify which company made the paint that poisoned him, and could not prove than any of the defendants specifically caused the poisoning, he could seek to hold liable all seven companies that manufactured lead paint pigments.

In *State v. Knapp*, the court held that certain blood-stained clothing should be excluded from evidence under the U.S. Constitution's Fifth Amendment because the evidence was discovered through the defendant's statement after the police had intentionally not given him a *Miranda* warning. The state then appealed to the U.S. Supreme Court, which held that the Fifth Amendment did not bar the clothing from being considered as evidence and sent the case back. On remand, the Wisconsin Supreme Court held that under the Wisconsin constitution, Article I, Section 8, the evidence should have been excluded.

State v. Dubose, decided the same day as *Knapp*, involved a "show-up," which resembles a line-up, except the witness sees only one suspect. The court relied heavily on social science studies and declared that the show-up was too suggestive and violated the defendant's right to due process of law. The court relied on Article I, Section 8, and stated that it would not interpret the Wisconsin constitution in "lock-step" with federal courts' interpretation of the U.S. Constitution. It then laid out more stringent restrictions on the use of "show-ups" than the rules announced by the U.S. Supreme Court. This case is an example of the "new judicial federalism," in which state courts interpret clauses in state constitutions that are the same or similar to clauses in the federal constitution differently, often granting more rights to individuals or putting greater restrictions on government.

In re Jerrell C.J., involved a fourteen-year-old suspected of armed robbery. The police handcuffed him to a wall for two hours and then interrogated him for five and a half hours before he confessed to the crime. On appeal, the court threw out the confession, ruling it was involuntary considering the defendant's age and the nature of the interrogation. The court went on to announce a new rule of evidence binding on all state courts. Under Article VII, Section 3, it exercised its supervisory authority over the state court system to require lower courts to exclude any custodial confession by a minor if the interrogation has not been recorded.

Two prominent federal judges wrote opposing law review articles analyzing these cases and further defining the shift in ideology. Diane Sykes, a judge on the Seventh Circuit Court of Appeals and a former Wisconsin Supreme Court justice, wrote first, decrying the court's abandonment of legal precedent, reliance on nonlegal sources, lack of deference to the other two branches of government, acting as a legislature in setting public policy, and generally failing to exercise its power judiciously, thereby endangering the state's economy and calling into question the stability and predictability of the legal system.[10] Lynn Adelman, a federal district court judge and former state legislator, co-authored an article with his former law clerk Shelley Fite, arguing that such criticisms were shortsighted and unfair because the search for justice and the fair administration of justice is more important than blind adherence to precedent.[11] They contended that the charge of activism indicated only disagreement with the results.

These opposing points of view paralleled those of the electorate, of which a majority favored the more conservative views. In the November 2008 election, Michael Gableman unseated justice Louis Butler, the first African-American justice in Wisconsin, in an exceptionally expensive and controversial election contest that was widely seen as the shifting of the tide. No sitting supreme court justice had lost an election since 1967. The court went from having a conservative minority to a conservative majority. Since that election, the court has stepped back from the new judicial federalism and generally follows U.S. Supreme Court decisions on individual rights issues. Although the framers intended for judicial offices to be nonpartisan, in recent years, the political parties have more and more overtly supported particular candidates, and some candidates have directly or indirectly declared their political party affiliation.

---

[10] Diane Sykes, "Reflections on the Wisconsin Supreme Court," *Marquette Law Review* 89 (2006): 723.

[11] Lynn Adelman and Shelley Fite, "Exercising Judicial Power: A Response to the Wisconsin Supreme Court's Critics," *Marquette Law Review* 91 (2007): 425.

▪ GENERAL TOPICS

I. The Public Purpose Doctrine

The public purpose doctrine of the Wisconsin constitution resembles the right to privacy of the U.S. Constitution—to see it in the document, one must peer between the lines and use some imagination. Nevertheless, it functions as does a constitutional provision: courts have stated that it does, and they have, based on this doctrine, ruled that statutes are unconstitutional. Despite its peculiar status, it is important because it constrains the use of public funds. It has two components, a general requirement that public funds may be used only for public purposes (in the case of state funds, the purpose must be a state purpose) and a requirement that the unit of government that imposes a tax must be the unit of government that spends the tax revenue.

Several attempts have been made to derive this doctrine from a particular state or federal constitutional provision. The court in *State ex rel. Wisconsin Development Authority v. Dammann* (1938), which concerned the prohibition against taking property without justly compensating the owner, looked to Article I, Section 13, and the equality provision, Article I, Section 1, of the state constitution. Another attribution, in *Heimerl v. Ozaukee County* (1949), was to the guarantee of a republican form of government in Article IV, Section 4 of the U.S. Constitution. Finally, the court in *State ex rel. La Follette v. Reuter* (1967) cited the requirement in Article VIII, Section 2 that no money may be paid out of the state treasury except by an appropriation made by law. All of these assertions are farfetched, particularly the one that would derive a state constitutional doctrine from the federal constitution. More recently, courts have conceded that the doctrine does not appear in the constitution and cannot be derived from any of its provisions, although they have continued to assert that it is well established and of constitutional dimensions See, e.g., *State ex rel. Singer v. Boos* (1969); *Hopper v. Madison* (1977).

In other words, the public purpose doctrine appears to be a judicial invention. But its questionable pedigree does not make it ill-advised. Wisconsin owes this doctrine, as it does a fair amount of its legal tradition, to Supreme Court Justice Luther Dixon. In *Soens v. City of Racine* (1860), asserted this doctrine in a case challenging the authority of the city of Racine to build piers, breakwaters, and other protections against the force of Lake Michigan was challenged. One commentators has claimed that Dixon's statement was mere dictum.[12] However, Justice Dixon invoked this doctrine in response to the final issue in the case: whether private property had been appropriated for public use or for private use. If the use was public and the tax in question had been imposed under

---

[12] Lewis R. Mills, "The Public Purpose Doctrine in Wisconsin: Part I," *Wisconsin Law Review* (1957): 40.

the city's taxing power it was therefore valid. If the use was private, the issue of whether private property had been taken without just compensation under Article I, Section 13 would arise. The circuit court judge had found that the purpose was private, but the supreme court disagreed and validated the tax. Thus, the public purpose doctrine, although judge-made, was founded on generally accepted conceptions of the government's taxing power.

In *Brodhead and others v. The City of Milwaukee and others* (1865), Justice Dixon put it this way: "[t]he legislature cannot create a public debt, or levy a tax, or authorize a municipal corporation to do so, in order to raise funds for a mere private purpose." Counsel on both sides had assumed this principle's validity and cited a Pennsylvania case as a precedent. The tax in question had been levied to pay bounties (financial rewards) to Civil War volunteers. Although the immediate beneficiaries were individuals, Justice Dixon considered that the bounties served a public purpose, and he therefore validated the tax. The commentator who thought that Dixon's statement in *Soens* was not necessary to the decision in that case called this the first public purpose case, but Justice Dixon wrote in his opinion that the principle had "frequently been affirmed by this court." He was correct. In addition to stating the doctrine in *Soens*, where it was essential to the decision, Dixon had also stated it in opinions in two earlier cases than *Brodhead*. In *Knowlton v. Supervisors of Rock County* (1859), he wrote in general terms that the taxing power allowed units of government to exact money "upon person or property for public uses." In *Hasbrouck v. The City of Milwaukee* (1860), he wrote, "[i]t is in view of the results, the public good thus produced, and the benefits thus conferred upon the persons and property of all the individuals composing the community, that courts have been able to pronounce them matters of public concern, for the accomplishment of which the taxing power might lawfully be called into action."

The history of the era in which the court developed the public purpose doctrine helps to explain Dixon's eagerness to treat it as a constitutional principle. The Panic of 1857 had recently devastated the country, leaving in its wake failed businesses, some of which had received governmental grants. Those defunct businesses would not repay governmental loans and would provide no other benefits in return for the loans. The blighted economy thus exacerbated the problems of municipal and state finance. Prudence counseled reining in the propensity of units of government to overextend themselves, especially to benefit private interests. That propensity derived in part from the need to develop the state's fledgling economy. Generally, the later a government begins developing the economy, the more important it is to infuse capital into that economy, and the more likely that public money will be needed for that purpose.

At the time, many of the beneficiaries of public expenditures were railroads. They exerted enormous influence on the legislature, in one session to the point of virtually controlling the legislature by means of disbursing free passes (which the ratification of Article XII, Section 11, in the Progressive era, brought to an end) and even cash. As well, Chicago was rapidly developing as a railroad center, a market, and a place where agricultural products were processed. The intensity of the battle for railroad lines and the power of the railroads is also illustrated by the legislature's investigation, in 1859, of the use by the 1856 legislature of the U.S. lands that were granted by the state to promote the building of railroads and of related corruption and bribery. Any Wisconsin municipality that had rail links to Chicago would most likely prosper; any Wisconsin municipality that did not would probably wither. In fact, competition among states and local units of government for economic and other kinds of development was intense and, so, too, was pressure on the legislature and local units of government to grant benefits directly to private entities or to expend money for narrow purposes. Some of those expenditures indirectly benefited the general public; others did not. Justice Dixon probably desired to increase the percentage that indirectly, at least, served a public purpose.

Several minor issues have arisen in cases addressing the scope of the public purpose doctrine. One is whether a need exists. If there is none, no purpose, much less a public purpose, exists. In striking down the Progressives' forest preservation act, the court in *State ex rel. Owen v. Donald* (1915) held that it violated many constitutional provisions in addition to the public purpose doctrine. On the latter issue, the court noted that, despite the legislature's statement of a need for forest preservation, there was no need, at least no present need. Determination of a need arguably was better left to the legislature, and the devastation of the state's forests made the court's determination at best questionable. Later courts did leave that kind of determination to the legislature, so *Donald* became an anomaly. In an early case, *Attorney General v. Eau Claire* (1875), the court decided that the public purpose must be stated in the act. For some time after the case was decided, if the legislature imagined that the public purpose doctrine might be an issue in litigation about a statute, it was likely to append a statement of purpose or intent to the bill that created the statute.[13] In two 1941 cases, *State ex rel. American Legion 1941 Conv. Corp. v. Smith* (1940) and *Disabled American Veterans Conv. Corp. v. Smith* (1940), the court inquired about the likelihood that the means adopted to effect the purpose were likely to work. Both cases involved state appropriations aimed at attracting conventions to the state, and in both the court held that, because there was no guarantee that the expenditures would secure a convention, the purpose was speculative and therefore improper.

If the state spends money, it must do so not only for a public purpose but for a statewide public purpose. This principle follows from the original connection of the public purpose doctrine to the taxing power. That is, it is logical to require that tax money raised by a unit of government should be spent by the unit of

---

[13] In 1969, an amendment to Article VIII, Section 7 required the legislature to state the public purposes when it incurred debt.

government for the benefit of the whole unit, not for the benefit of only part of it. Courts have been somewhat lenient about finding a statewide purpose. For example, spending money to acquire a convention that would be held in only one city was considered to fulfill a statewide purpose in *State ex rel. American Legion 1941 Convention v. Smith* (1940). Similarly, the court concluded that support for a major league baseball team that plays its home games in only one city fulfills a statewide public purpose. See *Libertarian Party v. State* (1996).

The decisions in public purpose doctrine cases depend heavily upon the facts and the justices' determination of whether those facts evince a public purpose. Accordingly, it makes sense to begin analyzing the central issues of these cases— whether there is a public purpose and, if the activity is the state's, whether the purpose is statewide—by listing the activities that have been held not to pass those tests, and then those that have been held to pass those tests. In those lists, some patterns can be discerned.

Courts have invalidated, on the ground of the public purpose doctrine, the following actions: paying funds to a private educational organization, *Curtis' Adm'r v. Whipple* (1869); paying funds to a railroad, *Whiting v. Sheboygan & Fond du Lac Railroad Co.* (1870); constructing a dam and leasing to manufacturers some of the water power that the dam would create, *Attorney General v. Eau Claire* (1875); spending funds to aid "habitual drunkards" in private institutions, *Wisconsin Keeley Institute Co. v. Milwaukee County* (1897); paying private debts, *State ex rel. Consolidated Stone Co. v. Houser* (1905); making a grant to a lumber company to lay pipe under a municipality's land, *Lakeside Lumber Co. v. Jacobs* (1908); a municipality's sale of land for $1 for construction of a factory, *Suring v. Suring State Bank* (1926); giving a "gift" in the form of a retirement benefit to an individual, *State ex rel. Smith v. Annuity and Pension Board* (1942); making an appropriation for veterans' housing authorities and city housing authorities, *State ex rel. Martin v. Giessel* (1948); and authorizing counties to contract with municipalities for work on private roads, *Heimerl v. Ozaukee County* (1949).

Courts have validated, despite attacks on public purpose grounds, the following: granting bonuses to Civil War recruits, *Brodhead and others v. The City of Milwaukee and others* (1865); committing delinquents to private, nonprofit institutions, *Wisconsin Industrial School for Girls v. Clark County* (1899); paying money to repair the damage caused by a cyclone, *State ex rel. City of New Richmond v. Davidson* (1902); paying veterans' bonuses, *State ex rel. Atwood v. Johnson* (1919); paying benefits to active teachers, *State ex rel. Dudgeon v. Levitan* (1923); paying unemployment relief, *Appeal of Van Dyke* (1935); refunding motor vehicle registration fees, *State ex rel. Larson v. Giessel* (1954); paying municipalities for sewage treatment plants, *State ex rel. La Follette v. Reuter* (1967); creation by counties of nonprofit organizations for industrial development, *State ex rel. Bowman v. Barczak* (1967); issuing state bonds for constructing interstate highways, *State ex rel. La Follette v. Reuter* (1967); expending funds for an incinerator and a waste disposal plant, *West*

Allis v. Milwaukee County (1967); appropriating money to a private medical school, *State ex rel. Warren v. Reuter* (1969); making pension payments, *State ex rel. Singer v. Boos* (1969); establishing a housing authority, *State ex rel. Warren v. Nusbaum* (1973); establishing an authority to promote solid waste recycling, *Wisconsin Solid Waste Recycling Auth. v. Earl* (1975); issuing industrial revenue bonds, *State ex rel. Hammermill Paper Co. v. La Plante* (1973); providing funds to a tenant union, a Spanish-American organization, and a day-care facility, *Hopper v. Madison* (1977); creating a district in which some of the property taxes and other funds would be used to benefit businesses in the district, *Sigma Tau Delta Fraternity House v. Menomonie* (1980); creating and appropriating funds to an authority that would encourage the construction of utilities, *State ex rel. Wisconsin Dev. Authority v. Dammann* (1938); providing state funds for private schools, *Davis v. Grover* (1992); and a combination of encouraging economic development and tourism, reducing unemployment, bringing capital into the state, and creating recreational opportunities, *Libertarian Party v. State* (1996).

One can see by examining the two lists that the percentage of invalidations has significantly declined. That is, the public purpose doctrine appears to have become less of an impediment to the use of public funds. As a court in *State ex rel. Warren v. Reuter* put it, it is a fluid doctrine that changes as conditions change. Indeed, the court has reversed its position on several issues, even though the facts in the cases have been substantially similar. Examples of subjects on which reversals occurred include: paying private, nonprofit organizations, *Curtis' Adm'r v. Whipple* (1869), *Wisconsin Industrial School for Girls v. Clark County* (1899); paying for-profit entities, *Whiting v. Sheboygan & Fond du Lac Railroad Co.* (1870), *State ex rel. Hammermill Paper Co. v. La Plante* (1973); and paying retirement benefits, *State ex rel. Smith v. Annuity and Pension Board* (1942), *State ex rel. Singer v. Boos* (1969).

The case that summarizes the major themes in the case law on the public purpose doctrine and accordingly is a useful summary of the concept is *State ex rel. Warren v. Nusbaum* (1972). There, the court conceded that the doctrine does not explicitly appear in the constitution but called it a "well-established constitutional tenet." The court accorded great weight to the legislature's determination that the law's purposes were public, although it reserved the right to evaluate that determination. It required the public benefit to be direct, although it approved benefits that fall more immediately on one group rather than being distributed equally among the state's people. It asserted that providing for the public's safety, health, education, morals, welfare, and comfort are public purposes. It reiterated that, if the state expends the funds in question, the benefit must be statewide, but conceded that dealing with local conditions would not necessarily violate that principle.

The second part of the public purpose doctrine is that a unit of government that raises a tax must be the unit of government that spends the proceeds of that tax. This is a logical concomitant to this doctrine's more general rule. As we have seen, the general doctrine has its roots in conceptions of government's taxing power, so it is fitting that one of the doctrine's rules applies solely to taxation. Also, it seems logical that a purpose is not truly public if one "public" provides money and another "public" reaps its benefits. Wisconsin courts, for over a century and a half, have affirmed this principle. See *Brodhead and others v. The City of Milwaukee and others* (1865); *State ex rel. New Richmond v. Davidson* (1902); *State ex rel. Garrett v. Froehlich* (1903); *State ex rel. Owen v. Donald* (1915); *State ex rel. Wisconsin Dev. Auth. v. Dammann* (1938); *State ex rel. American Legion 1941 Conv. Corp. v. Smith* (1940); *State ex rel. Warren v. Nusbaum* (1973); *Buse v. Smith* (1976); *Sigma Tau Delta Gamma Fraternity House v. Menomonie* (1980).

II. Priority of Constitutional Provisions

The Wisconsin constitution forbids, authorizes, and requires various behaviors. It has 137 sections, many of which contain more than one statement that performs one of those functions. Because of the large number of directions, one would expect conflicts, but there are no apparent internal inconsistencies. The difficulty arises regarding statutes that are based on the constitution or to which the constitution applies. For example, one section in the constitution may authorize behavior and another may forbid behavior. A statute based on the first constitutional provision might violate the other. In that instance, a court might be asked to decide whether one constitutional provision has priority over the other. If one does have priority, a statute based on the constitutional provision that has less priority will be void. Also, a statute based on a constitutional provision that requires an action may conflict with another constitutional requirement. The question for a court is whether one provision overrides the other. For instance, Article IV, Section 24 requires the proceeds of the state lottery to be used for property tax relief, while Article VIII, Section 1 requires uniform property taxation. Is a statute that implements the first requirement valid even if it violates the second requirement?

The supreme court settled this question early in its history. Like several other issues, this one was addressed by Chief Justice Luther Dixon, in *Bull v. Conroe* (1860). Dixon concurred "with the counsel for the respondent in the position that all parts of the constitution are equally binding and imperative." That is, constitutional provisions seemingly at odds must be harmonized. At the time of *Bull*, the exemption from execution of a judgment in Article I, Section 17 was different for agricultural property than for nonagricultural property. The plaintiff brought the case because the legislature, acting under Article XI, Section 1, had annexed his land to a municipality, thereby making it nonagricultural. The court decided that the plaintiff had had a right to an exemption but did not have the right to a particular exemption in perpetuity. In other words, the section that granted the exemption did not have priority over the section that governed the formation of municipalities. A statute, to be constitutional, had to conform to both provisions.

Seven cases followed the lead of *Bull*. One involved two sentences in the same section: Article X, Section 8. The court approved the withdrawal of school land from sale by the Commissioners of Public Lands despite the grant of power to the legislature to provide for the sale of that land in *State ex rel. Sweet and another v. Cunningham and others* (1894). In *Huber v. Martin* (1906), the court held that the legislature's authority under Article XI, Section 1 to form corporations and to dissolve them implied by that article did not permit it to violate the prohibition against impairing contracts in Article I, Section 12. The court in *Water Power Cases* (1912) invalidating one of the conservation laws that the 1911 legislature had passed, held that the legislature's authority to grant charters under Article XI, Section 1 did not override the prohibition in Article I, Section 13 against taking private land for public uses without adequately compensating the former owner. Similarly, the court in *State ex rel. Melms v. Young* (1920) held that a statute implementing the grant of power to the electors of a county to vote for their county's officials in Article XIII, Section 9 did not justify a violation of the requirement of uniform county government in Article IV, Section 23. The statute had required nonpartisan elections of county officials in counties that had a population of more than 250,000, but not in other counties.

Another case, *State ex rel. Sonneborn v. Sylvester* (1965), involved the authority to provide for county elections that derives from Article XII, Section 9. There the court invalidated a statutory scheme that provided for election of county officers by municipalities rather than county-wide, because the scheme in question violated the equal protection principle in Article I, Section 1. Finally, in *In Matter of Guardianship of Eberhardy* (1981), the court held that the grant to circuit courts of original jurisdiction in all matters in Article VII, Section 8 did not negate the power of the supreme court to superintend the legal system under Article VII, Section 3(1). The court ordered the circuit court not to take jurisdiction in a case about the sterilization of an incompetent person, although it did not deny that the circuit court had jurisdiction. In each of these cases, the court gave effect to both constitutional provisions that related to the statute that was the litigation's subject, rather than holding that one of the constitutional provisions overrode the other.

III. Apparent Grants of Legislative Power

The constitution, in Article IV, Section 1, unambiguously grants legislative authority to the legislature. Article IV, Section 17(2) states that "no law shall be enacted except by bill." The constitution is also rife with phrases that at first glance appear to grant power to the legislature to make laws on certain subjects. Their wording varies. Some examples include: "the legislature may by statute provide," Article I, Section 5; "the legislature by law may," Article I, Section 8(2) and (3); Article IV, Section 29; Article VII, Section 3; Article XI, Section 4 (the wording varies slightly among these provisions); and "shall be recognized by laws," Article I, Section 17; Article X, Sections 5, 6, and 8; Article XI, Section 1 (again, the wording varies). Although these phrases are ambiguous, one can confidently draw several inferences from the case law about their effects.

Before looking at the relevant case law, one needs to note two problems in addition to the ambiguity and variety of their wording. One is that Article X, Section 5 requires the legislature to present to the governor all the bills that it passes. That requirement makes it impossible for the legislature, by itself, to enact a law unless it overrides a gubernatorial veto. Presumably, then, the phrases that refer only to the legislature should be interpreted to mean the lawmaking process. The other problem is the ambiguity of the term "law." Passing a joint resolution, which does not require the governor's action, probably is not lawmaking. The court drew that distinction in *State ex rel. Reynolds v. Zimmerman* (1964). Under the statutes, administrative rules have the effect of law, Wis. Stat. § 227.01(13), but they are not law, so promulgating rules is probably not sufficient to fulfill whatever duty these phrases impose, or to exercise whatever power they confer.

One theme in the case law is that these phrases signify that the constitutional provision in which they appear is not self-executing. See, e.g., *Bull v. Conroe* (1860); *The Chicago, Milwaukee and St. Paul R'y Co. v. The State* (1881); *Kayden Industries, Inc. v. Murphy* (1967); *Forseth v. Sweet* (1968); *Chart v. Gutmann* (1969); *Kallembach v. State* (1986). A self-executing constitutional provision *by itself* forbids, authorizes, or requires behavior. An example is the right of free speech granted by Article I, Section 3. Simply on that provision's basis a person can attack a statute that he or she believes abridges that right. In contrast, Article VIII, Section 1 authorizes the nonuniform taxation of agricultural land and undeveloped land, both "as defined by law." Thus, an assessor may not value those kinds of land differently from the way that he or she values other kinds of land unless they have been defined by law. The last subsection of Article XIII, Section 12 states that the section is "self-executing." This section governs expulsion of elected officials, so the framers of the constitution prudently made it clear that its effectiveness did not depend upon the action of legislators, who might have an interest in making sure, by their inaction, that it never took effect.

Another theme in the case law is that the enigmatic phrases impose a duty on the legislature to act. Just as most of the cases in which courts interpret this kind of phrase to mean that the constitutional provision is not self-executing involve Article IV, Section 27 (concerning suits against the state), most of the cases that make the point about the duty to act involve Article VII, Section 15 (concerning justices of the peace), which has been repealed. An exception to this is a case that keeps cropping up in this account of the constitution, *Bull v. Conroe* (1860). There, Justice Dixon referred to "the laws required by that section [Article I, Section 17]," although he acknowledged that the court had no power to force the legislature to act. In two cases on Article VII, Section 15, courts interpreted the phrase as had Justice Dixon, determining that a phrase of this type meant that the legislature was required to act. See *State ex rel. Wood v. Goldstucker and Another* (1876); *Trogman v. Grover* (1908).

Courts have also frequently held that, in responding to one of these apparent grants of power, the legislature may not create a sham. All the cases in which the court took that position involved an earlier version of Article XI, Section 3. Before it was amended in 1926, that section required the legislature "to provide for the organization of cities and incorporated villages." The court in *Smith v. Sherry* (1880) held that combining noncontiguous land to create a village violated that section. Later, the plaintiff in *State ex rel. Town of Holland v. Lammers* (1902) successfully attacked a statute that allowed the creation of a village if certain population and size requirements were fulfilled. Then the creation of an even more obvious sham—a "village" composed of 465 acres of agricultural land, a settled area of thirty-eight and one-half acres (which was not adjacent to the agricultural land), and seventy-five acres that were under water—was held to be unconstitutional in *Fenton v. Ryan* (1909). Two years later the court in *Incorporation of Town of Biron* (1911) agreed that a village had to be a real village, not a sham, but found that the requirement was fulfilled. In yet another case, *Incorporation of Village of St. Francis* (1932), the court determined that a sham, not a village, had been created. Although these cases concern the same section of the constitution, the principle that emerges from them would probably apply to other sections as well.

Justice Dixon also sounded another theme in the case law on this issue in *Bull v. Conroe*: "I cannot assent to the doctrine that the discretionary power given to the legislature is absolute and unlimited, and it may not do violence to the clause [that gave it the power to specify the property that is exempt from execution after a judgment], as well by exempting too much as too little, or by protecting those things which are not of the necessary comforts of life as well as by refusing to protect those which are." In other words, Dixon believed that these phrases did not grant absolute power to the legislature and the governor to make laws as they saw fit. Rather, he believed that, even if a law was enacted on a subject to which one of the phrases applied, the courts had the power to rule it unconstitutional. Therefore, courts could read into the constitutional grant of lawmaking authority conditions and requirements. In too many cases to cite, the Wisconsin courts have followed Justice Dixon's lead, making it clear that the constitution's enigmatic phrases certainly do not grant absolute lawmaking power.

Three categories of cases bear close examination. Two consist of cases in which another general principle of constitutional law interacts with one of those enigmatic grants. The two principles that do so are the equal priority of all constitutional provisions and the public purpose doctrine. Cases in which the court held that one of the enigmatic grants of authority did not override another constitutional provision include: the provision for the sale of school lands in Article X, Section 8, *State ex rel. Sweet and another v. Cunningham and others* (1894); the provision in Article XIII, Section 9, allowing the legislature to direct the method of electing certain county officers, *State ex rel. Melms v. Young* (1920), and the provision in Article XI, Section 1, granting to the legislature the authority to create corporations and to alter and repeal their charters, *Attorney General v. Railroad Companies* (1874); *Huber v. Martin* (1906); *State ex rel. Northern Pac. R. Co. v. Railroad Commission* (1909); *Water Power Cases* (1912); and *State ex rel. Cleary v. Hopkins Street B. & L. Assoc.* (1935). The constitution grants, in whole or in part, to the legislature both the taxing power and the spending power by means of enigmatic phrases. Article VIII, Sections 1 and 5, grant taxing authority, and Article VIII, Section 2, implicitly grants spending authority. Accordingly, the public purpose doctrine, which limits both kinds of authority, occasionally interacts with one of these enigmatic grants, and all the cases mentioned in the essay on the public purpose doctrine are relevant here, too.

The third category worth examining involves a particular subject matter: the judiciary. Article VII, Section 7 grants to the legislature the authority to specify the terms of office and the compensation of circuit court judges. The court in *State ex rel. Pierce v. Kundert* (1958) held invalid a statute that created a term for one circuit court judge that was shorter than the terms of other circuit court judges, a salary for him that was less than that of other circuit court judges, and duties that were greater than those of other circuit court judges. Article VII, Section 8 specifies that circuit courts have original jurisdiction in all civil and criminal cases "[e]xcept as otherwise provided by law." However, the supreme court, rather than wait for the legislature to limit the circuit courts' jurisdiction, directed circuit courts to refrain from exercising their jurisdiction to allow the sterilization of persons who cannot give informed consent to the procedure in *In Matter of Guardianship of Eberhardy* (1981).

In summary, a reader's likely reaction to these enigmatic phrases—that they grant to the legislature specific power that supplements the general grant of power in Article IV, Section 1—proves to be less than accurate. Those phrases grant some power, but it is limited by the need to avoid shams, the requirement that other constitutional provisions not be violated, and the requirement that statutes based upon one of these grants may not be shams. The phrases also create a duty to legislate, and that duty has some urgency because the constitutional provisions that include those phrases have no effect unless a statute has been enacted.

IV. Interpretation of the Constitution

As the section-by-section commentary indicates, methods of interpreting the constitution are critical. We will see that Wisconsin courts often have arrived at meanings for constitutional provisions that differ dramatically from those that a layperson would adduce. Some of these surprising readings flow from the method of interpretation that the court used. Courts have at their disposal several such methods. No story of the Wisconsin constitution would be complete unless it explained those methods.

In the first case in which the supreme court interpreted the constitution, *State ex rel. Dunning v. Giles* (1849), it did so only obliquely. The case turned on Article XIV, Section 2, which preserved territorial laws that were "not repugnant to the constitution." The court, rather than specifying the constitutional provision to which the law was repugnant, made a sweeping statement about the spirit of the entire document: "I cannot believe that a constitution thus broad and catholic ever meant, by adopting an old provincial law, to extend the political disabilities of certain *inhabitants* of the territory to the *citizens* of the State." Thus the court adverted to the constitution's intent.

In the second case in which the supreme court interpreted a portion of the constitution, *State ex rel. Bond v. French* (1849), Judge Alexander W. Stow used a common-sense method. He wrote: "our only guide is the constitution, in construing which we are governed by the same general rules of interpretation which prevail in relation to statutes." Unfortunately, he did not state those rules; in its first term, the supreme court decided just two statutory construction cases, a sample too small to give one a clear idea of the rules the court considered appropriate. In one of those cases, *Whitney v. Powell* (1849), Stow adopted a literal interpretation of the statute, remarking that "on a careful examination" of it he thought that it had a particular meaning. In other words, he employed a principle that later came to be called the "plain meaning" rule: interpreting a text without recourse to any explanatory material or to an analysis of the intent that informs the text. In the other case, *Hardell v. McClure* (1849), the court stated, "if the policy of the act was not wholly misconceived, the courts were bound to give it a fair and liberal construction." This is a variation of another common method of statutory construction, the one that was loosely used in *State ex rel. Dunning v. Giles* (1849): trying to determine the statute's intent and then to interpret the statute to effect that intent. Some judges, in interpreting a statute, begin with this method; others refer to it if they believe that the statute is ambiguous. In *Hardell*, Judge Levi Hubbell reserved for himself judgment on the wisdom of the policy that the statute embodied. Presumably, had he found that policy to be "wholly misconceived," he would have either explicitly "interpreted" the statute to arrive at the result he wanted or he would have interpreted the statute as narrowly as possible, making it apply in as few instances as possible.

As one would predict from seeing that after only two cases courts deployed differing methods to interpret the constitution, later courts developed still more approaches. Of the methods, several appear only occasionally in the cases and three appear frequently. In a relatively recent case, *Thompson v. Craney* (1996), the court used all three of those methods. Because of the absence of unanimity and of consistent historical patterns, it makes the most sense to consider the methods separately.

One of the less frequently used methods is to determine the meaning of one constitutional provision by looking at other parts of the constitution. A dispute about the removal from office of a sheriff called into question the meaning of Article VI, Section 4 in *State ex rel. Rodd v. Verage* (1922), which gave the governor the power to remove sheriffs. The court used this method, narrowly, looking only at the rest of the section and concluded that the section's first sentence, which gave the electors the right to vote for sheriffs, implied that the governor did not have an absolute right to remove a sheriff but could do so only for cause. The court also concluded that the right to hold office was a property right. The court noted that the framers of the constitution could have, but did not, grant an absolute power of removal. These arguments are strained, and there was a more logical way to use the same method of interpretation to get to the result that the court achieved. That section of the constitution also provided that all officers who were in danger of removal had a right to learn of the charges against them and to answer those charges. Those two provisions imply that removal may be only for cause. A later court, in *State ex rel. Reynolds v. Zimmerman* (1964), used this comparative method in a much vaguer sense. The legislature had purported to redistrict the state without presenting a bill to do so to the governor for his consideration. Article IV, Section 3 gave the legislature the authority to redistrict and did not include "by law," which would have implied that a bill must be passed and presented to the governor. The court reasoned that the constitution as a whole established a "representative democratic form of government" and that, in keeping with that system, unilateral legislative action violated the constitution. The court thus declined to read the constitution literally.

Courts have also occasionally examined other constitutions as an aid to interpreting the Wisconsin constitution. An early example is *Attorney General ex rel. Schantz v. Brunst* (1854), in which the court relied upon interpretations of a provision in the New York constitution that was identical to the Wisconsin provision, Article VI, Section 4, to help it resolve the case. In *Wisconsin Central R. Co. v. Taylor County* (1881), the court asserted that examination of "earlier constitutions of the several [unnamed] states" and of the British constitution supported the contention that the state had plenary power to tax. Later, the plaintiff in *Milwaukee v. Horvath* (1966) argued that imposing a jail sentence for failing to pay a parking fine subjected her to involuntary servitude in violation of Article I, Section 2 of the state constitution and the Thirteenth Amendment of the U.S. Constitution. The court, noting that both constitutional provisions derived from the Northwest Ordinance, asserted that the cases in which the federal provision was interpreted were relevant and showed that the term meant not only confinement but requirement of labor.

In *Bablitch & Bablitch v. Lincoln County* (1978), which concerned the question whether a county was responsible for its sheriff's actions, the court examined New York cases because the relevant provision of the Wisconsin constitution, Article VI, Section 4, was based upon the New York constitution. This method has persisted until relatively recently. In a double jeopardy case, *State v. Barthels* (1993), the court used federal decisions on the U.S. Constitution's prohibition against creating double jeopardy to interpret a similar provision, Article I, Section 8, of the Wisconsin constitution. Federal cases interpreting parts of the U.S. Constitution often have been pertinent, or even controlling, in interpreting many portions of Article I.

Some justices have disputed the legitimacy of this method. As discussed previously, in the 1980s two Wisconsin Supreme Court justices expressed interest in adverting to the Wisconsin constitution if they believed that interpretations of an analogous provision in the federal Constitution did not sufficiently protect individual liberties. In that decade, one of them, Justice Abrahamson, wrote two opinions in which she took this approach. In one, a tax fraud case, an issue was whether the constitution's provisions that forbade issuing process to legislators, within fifteen days before and within fifteen days after a session, and that gave legislators immunity for words spoken in debate, Article IV, Sections 15 and 16, required that a subpoena directed to a legislator's aide be quashed. Abramson wrote in *State v. Beno* (1984) that, "in interpreting article IV, sections 15 and 16, of the state constitution, we are not bound by the construction given the speech and debate clause (article I, section 6) of the U.S. Constitution by the United States Supreme Court."

The minor theme of "practical" interpretation also sounds in cases in which the constitution is interpreted. In *Integration of Bar Case* (1943), which concerned whether attorneys may be required to be members of the State Bar of Wisconsin, a relevant statute that required the supreme court to issue orders about the organization of the bar brought into question the constitutional roles of the legislative and judicial branches of government. Justice Marvin B. Rosenberry first pointed out that the divisions between the two branches that the constitution created are not absolute, and that the constitution consists of principles rather than rules. This state of affairs necessitated interpreting the constitution to adapt its principles to the "practical affairs of government."

Six years later, in *State ex rel. Frederick v. Zimmerman* (1949), the same justice was confronted with an argument that "to be elected as now provided," which was added to Article VII, Section 4 in 1889, froze, as of that year, the statutory law on the election of judges. Rosenberry, in rejecting this interpretation, pointed out that no one in the state had understood the amendment in that way, and that to adopt that interpretation would invalidate all the judicial elections retroactively for decades. He implied, but did not explicitly state, that a "practical" interpretation was necessary. Later, in *Jacobs v. Major* (1987) another justice expressed skepticism about "practical" interpretations, conceding that the court had the power, perhaps the duty, to recognize changing conditions, but that "such action must be consistent with the clear meaning of the constitution."

One of the three major methods of interpreting the constitution is reading it literally, according to its plain meaning. Judge Stow in *State ex rel. Bond v. French*

(1849) used this method, although he was not explicit about it. A few years later, in *The Attorney General ex rel. Bashford v. Barstow* (1856), the court more clearly employed this method, rejecting arguments based upon the debates in the state and federal constitutional conventions and stating that "we must look to that instrument [the state constitution] for the purpose of determining this question." A later court differently expressed the same principle: "[i]f a difference exists it must exist by virtue of the organic law and not because the court may think that the framers of the law would have acted more wisely had they recognized the distinction and provided for it. Courts cannot supply what they deem to be unwise omissions from the constitution." *State ex rel. Van Alstine v. Frear* (1910). In a later case, *State ex rel. Reconstruction Finance Corp. v. Sanlader* (1947), the court listed kinds of analysis that could be used as an aid to interpreting part of the constitution, but added that they were relevant "only if [a provision's] language leaves it open to construction." That is, if the meaning is plain, the court should go no further.

Sometimes courts have asserted the plain meaning rule's validity but added qualifications to it. A common example is rejection of the plain meaning if it would lead to an "absurd" result. For example, in *State ex rel. Williams v. Samuelson* (1907), a court held that the plain meaning of Article VI, Section 4, which required all county officers, except judicial officers, to be elected was, if read literally, absurd because it made it impossible to enact a law that would allow the appointment of minor county officials. At first glance it may appear that the meaning of a constitutional provision is the meaning it has at the time of the litigation. However, in *B. F. Sturtevant Co. v. Industrial Comm.* (1925), the court stated that the relevant meaning is the one that would have been given to the provision when it was inserted in the constitution. In several cases, the court has stated that a constitutional provision ought to be interpreted in light of the purpose that it was intended to serve. See, e.g., *Kayden Industries, Inc. v. Murphy* (1967).

Thus, in constitutional interpretation cases courts have gradually eroded the plain meaning rule. Occasionally, courts have effectively abandoned the rule. One example is *State ex rel. Martin v. Heil* (1941), which arose because a governor-elect died before he assumed office. Under Article V, Section 7, if for certain specified reasons a governor can no longer serve, the lieutenant governor becomes governor. That section almost, but not quite, applied; the winning candidate was not yet a governor. Faced with this quandary, the court remarked that "[i]t is extremely important in the interpretation of constitutional provisions that we avoid determinations based purely on technical or verbal argument." The court meant that sometimes courts had to ignore a constitutional provision's plain meaning. The court did so, holding that the section's intent justified including the situation that was the subject of the case in the list of events that resulted in the lieutenant governor becoming governor. In effect, the court amended the constitution.

Sometimes courts have tried to ascertain the intent of the drafters of a constitutional provision not merely to elucidate the provision's meaning but to substitute for that meaning. That is, courts have held the intent, not the phrasing, paramount. Wisconsin courts adopted this method of interpretation quite early. It was used, for example, in *State ex rel. Comstock v. Joint School District* (1886). A later court clearly stated this rule, although it was more forceful about statutes than about the constitution: "[t]he familiar and elementary rule that it is the duty of the court to discover and give effect to the intent of the legislature in construing a statute is equally applicable to the constitution, and the intent and purpose of the framers of the constitution should therefore be a guide to its application and interpretation." *State ex rel. Zimmerman v. Dammann* (1930).

The first problem that arises in using this method is finding a way to determine the framers' intent. If the provision has not been amended since the 1848 constitution, Quaife's summary of the convention's debates and collection of contemporary newspaper articles is an invaluable resource.[14] The court in *In re Cannon* (1932) sought recourse to the common law (see the discussion on Article XIV, Section 13) to determine the meaning that the framers ascribed to the term "court." This tactic made sense because the undefined term was a legal one, and the framers of the constitution probably were thinking of its meaning in the common law. Other courts have used more than one source. The court in *Borgnis v. Falk* (1911) used "the conditions prevailing at the time . . . [and] the changed social, economic, and governmental conditions and ideals of the time, as well as the problems which the changes produced." The meaning of "changed" in this list is obscure, and many of the items are nebulous. On this subject, the court in *State ex rel. Zimmerman v. Dammann* (1930) stated, "[t]o discover that intent reference may be had to other provisions of the constitution, to the history of the times, the state of society at the time when the constitution was framed and adopted, and to prior well-known practices and usages." In addition to the vagueness of some of those entities and the difficulty of understanding the conditions in Wisconsin in 1848 in order to interpret a constitutional provision, proponents of this method must overcome skepticism about its inherent irrationality. One court, for example, commented that, if the framers intended that their understanding of a constitutional provision ought to be valid for all time, that "intention would entirely ignore those altered conditions which the mutations of time bring about, and would be tantamount to an egotistical declaration that when the constitution was framed the millennium had arrived and

---

[14] *See* Bibliographical Essay, Section III.

progress had reached its ultimate goal." *State ex rel. Van Alstine v. Frear* (1910). In addition, one has difficulty conceiving of the unitary intent of a body of persons.

Courts have also purported to uncover the intent of the framers of constitutional provisions by examining the laws that were enacted soon after the provision became part of the constitution. Upon the rehearing of a case about the right to the office of sheriff, the court in *State ex rel. Pluntz v. Johnson* (1922), after examining the language of Article VI, Section 4, examined part of the Revised Statutes of 1849. The court concluded that the relevant statute illustrated "contemporaneous legislative construction of this constitutional provision." That assertion is plausible because of the brief time span between ratification of the constitution and enactment of the relevant statute.

If the cases analyzed so far were the only ones on constitutional interpretation, one would be justified in asserting that the law on this subject lacks focus—that courts can choose among many methods of interpretation and, if so inclined, can choose a method that will yield the result that they desire. However, the Wisconsin Supreme Court in the last years of the twentieth century brought some stability to this area of the law. In three very important cases between 1974 and 1996 it followed the same method of interpreting the constitution, combining the three main methods that appeared earlier in the case law, although usually not all together. In *Board of Education v. Sinclair* (1974), the court's task was to interpret the requirement in Article X, Section 3 that schools be "free and without charge for tuition." First, the court examined the passage itself, citing a dictionary definition of "free" and using the context ("without charge for tuition") to help buttress its interpretation. Next, it tried to determine the framers' intent, not by recourse to the debates on the constitution, which would have been more convincing, but by consulting a history of education in the state. Then, it examined the first law enacted on the subject. To support its use of this method, it cited some of the cases already mentioned. The court determined that the use of "free" in the constitution did not prevent schools from charging for books and similar items. Recourse to the debates on the constitution rather than to a history of education to determine the framers' intent would have revealed a comment by delegate Vanderpoel that "there was a feeling of pride which restrained those who were unable to pay their proportion from sending their children to the common schools." A logical inference is that he, at least, thought that "free" meant without charge of any kind. Nevertheless, this rational method of interpretation was a significant step forward for the court in an important area of the law. The court employed this three-part approach in two important later cases, *Buse v. Smith* (1976) and *Thompson v. Craney* (1996).

Some of the people who created Wisconsin's constitutional history were remarkably good; some were not. Nevertheless, the document—the Wisconsin constitution—remains an impressive achievement, one that reflects the inherent goodness of the state. Adlai Stevenson, an astute observer, once remarked:

> the Wisconsin tradition meant more than a simple belief in the people. It also meant a faith in the application of intelligence and reason to the problems of society. It meant a deep conviction that the role of government was not to stumble along like a drunkard in the dark, but to light its way by the best torches of knowledge and understanding it could find. (Madison, Wisconsin, October 8, 1952).

PART TWO

The Wisconsin Constitution and Commentary

Believing that the relevant version of the constitution is the current one, we have neither included nor noted repealed sections. A commentary follows each section. Some of the commentaries are terse because the section to which they relate has rarely or never been changed or litigated. Commentaries on sections that are ambiguous or have often been amended or litigated are fairly long. We have briefly identified changes and explained in chronological order the judicial interpretations of some sections if that tactic most cogently addresses those sections, but we have not written a history of each section in the sense that Part One of this book is a history. Because of the great number of cases on the constitution, the commentary that follows is less than exhaustive. Some of our remarks depend upon the work of other scholars, which are cited in the bibliography to assist readers who require more detail than we are able to provide.

Preamble

We, the people of Wisconsin, grateful to Almighty God for our freedom, in order to secure its blessings, form a more perfect government, insure domestic tranquility and promote the general welfare, do establish this constitution.

The preamble has no legal effect but on rare occasions has been cited to support an argument that the constitution favors individuals' rights over governmental authority, See, e.g., *State ex rel. Zillmer v. Kreutzberg* (1902). One justice caught the preamble's tenor:

In this first utterance of our constitution is declared the keynote and dominating principle of the social organization established by it, namely, equality before the law of every individual. Whatever may be thought at this day by political scientists or theorists as to the ideal government or society, the conception of our forebears was a government not primarily for its own convenience, but for the protection of the individual rights of those who were to live under it. Government was not the end but merely the means to secure individual liberty and happiness. (*Nunnemacher v. State* (1906))

Article I

Declaration of Rights

Section 1
Equality; inherent rights.

All people are born equally free and independent, and have certain inherent rights; among these are life, liberty and the pursuit of happiness; to secure these rights, governments are instituted, deriving their just powers from the consent of the governed.

This section, which states the rights that form the basis of the constitution, has always very closely resembled the second and third paragraphs of the Declaration of Independence, and it is identical to part of the Virginia Declaration of Rights and portions of other states' constitutions. It was amended in 1982 to replace "secure these rights" with "serve these rights" and to make it gender-neutral. In 1986, it was amended again to return to "secure these rights." The phrasing indicates that the rights named are inherent and that the constitution protects them, not that the constitution creates those rights.

The presence in this section of "equally free" resembles the guarantee of equal protection of the laws found in the Fourteenth Amendment to the U.S. Constitution. In fact, that part of this section has the same effect. *Treiber v. Knoll* (1987); *Funk v. Wollin Silo & Equipment, Inc.* (1989). Treating individuals differently does not violate this section's requirement of equal protection of the laws if there is a reasonable basis for the difference. *State v. McManus* (1989). Because the section makes life, liberty, and the pursuit of happiness inherent rights, it also approximates the portion of the Fourteenth Amendment that forbids deprivation by the government of life, liberty, or property without due process of law. The state and federal provisions are "functional equivalents," *In re Reginald D. v. State* (1995), and this section has no independent function. Occasionally, the nature of "inherent rights" is an issue. For example, the right to be a candidate in an election is a political privilege, not an inherent right. *State ex rel. Frederick v. Zimmerman* (1949). An internet repository of criminal records maintained by the attorney general that incorrectly reports that an innocent person has a criminal record deprives him of a liberty interest in violation of this section. *Teague v. Schimel* (2017).

Wisconsin has developed its own interpretation of this section regarding only one issue, albeit a central issue of political theory: determining the proper balance between the authority of government and the rights of its citizens. Specifically, litigants have called on the courts to balance the rights that this section grants as against the state's police power: the authority of government to protect citizens' health, safety, and welfare or, more generally, "the inherent power of the government to promote the general welfare." *In re Reginald D. v. State* (1995). To balance the police power against individual rights one needs to determine "[h]ow far, consistently with freedom, . . . the rights and liberties of the individual member of society [may] be subordinated to the will of the government." *State ex rel. Zillmer v. Kreutzberg* (1902). This section clearly limits governmental power, but the individual rights that it specifies are also limited, by the police power. That power, although the constitution does not explicitly name it, has a constitutional significance and stature. *Kreutzberg.* The test that is used to determine the proper balance between state and citizen is flexible: the purpose for using the police power and the means employed to effect that purpose must be reasonable, a term that may be interpreted in a wide variety of ways. *State v. McKune* (1934).

As articulated in *Blake v. Jossart* (2016), the court analyzes equal protection claims in the following manner:

> A legislative classification satisfies the rational basis standard if it meets the following five criteria:
>
> (1) All classification[s] must be based upon substantial distinctions which make one class really different from another.
>
> (2) The classification adopted must be germane to the purpose of the law.
>
> (3) The classification must not be based upon existing circumstances only. [It must not be so constituted as to preclude addition to the numbers included within a class.]

(4) To whatever class a law may apply, it must apply equally to each member thereof.

(5) That the characteristics of each class should be so far different from those of other classes as to reasonably suggest at least the propriety, having regard to the public good, of substantially different legislation.

Equal protection came into play, for example, in *Ferdon v. Wisconsin Patients Comp. Fund* (2005), which concerned limits on damage awards in medical malpractice cases. Injured parties affected by the limits claimed that they were as a distinct class treated unfairly and the monetary cap did not bear a reasonable relationship to a legitimate government purpose. The court in *Ferdon* held the statutory cap on non-economic medical malpractice damages violated equal protection, but it later overruled that decision, holding in *Mayo v. Wisconsin Patients Comp. Fund* (2018) that *Ferdon* had invaded the province of the legislature's policymaking authority.

The legislature cannot create three methods for appealing a property tax assessment and deny one of them to property owners in populous counties unless there is a rational distinction between populous counties and other counties relating to assessment appeals. The statute at issue provided three avenues of appeal: (1) file for certiorari review in circuit court; (2) file a complaint to the Department of Revenue followed by certiorari to circuit court; (3) or pay the tax and then sue the county, resulting in a de novo review (a complete court trial). The statute denied the third option to residents of counties with a population greater than 500,000 (Milwaukee County). The third option was also the method most likely to result in a fairer and more thorough review. The court found no rational basis for the denial and held the statute violated equal protection. *Nankin v. Village of Shorewood* (2001).

In 2008, the legislature changed the method for contesting a property tax assessment, allowing cities and villages to opt out of full-scale de novo court review of the board of review, so landowners in those cities could only use the more limited certiorari method. The statute enhanced the certiorari process to provide a fuller review of the assessment. However, the court held that property owners in the opt-out counties received a less effective review, in violation of the equal protection clause. *Metropolitan Associates v. City of Milwaukee* (2011).

A statute that prohibits cities from withholding union dues from employees' paychecks but does not prohibit withholding other groups' dues does not violate the equal protection clause. *Madison Teachers, Inc. v. Walker* (2014).

Although the statutes setting the funding for public schools provide varying amounts of money for various school districts, the funding system does not violate the equal protection clause. *Vincent v. Voight* (2000). *Vincent* discusses, but does not resolve, whether the equal protection clause requires equalization of *inputs* (money) or equalization of *outcomes* (educational achievement).

Due process of law requires that the people must have fair notice of which acts constitute crimes. *State v. Neumann* (2013).

A trial court did not violate a defendant's due process rights when it considered a presentence investigation report that contained a computer-generated estimate of the probability that a defendant would commit further crimes, and based part of that estimate on the defendant's sex and part upon unreleased proprietary confidential information. *State v. Loomis* (2016).

A statute that requires a person who has been civilly committed as a sexually violent offender to present facts to show that he or she should be given a discharge trial does not shift the burden of persuasion to the petitioner and therefore does not violate due process. *State v. Hager* (2018).

Section 2
Slavery prohibited.

There shall be neither slavery, nor involuntary servitude in this state, otherwise than for the punishment of crime, whereof the party shall have been duly convicted.

As its title indicates, this section, which derives from part of the Northwest Ordinance, made Wisconsin a free state. It resembles the Thirteenth Amendment of the U.S. Constitution, so federal decisions on the federal provision have been applied to this section, even though it predates the federal provision. *Milwaukee v. Horvath* (1965). This section has not been amended, and the two cases addressing it involve not slavery but penal conditions. Those cases make it clear that the reference to "crime" includes misdemeanors, *In re Ferdinand Bergin* (1872), and nonpayments of forfeitures for violations of a municipal ordinance, *Horvath*. In the latter case the punishment was a fine, which, along with incarceration, is one of the penalties for a crime, even though the punishment for a violation of an ordinance is a forfeiture: a civil, not a criminal, penalty. The court in the latter case also noted in passing that, even if it had held the other way on the issue of whether a crime was involved, imprisonment without the requirement of labor does not amount to involuntary servitude.

Section 3
Free speech; libel.

Every person may freely speak, write and publish his sentiments on all subjects, being responsible for the abuse of that right, and no laws shall be passed to restrain or abridge the liberty of speech or of the press. In all criminal prosecutions or indictments for libel, the truth may be given in evidence, and if it shall appear to the jury that the matter charged as libelous be true, and was published with good motives and for justifiable ends, the party shall be acquitted; and the jury shall have the right to determine the law and the fact.

This section establishes and limits the freedom of speech and publication. It has not been amended. It derives from provisions in other states' constitutions and is similar to, but more elaborate than, the prohibition in the First Amendment of the U.S. Constitution against laws "abridging the freedom of speech." Placing a declaration of the right to free speech in the same section as a statement on libel implicitly recognizes that the latter is an exception to the former. Civil libel cases have been based upon federal case law, and this section has played no part in them. This section, however, as its wording indicates, does apply to criminal libel cases, which are based on a statute, Wis. Stat. § 942.01. Defamation is a misdemeanor. This section has been relevant to two criminal libel cases, which indicate that a defendant who has made a defamatory statement will escape liability for it only if he or she proves that the statement is true, that his or her motives were good, and that the ends he or she intended to effect with the statement were justifiable. *State v. Herman* (1935). Although this section states that the jury shall determine the law, a task that judges almost always assume, a judge may instruct the jury on the law. *Branigan v. State* (1932).

Because this section and the First Amendment have the same subject matter, one needs to clarify the relation between the two provisions. On that matter one can divide the cases in which this section is an issue into four categories. The first includes cases in which the court has explicitly stated that the two provisions have identical effects. An example is the statement that "[s]ecs. 3 and 4, art. I of the Wisconsin constitution, guarantee the same freedom of speech and right of assembly and petition as do the First and Fourteenth amendments of the U.S. Constitution." *Lawson v. Housing Authority* (1955). The court in *Lawson* relied upon some of the many First Amendment cases as precedents. The court later reached the same conclusion in an obscenity case. *County of Kenosha v. C & S Management, Inc.* (1999).

Another case in this category held that certain Wisconsin statutes that regulated money raised and spent for political speech, such as issue advocacy, violated this section. Statutes may require only the reporting of expenditures for "express advocacy" that clearly relate to supporting the election or defeat of a particular candidate for public office. Ordinary political speech about issues, policy, and public officials ("issue advocacy") is protected by the First Amendment and this section. The court held that a statute that prohibited close coordination between a candidate and an issue group was unconstitutional because it prohibited protected speech. The dissent noted that "no opinion of the United States Supreme Court or a federal court of appeals has established that the First Amendment forbids regulation of, or inquiry into, coordination between a candidate's campaign committee and issue advocacy groups." *State ex rel. Two Unnamed Petitioners v. Peterson* (2015).

The second category consists of cases in which the court has acknowledged that both provisions were at issue, made no statement about the relationship between the two, and used federal cases as precedents, thereby implying that the two provisions have the same effect. See, e.g., *State v. I, A Woman-Part II* (1971).

A third category consists of cases in which the court stated that the two provisions have different effects, but then used only federal cases or cases from other states, or both, as precedents, thus failing to distinguish between the two provisions' effects. An example is a decision in which the court stated, "a state may permit greater freedom of speech than the Fourteenth amendment would require, although it may not permit less," and then used only one federal case and one case from another state as precedents. *McCauley v. Tropic of Cancer* (1963).

The fourth category of cases includes those in which this section actually affects the result. In one, *Jacobs v. Major* (1987), the plaintiffs did not raise the First Amendment as an issue, thereby forcing the court to decide the case on the basis of this section. The court examined this section's wording and held that "no laws shall be passed to restrain or abridge the liberty of speech or of the press" applies only to action by the state, not to action by citizens. Surprisingly, especially in light of the phrase's clear meaning and the dissent's reminder that the framers of the state constitution had rejected a free speech provision that resembled the one in the U.S. Constitution, the court held that the language, "[e]very person may freely speak, write and publish his sentiments on all subjects" bars only state, not private, interference with those rights. The court apparently thought that it had justified its conclusion by declaring that many provisions in the Wisconsin constitution apply only to state action.

A group of cases concerning freedom of the press also belong in this fourth category. The U.S. Supreme Court has held that reporters enjoy no privilege under the First Amendment to protect their sources, but "[i]t goes without saying, of course, that we are powerless to bar state courts from responding in their own way and construing their own constitutions to recognize a newsman's privilege, either qualified or absolute." *Branzburg v. Hayes* (1972). A few years later a Wisconsin court accepted the invitation in *Zelenka v. State* (1978). It held that *Branzburg* could be restricted to its narrow holding—that the lack of a privilege applied only in grand jury proceedings—because the court there was referring to possible privileges in other kinds of cases, and that *State v. Knops* (1971), a Wisconsin case that recognized a limited privilege for reporters, could have been decided based upon this section, although the court decided it based upon the First Amendment. Thus, this section created a journalist's privilege, even though that privilege was first recognized by a Wisconsin court in a First Amendment case. Despite the twists and turns of the logic, the invitation to state courts in *Branzburg* made such a conclusion reasonable. The privilege, rather than being absolute, is subject to a balancing against "the societal values favoring disclosure." *Zelenka.*

The court has held that the journalist's privilege does not grant a reporter greater access to an airplane crash scene than would be afforded to the public. *City of Oak Creek v. King* (1988).

A statute that required a defendant charged with distribution of child pornography to prove he or she did not know the age of the child (rather than requiring the state to prove that the defendant did know the child's age) violated the free speech guarantees of this section. *State v. Zarnke* (1999).

Section 4
Right to assemble and petition.

The right of the people peaceably to assemble, to consult for the common good, and to petition the government, or any department thereof, shall never be abridged.

This section, which grants the rights to petition the government and to assemble, has not been amended. It resembles a portion of the First Amendment of the U.S. Constitution. However, it adds to the purpose for assembling stated there, petitioning the government, the purpose of consulting for the common good. One could thus infer that the framers of the constitution intended that this addition cover instances in which the government has failed to make sufficient efforts to promote the public good, so that citizens must respond to that deficiency. Thus, like the preamble and several other portions of the Wisconsin constitution, that part of this section emphasizes that the ultimate power in the state rests in the people, not in the government.

The right to assemble that this section grants is the same as under the U.S. Constitution. *Lawson v. Housing Authority* (1955). Government may reasonably regulate and limit the right to assemble. *State v. Givens* (1965). Such regulation is subject to the prohibitions against vagueness and overbreadth that have been developed in the case law interpreting the U.S. Constitution. *Milwaukee v. K. F.* (1988). Reasonable disorderly conduct ordinances and reasonable enforcement of them do not violate this section. *Givens.* The right to assemble does not protect purely commercial activity that violates zoning ordinances. *Town of Richmond v. Murdock* (1975). The right to assemble does not include the right to nominate candidates for the U.S. Senate in party conventions, as opposed to primary elections. *State ex rel. Van Alstine v. Frear* (1910). However, the right to assemble makes it unconstitutional for a public housing authority to deny lodging to a person who refuses to certify that he or she does not belong to a "subversive" organization. *Lawson.*

Like the right to assemble, the right to petition the government is not unbounded and may be reasonably regulated and circumscribed. *Madison Joint School Dist. No. 8 v. WERC* (1975). In interpreting this right, state courts have examined U.S. Supreme Court cases that interpret the federal right. *Id.* Some litigants eschew this section when they could use it and base their cases on the federal equivalent. The exact relationship between the two provisions remains murky. The right under this section is that which existed at the time when the constitution was ratified. *In re Stolen* (1927). The considerable development of the case law since *In re Stolen* casts doubt on the viability of its holding, although no case has explicitly overruled it.

The right to petition governmental agencies does not include the right to park near the building where the agency is located. *Madison v. McManus* (1969). The right to petition also does not include the right of persons who are not parties in a case to attempt to influence a court with a petition, because that tactic departs from acceptable judicial procedure. *Stolen.* A later court came to the same conclusion on the right to petition a court but gave a different reason: petitioning amounts to the unauthorized practice of law. *State ex rel. Baker v. County Court* (1965). This section does not require that a statutory grant of the right to petition cities on certain matters also include villages on the same matters. *State ex rel. Poole v. Menomonee Falls* (1972). The right to petition does not justify union members, by speaking at a school board meeting, abridging a union's exclusive right to bargain. *Madison Joint School Dist. No. 8.* A statute forbidding municipal employers from collecting union dues does not violate the employees' right to assemble and petition the government. *Madison Teachers, Inc. v. Walker* (2014).

Section 5
Trial by jury; verdict in civil cases.

The right of trial by jury shall remain inviolate, and shall extend to all cases at law without regard to the amount in controversy; but a jury trial may be waived by the parties in all cases in the manner prescribed by law. Provided, however, that the legislature may, from time to time, by statute provide that a valid verdict, in civil cases, may be based on the votes of a specified number of the jury, not less than five-sixths thereof.

This section prescribes the scope of the right to a jury trial. Its original version remains as the first sentence. An amendment added the second sentence in 1922. "At law" means as opposed to at equity. In England, a separate system of equity courts, under the chancellor's direction, provided relief that was not available under the common law (the system of judge-made, as opposed to statutory, law that extended over the entire country and that was later adapted for use in this country). Wisconsin courts no longer distinguish between law and equity except for a few purposes, one of which is determining the scope of the right to a trial by jury that this section grants. The Seventh Amendment to the U.S. Constitution requires jury trials in cases under the common law in which the amount at stake is at least $20.

One can tersely state this section's main effects. The right to a trial by jury is not quite "inviolate." The primary exceptions are straightforward. The right applies only to the kinds of cases to which it applied when the constitution was ratified, which does not include, for example, election contests. *Burke v. Madison* (1962). A statute may extend the right to a jury trial and may even do so indirectly; for example, by requiring a trial de novo. *Village of Menomonee Falls v. Michelson* (1981). And the parties may waive their rights to a jury in a pre-litigation contract even if a party did not knowingly and voluntarily sign the waiver. *Parsons v. Associated Bank-Corp.* (2017).

The limitations on the right to a jury trial in cases at law in 1848 can be clarified by naming some kinds of cases to which that right does not apply. By specifying that the right to a trial by jury applies to "all cases at law," this section indicates that it does not apply to actions at equity. *Norwest Bank Wis. Eau Claire v. Plourde* (1994). A party charged with violating a municipal ordinance has no constitutional right to a jury trial, although a statute may grant that right. *Village of Oregon v. Waldofsky* (1993). The amount of protection that a court will give to the right to a jury trial—for example, the rigor of the procedures that it establishes for waiving that right—depends upon whether the right derives from the constitution or from a statute. Defendants have no right to a jury trial in proceedings during which a judge determines the amount of restitution that they owe to their victims. *State v. Dziuba* (1989). Because in 1848 no statute prohibited unfair labor practices cases, no one has a right to a jury trial in that kind of case. *General D. & H. Union v. Wisconsin E. R. Board* (1963). Eminent domain proceedings under Article I, Section 13, being purely statutory, are not "cases at law," so there is no constitutional right to a jury trial in them, and the procedures applicable to them may be specified by statute. *State ex rel. Allis v. Wiesner* (1925). Legal actions in which a litigant seeks only an injunction were, under the common law, cases in equity, so no right to a jury trial exists in them. *Upper Lakes Shipping v. Seafarers' I. Union* (1964). Because no juvenile proceedings were held in 1848, there is no constitutional right to a trial by jury in them, although a statute grants that right. *In Interest of N. E.* (1985). Because in England ecclesiastical courts, not the common-law courts, decided probate cases, there is no constitutional right to a jury trial in cases about the rights under a will. *In the matter of the will of Timothy Jackman–First Appeal* (1870). Because workers' compensation has replaced legal actions against employers for torts and no cases of that kind existed in 1848, parties have no constitutional right to a jury trial in those cases. *Messner v. Briggs & Stratton Corp.* (1984).

The court of appeals stated a general rule: this section limits the right to a jury to actions "at law," and the right applies only to actions that were "at law" when the constitution was ratified. In causes of action that are based on a statute, a jury is not available unless the statute codifies a cause of action that was recognized in common law in 1848. *State v. Ameritech Corp.* (1994). The supreme court later rejected the test in *Ameritech* as being too narrow—that a jury could be available even if the statute did not narrowly follow the pre-1848 common law but provided a cause of action that was the *essential counterpart* of a common-law claim. *State v. Ameritech Corp.* (1995). If the cause of action was not available at common law in 1848, the right to a jury will then depend upon whether the legislature explicitly included the right to a jury when it created the cause of action. *Village Food & Liquor Mart v. H & S Petroleum* (2002).

The court has come to refer to the test for a right to a jury as the "*Village Food test.*" The court has commented on the difficulty in applying this test and held that a statutory cause of action is only an "essential counterpart" of a common-law cause of action if it has a similar purpose. *Harvot v. Solo Cup Company* (2009). For example, the court held that the common-law claim of "cheating" is an essential counterpart to Medicaid fraud. *State v. Abbott Laboratories* (2012). The court also held that if a statutory cause of action is not clearly based upon the common law, the right to a jury is only available if the statute explicitly provides that right. *Harvot.*

Certain rights pertinent to jury trials follow implicitly from the right to such a trial that this section explicitly grants. Regardless of a statute to the contrary, the right to a jury trial includes the right to a jury of twelve persons. *Norval v. Rice and wife* (1853). That rule is in effect because common-law juries consisted of twelve persons. A defendant may waive the right to a jury of twelve persons, but only by following the procedures for effecting that waiver, and a trial will then proceed with eleven jurors. *State v. Cooley* (1981). Except as provided in this section's second sentence, the right to a jury trial also includes the right to a unanimous verdict, so that it will be clear that each juror is convinced beyond a reasonable doubt that each element of the criminal offense that was charged has been proved. *State v. Lomagro* (1983). Determining whether the jury is unanimous may become difficult if more than one action might result in a conviction, or if the state has charged more than one crime. In such cases, the court first determines whether the jury has heard evidence of either more than one crime or more than one means of committing one crime. *Manson v. State* (1981). If the defendant might have committed more than one crime, the jury must achieve unanimity about each. If the defendant might have used more than one means to commit a crime, the jury need be unanimous only if the means differ conceptually. The right to a trial by a jury also includes the right to ask for a new trial. *Malinowski v. Moss* (1928).

Even if a party has a right to a jury trial, a jury does not have an absolute right to decide the case. In general, juries decide matters of fact, and judges decide matters of law. However, the right to a trial by jury does not preclude a judge from deciding, "as a matter of law," certain factual issues, which frequently occurs. A judge's offering a plaintiff who has won a case the choice between accepting lower damages than the jury awarded and beginning a new trial does not violate the right to a trial by a jury, because under either option a jury will at least initially decide the amount of damages. *Lucas v. State Farm Mut. Automobile Ins. Co.* (1962). A judge may direct a verdict (require a jury to decide in a certain way) on an issue, even if a jury usually makes the decision on that issue, without violating this section. *Wendel v. Little* (1961).

Courts have resolved several miscellaneous issues related to this section, once to repel a challenge to the courts' operation and twice to strengthen the rights that this section grants. Requiring litigants to pay fees does not violate this section because the territorial courts charged fees and this section has the meaning that it had for the framers of the constitution, although imposing a fee may not unreasonably regulate the right to a jury trial. *County of Portage v. Steinpreis* (1981). Using a test case without the consent of all of the parties violates the right to a jury trial of the parties who are thus precluded from having a trial. *Leverence v. PFS Corp.* (1995). If this section's second sentence makes a less-than-unanimous verdict acceptable, the verdict is nevertheless invalid unless the same ten jurors (the number that the related statute specifies) agree on each issue necessary for the decision. *Mueller v. Brunn* (1982). That result occurs because under the common law defendants had a right to a special verdict.

The court of appeals held that because Article XIV, Section 13 authorizes the legislature to modify the common law, it can limit the right to a jury that was available under the common law. *Guzman v. St. Francis Hospital, Inc.* (1999). The dissent pointed out that, although the legislature can modify the common law, the right to a jury is guaranteed by this section.

Section 6
Excessive bail; cruel punishments.

Excessive bail shall not be required, nor shall excessive fines be imposed, nor cruel and unusual punishments inflicted.

This section, which provides rights for criminal defendants and persons who have been convicted of crimes, has not been amended. With the exception of the second "shall," it is identical to the Eighth Amendment of the U.S. Constitution. For this reason, Wisconsin courts have occasionally relied upon federal opinions in cases on the Eighth Amendment as precedents in applying this section.

The Wisconsin standard for judging the reasonableness of a fine derives from a legal encyclopedia, *Corpus Juris Secundum*. Because courts have also adapted that standard for cases on the reasonableness of punishments, *State v. Pratt* (1967), *Steeno v. State* (1978), it is worth quoting at length:

> The courts are reluctant to say that the legislature has exceeded its power in authorizing excessive fines, and as a general rule will not do so except in a very clear case. . . . In order to justify the court in interfering and setting aside a judgment for a fine authorized by statute, the fine imposed must be so excessive and unusual, and so disproportionate to the offense committed, as to shock public sentiment and violate the judgment of reasonable people concerning what is right and proper under the circumstances. (*State v. Seraphine* (1954))

The case in which that standard first appeared is the only significant case about a fine's propriety, but courts have often decided whether a punishment is cruel or unusual. Anyone who attacks a sentence based upon this section faces heavy odds. First, a court presumes that a sentence established by statute is reasonable: "punishment established by a democratically elected legislature is presumed valid, and a 'heavy burden rests on those who would attack the judgment of the representatives of the people.'" *State v. Hermann* (1991). Various statutory requirements for sentences do not, in themselves, violate this section: enhanced penalties for repeat offenders, *Hanson v. State* (1970), mandatory minimum sentences, *Hermann*, and mandatory imprisonment, *Steeno*.

Second, appellate courts assume that a trial judge's imposition of a sentence accords with this section. *State v. Teynor* (1987). However, a sentence or fine that is within the minimum and maximum limits that a statute establishes is not for that reason necessarily constitutional. *Hanson*. Also, the trial judge must indicate in the trial record the reasons for the punishment. *State v. Lynch* (1981). If the judge fails to do so, the appellate court will look in the record for justification for the punishment: it will, in effect, do the trial judge's work, and if the appellate court finds no justification in the record, it will overturn the sentence. In *McCleary v. State* (1971), the most promising part of the record consisted of speculation in the presentencing report by a probation and parole officer who had recently been a graduate student in philosophy that the defendant's early reading of Karl Marx had made him antisocial. The Supreme Court, which overturned the sentence, was not impressed:

> Reading the long disproved labyrinthine syllogistic "economic science" of Karl Marx is not a crime, though perusal of its turgid marshalling of preconceived prejudices may well be a form of punishment. It is ridiculous to assume, despite McCleary's ambivalence toward his society, that his check passing at Kroger's constituted a subversive political economic conspiracy to hasten the "withering away" of the state. The Marxist theory of "socialist inevitability" does not rely on check forgers to hasten the disintegration of the state.

A number of arguments that particular circumstances make a punishment cruel and unusual have failed: the trial judge did not use the American Bar Association's sentencing guidelines, *Teynor*; the trial judge used a statutory option of limiting the prisoner to bread and water for part of the sentence, *Spencer v. State* (1907); the age of the defendant (seventy-two) made the sentence equivalent to life imprisonment, *Boyd v. State* (1935); the sentence differed from the co-defendant's, *State v. Studler* (1973); and the convicted person could not get needed treatment because of the type of sentence, *State v. Lynch* (1981). In all these cases, the court determined whether the punishment was cruel. In the only case addressing unusual rather than cruel punishment, the court held that revoking a corporation's charter did not violate this section. *State v. Golden Guernsey Dairy Cooperative* (1950).

A sentence of life imprisonment without the possibility of parole does not shock the public conscience and is not "cruel" when the defendant has been convicted of a third serious felony. *State v. Lindsey* (1996). It is not cruel and unusual punishment to sentence a fourteen-year old boy, convicted of murder, to a life sentence without possibility of parole. *Ninham v. State* (2011).

Section 7
Rights of accused.

In all criminal prosecutions the accused shall enjoy the right to be heard by himself and counsel; to demand the nature and cause of the accusation against him; to meet the witnesses face to face; to have compulsory process to compel the attendance of witnesses in his behalf; and in prosecutions by indictment, or information, to a speedy public trial by an impartial jury of the county or district wherein the offense shall have been committed; which county or district shall have been previously ascertained by law.

This section, which grants certain rights to criminal defendants and has not been amended, closely resembles the Sixth Amendment of the U.S. Constitution. The right to confront witnesses that it grants is the same as the corresponding right under that amendment. *State v. Patino* (1993); *State v. Jenkins* (1992). However, Wisconsin has developed its own case law, without constraints imposed by federal courts' interpretations of the federal provision, on the other rights that this section grants.

This section creates several rights that exist almost completely independently of one another. The first is the right to be heard by oneself and counsel. That right, in turn, raises several issues. One is the propriety of a judge's contact, in the absence of both the defendant and the defendant's counsel, with a jury during its deliberations.

The other issues divide into two categories. The first includes issues about the right to be heard by counsel. That, of course, does not mean that an attorney must hear the defendant, but that the defendant has a right to be represented by counsel: to be heard *by means of* counsel. The right attaches well before trial, during interrogation by the police. On this point, Wisconsin follows federal case law, specifically *Edwards v. Arizona* (1981). The defendant's right to be heard does not include the right to lie, and the right to counsel includes a duty on the attorney's part to bring forth only truthful evidence. *State v. McDowell* (2004). The defendant's right to testify has been deemed fundamental under this section. If a defendant waives the right to testify, the court must conduct an evidentiary hearing to determine if the waiver was knowingly, voluntarily, and intelligently made. *State v. Weed* (2003).

Police must notify persons whom they interrogate of their right to counsel. If the person invokes that right, the police must stop the interrogation and may not resume it unless the suspect initiates a conversation and knowingly waives this right. If the suspect makes a statement that might or might not be a request for an attorney—such as, "[d]o you think that I need an attorney?"—the police must stop the interrogation, except for asking questions about that statement, until they resolve the ambiguity. *State v. Walkowiak* (1994). However, the court has more recently ruled that if the suspect says, "How can I get an attorney here because I don't have enough to afford one?" the questioning may proceed. *State v. Subdiaz-Orsorio* (2014).

The right to counsel remains in effect until the very end of the legal process, the announcement of the jury's verdict. The absence of a defendant's counsel at that point, unless the defendant has knowingly, voluntarily, and unequivocally waived the attorney's presence, is a constitutional error requiring a reversal of the conviction and a new trial or dismissal of the charges. *State v. Behnke* (1990).

Exceptions to the general rule about the right to counsel exist; in certain circumstances, a defendant may constitutionally be without counsel, either temporarily or permanently. Counsel may withdraw from a case, but only with the court's permission, after a hearing, if the judge determines that there is good cause for the withdrawal. *State v. Batista* (1992). A defendant may also waive the right to counsel if he or she follows the proper procedures. *Pickens v. State* (1980). That is, a defendant, because this section grants the right to be "heard by himself," may represent himself or herself if the right is knowingly, clearly, unequivocally, and voluntarily waived, and if the defendant is competent to proceed unrepresented. *State v. Haste* (1993). If a defendant fails to prove he or she is competent to proceed, the court will appoint counsel. *Haste*. If a criminal defendant wishes to represent himself or herself, the court must determine if the defendant made a deliberate choice and knows the difficulties of self-representation, the seriousness of the charge, and the possible penalties. *State v. Klessig* (1997).

The right to counsel arises frequently regarding defendants who cannot afford legal representation. A person who cannot afford an attorney has a right to one under this section and will be represented either by the State Public Defender's office or by a private attorney who will be paid with public funds. The State Public Defender's office has guidelines for establishing whether a defendant can afford an attorney, but those guidelines do not bind courts in their determinations of whether to provide an attorney at state expense. *Appointment of Counsel in State v. Pirk* (1993). An indigent may not discharge a counsel whom the state pays, although a court may approve a substitution for good cause, such as a breakdown in communication. *State v. Clifton* (1989). An indigent may not manipulate his or her right to a court-appointed attorney to disrupt or delay a trial. *Rahhal v. State* (1971).

A criminal defendant has the right not only to counsel but also to *effective* counsel. Ineffective representation justifies reversing a conviction. This right does not apply in civil cases; regarding them, the remedy is suing the attorney for malpractice. *Village of Big Bend v. Anderson* (1981). In 1973, the court announced the applicable standard for effectiveness of counsel would be representation "equal to that which the ordinarily prudent lawyer, skilled and versed in criminal law, would give clients who had privately retained his services." *State v. Harper* (1973). However, if a defendant argues that he or she has had ineffective representation by counsel under both the U.S. Constitution and this section, a court might rely only upon the former, as interpreted by a federal case,

Strickland v. Washington (1984): the performance must be deficient and so prejudice the defense that the result cannot be said to be reliable. *State v. Johnson* (1985).

Several cases deal with the effectiveness of counsel when the defendant is a noncitizen at risk of deportation if convicted of the crime. The U.S. Supreme Court has ruled that, if the defendant wishes to plead guilty, counsel must inform him of that risk. *Padilla v. Kentucky* (2010). Wisconsin has a relaxed approach to this duty. *State v. Ortiz-Mondragon* (2015); *State v. Shata* (2015).

Under this section, a criminal defendant, generally, has the right to be present throughout the trial. However, that right does not include the right to be present when only matters of law are being discussed, *Leroux v. State* (1973), or when administrative matters, such as providing for security during the trial, are discussed, *State v. Clifton* (1989). A statute, Wis. Stat. § 971.04(2), specifies the procedure that defendants must use to waive their right to be present.

The right to demand the nature and causes of an accusation applies to the complaint and to the information, which the court issues at the end of a preliminary hearing in a felony case if it determines that there is probable cause to believe that the defendant has committed a crime. These documents must be sufficiently clear to state an offense to which the defendant can plead, and for which he or she can prepare a defense; and they must ensure that a decision in the ensuing case will bar another prosecution for the same offense. *Holesome v. State* (1968). That is, this requirement's purposes are to be fair to the defendant and to avoid placing the defendant in double jeopardy, not to erect a high barrier for the prosecution. This requirement does not prevent a defendant from being convicted of a lesser-included offense if a higher offense has been specified in the complaint or information. *Holesome.* An offense is lesser-included if it is impossible to commit a higher offense (an offense that results in a more severe penalty) without committing the offense in question, if both offenses derive from the same transaction, and if they have the same nature, except for the degree of their seriousness. The state need not precisely state the time when the offense was alleged to have been committed if that time is not a material element of the offense, but it may be imprecise on that matter only if it fulfills the other requirements that apply to the complaint. *State v. George* (1975). If the offense is continuous, the document need not allege the circumstances of each act if it provides a "plain, concise statement of the elements of the offense and uses the wording of the statute that specifies the crime." *State v. Copening* (1981). In general, however, if the document fully advises the defendant of the accusation's nature and cause, it need not repeat the wording of the pertinent criminal statute. *Manson v. State* (1981).

Generally, "absent a constitutional provision, statute, or evidentiary rule to the contrary, the law is entitled to every person's evidence." *State v. Migliorino* (1992). More limited, and probably more accurate, descriptions of the witnesses who may be compelled are those who can offer "relevant and material evidence" for the party who wishes to compel their attendance, *State v. Groppi* (1969), and those whose testimony "will lead to competent, relevant, material and exculpatory evidence," *State ex rel. Green Bay Newspaper v. Circuit Court* (1983). A defendant may compel a district attorney's testimony. *State v. Wallis* (1989). Neither the right to privacy nor the fact that the persons whose testimony was sought were at a medical facility when they witnessed the act in question (and thus asserted the privacy of their relation to their physician) creates an exception to this right. *State v. Migliorino* (1992). The right to compel witnesses includes the right to discover their identities. *Migliorino*. Although a criminal defendant has the right under this section to cross-examine all prosecution witnesses, a defendant cannot demand to confront a witness if he or she has made that witness unavailable at trial. This rule is called the "forfeiture by wrongdoing doctrine." In such cases, the judge conducts a separate hearing on the question of whether the accused caused the absence of the witness. *State v. Jensen* (2007).

A toxicology report prepared as part of an autopsy is not "testimonial" because its primary purpose was not to create evidence and, therefore, the lab technician who prepared it is not subject to a criminal defendant's cross-examination under the confrontation clause. *State v. Mattox* (2017). *Mattox* is another example of the court following the opinions of the U.S. Supreme Court where the text of the Wisconsin constitution is similar but not identical to the U.S. Constitution. The dissent noted that the U.S. Supreme Court has never settled on a single test for "primary purpose," but has articulated five different formulations of the test and stated that the proper test of whether the document is testimonial is if it is "potentially relevant" to a possible criminal case.

The decision in *Barker v. Wingo* (1972), a federal case, states the factors that a court must consider in determining whether a defendant has had a speedy trial: the length of the delay, the reasons for the delay, whether the defendant asserted a denial of this right, and the degree of prejudice to the defendant. *Scarborough v. State* (1977). This right prevents oppressive pretrial incarceration, prevents anxiety, prevents impairment of a defense, and, in a few circumstances, makes possible concurrent sentences. *Hipp v. State* (1977). The right to a speedy trial arises when the state issues the complaint and warrant, so it does not apply to delays in investigation or in serving the warrant. *State v. Lemay* (1990). This right interacts with the issue of whether a defendant knowingly pled guilty, because a defendant may argue that he or she did not know that a guilty plea would extinguish the right to assert that the trial was not speedy; if a defendant makes this argument, a court must first determine whether there has been a speedy trial. *Hatcher v. State* (1978).

In 2009, the court clarified its use of the terms "forfeiture" and "waiver." A trial judge removed the defendant's family from the courtroom, some of whom had been called as witnesses. The defendant did not object to the removal but asserted his right to a public trial on appeal. The supreme court held that the defendant had forfeited his right to a public trial under the Sixth Amendment to the U.S. Constitution. The court defined "forfeiture" as the failure to make the timely assertion of a right, and "waiver" is the intentional relinquishment or abandonment of a known right. *State v. Ndina* (2009).

The right to an impartial jury of the county or district has three components. The first is the right to a jury trial, which applies to misdemeanors as well as felonies. *State ex rel. Murphy v. Voss* (1967). A defendant may waive this right, but only by following the statutory procedures. *State ex rel. Sauk County D. A. v. Gollmar* (1966). Only the defendant, not the defendant's counsel, may waive the right to a jury trial. *State v. Livingston* (1991). To be effective, the waiver must be knowing, voluntary, and on the record. *Krueger v. State* (1978).

Second, a defendant has a right to an impartial jury. If a potential juror gave inaccurate or incomplete answers on the jury questionnaire, an appellate court will reverse the conviction if it believes that it is more probable than not that the juror was biased. *State v. Wyss* (1985). The court has set out guidelines for determining if a juror can be impartial. "Statutory bias" means a juror has a financial interest in the case or is related by blood to a party or a witness, in accordance with Wis. Stat. § 805.08(1). "Subjective bias" means bias observed through the prospective juror's words and demeanor that reveal bias in the state of mind. "Objective bias" means bias that would naturally occur in a person in the prospective juror's position. *State v. Faucher* (1999). For example, a trial judge's mother, sitting on a jury, illustrates objective bias, which violates this section. *State v. Tody* (2009). If a hearing-impaired juror cannot hear all of the testimony, an impartial jury has not tried the defendant. *State v. Turner* (1994).

Third, a defendant has a right to a trial by a jury of the county where the crime was committed. A defendant implicitly waives this right if, during jury selection, he or she or his or her attorney does not question the potential jurors to ensure that they reside in the county. *State v. Wyss* (1985). A defendant may ask that the trial be moved to a different county, but a judge cannot move the trial without the defendant's assent. *State v. Mendoza* (1977).

The constitution guarantees defendants a right to a twelve-person jury, which was the rule at common law when the constitution was adopted. A statute providing for six-person juries in misdemeanor cases violates this section. *State v. Hansford* (1998).

This section guarantees a criminal defendant the right to "meet the witnesses face to face," which is the equivalent to the U.S. Constitution's Confrontation Clause. This rule precludes hearsay evidence, which generally consists of statements made outside of court that are either written or repeated in court by a different witness. However, if the defendant caused the person who made the statement to be unavailable at the trial, he or she has forfeited the right to confront the witness and the hearsay evidence may be considered. *State v. Jensen* (2007). The defendant's action to prevent the witness from testifying must have been intentional. *State v. Baldwin* (2010).

Section 8
Prosecutions; double jeopardy; self-incrimination; bail; habeas corpus.

(1) No person may be held to answer for a criminal offense without due process of law, and no person for the same offense may be put twice in jeopardy of punishment, nor may be compelled in any criminal case to be a witness against himself or herself.

(2) All persons, before conviction, shall be eligible for release under reasonable conditions designed to assure their appearance in court, protect members of the community from serious bodily harm or prevent the intimidation of witnesses. Monetary conditions of release may be imposed at or after the initial appearance only upon a finding that there is a reasonable basis to believe that the conditions are necessary to assure appearance in court. The legislature may authorize, by law, courts to revoke a person's release for a violation of a condition of release.

(3) The legislature may by law authorize, but may not require, circuit courts to deny release for a period not to exceed 10 days prior to the hearing required under this subsection to a person who is accused of committing a murder punishable by life imprisonment or a sexual assault punishable by a maximum imprisonment of 20 years, or who is accused of committing or attempting to commit a felony involving serious bodily harm to another or the threat of serious bodily harm to another and who has a previous conviction for committing or attempting to commit a felony involving serious bodily harm to another or the threat of serious bodily harm to another. The legislature may authorize by law, but may not require, circuit courts to continue to deny release to those accused persons for an additional period not to exceed 60 days following the hearing required under this subsection, if there is a requirement that there be a finding by the court based on clear and convincing evidence presented at a hearing that the accused committed the felony and a requirement that there be a finding by the court that available conditions of release will not adequately protect members of the community from serious bodily harm or prevent intimidation of witnesses. Any law enacted under this subsection shall be specific, limited and reasonable. In determining the 10-day and 60-day periods, the court shall omit any period of time found by the court to result from a delay caused by the defendant or a continuance granted which was initiated by the defendant.

(4) The privilege of the writ of habeas corpus shall not be suspended unless, in cases of rebellion or invasion, the public safety requires it.

This section creates another set of rights for criminal defendants. Its original version made persons answerable for criminal offenses only after a presentment—a charge by a grand jury—or an indictment by a grand jury, except in certain kinds of cases, and it required release on bail except for capital offenses if the proof was evident or the presumption great. In 1870, an amendment substituted a requirement of due process of law for the requirements of a presentment or indictment. A 1982 amendment added subsections (2) and (3). Other parts of the constitution grant the power to issue all writs, including the writ of habeas corpus to the supreme court, Article VII, Section 2, the courts of appeals, Article VII, Section 5, and the circuit courts, Article VII, Section 8. The Fifth Amendment of the U.S. Constitution also grants the three rights in subsection (1). The due process right under this section is the same as it is under federal law. *State v. Greenwold* (1994). Interpretation of the double jeopardy prohibition is guided by federal decisions. *State v. Barthels* (1993). The federal Constitution's provision on double jeopardy protects against a second prosecution for the same offense after acquittal, a second prosecution for the same offense after conviction, and multiple punishments for the same offense; it is based upon principles of fairness and finality. *State v. Comstock* (1992). Accordingly, these two provisions now have little or no independent relevance in Wisconsin.

The 1982 amendment made irrelevant many of the existing cases on bail. It also focused on "the administration of bail on individual defendants." *Demmith v. Wisconsin Judicial Conference* (1992). The legislature and the judiciary share power on the issue of bail. *Demmith*. Denying the right of a person to drive without a valid driver's license is a reasonable condition that protects members of the community from serious bodily harm if the accused person has charges of driving without a valid driver's license pending. *State v. Dennis* (1987).

Although the Fifth Amendment of the U.S. Constitution also protects against self-incrimination, the protection under this section has not been subsumed within the federal right, notwithstanding that some of the federal case law has influenced the Wisconsin courts. This protection "exists whenever a witness has a real and appreciable apprehension that the information requested could be used against him in a criminal proceeding." *In Matter of Grant* (1978). The protection, therefore, might arise in a civil trial, but it usually arises during an investigation leading to a criminal trial or during a criminal trial. Most frequently it is an issue during contact with a police officer or in court, but it may also arise during contact, which a police officer instigates, with someone who is not a police officer, such as a relative. *State v. Lee* (1984). Under federal law, police officers must advise persons whom they take into custody or otherwise deprive of freedom that they have the right to remain silent. *Miranda v. Arizona* (1966). On this subject Wisconsin courts have usually deferred to federal decisions. To determine whether a warning must be given, a person is deprived of freedom if his or her freedom is curtailed to a degree associated with an arrest; that degree exists if a reasonable person in the defendant's situation would have considered himself or herself to be in custody, considering the degree of restrictions that all of the circumstances create. *State v. Pounds* (1993). Defects in the warning that a police officer gives may be negated by the suspect's attorney explaining a suspect's rights to him or her. *Jones v. State* (1970). Statements that a defendant makes before a police officer gives him or her these warnings, if the warnings are required, are not admissible at trial. *State v. Oliver* (1978).

The most significant kind of self-incriminating statement is of course a confession, "a voluntary admission or declaration by a person of his agency or participation in a crime." *Moore v. State* (1936). A statement might be a confession even if a person makes it to someone who is not a police officer, for example, a polygraph examiner. *Barrera v. State* (1980). The protection against self-incrimination, as it relates to confessions, applies also in civil cases. *In Matter of Grant* (1978). To summarize, confessions are admissible to prove guilt only if a police officer gives the warnings that *Miranda v. Arizona* requires and if the confession is voluntarily made. *Scales v. State* (1974). However, confessions that are not otherwise admissible because they do not fulfill those two requirements are admissible to impeach the defendant about statements that contradict those that otherwise may not be admitted. *State v. Schultz* (1989).

The right against self-incrimination extends only to "testimonial utterances." *Barron v. Covey* (1955). For example, it does not include physical examinations, *Green Lake County v. Domes* (1945); blood tests and urinalyses, *Barron*; identification of a person's voice or physical characteristics, *State v. Isham* (1975); a breathalyzer test, *State v. Albright* (1980); a psychiatric examination offered as evidence during the phase of a criminal trial when the defendant's psychological condition is the issue, *State v. Lindh* (1991); or evidence of payment of an occupational tax on a controlled substance, the possession of which is illegal, *State v. Heredia* (1992).

As to the issue of self-incrimination during encounters with police officers, even if a statement is self-incriminating, it may be admitted into evidence if the suspect made it voluntarily. In determining voluntariness a court examines the "totality of the circumstances," and balances the defendant's characteristics against the pressures to which he or she has been subjected, considering the defendant's age; whether the defendant was apprised of his or her rights; whether the defendant requested counsel; the length and conditions of the interrogation; and whether the police used any physical or psychological pressures, inducements, methods, or stratagems. *State v. Hockings* (1979). Thus, the court must balance factors based upon a plethora of facts and make a judgment. Many such decisions turn on whether the statement was voluntary. A trial court determines in a separate hearing (out of the presence of the jury) the admissibility of incriminating statements. *State ex rel. Goodchild v. Burke* (1965). As to this issue, the state has the burden of proving beyond a reasonable doubt that the statement was voluntary. *State v. Cumber* (1986). An appellate court will accept a trial court's determination about the voluntariness of a statement unless the determination is against the "manifest weight and clear preponderance of the evidence." *Turner v. State* (1977).

Because the determination of whether a statement was voluntary depends to such a great extent on the facts surrounding the statement, it is useful to examine some representative fact situations. The defendant's subnormal intelligence does not require a finding that his or her statement was involuntary, unless he or she could not understand the meaning and effect of the statement or of the waiver of his or her constitutional rights. *State v. Cumber* (1986). A police officer's accurate claim that he or she can produce evidence of guilt does not make a statement involuntary; neither does the self-imposed coercion of a suspect's desire to be with his or her spouse. *Blaszke v. State* (1975). Interrogation at a late hour and at a time when the suspect has had insufficient sleep does not make a statement involuntary if that interrogation occurs shortly after commission of the crime. *State v. Verhasselt* (1978). A suspect's nervous condition and lack of education do not make his or her statement involuntary if he or she has had experience with the criminal justice system. *State v. Schneidewind* (1970). Neither presentation of polygraph evidence that would be damaging to a defendant nor religious discussion make a statement involuntary. *Barrera v. State* (1980). A police officer's use of deceit in eliciting a statement does not by itself make that statement involuntary, although it is an element to be considered in the totality of the circumstances. *State v. Fehrenbach* (1984); *State v. Woods* (1984). However, an unreasonably long detention of a suspect will make a statement, whether voluntary or involuntary, inadmissible. *Wagner v. State* (1979).

The protection against self-incrimination relates to the right to counsel under Article I, Section 7. Under federal law, police officers are required, in the same circumstances in which they are required to inform a person of his or her right to remain silent, to inform a person that he or she has a right to counsel. *Miranda v. Arizona* (1966). However, they may omit that information if doing so is necessary to protect either the general public or a particular individual. *State v. Camacho* (1992). As to the consequences of that request for counsel, Wisconsin follows a U.S. Supreme Court decision, *Edwards v. Arizona* (1981), and requires interrogation to stop if a suspect requests an attorney. *State v. Lee* (1985). However, if a suspect initiates a conversation after he or she requests counsel and before counsel arrives, interrogation may proceed. *State v. Price* (1982). A suspect may waive the right to counsel, and if that waiver is voluntary, interrogation may proceed. *Woods.*

The second category of instances related to this section's protection against self-incrimination involves proceedings in court. At that point, a significant exception to the protection arises. The prosecution may, under a number of statutes, ask the judge to grant immunity from prosecution to a witness who has claimed such protection. If the relevant statute's terms apply, the court may grant the immunity. A grant of immunity cancels the protection against self-incrimination. *State ex rel. Jackson v. Coffey* (1978). This transaction consists of exchanging testimony for a grant of immunity from prosecution, but that immunity extends only to the crimes to which the testimony relates. *State v. Hall* (1974). Immunity applies to slightly more than a criminal trial's main phase. It applies also in the dispositional phase of proceedings against a juvenile. *State v. J. H. S.* (1979).

Remaining silent and refusing to answer questions invoke the protection against self-incrimination. In fact, the protection against self-incrimination is often called the right to remain silent. That right comes into existence at the moment of contact with a police officer, even before an arrest is made. These actions, and the protection that they invoke, would be of little value if the prosecution could use them during a trial as evidence of guilt. For that reason, in general, comments on a defendant's silence are a constitutional error; that is, absent substantial mitigating circumstances, they require a judge to declare a mistrial. It is usually clear whether someone has commented on the defendant's silence, so the issue in these circumstances almost invariably is whether anything sufficiently mitigates that comment. The comment is a harmless error if it has little effect on the jury's deliberations. *State v. Fencl* (1982). If the defendant's counsel objects immediately after the comment but neglects to ask the judge either to declare a mistrial or to give the jury an instruction that would negate the comment's effect, a court need not declare a mistrial. *Neely v. State* (1978). However, if a detective testifies that the defendant refused to answer a question during interrogation, there is a constitutional error because the remark was "designed to demonstrate a tacit admission of guilt on the part of the defendant." *Odell v. State* (1979).

The provisions of this section are identical to those of the U.S. Constitution's Fifth Amendment in prohibiting self-incrimination by a defendant in police custody in the absence of a lawyer, and therefore the courts have not interpreted the Wisconsin constitution to afford greater protections. *State v. Jennings* (2002) illustrates most clearly the concept of "lock-stepping" state constitutional decisions to those of the U.S. Supreme Court. Lock-stepping often arises in the context of search and seizure cases. *State v. Tompkins* (1988).

In a case involving the civil commitment of a sexually violent offender, followed by a criminal prosecution for the sex offenses, this section's prohibition against double jeopardy applies if the civil commitment proceeding was punitive. If the intent and the effect of the civil proceeding was not punitive, then the criminal prosecution may proceed. *State v. Rachel* (2002).

Because this article grants rights that are nearly identical to those in the U.S. Bill of Rights, the Wisconsin Supreme Court usually follows the interpretations of the U.S. Supreme Court in similar cases. There are exceptions. In a murder case, the Wisconsin Supreme Court held that, under the Fifth Amendment, certain blood-stained clothing could not be used in evidence because the police intentionally did not give the defendant a *Miranda* warning. The state appealed, and the U.S. Supreme Court held that, considering its recent decision in a similar case, such evidence could be used, *U.S. v. Patane* (2004), and sent the case back to Wisconsin. Then, the Wisconsin court held that the illegally obtained evidence could not be used in the trial under this section. *State v. Knapp* (2005).

Another case in which the court varied from the federal decisions involved a "show-up" where, immediately after his arrest for armed robbery, the police confronted the defendant face to face with a witness to the crime who identified him as the offender. Rulings under the federal constitution allow the use of show-ups. However, the Wisconsin court, citing this section, held that because show-ups suggest that the person being viewed is guilty and are prone to identification errors, such evidence cannot be used at trial unless the police follow the court's list of procedures to prevent suggestiveness. *State v. Dubose* (2005).

Section 9
Remedy for wrongs.

Every person is entitled to a certain remedy in the laws for all injuries, or wrongs which he may receive in his person, property, or character; he ought to obtain justice freely, and without being obliged to purchase it, completely and without denial, promptly and without delay, conformably to the laws.

This section creates, in very general terms, a right to recourse in the courts. It has not been amended. One can trace its purpose back to *Magna Carta*, the drafters of which, in response to the bribes that were endemic in England's legal system during the middle ages, included "[w]e will not sell the right and justice to anyone, nor will we refuse it, or put it off." The rights that this section creates resemble the right to due process that the Fourteenth Amendment mandates: "nor shall any State deprive any person of life, liberty, or property, without due process of law." However, the federal provision applies only to a state action.

The opinion in an early case, *Flanders v. The Town of Merrimack and another* (1880), captures this section's attempt to ensure not that perfect justice, but a reasonable approximation of it, will be rendered:

The remedy to which a party is entitled is frequently uncertain until made certain by the judgment of the court; litigation has always been attended with expense; delays have always occurred in the progress of law suits; and parties have often failed, through defect of proof or other causes, to get their just rights at the end of litigations. Notwithstanding the declaration in the constitution, doubtless these things will continue to happen; for there has not yet been developed sufficient wisdom on earth to establish a system of jurisprudence free from these hindrances to absolute justice; and the framers of the constitution never supposed that they could do so in a paragraph, and did not attempt it. The declaration simply means that laws shall be enacted giving a certain remedy for all injuries or wrongs, and that the rights of every suitor shall be honestly and promptly adjudicated, and enforced in conformity with the laws.

A terser way to phrase this is that this section grants not the remedy that a litigant wants but a "day in court." *Metzger v. Department of Taxation* (1967).

This section allows courts to create remedies and procedures if the existing ones are inadequate. For example, fired teachers who have the right, under a statute, to appeal only to their school board, which is also their adversary in the proceedings, may, notwithstanding that statute, appeal to a county court. *Hortonville Ed. Asso. v. Joint Sch. Dist. No. 1* (1975). Because the procedures for appealing the waiver of a juvenile into adult court often take a long time, occasionally resulting in the juvenile becoming an adult before the trial begins, a court may create more expeditious procedures. *In Interest of D. H.* (1977). Because no statute gave an adequate remedy to phonograph record companies for pirated products, and because a court concluded that "it is the duty of this court to act in circumstances where it is apparent that a wrong has been committed, and to furnish a remedy for that wrong when to do so is in accordance with previous statements of this court and would be fully consistent with the legislatively expressed policy of this state," the court created a remedy for the record company. *Mercury Record v. Economic Consultants* (1974).

The right to a remedy has limits. Despite an early case, *State ex rel. Wickham v. Nygaard* (1915), to the contrary, this section does not mandate a remedy if one did not exist at common law when the constitution was ratified. Accordingly, this section does not aid persons who wish to assert claims against a local unit of government for negligence, *Firemen's Insurance Co. v. Washburn County* (1957); persons who assert a wrongful death claim against their fathers because of the deaths of their mothers, *Cogger v. Trudell* (1967); or children who assert alienation of affection claims because of attentions paid to one of their parents, *Scholberg v. Itnyre* (1953). Because this section creates no rights, it does not add remedies or procedures to those granted by statute regarding workers' compensation claims. *Messner v. Briggs & Stratton Corp.* (1984). If a subject, such as rate making for utilities is "legislative," a term that the court does not define, this section does not avail a litigant. *Kimberley-Clark Corp. v. Public Service Comm.* (1983). If a statute of limitation extinguished a claim, this section will not revive it. *Neuhaus v. Clark County* (1961); *Miller v. Luther* (1992).

A child with serious lead poisoning, who had eaten lead paint chips or dust, won a damage award from his parents' landlords and then sued various paint manufacturers. He claimed that his illness resulted from both the landlords' negligence and the wrongdoing by paint companies in using lead in their paints. Citing to this section, the court in *Thomas v. Mallett* (2005) held that, if a person has suffered a wrong that was caused by more than one defendant, recovery from one or more defendants does not absolve other defendants from liability.

In 1997, confronted with a statute of repose, the supreme court held that, because the plaintiff could not have discovered the cause of action before the period of repose ran out, the statute violated this section. *Estate of Makos v. Wisconsin Health Care Fund* (1997). Three years later, the court overruled *Makos* and held that statutes of repose represent policy decisions that only the legislature should make. *Aicher v. Wisconsin Patients Compensation Fund* (2000). The court held that the constitution gives *reasonable* access to the courts, not unlimited access.

The meaning of many of the words and phrases in this section has been litigated. "Every person" includes illegal aliens. *Arteaga v. Literski* (1978). "Certain remedy" does not mean certainty of recovery, *Neuhaus v. Clark County* (1961), but access to the courts, *Messner v. Briggs & Stratton Corp.* (1984). "Injuries" does not mean every kind of injury, but only those that result from "an infringement of a legal right or failure to discharge a legal duty." *Scholberg v. Itnyre* (1953). "Wrongs" means "those resulting from an invasion of a party's legal right." *Ross v. Ebert* (1957). "Freely" does not mean that one may practice law without a license to avoid the expense of hiring an attorney, *State ex rel. Baker v. County Court* (1965), or that fees assessed by courts, such as jury fees, violate this section, *County of Portage v. Steinpreis* (1981). However, "freely" does mean that a judge may not require a litigant to forfeit a substantial sum if a contest over a will fails. *Will of Keenan* (1925). If the issue is the right to justice "without delay," no inflexible standards exist; a court must examine each instance. *Will v. H. & SS Department* (1969). In fact, time limits that a statute imposes on courts are not necessarily binding. *Anderson v. Eggert* (1940). However, a court's ruling on the merits of a case before it rules on the constitutionality of the statute at issue violates this section because one of the parties would have won if the statute were ruled unconstitutional, and thus would not have had to endure the delay caused by considering the merits. *Werner v. Milwaukee Solvay Coke Co.* (1948). "Conformably to the laws" means that "the justice to be administered by the courts is not an abstract justice conceived of by the judge, but justice according to law." *State ex rel. Department of Agriculture v. McCarthy* (1941). This "gives the legislature the power to regulate the remedies for wrongs," rather than establishing a common-law right. *Kerner v. Employers Mut. Liability Ins. Co.* (1967).

Section 9M
Victims of crime.

This state shall treat crime victims, as defined by law, with fairness, dignity and respect for their privacy. This state shall ensure that crime victims have all of the following privileges and protections as provided by law: timely disposition of the case; the opportunity to attend court proceedings unless the trial court finds sequestration is necessary to a fair trial for the defendant; reasonable protection from the accused throughout the criminal justice process; notification of court proceedings; the opportunity to confer with the prosecution; the opportunity to make a statement to the court at disposition; restitution; compensation; and information about the outcome of the case and the release of the accused. The legislature shall provide remedies for the violation of this section. Nothing in this section, or in any statute enacted pursuant to this section, shall limit any right of the accused which may be provided by law.

The first sentence of this section does not create a right for crime victims but describes the general policy of the state. *Schilling v. Crime Victims Rights Board* (2005). The court relied in part upon this section to deny a public records request for videotapes of a district attorney's training presentation regarding prosecution of online child exploitation and victim confidentiality in the interest of protecting the privacy of crime victims. *Democratic Party of Wisconsin v. Wisconsin Department of Justice* (2016).

In a case where the prosecutor and defendant made a plea agreement, it was not an error to allow a police officer to make a statement to the court recommending a harsher sentence because the officer had been shot while making the arrest and was therefore a victim. All victims of a crime have a constitutional right to speak to the court at the time of disposition. *State v. Stewart* (2013). This section does not empower the legislature to create an executive-branch board with the authority to discipline judges; that power is a core function of the judiciary. *Gabler v. Crime Victims Rights Board* (2016).

Section 10
Treason.

Treason against the state shall consist only in levying war against the same, or in adhering to its enemies, giving them aid and comfort. No person shall be convicted of treason unless on the testimony of two witnesses to the same overt act, or on confession in open court.

This section, which defines treason and specifies the requirements for proving it, has not been amended or litigated. It belongs to the small group of provisions that are based on the notion that the state resembles a sovereign state, in the sense that it can make war and be the victim of treason. Other provisions in this group include Article I, Section 20; Article IV, Section 29; Article V, Section 4; Article V, Section 7(2); and Article VIII, Section 7.

Section 11
Searches and seizures.

The right of the people to be secure in their persons, houses, papers, and effects against unreasonable searches and seizures shall not be violated; and no warrant shall issue but upon probable cause, supported by oath or affirmation, and particularly describing the place to be searched and the persons or things to be seized.

This section, which grants rights to persons who are suspected of committing a crime, has not been amended. Except for trivial differences, it is identical to the Fourth Amendment of the U.S. Constitution. For decades, however, this section had different effects than its federal counterpart. For example, Wisconsin adopted an exclusionary rule—a rule forbidding the use of improperly obtained evidence in criminal trials—thirty-eight years before the U.S. Supreme Court mandated such a rule for states. *Hoyer v. State* (1923). In fact, a considerable body of case law interpreting this section without reference to federal cases had developed. However, this section more recently had been held to have the same effects as the federal provision, so that federal case law controls Wisconsin cases and this section no longer has any independent meaning. *State v. Buchanan* (1993); *State v. Fry* (1986); *State v. Guzman* (1992). More recent decisions in this area by the U.S. and Wisconsin Supreme Courts have steadily eroded the rights protected by the Fourth Amendment and, by extension, this section.

A police officer had probable cause under the state littering law to stop a vehicle when the passenger tossed a cigarette butt out the window; therefore, the resulting drunk driving charge against the driver did not violate this section. *State v. Iverson* (2015). A police officer may make a traffic stop if the officer has a reasonable suspicion that a traffic law is being or has been broken. In a case where an officer stopped a car for having an air freshener hanging from the rearview mirror, which was not a violation of the traffic laws, the stop was held reasonable under this section and the evidence found in a search of the car was admissible in court. *State v. Houghton* (2015).

A "dog sniff" of an automobile by a trained and reliable dog can be the source of probable cause to search the vehicle, and no warrant is required for the dog to sniff the car. *State v. Arias* (2008).

Under the community caretaker doctrine, no search warrant is needed for a police officer to search each room in a house where a bloody beating victim lived after the victim was taken to the hospital. The search, which resulted in the victim's brother being convicted of possession of drugs, did not violate this section. *State v. Matalonis* (2016). Likewise, under the "exigent circumstances doctrine," the police did not need a warrant to order a blood draw in the emergency room from a defendant who had overdosed on heroin because heroin in the blood dissipates quickly. *State v. Parisi* (2016).

The U.S. Supreme Court has said that the "inevitable discovery doctrine" allows the state to use evidence in a trial that was obtained illegally if that evidence would have been eventually discovered by legal means, and the state does not have to prove absence of bad faith on the part of the police. *Nix v. Williams* (1984). Although the Wisconsin court has acknowledged its authority to find greater protection under this section than that afforded by the U.S. Supreme Court, the court has followed *Nix*, holding that evidence obtained in violation of the *Miranda* rule is admissible even in a case where the court found that the police had engaged in "flagrant" and "reprehensible" violations of the defendant's rights. *State v. Jackson* (2016).

The extent to which the police need a warrant to locate a defendant by cell phone tracking brings an important new aspect to the law governing searches. In two cases, the court seemed to say that a warrant is needed, but found "exigent circumstances" sufficient to justify a warrantless search and a search based on a defective warrant. "[T]racking a phone on a public roadway is not a violation of the Fourth Amendment because there is no legitimate expectation of privacy on public roadways." *State v. Subdiaz-Osorio* (2014). In a companion case, the police obtained a court order to track the cell phone, and when they found it, they entered the home and seized the phone and other evidence. The court held that although the warrant authorized cell phone tracking and not a search of a home, the error was harmless. *State v. Tate* (2014).

Many of the search and seizure cases in the twentieth century involved the police taking a blood sample from an objecting or unconscious suspect of a crime or requiring one to take a breath test. The U.S. Supreme Court has set limits for these kinds of searches. Blood tests require a warrant unless the circumstances present a recognized exception to the warrant requirement. There is no "per se" rule that allows the police to obtain a blood draw from a drunken driving suspect without a warrant. *Missouri v. McNeely* (2013). Breath tests incident to an arrest for drunken driving, being less invasive, do not require a warrant. *Birchfield v. North Dakota* (2016).

The court upheld a warrantless blood draw under the exigent circumstances doctrine in a case attacking the implied consent statute. As an injured motorcyclist was lying unconscious in a hospital bed, a deputy sheriff asked him if he would consent to a blood draw. The defendant did not respond, so the deputy directed the medical staff to draw blood. The court did not rule on the statutory issue of whether a motorist grants implied consent to a blood draw by the act of using the highway but held the exigent circumstances justified the blood draw. *State v. Howes* (2017). However, the court has ruled that if the police misstate the consequences of refusing a blood draw, the defendant's consent to the draw was invalid and the evidence should be suppressed. *State v. Blackman* (2017).

Section 12
Attainder; ex post facto; contracts.

No bill of attainder, ex post facto law, nor any law impairing the obligation of contracts, shall ever be passed, and no conviction shall work corruption of blood or forfeiture of estate.

This section prevents the enactment of certain kinds of laws. It has not been amended. Article I, Section 9 of the U.S. Constitution prohibits Congress from passing bills of attainder and ex post facto laws. Article I, Section 10 of the U.S. Constitution prohibits the states from passing the three kinds of laws specified in this section. "Corruption of blood" is the incapacity to acquire property by inheritance and to transfer property at death.

A bill of attainder is a legislative act that inflicts punishment without a judicial trial. *Christie v. Lueth* (1953). Prohibiting persons from obtaining property by killing someone does not violate either the prohibition against bills of attainder or the prohibition against corruption of blood. *Estate of King* (1952). If a right never vested, refusing to grant it is not punishment and thus there is no bill of attainder. *Id.* A direction by a common council to a chief of police to bring charges against an officer is not a bill of attainder because it inflicts no punishment. *Christie v. Lueth* (1953). Denying a license is not a criminal penalty, so no bill of attainder can result from that action. *Wis. Bingo Sup. & Equip. Co. v. Bingo Control Board* (1979).

An ex post facto law is one "which punishes as a crime an act previously committed, which was innocent when done; which makes more burdensome the punishment for a crime after its commission, or which deprives one charged with a crime of any defense available according to law at the time when the act was committed." *State v. Thiel* (1994). The prohibition against that kind of law applies only to criminal laws. *State ex rel. Prahlow v. Milwaukee* (1947). Since 1974, courts have interpreted this section's prohibition against ex post facto laws in accordance with U.S. Supreme Court decisions on the ex post facto provision of the U.S. Constitution. *State ex rel. Mueller v. Powers* (1974).

By examining *Mueller* and a few other cases, one can see the current state of the law on this subject. Applying a statute that was enacted after a person was placed on probation and that allowed a sentence that resulted from a revocation of parole to be consecutive to another sentence, rather than applying the statute in effect when the person was placed on probation that required the sentence in that instance to begin when the person entered prison for another offense, violates this section. *State v. White* (1979). Applying a formula for calculating good time (advancement of a prisoner's release date because of good behavior in prison) that went into effect after the person was released and had his or her parole revoked and that disadvantages the person violates this section. *State ex rel. Eder v. Matthews* (1983). However, a court's modification of the method of calculating good time, based upon its interpretation of a statute, does not violate this section, because this section applies to judicial interpretations of statutes only if those interpretations are unforeseeable. *State ex rel. Parker v. Fiedler* (1993). Calculating the date when a person becomes eligible for parole based upon a statute that was enacted after the person was convicted, if the new calculation disadvantages the person, violates this section. *Powers.* Applying a law that was enacted after a person was convicted by a tribal court of driving while intoxicated and that allowed counting that kind of conviction in determining the punishment for a later conviction for the same offense does not violate this section because it affects the later conviction, not the earlier conviction. *State v. Schuman* (1994). Applying a statute that was enacted after a person was sentenced and that places conditions on the person's possession of firearms that are stricter than were the terms of his or her release does not violate this section because the statute's purpose is to protect others' safety, not to punish. *Thiel.* Applying new rules on the minimum length of time that persons who serve life sentences must be confined to maximum security prisons does not violate this section because those rules' purposes are to prevent escape and reduce risks within the prison, not to punish. *Burruss v. Goodrich* (1995). Applying a new statute that allows civil commitment of persons who have served prison terms for sexually violent crimes does not violate this section, because its purpose is to safeguard the public, not to punish. *State v. Carpenter* (1995).

In short, during the last few years the protections under this section have been diminished as court has balanced other factors against those protections. Most often the court has done so by concluding that a law that clearly increased punishments also had another, primary purpose. For example, a statute that became effective after a defendant committed a crime, but before she was sentenced, was not an ex post facto law because it was not a punishment. The court held a statutory DNA surcharge for persons convicted of a felony not a punishment, using an "intents and effects" test. The court determined that the legislature did not have a punitive intent in passing the law, and that the surcharge was not punitive. *State v. Scruggs* (2017). And in *State v. Muldrow* (2018), the court held a court order requiring a person convicted of sexual assault to wear a GPS tracking ankle bracelet for life was not a punishment, as the intent was to protect the public.

In cases about impairment of contract, the first issue is whether there is a contract. If there is an express, valid contract, even if it is oral, this question presents little or no difficulty. The difficulty arises in cases involving an implied contract or "contractual rights." For decades, courts had difficulty with cases involving public employees and, in particular, those in which they had to decide whether the employees had contractual rights to pension benefits. However, since 1945 the public employee retirement statutes have included a statement that the participants in that retirement system have a contractual right to the system's benefits, Wis. Stat. § 40.19(1). An impairment is a change in the obligations that the contract specifies. *Burke v. E. L. C. Investors, Inc.* (1982).

Because the U.S. Constitution forbids states from enacting laws that impair contracts, many federal cases deal with this issue. Although that does not mean that state courts are bound by those decisions, many, including the Wisconsin courts, do rely upon them. *Chappy v. LIRC* (1987). The reliance has increased in recent years, so that the protection under this section has very little independent effect. A review of the analysis that federal courts currently undertake in impairment of contract cases, as Wisconsin courts understand it, is thus pertinent. The prohibition is not absolute but subject to the state's police power. Adjudication of these cases requires a balancing of interests. First, courts determine the extent of the impairment. At that stage courts consider, among other things, whether the parties to the contract reasonably relied on its express terms, as indicated by whether the industry has been regulated previously, whether a basic term of the contract was altered, and whether liability was significantly increased. The more severe the impairment, the more important must be the public purpose that is the reason for the impairment. If there is a legitimate public purpose, the legislation must create reasonable conditions and be appropriate to the purpose. However, because local units of government are creatures of the state, the state may impair their contracts if the other party to the contract consents. *Douglas County v. Industrial Comm.* (1957). That is, the rights in a contract between a municipality and a private person that may not be impaired are those of the private person.

Older cases approved the impairment only if it addressed an emergency or temporary situation, but the modern view approves statutes that serve an important public purpose. *Wis. Prof. Police Ass'n v. Lightbourn* (2001).

Section 13
Private property for public use.

The property of no person shall be taken for public use without just compensation therefor.

This section, which protects property from appropriation for public uses, has not been amended. It is almost identical to part of the Fifth Amendment to the U.S. Constitution, which refers to "private property" rather than to "property." Despite this similarity, judicial interpretation of this section differs from judicial interpretation of the federal provision. Unlike the equivalent section of many other state constitutions, this section refers only to taking private property, not to both taking and damaging property.

In recognition of the need to pay just compensation for a taking, statutes provide the rules under which the state and other entities that have the right to condemn property may acquire property or rights to property under their power of eminent domain. The clear majority of cases arise when a property owner alleges that a governmental agency has taken his or her property without commencing the statutory procedures and thus without paying compensation. These cases are inverse condemnation cases. *Zinn v. State* (1983). A property owner may begin litigation of this type even if a unit of government has only done some things leading to condemnation short of actually acquiring the property. *Vivid, Inc. v. Fiedler* (1993). Because this section is self-executing, the state's sovereign immunity does not protect it from inverse condemnation suits. *Retired Teachers Ass'n v. Employe Trust* (1995).

Because this section does not require compensation for damage, but only for a taking, a property owner must prove that there has been a serious interference with his or her property rights. The difference between a unit of government's permissible interference with property and a taking is a matter of degree. *Nagawicka Island Corp. v. City of Delafield* (1983); *Just v. Marinette County* (1972). Causing "indirect damages" or "consequential damages" does not amount to a taking. *Howell Plaza, Inc. v. State Highway Comm.* (1979). Those two terms refer to damages that flow from the results of an act. In inverse condemnation cases, a court must assess the interference's severity. However, courts have developed some principles for use in these cases. Because of the overriding importance of facts, one may best elucidate this section by analyzing some cases in which courts held the governmental action to be a taking and some other cases in which courts held the governmental action not to be a taking.

Several important principles arise from a case in which the erroneous determination of the ordinary high-water mark of a lake, which in turn determined the division of ownership rights between the state and the owner of the shoreland, was held to be a taking. *Zinn.* A plaintiff need not demonstrate that the unit of government intended to take property, as some earlier cases had indicated. A temporary interference for regulatory reasons—to protect health, safety, or welfare—can be a taking. A legally enforceable restriction that negates all or nearly all of an owner's beneficial use—the enjoyment of the rights that result from ownership—is a taking.

The following actions are takings: using the assets of some retirees, rather than the state's general purpose revenue, to fund increased benefits for other retirees, *Retired Teachers Ass'n v. Employe Trust* (1995); refusing to issue a liquor license or to renew a theater license if the purpose—an action's purpose is relevant, although an intent to take or not to take is irrelevant—is to force the applicant for, or the owner of, the license and the property to convey the property that the city wishes to acquire to the city, *Mentzel v. City of Oshkosh* (1988); ordering a property owner to build a drainage ditch, because the ditch deprives the owner of all beneficial use of the land on which it is built, *Otte v. DNR* (1987); requiring disclosure of data and of core samples obtained to determine whether mining is feasible, because there is no police power reason for disclosure, *Noranda Exploration, Inc. v. Ostrom* (1983); requiring overhead utility lines to be buried, because there is a public benefit and a statute implies that such a result should be accomplished by using the statutory procedures, *Public Service Corp. v. Marathon County* (1977); constructing a water patrol station that interferes with navigation, *W. H. Pugh Coal Co. v. State* (1990); depriving the owner of shoreland of swimming, boating, and bathing, *Bino v. Hurley* (1956); and forbidding hunting in a designated area, which increased the damage that birds caused to the crops of the owner of nearby property, *State v. Herwig* (1962).

There was no taking in the following instances: raising the water level on the basis of a shoreline zoning ordinance, because of the state's duty to protect navigation under Article IX, Section 1 and because the restriction is a reasonable one for the owner to bear, *Just v. Marinette County* (1972); requiring construction of a sidewalk, because the police power was being exercised, *Stehling v. City of Beaver Dam* (1983); denying access to a highway, under the police power, if other means of access are available, *Surety Savings & Loan Asso. v. State* (1972); building a subway station, because the interference with access and a view are merely consequential damages, *Randall v. City of Milwaukee* (1933); forcing the loss of forty-two parking spaces, because that is merely consequential, *More-Way North Corp. v. State Highway Comm.* (1969); and declining to renew a fishing permit, because nothing was taken, there being no property right to the permit, *LeClair v. Natural Resources Board* (1992). The construction of a pedestrian bridge across a highway that obscures the view of an advertising sign is not a taking because the sign's owner does not have a property interest in having the sign be viewable. *Adams Outdoor Advertising v. City of Madison* (2018).

Generally, if property rights are interfered with under the eminent domain power in order to benefit the public, the property owner receives just compensation, but if the taking is appropriate under the police power, the property owner is not entitled to compensation. *Just v. Marinette County* (1972). However, if the interference was done under the police power and the "degree of damage to the [property owner] far exceeds the alleviation of potential public harm," the owner may receive compensation in eminent domain proceedings under the statutes or the unit of government should buy the property. *Nagawicka Island Corp. v. City of Delafield* (1983).

A compensable taking occurs if a city-owned airport extends its runways by 1,500 feet, enabling low and frequent overflights on neighboring properties that directly and immediately interfere with the enjoyment and use of the land. *Brenner v. City of New Richmond* (2012).

If a property owner loses all use of his or her property because of a taking, calculation of the damages begins with the property's fair market value. *Kruescher v. Wisconsin Elec. Power Co.* (1965). Fair market value is the value that the property would have if it were put to its highest and best use. *Bembinster v. State* (1973). The best indicator of that value is the value of similar property. *Kreuscher.* If no similar property exists, the best indicator is the income that the property generates. *Leathem Smith Lodge, Inc. v. State* (1980). If the owner loses only a part of the value of the property, calculation of the damages, as a statute specifies, begins by determining the difference between the property's value before the taking and its value after the taking. *DeBruin v. Green County* (1976). In addition, the property owner is entitled to compensation for secondary monetary losses such as lost rents, *Luber v. Milwaukee County* (1970), and attorney fees for appellate work that were caused in part by the state's desultory litigation and to interest on the sum of the damages, *W. H. Pugh Coal Co. v. State* (1990).

The concept of property interest forms the core of takings law—if there is no vested property interest, there can be no taking. The court has taken varying approaches to what constitutes ownership in state-held funds. The court has held that each participant in a public retirement system has a property interest in the system as a whole. *Wisconsin Retired Teachers Assoc., Inc. v. Employe Trust Funds Board* (1997). In a case involving the participants in the Wisconsin Retirement System, although the court found that "each participant has a broad property interest in the WRS as a whole," it upheld a statute that transferred $200 million from one of the subfunds of the system to forgive employer debts. *Wis. Prof. Police Ass'n v. Lightbourn* (2001.) The court struck down a statutory transfer of $200 million from the Injured Patients and Families Compensation Fund, finding that healthcare providers, who pay assessments similar to insurance premiums into the fund, have an "equitable interest" in the fund and, therefore, a transfer from the fund is a taking. *Wisconsin Medical Society v. Morgan* (2010).

Section 14
Feudal tenures; leases; alienation.

All lands within the state are declared to be allodial, and feudal tenures are prohibited. Leases and grants of agricultural land for a longer term than fifteen years in which rent or service of any kind shall be reserved, and all fines and like restraints upon alienation reserved in any grant of land, hereafter made, are declared to be void.

This section, which precludes certain feudal forms of property ownership, has not been amended. One can trace "allodial" back to the eleventh century, when it meant that a person had full rights to own, use, and transfer land. As the rest of the first sentence implies, that term contrasts with feudal rights to land, under which ownership was restricted.

In the first case addressing this section, the supreme court admitted to being almost swayed by an argument that "allodial" meant that landowners held those rights also against the legislature, which, if that were the correct meaning of the term, could not, for example, forbid oral transfers of land. *Barker, Receiver, etc., v. Dayton and Another* (1871). The court, however, considered the context in which the word appeared and decided that it merely was an antonym of "feudal."

In a case about the rights to an inheritance, the issue about whether some of the decedent's children who might have rights were "legitimate" arose. *Frame and Others v. Thormann* (1899). The court held that it made no difference because this section gave the decedent the right to dispose of his property to whomever he chose. In *Mutual Fed. S. & L. Assoc. v. Wisconsin Wire Works.* (1973), "restraints upon alienation" of property was an issue, and the court held that that phrase did not invalidate an acceleration clause—a clause that requires the buyer to pay the balance of the sale price immediately upon the occurrence of a specified event—in the contract for sale. The court took the same position when it reheard the case. *Mutual Fed. S. & L. Asso. v. Wisconsin Wire Wks.* (1973).

Section 15
Equal property rights for aliens and citizens.

No distinction shall ever be made by law between resident aliens and citizens, in reference to the possession, enjoyment or descent of property.

This section, which protects resident aliens' property rights, has not been amended. Although a few cases involving *nonresident* aliens have been litigated, see, e.g., *Lehndorff Geneva, Inc. v. Warren* (1976), this section has not been litigated.

Section 16
Imprisonment for debt.

No person shall be imprisoned for debt arising out of or founded on a contract, expressed or implied.

This section, by precluding imprisonment for debts that arise from contracts, conjures up memories of nineteenth-century debtors' prisons, including the one where Charles Dickens' family spent some time because of his father's debts. It has not been amended. Although there was an expressed contract in one case, *In re Mowry* (1860), nearly all of the cases have involved an implied contract: the actions of the parties indicated that they had come to a tacit agreement. The other important term in this section is "imprisonment." Subjection to a writ of *ne exeat*—an order not to leave the jurisdiction of the court that issued the writ—is not imprisonment. *Dean v. Smith* (1868).

In only one case, *In re Blair* (1854), in which this section was an issue did the court release the plaintiff from prison. The executor of an estate had kept some of the estate for himself. Although there was no express contract, accepting the position of executor implied a duty to distribute the estate's assets to the proper persons. Failure to do so created a debt. If the court had ordered the executor to dispose of the estate's assets properly, and he had refused and the court had then held him in contempt, the contempt would have justified imprisonment. However, imprisonment for a mere debt violated this section.

A justice in an early case composed the theme that sounds continually throughout the cases on this section: "[i]t does not follow, necessarily, because a party owes a debt, and is imprisoned until he pays the same sum of money, that he is imprisoned for a debt." *In re Meggett* (1900). If there is no contract, or if the court may not under the circumstances find anyone in contempt, or if the debt is someone else's (a divorced spouse had failed to pay the other spouse's attorney's fees, as the divorce agreement specified), the debtor may be imprisoned. *O'Connor v. O'Connor* (1970). By far the most common occurrence in the cases, however, is holding that not a debt but a wrongful act that results in an obligation to pay money justifies imprisonment. Examples of such wrongful acts include: contempt of court, *In re Milburn* (1883), *In re Meggett* (1900), *Wisconsin E. R. Board v. Mews* (1965); a tort, *Toal v. Clapp and another* (1885), *Cotton v. Sharpstein* (1861), *In re Mowry* (1860); passing worthless checks, *Locklear v. State* (1979), *State v. Croy* (1966); trespass, *Howland v. Needham* (1860); a crime, *State v. Roth* (1983), *Baker v. The State* (1882), *Pauly v. Keebler* (1921); and failure to pay child support, *State v. Lenz* (1999).

Section 17
Exemption of property of debtors.

The privilege of the debtor to enjoy the necessary comforts of life shall be recognized by wholesome laws, exempting a reasonable amount of property from seizure or sale for the payment of any debt or liability hereafter contracted.

This section, which protects the property of debtors, has not been amended. It differs considerably from the section on this subject in the 1846 version of the constitution. The prior version was specific and favorable to debtors, and it was one of the reasons the voters did not ratify that constitution.

The first half of this section appears to be a quaint expression of hope that the legislature will protect debtors, and because of it courts have interpreted liberally, in favor of debtors, statutes exempting property from seizure by their creditors.

Another reason for this kind of interpretation is the "strong public policy in this state to protect the homestead exemption." *Schwanz v. Teper* (1974). The court has announced this principle many times, sometimes in cases in which this section is an issue, sometimes in cases in which it is not an issue. See, e.g., *Julius v. Druckery* (1934); *Northwest Securities Co. v. Nelson* (1927).

One example of a liberal reading of this section is allowing an exemption for the total amount of an employee's pension, even though this section authorizes exemptions only up to a "reasonable amount." *North Side Bank v. Gentile* (1986). Another example is interpreting a statute that exempted property that was located outside a city or village only if it was agricultural to include all homesteads that were not in cities or villages, because "an exemption law which protects only certain classes of debtors" would be unconstitutional. *Binzel v. Grogan* (1886). Even if a debtor has sold nonexempt property and used the proceeds to buy exempt property, thus foiling his creditors, that recently acquired property remains exempt, and the creditor may not seize it but may only attack the sale of the nonexempt property. *Comstock v. Bechtel* (1885). However, this section is not self-executing; laws must be enacted to make it effective, and only property that a statute (liberally interpreted) exempts will be exempt. *Williams v. Smith* (1903).

There are a few exceptions to the rule of liberal, pro-debtor interpretation of this section. Because an exemption is "a personal privilege of each debtor," there are no joint exemptions, such as exemptions for property held in joint tenancy. *Russell and another v. Lennon* (1876). Similarly, there is no exemption for property that a partnership owns; the partners must divide the property or dissolve the partnership to qualify for an exemption. *O'Gorman v. Fink* (1883).

Section 18
Freedom of worship; liberty of conscience; state religion; public funds.

The right of every person to worship Almighty God according to the dictates of conscience shall never be infringed; nor shall any person be compelled to attend, erect or support any place of worship, or to maintain any ministry, without consent; nor shall any control of, or interference with, the rights of conscience be permitted, or any preference be given by law to any religious establishments or modes of worship; nor shall any money be drawn from the treasury for the benefit of religious societies, or religious or theological seminaries.

This section was amended in 1982 to make its phrasing gender-neutral. This is the Wisconsin version of the First Amendment's establishment of religion clause and free exercise clauses. In many cases both this section and its federal counterpart are at issue. This section provides stronger protection for the free exercise of religion than the First Amendment. *Noesen v. Dept. of Reg., Pharm., Exam. Bd.* (2008). Related sections are Article X, Section 3, which forbids sectarian instruction in the public schools but allows released time for religious instruction; and Article I, Section 23, which allows the state to transport pupils to religious schools.

A 1994 case made it necessary to determine definitively whether this section differs from the First Amendment's similar provisions. In *King v. Village of Waunakee*, the court held that the two provisions are equivalent, although the forceful dissent pointed out that they used different means to achieve their results. After using the kind of analysis that was used in recent U.S. Supreme Court cases and dealing briefly with this section, mainly by making assertions rather than arguments, the court, demonstrating its willingness to interpret this section's prohibition against establishment of religion as weak, held that a village's display of a nativity scene, along with several clearly secular decorations, did not violate the section, because the display had a purely secular purpose.

The tradition of considering this section independently of the First Amendment began with an early case on Article X, Section 3, *State ex rel. Weiss and others v. District Board, etc.* (1890). The court there wrote, "Wisconsin, as one of the later states admitted into the Union, having before it the experience of others, and probably in view of its heterogeneous population, . . . has, in her organic law, probably furnished a more-complete bar to any preference for, or discrimination against, any religious sect, organization, or society than any other state in the Union." In a later case concerning this section, *State ex rel. Reynolds v. Nusbaum* (1962), the court approvingly quoted those words. And in *State ex rel. Warren v. Reuter* (1969), the court stated "that Article I, Section 18 is more prohibitive than the first amendment of the federal constitution." In *State v. Fuerst* (1994), the court remarked that "we recognize that the United States and Wisconsin Constitutions each afford an independent protection of a person's religious freedom." In several cases involving both constitutional provisions, after analyzing the facts under the First Amendment, courts have turned to the Wisconsin constitution. *State ex rel. Warren v. Nusbaum* (1972); *State ex rel. Warren v. Nusbaum* (1974); *State ex rel. Holt v. Thompson* (1975).

King v. Village of Waunakee only appears to overturn this precedent; it does not actually do so. If it did overturn the other cases, the court would most likely would have said so. In fact, the court wrote that, pursuant to *State ex rel. Reynolds v. Nusbaum* (1962), with its strong language about the difference between this section and the First Amendment, this section "may be 'less flexible' than the First Amendment." These are not the words of a court that is overruling a decision. The explanation is quite simple: the plaintiff in *King* made the tactical error of conceding that this section and the First Amendment had identical meanings, so the court, being limited by the way in which the case was presented, made the same assumption. The validity of this analysis is buttressed by a case that was decided during the previous year, *In re Marriage of Lange v. Lange* (1993). There, the court held that if a plaintiff does not assert that this section and the First Amendment differ, it will rely only upon a First Amendment analysis. In short, *King* did not reverse the law on this section, and a plaintiff may take advantage of the differences between this section and the First Amendment by asserting that the two provisions differ. If a plaintiff does not do so, the court will resort to an analysis based on First Amendment cases.

The type of analysis will depend upon whether the issue is free exercise or the alleged establishment of religion. If it is the former, the court will balance the burden placed on religion against the governmental interest that placing that burden furthers. For example, if a crime is involved, the legislature has decided that the governmental interest is extremely important, *State v. Peck* (1988), but if the burden is merely collecting sales tax revenue and turning it over to the state, it will be deemed lighter than the impediment that it creates for religion, *Kollasch v. Adamany* (1980) (reversed on other grounds).

This section has been litigated most frequently in three kinds of cases. The first category is criminal cases. Imposing a criminal penalty on a grower of marijuana for his or her personal use does not violate this section even if the Native American Church, of which the defendant was a member, requires that use. *State v. Peck* (1988). A conviction for practicing medicine, in the form of using prayer to heal, without a license does not violate this section. *State v. Harrison* (1951). In contrast, because of this section the lack of religious beliefs may not be a factor in criminal sentencing. *State v. Fuerst* (1994).

The second important category of cases is actions involving the family. A judicial order in a custody case stating that a mother has the right to determine the religion of the children does not violate the father's rights under this section. *In re Marriage of Lange v. Lange.* However, a court may not base its decision about custody rights on the fact that it prefers one parent's religious views. *In re Marriage of Gould v. Gould* (1984).

The most important category of cases under this section involve education. A nonsectarian prayer at a high school graduation ceremony, being a "mere incident," does not violate this section. *State ex rel. Conway v. District Board* (1916). Requiring all private schools, including religious ones, to fill out a form about children who have exceptional educational needs does not place a burden on religion and thus is constitutional. *State ex rel. Warren v. Nusbaum* (1974). Busing pupils to religious schools aids religious societies and therefore is unconstitutional. *State ex rel. Reynolds v. Nusbaum* (1962). That decision led to the ratification of Article I, Section 23, which makes the practice constitutional. Releasing children from public school so that they may receive religious instruction is constitutional. *State ex rel. Holt v. Thompson* (1975). Providing aid to a medical school that has severed its ties to the Jesuit university of which it had been a part is constitutional, *State ex rel. Warren v. Reuter* (1969), but providing revenue, under a contract to educate dentists, to a dental school that is still part of that Jesuit university violates this section, *State ex rel. Warren v. Nusbaum* (1972).

The court seemed to have relaxed this section's rigor in a case challenging the Milwaukee Parental Choice Program. The program reimbursed costs to parents who send their children to sectarian schools. Focusing on the "primary effect" of the statute, the court held that the primary effect of the law was not to advance any particular religion but to allow parents to guide their children's educational development. *Jackson v. Benson* (1998).

This section's freedom of conscience clause applies to both individuals and groups of individuals. As a result, a church's choice of ministers is exempt from employment statutes under a "ministerial exception" doctrine. This exception includes teachers in a church school whose teaching includes religious instruction fundamental to the mission of the school. Therefore, a teacher's claim that she was dismissed because of her age is barred because she was an ecclesiastical employee. *Coulee Catholic Schools v. Labor and Industry Review Commission* (2009).

There are a few cases under this section on other areas of the law. Requiring the collection of sales taxes by a religious organization is not an unconstitutional burden. *Kollasch v. Adamany* (1980) (reversed on other grounds). Requiring nonresident solicitors of funds, including funds for religious purposes, to register and pay a fee does not create an unconstitutional burden. *Washburn v. Ellquist* (1943). Forbidding religious services, except Easter sunrise services, in county parks violates this section. *Milwaukee County v. Carter* (1950). Making a bequest in a will contingent on a person regularly attending a particular church does not interfere with religious freedom, the choice being the potential recipient's and the decedent having the right to dispose of his or her property as he or she wishes. *In re Paulson's Will* (1906). Requiring the members of a voluntary association to be Roman Catholics is constitutional. *Barry v. Order of C. K.* (1903). Suspending a person who is a director and officer of a corporation for misfeasance, by causing the person, according to his religion, to fall from grace, does not violate this section. *John v. John* (1989). Removing a pastoral associate for religious reasons, if the person has refused to accept a position for which particular religious beliefs are not required, does not violate this section. *Shudarek v. Labor & Industry Rev. Comm.* (1983).

In *State v. Miller* (1996), the court relied explicitly upon this section rather than the First Amendment, saying that the "state constitution provides an independent basis" for deciding the case, which involved Old Order Amish charged with breach of a statute that requires the use of a triangular red and orange slow-moving vehicle symbol. Following their church rules, they had used white reflective tape instead because they consider red and orange symbols garish, in violation of their church's fundamental principles. The court followed an analysis (derived from several federal court cases) that balances the burden of a statute upon a sincerely held religious belief against the need to address a compelling state interest. The court concluded that the white reflective tape used by the Amish, which is more reflective than the slow-moving vehicle symbol, is less restrictive—therefore the statute, as applied, violated this section's guarantee of freedom of conscience.

Section 19
Religious tests prohibited.

No religious tests shall ever be required as a qualification for any office of public trust under the state, and no person shall be rendered incompetent to give evidence in any court of law or equity in consequence of his opinions on the subject of religion.

This section, which forbids establishing religious tests for holding public office, has not been amended or litigated.

Section 20
Military subordinate to civil power.

The military shall be in strict subordination to the civil power.

This section has not been amended or litigated. It is one of a few sections based upon the notion that the state enjoys the status of a sovereign entity. Other such provisions include Article IV, Section 29; Article V, Section 4; Article V, Section 7(2); and Article VIII, Section 7(1). Those sections, along with other considerations, were cited to justify granting bonuses to World War I veterans. *State ex rel. Atwood v. Johnson* (1919).

Section 21
Rights of suitors.

(1) Writs of error shall never be prohibited, and shall be issued by such courts as the legislature designates by law.

(2) In any court of this state, any suitor may prosecute or defend his suit either in his own proper person or by an attorney of the suitor's choice.

This section both grants the right to appeal lower courts' decisions and allows persons to serve as their own attorneys. It originally read: "[w]rits of error shall never be prohibited by law." It was amended in 1977. The material added had been Article VII, Section 20. A writ of error is an order issued by an appellate court directing a trial court to send it the record so that the case can be appealed. Thus, the first subsection guarantees the right to appeal trial courts' decisions. However, Article I, Section 8, which prohibits placing a defendant in double jeopardy, and the Fifth Amendment of the U.S. Constitution, preclude the state from appealing a verdict of acquittal in a criminal case. Article VII, Sections 3(2) and 5(3) establish the appellate jurisdiction of the supreme court and the courts of appeals.

This section grants the appeal rights that existed at the time when the constitution was ratified. *Jackson v. The State* (1896); *Aetna Accident & Liability Co. v. Lyman* (1913). At that time, the right to appeal attached "only after judgment in an action at law in a court of record, or after an order in the nature of a final judgment, to correct some supposed mistake in the proceedings in respect to such judgment or order." *Jackson*. A motion for a new trial that was made after a judgment was issued does not justify a writ of error. *Id*. Even after a statute was enacted allowing writs of error to be issued upon requests for new trials, the appeal had to be directed at the judgment and not be a request for a new trial. *Ullman v. State* (1904). This section does not apply to requests for an injunction against a clerk of circuit court and a sheriff, *Martin v. State* (1941), or to appeals of a judge's rulings and directions, *Lovesee v. State* (1908).

Even though the right to appeal is nearly absolute, reasonable laws may be enacted to regulate the procedures by which parties may exercise it. Setting reasonable time limits for making appeals is constitutional. *Scheid v. State* (1973); *O'Donnell v. State* (1906). However, requiring that appeals of convictions for murder may be made only with the approval of at least one justice of the supreme court violates this section. *State v. Raines* (1948).

The portion of this section about the right to prosecute suits has rarely been litigated. It does not require a party to obtain an attorney—in fact, it explicitly allows parties to represent themselves—so a judge may not dismiss a case because a party has failed to comply with the judge's demand that the party obtain an attorney. *Hlavinka v. Blunt, Ellis & Loewi, Inc.* (1993). A non-attorney may not file a notice of appeal on behalf of a corporation; corporations are not natural persons and are not persons for purposes of subsection (2). *Jadair, Inc. v. U.S. Fire Insurance Co.* (1997). Even though a statute requires that a person who is at risk of commitment to an institution in a case have counsel, that counsel may be the person who is at risk. *In Matter of Condition of S. Y.* (1991). "Proper person" means personally, not that counsel must be an adult and competent. *Id*.

Section 22
Maintenance of free government.

The blessings of a free government can only be maintained by a firm adherence to justice, moderation, temperance, frugality and virtue, and by frequent recurrence to fundamental principles.

This section, which seems to be a civics lesson rather than a constitutional provision, has not been amended or litigated. However, it has been used as a guide to interpreting the constitution's general purpose and influenced the decisions in a few cases. For example, one court stated, "[w]hen things as monstrous as this are contemplated as within the language of the statutory provisions under consideration it behooves us to heed the admonitions of sec. 22, art. I, of our state constitution . . . and to consider and determine whether the thing attempted is contrary to those principles." *Stierle v. Rohmeyer* (1935).

Section 23
Transportation of school children.

Nothing in this constitution shall prohibit the legislature from providing for the safety and welfare of children by providing for the transportation of children to and from any parochial or private school or institution of learning.

This section permits using public money to transport children to and from parochial schools. In 1945, the Wisconsin attorney general wrote that a bill authorizing spending public money for that purpose would violate Article I, Section 18. 34 Op. Att'y Gen. 127. During the next year, the electors failed to ratify a constitutional amendment that would have allowed this kind of transportation. In 1961, another attorney general, noting with approval the earlier opinion, wrote that that use of public money would violate both Article I, Section 18 (on freedom of religion and the establishment of religion) and the public purpose doctrine and perhaps would violate Article X, Section 3 (on sectarian instruction in the public schools). 50 Op. Att'y Gen. 132. Shortly thereafter, the court confirmed the opinions of the two attorneys general by holding that public money may not be used to bus children to or from parochial schools. *State ex rel. Reynolds v. Nusbaum* (1962). In 1965, the legislature began the process of amending the constitution to create this section, which was ratified in 1967.

Section 24
Use of school buildings.

Nothing in this constitution shall prohibit the legislature from authorizing, by law, the use of public school buildings by civic, religious or charitable organizations during nonschool hours upon payment by the organization to the school district of reasonable compensation for such use.

This section, added by amendment in 1972, allows certain kinds of nonprofit organizations, including religious organizations, to use school buildings. Since its inclusion in the constitution this section has not been amended or litigated. A court's holding that using public school property to aid religious groups to spread their faith violated Article I, Section 18 made this amendment necessary if school buildings were to be used by religious organizations. *Milwaukee County v. Carter* (1950).

Section 25
Right to keep and bear arms.

The people have the right to keep and bear arms for security, defense, hunting, recreation or any other lawful purpose.

Section 25 was adopted in 1998. It preserves the fundamental right to bear arms, but subject to reasonable regulation. This section did not create a right to carry a weapon but protects a fundamental right that has always existed. *Wisconsin Carry, Inc. v. City of Madison* (2017).

Although this section does not mention statutory regulation, the legislature has the inherent police power to control the time, place, and manner of concealed carry of weapons. Therefore, a statute prohibiting the concealed carry of dangerous weapons is valid. *State v. Cole* (2003). The court further considered the constitutionality of the concealed carry statute in a case in which a store owner who had concealed a pistol in his pocket, in his own store located in a high crime area, who had been robbed before, was convicted of concealed carry. The court held the case should go back to the trial court on the questions of whether the defendant had a substantial need to carry the weapon and a reasonable alternative to concealing it. *State v. Hamden* (2003). The following year, the court reaffirmed its holding in *Hamden* and held that this section did not give a store owner the right to conceal several weapons in his car. *State v. Fisher* (2004). A statute that prohibits felons from possessing guns does not violate this section. *State v. Pocian* (2013). The court of appeals has held that mere possession of a switchable knife in one's home for self-defense is protected under this section and the Second Amendment. *State v. Herrmann* (2015).

Section 26
Right to fish, hunt, trap, and take game.

The people have the right to fish, hunt, trap, and take game subject only to reasonable restrictions as prescribed by law.

Section 26 was adopted in 2003. This section codifies the right to hunt that existed at common law. *Wisconsin Citizens Concerned for Cranes and Doves v. Wis. D.N.R.* (2004). It has not been amended.

Article II

Boundaries

Section 1
State Boundary.

It is hereby ordained and declared that the state of Wisconsin doth consent and accept of the boundaries prescribed in the act of congress entitled "An act to enable the people of Wisconsin territory to form a constitution and state government, and for the admission of such state into the Union," approved August sixth, one thousand eight hundred and forty-six, to wit: Beginning at the northeast corner of the state of Illinois—that is to say, at a point in the center of Lake Michigan where the line of forty-two degrees and thirty minutes of north latitude crosses the same; thence running with the boundary line of the state of Michigan, through Lake Michigan, Green Bay, to the mouth of the Menominee river; thence up the channel of the said river to the Brule river; thence up said last-mentioned river to Lake Brule; thence along the southern shore of Lake Brule in a direct line to the center of the channel between Middle and South Islands, in the Lake of the Desert; thence in a direct line to the head waters of the Montreal river, as marked upon the survey made by Captain Cramm; thence down the main channel of the Montreal river to the middle of Lake Superior; thence through the center of Lake Superior to the mouth of the St. Louis river; thence up the main channel of said river to the first rapids in the same, above the Indian village, according to Nicollet's map; thence due south to the main branch of the river St. Croix; thence down the main channel of said river to the Mississippi; thence down the center of the main channel of that river to the northwest corner of the state of Illinois; thence due east with the northern boundary of the state of Illinois to the place of beginning, as established by "An act to enable the people of the Illinois territory to form a constitution and state government, and for the admission of such state into the Union on an equal footing with the original states," approved April 18th, 1818.

The 1848 constitutional convention included in this section, which describes the state's boundaries, an additional paragraph stating its preference for a change in those boundaries. In the act admitting Wisconsin to the Union, Congress rejected that proposal. As the section indicates, the constitution's framers borrowed the description of the state's boundaries from a federal law, the enabling act, 9 U.S. Stat. 56. The lack of precision is notable. Part of the problem derives from references to old maps and an Indian village, part from references to rivers, the courses and main channels of which change. The boundaries matter because they delineate the reach of the state's laws. For example, the fishing laws of Wisconsin and Minnesota might differ regarding an action on a border river, and if so, it would matter whether one were in Wisconsin or Minnesota.

In two cases that the court decided in 1903, it reaffirmed the statement in the constitution that in the area where the Mississippi River flows between Minnesota and Wisconsin its main channel is the boundary between the two states, and that neither state has jurisdiction over the river's entire breadth. *Roberts v. Fullerton* (1903); *Franzini v. Layland* (1903). A few years later the court decided a case about the part of the border that traverses Lake Superior. *Independent Tug Line v. Lake Superior L. & B. Co.* (1911). Out-of-state corporations had to register their articles of incorporation with the secretary of state before beginning operations in Wisconsin. A corporation that had a contract to tow logs across part of Lake Superior had failed to file, and argued that, the lake being international waters, the corporation could operate on it. But the court concluded that the corporation did part of the towing well within Wisconsin's borders.

The following year, the court decided another case involving the portion of the boundary between Wisconsin and Minnesota that runs down the Mississippi River, *State v. Bowen* (1912). There, the court held that the main channel referred to in this section meant the main channel at the time of ratification of the constitution, unless the channel was changed by two natural processes: erosion and accretion. The boundary did not change because a bridge diverted a river's flow. But when Wisconsin's and Iowa's fishing laws are similar, Wisconsin can take jurisdiction over illegal clamming in the Iowa waters of the Mississippi River. *State v. Beck* (1996).

Section 2
Enabling act accepted.

The propositions contained in the act of congress are hereby accepted, ratified and confirmed, and shall remain irrevocable without the consent of the United States; and it is hereby ordained that this state shall never interfere with the primary disposal of the soil within the same by the United States, nor with any regulations congress may find necessary for securing the title in such soil to bona fide purchasers thereof; and in no case shall nonresident proprietors be taxed higher than residents. Provided, that nothing in this constitution, or in the act of congress aforesaid, shall in any manner prejudice or affect the right of the state of Wisconsin to 500,000 acres of land granted to said state, and to be hereafter selected and located by and under the act of congress entitled "An act to appropriate the proceeds of the sales of the public lands, and grant pre-emption rights," approved September fourth, one thousand eight hundred and forty-one.

This section is Wisconsin's assent to the federal law that allowed it to begin the process of becoming a state. The constitutional text refers to "the act" rather than citing to it; the citation is 9 U.S. Stat. 56. In accepting the enabling act, the new state of Wisconsin agreed to three conditions that appear in the act but not in this section. That general acceptance bestowed on those conditions a constitutional status. One is that Wisconsin and all bordering states have concurrent jurisdiction over the Mississippi River and all other rivers and waters that form part of the borders between Wisconsin and neighboring states. Although the constitution recites that the state's boundary lies at the center of the main channel of the Mississippi River, the act of Congress admitting Wisconsin into the union granted concurrent jurisdiction over the entire river where it forms a border between Wisconsin and Minnesota or Iowa. *State v. Nelson* (1979); *State v. Beck* (1996). Concurrent jurisdiction means both states have the power to prosecute crimes if the states have similar laws.

A second condition is that the navigable waters leading into the boundary waters are "common highways" and forever free—that is, no "tax, duty, impost, or toll" may be charged for travel on them. Actually, there is no doubt about the constitutional status of conditions very similar to these. Article IX, Section 1 states nearly the same conditions, although the second condition is somewhat modified. In that section carrying places are also made common highways and free, but the waters to which those principles apply is limited to those that lead to the Mississippi or St. Lawrence rivers. The third condition is that federal laws that are not "locally inapplicable" have the same force in Wisconsin as they have elsewhere in the United States. Article VI of the federal Constitution, which includes the Supremacy Clause, achieves the same result.

The enabling act also contains material that does not have the force of the constitution. Some of this material consists of statements that a federal district court will be established and a judge and clerk for it and a federal attorney will be appointed to it; and, until the next (1850) federal census, Wisconsin will be entitled to two representatives to Congress. Other material that appears in the enabling act and does not have the force of the constitution consists of offers by the federal government that the constitutional convention may accept. If the convention does accept them, they are binding on the United States. Those offers include setting aside "section sixteen" in each township for the use of schools, conveying to the state two entire townships for the use of a university, allowing the legislature to select ten sections from the unappropriated lands to be used to complete the state's public buildings, and granting to the state as many as twelve salt springs and six sections of land adjoining them. A section is one square mile; thirty-six constitute a standard township, and each section in a township is numbered, making section sixteen readily identifiable.

Surprisingly, this section has been both amended and a peripheral part of a legal case. The original version stated "no tax shall be imposed on land the property of the United States," which was deleted in 1951. The statement in Article VI of the U.S. Constitution that that document and the laws of the United States are the supreme law of the land validates any federal law forbidding states from taxing federal property. The principle of intergovernmental tax immunity (one unit of government may not tax another), although it does not have the force of a constitutional provision, also would most likely prevent a state from taxing federal property. However, the federal government has occasionally waived its right to a tax exemption, so removing that clause from the state constitution allowed Wisconsin to take advantage of such waivers. The prohibition against imposing higher taxes on nonresidents, which, because of its context, probably refers only to property taxes, is narrower than the requirement of uniform property taxation in Article VIII, Section 1. That promise and the promise never to interfere with the disposal of the "soil" in the state are conditions of grants of federal land to the state, as specified in the 1846 enabling act. That act required these two provisions to be included in the constitution and specified that they are "irrevocable without the consent of the United States," phrasing that this section echoes. These provisions and the statement of the boundaries in the previous section are the only parts of the constitution that the state may not unilaterally amend.

The case in which this section figured was about the validity of the federal Homestead Act's prohibition against seizing for debts land acquired under that act. *Gile and another v. Hallock* (1873). The court pointed out that provisions of the federal Constitution gave Congress the power to regulate the territory it had conveyed, Article IV, Section 2(2), and that the "supremacy clause" justified such regulation. *Gile* cited to the promise that was made in this section not to interfere with the federal government's disposition of its land, but, because the U.S. Constitution disposed of the case, that reference was not necessary to deciding the case and therefore has no precedential value.

Article III

Suffrage

This article originally consisted of six sections, which specified qualifications for voting, the most limiting of which were being white, male, and at least twenty-one years old; declared persons who were under guardianship "non compos mentis" (not having control of their mind) or insane could not vote; required secret ballots in almost all elections; specified that leaving Wisconsin on state or federal business did not deprive persons of residency for voting purposes; decreed that military personnel were not residents of the state merely because they were stationed in it; and authorized laws to deny the vote to certain criminals and persons who bet on elections. During 1882 the first section, on qualified electors, was amended to delete "white" wherever it occurred. That amendment recognized the decision in *Gillespie v. Palmer* (1866) that the electors had voted during 1849 to extend the suffrage to African-Americans. A 1908 amendment altered the provision on persons of foreign birth to provide that to be eligible to vote, they must have declared, before December 1, 1908, their intentions to become citizens, and that their right to vote under that provision expired on December 1, 1912. In 1934 this section was amended to delete voting restrictions that had been imposed on women, persons who were born in other countries, and American Indians. Finally, in 1986 an amendment reorganized this article and amended it into its present form. Earlier versions of this article were litigated, but the changes that were made rendered some of that litigation irrelevant.

Section 1
Electors.

Every United States citizen age 18 or older who is a resident of an election district in this state is a qualified elector of that district.

This section specifies the requirements for voting. In the litigation that is relevant to its current version, two topics dominate. The first is the section's scope, specifically whether it grants an absolute right to vote. Courts have ruled that this section bestows the right to vote, but it does not prevent regulation by statute of voting if the regulation does not in effect impair that right. *State ex rel. McGrael v. Phelps* (1910) neatly illustrates these principles. The Milwaukee County Democratic candidates who had received the most votes in their primary litigated the refusal of the board of county canvassers—the officials who counted the votes and performed other administrative duties related to elections—to place their names on the general election ballot as their party's candidates. The board had refused to do so because of a statute that specified that, only if all the candidates whose names appeared on a ballot as representatives of a party in the aggregate receive at least 20 percent of the votes cast (presumably in the jurisdiction) for their party's nominee for governor in the previous election, would the winning candidate be listed on the general election ballot as the party's candidate for the office. The court first disposed of the notion that voting was a privilege, not a right. It then held that, under the police power, the state could regulate elections to prevent abuse and promote efficiency if the regulation was reasonable. The court concluded that the statute reasonably regulated voting. A few years later, the court defined reasonable regulation of voting as regulation that stopped short of materially impairing the right of electors to choose freely. *State ex rel. Barber v. Circuit Court* (1922). In *Barber*, the issue was the right to vote for a candidate who, if elected, would be ineligible to serve.

Requiring photo identification at the polling place does not add a qualification to vote in addition to those listed in this section. *League of Women Voters Network v. Walker* (2014). In a companion case, the court adopted a "saving construction" of the photo I.D. statute that would forbid the Department of Transportation from enforcing its rules on issuing photo identification that require documents that would cost the applicant a fee to obtain. *Milwaukee Branch N.A.A.C.P. v. Walker* (2014).

The other dominant topic in the cases on this section is the age requirement. A statute required that candidates for the office of county supervisor be qualified electors at least ten days before the earliest day on which they could circulate nomination papers. A county clerk had refused to accept the nomination papers of a potential candidate for county supervisor who would become twenty-one (at the time, the age at which persons could begin to vote) before election day but did not satisfy the statutory requirement. In *Cross v. Hebl* (1970), the court held that this section allows the legislature to define residency (all the cases on that issue rest on the applicable statutes, not on this section), but does not give the legislature the right to add requirements to the age requirement that this section states. The court then held that this section meant that an elector need not turn twenty-one until election day and that, therefore, the plaintiff was eligible to run for county supervisor.

Section 2
Implementation.

Laws may be enacted:

(1) Defining residency.

(2) Providing for registration of electors.

(3) Providing for absentee voting.

(4) Excluding from the right of suffrage persons:

(a) Convicted of a felony, unless restored to civil rights.

(b) Adjudged by a court to be incompetent or partially incompetent, unless the judgment specifies that the person is capable of understanding the objective of the elective process or the judgment is set aside.

(5) Subject to ratification by the people at a general election, extending the right of suffrage to additional classes.

Requiring photo identification is part of the registration process at the polls and does not create an unconstitutional bar to voting. The requirement provides a reasonable means of furthering the state's interest in protecting the integrity of the electoral process. Requiring a voter to furnish photo identification is no different from requiring a voter to state his or her name and address to confirm that the voter is the person shown on the registration list. *League of Women Voters Network v. Walker* (2014).

Section 3
Secret ballot.

All votes shall be by secret ballot.

This section originally made an exception for "township" offices. The correct term would have been "town," which refers to a unit of government, not "township," which refers to a unit of measure that applies to land. This section has not been litigated.

Article IV

Legislative

Section 1
Legislative power.

The legislative power shall be vested in a senate and assembly.

This section vests legislative power in the two houses of the legislature, just as Article V, Section 1 vests executive power in the governor and Article VII, Section 2 vests judicial power in the court system. The combination of the three sections creates the separation of powers doctrine. For an analysis of that doctrine, see the commentary on Article VII, Section 2. Because Article V, Section 10 requires the presentation to the governor for approval or veto of all bills that pass the legislature, one needs to distinguish between legislative power and law-making power (which the legislature and the governor share). However, the legal opinions on this article conflate the two powers, just as other parts of the constitution refer to the legislature making laws.

Courts frequently recognize the large scope of the legislature's powers by expressing great deference to that branch of government. A reader of legal opinions finds many statements like "the framers of the Wisconsin constitution vested the legislative power of the state in a senate and assembly. The exercise of such power is subject only to the limitation and restraints imposed by the Wisconsin constitution and the constitution and laws of the United States." *State ex rel. McCormack v. Foley* (1962). The explicit constitutional limits on legislative power include Article I, Section 12 (prohibiting bills of attainder, ex post facto laws, and laws impairing contracts) and Article I, Section 31 (prohibiting special and private laws on enumerated subjects). The constitution also creates, in many of the sections of Article I, individual rights that legislative enactments may not violate. Even apparent constitutional grants of legislative power are not absolute. In other words, the legislature has significantly less than plenary power.

Courts are also deferential to legislative enactments when their constitutionality is challenged: "all legislative acts are presumed constitutional, a heavy burden is placed on the party challenging constitutionality and if any reasonable doubt exists it must be resolved in favor of the constitutionality of the statute." *In Matter of Guardianship of Nelson* (1980). That is, the burden of proof—beyond a reasonable doubt—is the same in that kind of case, even if basic rights are at issue, as it is in criminal cases. In fact, if a statute might be read in more than one way, courts will choose the interpretation that will sustain the statute. *State ex rel. Strykowski v. Wilkie* (1978). If, in order to make it more likely that a statute will be found to be constitutional, the legislature has added to a statute, or to a bill that creates a statute, a statement of its purpose, courts usually accept that statement's validity. *State ex rel. Thomson v. Giessel* (1953). However, if the legislature has added such a statement, a court, in deciding whether the statute is constitutional, will examine only the purpose that that statement specifies, rather than searching for another purpose. *Milwaukee Brewers v. DH&SS* (1986).

Individualized tests for constitutional validity apply to two kinds of statutes. First, if a statute makes a classification, it will be upheld if any rational basis or reasonable set of facts justifies that classification. *Committee to Retain Byers v. Elections Board* (1980). However, many constitutional provisions require uniformity and thus cast doubt on any classifications in statutes on their subject matter. Those provisions are Article IV, Section 23 (uniformity of town government); Article VIII, Section 1 (uniformity of property taxation); Article X, Section 3 (uniformity of the public schools); and Article XI, Section 3 (uniformity of city and village government). Second, if statutes enacted based on the police power "do not contravene significant constitutional or inherent rights of individuals, if the classification on which they are based is reasonable, if they are within the scope of the police powers of the state, [and] if they are appropriately related to a proper purpose of such police power," they will not be invalidated. *Bisenius v. Karns* (1969).

One of the main issues regarding this section is the relation between the legislature and administrative agencies, which are part of the state government's executive branch. Those agencies are creatures of the legislature. *State ex rel. Thompson v. Nash* (1965). The leading case on this issue, *Clintonville Transfer Line v. Public Service Comm.* (1945), sets forth the law on this subject:

1. The power to declare whether there shall be a law; to determine the purpose or policy to be achieved by the law; and to fix the limits within which

the law shall operate is vested in the legislature and may not be delegated, but when the legislature has laid down the fundamentals of the law, it may delegate to administrative agencies such legislative powers as may be necessary to carry into effect the general legislative purpose.

2. The powers exercised by administrative agencies are legislative and not judicial in their nature.

3. If in the exercise of delegated power the constitutional rights of a citizen are impaired, his rights will be protected by a court.

4. So long as an administrative agency acts within the scope of the powers granted to it without impairing the constitutional rights of a citizen, its findings of fact are subject to review by the courts only to the extent and in the manner prescribed by the legislature.

5. It is not competent for the legislature, even in a circumscribed field, to grant to an administrative agency unlimited legislative power. The power granted must be exercised in accordance with standards and limitations fixed by the legislature.

6. If no appeal or comparable procedure is prescribed for review, none exists. In the absence of legislative authorization to review the facts, administrative determinations can be reviewed only by certiorari [certifying the record of the agency's proceedings to a court for review], in which only questions of law are raised.

These principles require only minimal modification and amplification. Administrative agencies have not only the powers that the legislature expressly grants them, but those that may be implied from the applicable statutes. *American Brass Co. v. State Board of Health* (1944). Agencies may exercise limited judicial functions: "administrative boards may constitutionally exercise such judicial power as is incidental to their administration of the particular statutes which the legislature has given them to administer." *State ex rel. Volden v. Haas* (1953). As administrative agencies have proliferated, making more rules, it has become necessary to establish those agencies' relation to the legislature regarding that function. They may promulgate rules only within the scope, express or implied, of the statutes that the rules interpret. *Brown County v. H & SS Department* (1981).

The legislature also relates to local units of government in ways that affect the scope of its powers. The legislature has nearly supreme authority over them. The state constitution is virtually the only restraint upon that authority. *State ex rel. Martin v. Juneau* (1941). The most important constitutional limit is the grant of home rule power in Article XI, Section 3. Moreover, local units of government have no rights under the federal Constitution against the state. *Madison Metropolitan Sewerage Dist. v. Committee* (1951). The legislature may cede portions of its authority to municipalities regarding matters of purely local concern. *Fish Creek Park Co. v. Bayside* (1957).

In fact, delegation of legislative power is a major issue related to this section. One can most easily understand this issue in regard to the delegation of judicial power. The legislature may delegate any truly judicial power to the judicial branch of government. *In re Rules of Court Case* (1931). One may accurately draw the line between legislative and judicial power by remembering that "what is 'desirable' or 'advisable' or 'ought to be' is a question of policy, not a question of fact. What is 'necessary' or what is 'in the best interest' is not a fact and its determination by the judiciary is an exercise of legislative power when such involves political considerations and reasons." *In re City of Beloit* (1968). For example, the power to draw municipal boundaries is not judicial, *In re Incorporation of Village of North Milwaukee* (1896); neither is the power to annex property, *In re City of Beloit* (1968). Court procedure, however, is a judicial matter. *In re Rules of Court Case* (1931).

The propriety of delegating legislative power to nonjudicial bodies is less clearcut. Certainly, the legislature may not delegate the power to make a law, such as allowing trade or industrial groups or associations to propose "laws" that would be codes of fair competition, which the governor could modify. *Gibson Auto Co. v. Finnegan* (1935). Unfortunately, the limits of the delegation of legislative power to entities other than the judiciary and private citizens are unclear. Until 1928 courts decided this kind of case by examining the nature of the power that had been delegated; that year, in *State ex rel. Wis. Inspection Bureau v. Whitman* (1928), another method of analysis superceded that one. However, one cannot be absolutely sure about the method that replaced it. Taking in chronological order five important cases on this issue indicates the lack of consistency in this area. In the first case the court held that the legislature may delegate its power to fill in a statute's details if the statute specified standards. *Milwaukee v. Sewerage Comm.* (1954).

Next, the court, although recognizing that the statute in question did not specify standards, upheld the statute's delegation of legislative authority because the statute had a clear purpose and because procedural safeguards (review of administrative rulemaking by a legislative committee) and judicial safeguards (the opportunity to litigate) existed. *Chicago & Northwestern Ry. Co. v. Public Service Comm.* (1969). In a case that was decided two years later, the court adhered to the rule that "a delegation of legislative power will be upheld if the purpose of the delegating statute is ascertainable and there are procedural safeguards to [e]nsure that the board or agency acts within the legislative purpose," and the court added that there must be standards. *Watchmaking Examining Board v. Husar* (1971). In the next case, *Westring v. James* (1976), the court conceded that the statute established standards that were "exceedingly general" rather than definite but concluded that the clarity of the statute's purpose and the existence of procedural safeguards validated the rulemaking. In 1984, in *Gilbert v. Medical Examining Board*, the court explicitly required an ascertainable purpose and safeguards and alluded frequently to the clarity of the statute's standards, which suggests that clear standards might again be a requirement. The requirement of a clear purpose and procedural safeguards are common threads, and one senses some flexibility in this kind of case, but the courts sometimes require standards, sometimes waive them, and sometimes are unclear about whether they are required.

"[A] governor's power to craft legislation necessarily must have constitutional limits. A write-in veto power which extends beyond the reduction of appropriation amounts intrudes too far into the constitutional grant of legislative power vested in the senate and the assembly." *Risser v. Klauser* (1997).

Section 2
Legislature, how constituted.

The number of the members of the assembly shall never be less than fifty-four nor more than one hundred. The senate shall consist of a number not more than one-third nor less than one-fourth of the number of the members of the assembly.

This section has not been amended or litigated. There now are thirty-three senators and ninety-nine representatives to the assembly.

Section 3
Apportionment.

At its first session after each enumeration made by the authority of the United States, the legislature shall apportion and district anew the members of the senate and assembly, according to the number of inhabitants.

This section begins a sequence of three about redistricting the legislature. Although the guarantee of equal protection of the laws in the Fourteenth Amendment of the U.S. Constitution protects voters, the Wisconsin cases on these three sections are still valid. That is, litigants may challenge districting and apportionment plans on the basis of either constitution. This section's original form required apportionment—assigning seats in the legislature to districts—and districting—drawing the boundaries of the districts for the state senate and assembly—in 1855, every ten years thereafter and after each federal census. It required that the legislature undertake these actions based upon population, not including American Indians who were not taxed, and soldiers and officers of the army and navy. In 1910, the voters ratified an amendment that deleted the requirement that the legislature reapportion and redistrict every ten years after 1855. Accordingly, the legislature now performs those functions every decade, not every five years. In 1910, the prohibition against counting nontaxed American Indians in the population was deleted. In 1982, the prohibition against counting military personnel was deleted.

Because this section not only directs the legislature periodically to perform actions but also affects the legislature's composition, any litigation concerning it raises delicate issues about the judiciary's relationship with the legislature. In other words, this kind of litigation implicates the doctrine of separation of powers. In addition to the presumption of constitutionality that courts customarily grant to legislative enactments, the courts presume that apportionment and districting plans are equitable. *State ex rel. Bowman v. Dammann* (1932). At first, the courts thought that they could not compel the legislature to perform these two actions to adjust apportionment schemes that were valid when they were enacted, despite this section's mandatory nature. *State ex rel. Broughton v. Zimmerman* (1952); *State ex rel. Martin v. Zimmerman* (1946). However, a later court explicitly overruled the two earlier cases on this point. *State ex rel. Reynolds v. Zimmerman* (1964). Indeed, the court in that case gave the legislature and the governor a deadline to produce an acceptable apportionment and districting plan, and, upon the failure of the other two branches of government to meet that deadline, drew its own plan and declared it to be in effect.

Although this section does not quite say so—it states, "according to the number of inhabitants"—it requires an approximation of equal representation, which is also required by the Fourteenth Amendment. The legislature need not create districts that result in exactly equal representation, but "there should be as close an approximation to *exactness* as possible." *The State ex rel. Lamb v. Cunningham, Secretary of State* (1892). The kind of effort that will not pass constitutional muster is clear:

> If . . . there is such a wide and bold departure from this constitutional rule [of equal representation] that it cannot possibly be justified by the exercise of any judgment or discretion and that evinces an intention on the part of the legislature to utterly ignore and disregard the rule of the constitution in order to promote some other object than a constitutional apportionment, then the conclusion is inevitable that the legislature did not use any judgment or discretion whatever. *Id.*

One can understand the degree of allowable deviation from perfectly equal representation only by examining some statistics from the cases on this section. In one case, the court accepted a deviation in the population of assembly districts from 55.1 percent of the average (the population of the state divided by the number of districts) to 199.3 percent of the average, because it presumed that the plan was fair and because the plaintiff did not overcome that presumption. *State ex rel. Bowman v. Dammann* (1932). In that case, a misreading of the next section that resulted in requiring that county borders not divide assembly districts made equal representation more difficult to achieve. A plan that created assembly districts that ranged in population from 8,626 to 25,111 was too far from creating equal representation to be constitutional. *Lamb*. A plan that created senate districts that ranged from 74,293 to 208,343 and assembly districts that ranged from 19,651 to 87,486 was also too far from equal to be constitutional. *Zimmerman*.

Because this section requires the legislature to reapportion and redistrict during the first legislative session after each federal census, the timing of these actions might be—and, in fact, has been—an issue and therefore the subject of litigation. The legislature has erred both by failing to do such work in time and by doing it too early. As mentioned, a court has given the legislature a deadline and, after the deadline passed, put its own plan into effect. *Zimmerman*. A legislature may not reapportion and redistrict more than once in the period between federal censuses. *Id*. However, changes in apportionment and districting that occur between those that follow a federal census and the next federal census are constitutional if they "result incidentally from the exercise of the acknowledged power of the legislature to organize counties, towns and cities, and change the boundaries of such as are already organized." *Slauson et al. v. The City of Racine* (1861).

The courts have also decided several minor issues related to this section. A reapportionment and redistricting plan may have a delayed effective date. *State ex rel. Broughton v. Zimmerman* (1952). It may be contingent on the results of an advisory referendum. *Id*. Although the section refers to the legislature performing these tasks, no plan is valid unless it has been presented to the governor and either signed by him or her or passed notwithstanding a gubernatorial veto. *State ex rel. Reynolds v. Zimmerman* (1964).

Section 4
Representatives to the assembly, how chosen.

The members of the assembly shall be chosen biennially, by single districts, on the Tuesday succeeding the first Monday of November in even-numbered years, by the qualified electors of the several districts, such districts to be bounded by county, precinct, town or ward lines, to consist of contiguous territory and be in as compact form as practicable.

This is the second of three sections about redistricting the legislature, and it also contains details about elections. This section's first version provided for annual elections of members of the assembly. In 1882, it was amended to make the elections biennial, although the amendment also stated that the biennial election was to occur on the Tuesday after the first Monday in November after the amendment was adopted, which implies that there was to be only one election. This slip was ignored for 101 years. In 1982, an amendment replaced the problematic phrase with the reference to even-numbered years.

Although this section, after its first amendment, required that assembly districts "be bounded by county, precinct, town, or ward lines," the court held unconstitutional a redistricting plan that resulted in some assembly districts containing territory in more than one county. *The State ex rel. Lamb v. Cunningham, Secretary of State* (1892). That is, despite the use of "or" rather than "and" in this section, the court interpreted it to require that, although counties may be divided into assembly districts, each county must by itself consist of at least one district. A later court, although it held that requiring districts to be apportioned according to population in turn requires only minimal deviation in districts' populations, also held that a plan may not combine a county with part of another county to form an assembly district. *State ex rel. Reynolds v. Zimmerman* (1964).

This section was pertinent to three annexation cases. In one, although the court had invalidated the annexation because no referendum was held, it also said that the annexation violated this section because it would have placed one ward in two assembly districts. *Wauwatosa v. Milwaukee* (1951). In another annexation case, the court validated an annexation that split a municipality between two assembly districts and that resulted in an assembly district that included parts of two counties, but the court nullified the changes to the assembly districts. *Fish Creek Park Co. v. Bayside* (1957).

Section 5
Senators, how chosen.

The senators shall be elected by single districts of convenient contiguous territory, at the same time and in the same manner as members of the assembly are required to be chosen; and no assembly district shall be divided in the formation of a senate district. The senate districts shall be numbered in the regular series, and the senators shall be chosen alternately from the odd and even-numbered districts for the term of 4 years.

This is the third in a sequence of three sections about redistricting the legislature, and it also includes some provisions about elections. This section's first version decreed that senators' terms are two years, and it staggered the terms by stating that during the transition to longer terms the senators who were elected from odd-numbered districts would serve only one year. An 1881 amendment changed senators' terms of office to four years and included a transitional provision that allowed senators who were in office when the amendment was ratified to complete their terms; after that, the odd-numbered and even-numbered district seats would continue to be filled alternately. An amendment that was ratified in 1982 deleted the transitional material that the previous amendment inserted. Although redistricting plans that include drawing the boundaries of senate districts have been litigated, this section has not been necessary to the decision in any of them.

Section 6
Qualifications of legislators.

No person shall be eligible to the legislature who shall not have resided one year within the state, and be a qualified elector in the district which he may be chosen to represent.

This section, which establishes qualifications for legislators, has not been amended or litigated. Article III, Section 1 defines "qualified elector" for purposes of this section.

Section 7
Organization of legislature; quorum; compulsory attendance.

Each house shall be the judge of the elections, returns and qualifications of its own members; and a majority of each shall constitute a quorum to do business, but a smaller number may adjourn from day to day, and may compel the attendance of absent members in such manner and under such penalties as each house may provide.

This section creates some prerogatives for legislators. It has not been amended, and it has been the subject of only one case. *State ex rel. Elfers v. Olson* (1965). In that case, a board of canvassers—a group of officials who count votes and perform other administrative functions for elections—determined that a candidate for the assembly had won an election by thirteen votes. After a recount, he was declared the winner by seven votes. The circuit court declared him the winner by five votes. After he took his seat, the assembly declared his opponent the winner by one vote. The supreme court candidly admitted that courts dislike considering political questions and pointed out that this section gave the assembly the right to judge its members' elections. As a result, the court ruled that the assembly had decided an election, not expelled a member, in which case Article IV, Section 3 would have applied. According to the court, it had no authority to consider, much less to reverse, the assembly's judging of a member's election.

Section 8
Rules; contempts; expulsion.

Each house may determine the rules of its own proceedings, punish for contempt and disorderly behavior, and with the concurrence of two-thirds of all the members elected, expel a member; but no member shall be expelled a second time for the same cause.

This section, which grants certain prerogatives to the legislature, has not been amended. Courts in two cases defined the scope of the legislature's authority to determine its own rules, although in neither case did they mention this section. In the first of them the court held that it would look at the legislature's journals to determine whether a bill was passed, but would not inquire beyond that to determine whether the legislature passed the bill according to legislative rules. *McDonald and another v. The State* (1891). Journal entries are required by several constitutional provisions: Article IV, Section 20; Article V, Section 10; Article VIII, Section 8; and Article XII, Section 1. A later court, considering the validity of a vote on whether to override a veto for which certain legislators had paired (one who would vote yes and one who would vote no, agreeing with each other not to vote), adopted the same limit on its inquiry. *Integration of Bar Case* (1943). In *Wisconsin Solid Waste Recycling Auth. v. Earl* (1975), the court mentioned this section, holding that a statutory requirement that the joint committee on finance introduce a bill to appropriate money to an authority (a quasi-public entity) was merely a rule of committee procedure and thus did not violate this section.

The legislature's authority to punish for contempt was an issue in one case, but again the court did not mention this section. *In re Falvey and Kilbourn v. Massing* (1858). In *Massing*, the court held valid one of the legislature's sergeants-at-arms detaining a person who had refused to answer the questions of a committee investigating bribery, corruption, and the use of lands that the U.S. government had granted to the state. The major contempt case, *State ex rel. Groppi v. Leslie* (1969), evolved from a takeover of the assembly chamber to protest the size of welfare payments. After expelling the protesters, the assembly found the leader of the protest in contempt and ordered him jailed. The court determined that making it impossible for one house of the legislature to conduct its business was an act of contempt and that a person may be summarily held in contempt.

Article VI, Section 4(4); Article VII, Sections 1, 11, and 13; and Article XIII, Section 12 also address the removal of officials.

Section 9
Officers.

(1) Each house shall choose its presiding officers from its own members.

(2) The legislature shall provide by law for the establishment of a department of transportation and a transportation fund.

This section's original form recognized that the senate would need a temporary president because the lieutenant governor served as that body's presiding officer and would not always be available to preside. A 1979 amendment deleted that provision; the senate now elects its president. That amendment also required each house to select its officers from among its members. Only one case is pertinent to this section, *Tenney v. the State* (1871), in which the assembly had directed one of its committees to reorganize the state's tax laws, and the committee had hired a local attorney to do that work. The attorney sued because he thought that the pay was inadequate. Before reaching that issue, the court had to decide whether the assembly had the authority to hire him. It resorted to this section and decided that, although the attorney was hired to be a committee clerk, he was an "officer" because that term meant a person "authorized to perform a public duty." It would seem that the general grant of legislative power to the legislature in Article IV, Section 1 would have been a more logical source of the power to hire the attorney. Also, the case makes little sense considering the later change to this section that requires the legislature to elect its officers from among its members. If it were followed literally, each of the hundreds of positions in the legislative branch of the state government would have to be filled by election from among the legislature's members.

The second clause was added in 2014 to prevent the governor from transferring money from the transportation budget to the education budget.

Section 10
Journals; open doors; adjournments.

Each house shall keep a journal of its proceedings and publish the same, except such parts as require secrecy. The doors of each house shall be kept open except when the public welfare shall require secrecy. Neither house shall, without consent of the other, adjourn for more than three days.

This section, which imposes some duties on the legislature, has not been amended. Legislative journals conclusively prove the legislature's action. *Integration of Bar Case* (1943). Accordingly, their entries determine which bills, in which form, the legislature has enacted and therefore determine the contents of Wisconsin's statutes. Courts will not accept other evidence, such as a memorandum, that purports to show errors in the journal. *Id.* Courts have both read the journals absolutely literally and have read them so as to correct an obvious error. An example of the former was refusing to accept that a reference to bill "258A" (Assembly Bill 258) was a clerical error and that the reference should have been to bill "258S" (Senate Bill 258). *The State v. Wendler* (1896). As a result, the court held that Senate Bill 258 had not been enacted.

However, another court agreed that "was read a third time" following a list of bills really meant "were read a third time," so that all of the bills in the list had been read three times. *Bound v. The Wisconsin Central Railroad Company* (1878). Under the legislature's rules, neither house may pass a bill unless it has been read three times. (In the legislature's early days, bills were read in their entirety three times; now only the portion that specifies the topics to which they relate is read three times.) Although a legislative journal conclusively specifies the action taken on each bill, it does not conclusively determine a bill's contents. *Milwaukee County v. Isenring and others* (1901).

The legislature did not violate this section by conducting a joint conference committee meeting in the senate parlor, a room too small to accommodate every person who might have wished to observe the proceeding. *State ex rel. Ozanne v. Fitzgerald* (2011).

Section 11
Meeting of legislature.

The legislature shall meet at the seat of government at such time as shall be
provided by law, unless convened by the governor in special session, and when
so convened no business shall be transacted except as shall be necessary to accomplish the special purposes for which it was convened.

This section deals with meetings of the legislature, in particular with special
sessions. Its original version authorized the legislature to meet once a year unless the governor convened it. An 1881 amendment made legislative sessions
biennial. That amendment also elaborated on the governor's convening of the
legislature, denominating those occasions special sessions and limiting them to
business necessary to accomplish the purposes for which the governor called
the session. This section adds another germaneness requirement. The rules of
the legislature require that amendments and substitute amendments be germane to the bills that they affect. This constitutional provision requires that
all special session legislation be germane to the session's purpose, as stated in
the governor's call of the special session. That requirement of germaneness also
applies, by legislative rule, to extraordinary sessions that the legislature calls.
This requirement occasionally makes it necessary to amend a call. In 1968, this
section was amended to replace the reference to biennial sessions with the current general reference to the meeting time.

The significant case law on this section has addressed the requirements for
special sessions. The governor may call them when the legislature is meeting in a
regular session, so that the legislature will be meeting in both kinds of session at
the same time. *State ex rel. Groppi v. Leslie* (1969). During the Great Depression,
a governor had called a special session for several purposes, including "[t]o make
provision for the relief of unemployed citizens in co-operation with county and
local authorities; such relief preferably to take the form of employment on necessary public works, including forestry, and/or of providing the necessities of
life when work cannot be provided." During the special session, a law to impose a temporary income tax, the proceeds of which were to be distributed to
municipalities on a per capita basis, was enacted. Because the relief that they
were paying to the unemployed strained the municipalities' budgets, the court
held that this infusion of revenue helped to achieve the stated purpose of providing the necessities of life to the unemployed. *Appeal of Van Dyke* (1935). The
legislation that created the tax thus being germane to the call of the session, its
enactment did not violate this section.

Section 12
Ineligibility of legislators to office.

No member of the legislature shall, during the term for which he was elected,
be appointed or elected to any civil office in the state, which shall have been

created, or the emoluments of which shall have been increased, during the term for which he was elected.

This section, which is designed to prevent legislators from using their office for their own gain, has not been amended. It is to be construed in favor of declaring members of the legislature eligible for offices. *State ex rel. Johnson v. Nye* (1912); *State ex rel. Zimmerman v. Dammann* (1930). Changing the source of funding for a position that does not increase the salary for the position does not violate this section. *Nye*. Because the section is designed to prevent legislators from using their position to increase their income, a pay increase that a constitutional amendment causes does not violate this section. *Dammann*.

Section 13
Ineligibility of federal officers.

No person being a member of congress, or holding any military or civil office under the United States, shall be eligible to a seat in the legislature; and if any person shall, after his election as a member of the legislature, be elected to congress, or be appointed to any office, civil or military, under the government of the United States, his acceptance thereof shall vacate his seat. This restriction shall not prohibit a legislator from accepting short periods of active duty as a member of the reserve or from serving in the armed forces during any emergency declared by the executive.

This section, which deals with holding more than one public office, was amended during 1966 to add the last sentence.

Section 14
Filling vacancies.

The governor shall issue writs of election to fill such vacancies as may occur in either house of the legislature.

This section has not been amended or litigated.

Section 15
Exemption from arrest and civil process.

Members of the legislature shall in all cases, except treason, felony and breach of the peace, be privileged from arrest; nor shall they be subject to any civil process, during the session of the legislature, nor for fifteen days next before the commencement and after the termination of each session.

This section, which is designed to prevent a possible disruption of the legislature's business, has not been amended. It resembles Article I, Section 6 of the U.S. Constitution, although federal courts' interpretations of that provision do not bind state courts. *State v. Beno* (1984). "Felony" has the same meaning it had in the common law at the time that the constitution was ratified; accordingly, it does not include bribery, although that act was, under the statutes that were in effect at the time of the case, a felony. *State ex rel. Isenring v. Polacheck* (1898). "Process" includes a subpoena to appear in court, and the privilege under this section does not extend to legislative aides, because its purpose is to guarantee representation of the people in a legislative district. *Beno.*

At the time the constitution was adopted, civil cases not based upon contract disputes arrest were initiated by arresting the defendant. This section's phrase "treason, felony and breach of the peace" includes all crimes; therefore a legislator's immunity from arrest only shields him or her from service of process in *civil* cases. *State v. Burke* (2002).

Section 16
Privilege in debate.

No member of the legislature shall be liable in any civil action, or criminal prosecution whatever, for words spoken in debate.

This section, the purpose of which is to promote robust legislative debate, has not been amended. It resembles Article I, Section 6 of the U.S. Constitution, but federal courts' interpretations of that provision do not bind state courts. *State v. Beno* (1984). Like the previous section, it does not apply to legislative aides. *Id.* The reference to "liable in any civil action" includes liable to be subpoenaed to appear, and "words spoken in debate" includes more than the words spoken on the legislature's floor; it also includes "matters that are an integral part of the processes by which members of the legislature participate with respect to the consideration of proposed legislation or with respect to other matters which are within the regular course of the legislative process." *Id.*

The speech and debate clause protects legislators engaged in legislative activity, but political activity such as managing a political party caucus staff in campaign activities is not protected. *State v. Chvala* (2004). This section does not create any right to keep legislative communications secret. *Custodian of Records v. State* (2004).

Section 17
Enactment of laws.

(1) The style of all laws of the state shall be "The people of the state of Wisconsin, represented in senate and assembly, do enact as follows:"

(2) No law shall be enacted except by bill. No law shall be in force until published.

(3) The legislature shall provide by law for the speedy publication of all laws.

This section creates a formal requirement and a substantive requirement applicable to lawmaking. An amendment that was ratified in 1977 added the material that is now subsection (3) and that, along with a requirement that the judicial decisions that it was deemed expedient to publish be published speedily, had originally appeared in Article VII, Section 21. That amendment also moved the second sentence of subsection (2) from Article VII, Section 21 and in the process deleted "general," which had modified "law" and had been the subject of some cases. Accordingly, some, but not all, of the cases in which former Article VII, Section 21 was at issue are pertinent to this section. The first subsection recognizes the fact that the ultimate authority rests in the people, not in the government, which accords with the preamble. The statement that is included within the quotation marks appears on every bill that is drafted for the legislature and on every act. Originally entire bills were published, but now only notices of enactment are published. A statute, Wis. Stat. § 991.11, states that every act, except those that specify otherwise, becomes effective on the day after publication.

This section's purpose is "protection of the people, by preventing their rights and interests from being affected by laws which they had no means of knowing." *Clark v. City of Janesville* (1860). It contains two words the definitions of which are crucial in determining its effect. The first of those words is "law." In the context of the requirement to publish in subsections (2) and (3), "law" means an "act of the legislature which has been deposited in the office of the secretary of state, properly authenticated by the presiding officers of the two houses and approved by the governor to become effective as a rule of conduct when published." *State ex rel. Martin v. Zimmerman* (1939). Three years later, the court ignored this sensible definition in a case in which it was held that "law" means statute, *Wentworth v. Racine County* (1898), thereby obscuring the meaning of "law." *Whitman v. Department of Taxation* (1942). In the latter case, the court held that an administrative rule of the Tax Commission was a law, so that it had to be published to be effective. Although admitting that there was no evidence that the rule had been published, the court cited a case that held that public officials are to be presumed to have done their duty and that publication may therefore be assumed. It would have been much simpler to hold that administrative rules are not laws; a current statute states that they have the effect of laws, which indicates that they are not themselves laws, Wis. Stat. § 227.01(13). It would also have been more logical to do that, because if administrative rules are laws, the statement in the section that no law may be enacted except by bill destroys the distinction between administrative rules and statutes. "Law" does not mean a county board's resolution. *Wentworth*.

The other crucial term is "publication." In general, as the phrase "provide by law" implies, to be effective publication must be according to statutory procedures. *Clark v. City of Janesville* (1860); *State ex rel. Cothren v. Lean* (1859); *Mills v. Town of Jefferson* (1865). For example, publication only in the newspapers of the city that the law affects is not acceptable if it does not comply with statutory procedures. *Clark*. Publication in a volume of private laws (laws that have a very limited scope) well after enactment, notwithstanding the requirement of "speedy publication," is acceptable, although a law published then does not take effect until publication of the volume that includes it. *Id.* That manner of publication is acceptable even if the law is general and should have been published as are general laws. *In re Boyle* (1859).

However, publication of a law after a statutory time limit has passed invalidates that law. *State ex rel. Cothren v. Lean* (1859). Publication by means that the law itself specifies, rather than by statutory means that apply generally, does not invalidate the law. *Mills v. Town of Jefferson* (1865). If an act is effective only upon ratification by the electors at a referendum, publication after enactment of the bill and before the referendum suffices; the law need not also be published after ratification. *State ex rel. Van Alstine v. Frear* (1910). If a governor vetoes part of a bill, only the parts of the bill that are either not vetoed or the veto of which is overridden by the legislature need be published. *State ex rel. Wisconsin Tel. Co. v. Henry* (1935). If a law is published a second time to correct an error that does not "change the substance or legal effect of the statute," the law takes effect upon the first publication. *Smith v. Hoyt* (1861). The secretary of state, who, prior to 2013, was responsible for publishing laws, had no authority under this section to refuse to publish a law because he or she believes it to be invalid. *State ex rel. Martin v. Zimmerman* (1939). Although courts decided some of these cases when complete texts of laws were published, the cases, except for the case on vetoes, remain relevant because their principles also apply to publication only of the matters to which the law relates, which is the present practice.

A labor contract that was referred to in a bill ratifying the contract did not itself become law because the legislature did not enact the contract as a bill and did not publish it. *Milwaukee Journal Sentinel v. D.O.A.* (2009). The contract prohibited disclosure of employee names and purported to amend the Public Records Law accordingly.

Courts have no authority to enjoin the publication of an act of the legislature. *State ex rel. Ozanne v. Fitzgerald* (2011).

Section 18
Title of private bills.

No private or local bill which may be passed by the legislature shall embrace more than one subject, and that shall be expressed in the title.

This section, which restricts the legislature's ability to pass laws that have limited application, has not been amended. It relates to Article IV, Section 31, which prohibits special and private laws on specified subjects, and to Article IV, Section 32, which authorizes general laws on the subjects about which special and private laws may not be enacted. In several cases plaintiffs have challenged legislation based upon both this section and Article IV, Section 31. This section's purposes are to encourage the legislature to devote its time to matters that affect the entire state, to preclude favoritism and discrimination, and to alert the members of the legislature to the subject matter of the legislation that they consider. *Milwaukee Brewers v. D. H. S. S.* (1986). Wisconsin enacts biennial budgets, and often during the years between those acts it enacts budget adjustment legislation. Both kinds of acts, rather than containing only appropriations and material inextricably related to them, also contain hundreds of pages of legislation on general policy matters. Those bills thus cover many subjects, and they have general titles. For these reasons, this section's prohibition of private and local laws that embrace more than one subject and its requirement that a bill's title must express the subject of any private or local provision contained in the bill are very important.

Regarding most of the constitutional provisions that form the grounds of challenges to legislation, courts presume that the statute is constitutional, so a challenger must overcome that presumption to prevail. In cases concerning this section, however, because the challenger is alleging that the legislature has "violated a law of constitutional stature which mandates the form in which bills must pass," courts will not automatically presume that a law is constitutional. *Brookfield v. Milwaukee Sewerage* (1988). However, they will make that presumption if they find evidence that the legislature adequately considered the issue in question. *Davis v. Grover* (1992).

The most basic question that appears in cases concerning this section is whether a law (actually, a bill or part of a bill) is private or local. Local laws apply only to particular places, and private laws apply only to particular persons or things. *Soo Line R. Co. v. Transportation Dept.* (1981). The courts use two processes to determine whether, under this section, a law is, on the one hand, private or local or, on the other hand, general. *Brookfield v. Milwaukee Sewerage* (1988). The nature of the law determines which of the processes the court will use. If a law is explicitly private or local, it avoids this section's requirements (has a single subject and expresses that subject in its title) only if "relates to a state responsibility of statewide dimension and its enactment will have a direct and immediate effect on a specific statewide concern or interest." If a law is not explicitly private or local but is framed so as to have only a private or local effect, it fulfills this section's requirements if it fulfills the requirements for general laws that apply to Article IV, Section 31: the classification is based on substantial distinctions that make each class really different from the others, the classification is germane to the law's purpose, the classification is open (the composition of the classes later might change), if the law applies to a class, it applies to all of the members of the class, and the characteristics of each class are so different from those of the other classes that, considering the public good, it is proper to apply substantially different legislation to those classes.

The courts have only loosely enforced the one-subject rule: "subjects . . . subordinate to, and naturally or necessarily connected with the primary or leading subject of the bill, may be included in the bill without rendering the act double or multifarious." *Mills v. Charleton, County Treasurer, and others* (1872). A bill's unity is to be sought in its intended end, not in its details. *Evans v. Sharp* (1872). To be on one subject, a bill need only have the same general subject throughout. For example, a bill, the dominant purpose of which was to create a wildlife refuge, had one subject even though it also accomplished secondary, related purposes. *State ex rel. Hammann v. Levitan* (1929). A bill that authorized improving certain streets and a tax to pay for the improvements had a single subject. *Warner v. Knox, imp.* (1880). A bill that authorized improving a highway, building bridges and viaducts over it, and funding those works had a single subject. *Harrison v. The Board of Supervisors of Milwaukee County, imp.* (1881). A bill that authorized building a railroad and provided a means to pay for it had a single subject. *Phillips and others v. The Town of Albany and others* (1871).

The title of a bill includes the relating clause (a statement of the bill's purpose or effect) and, in most cases, a list of the statutory sections that the bill creates or affects. Recognizing that most relating clauses are brief and general, courts have liberally construed them and usually have found them fully relate to a bill's contents. This section requires a bill's title to state the bill's contents so that legislators and the public are advised of the bill's real nature and subject matter and so that fraud and surprises are avoided. *Soo Line R. Corp.* The title need not completely describe the bill's content: "the court is not to set aside or declare an act void because the subject was not as fully or as unequivocally expressed as it might otherwise have been." *Mills v. Charleton, County Treasurer, and others* (1872). For example, although a bill applies to only one geographical area, the title need not identify that area but may use such expressions as "certain." *Phillips and others v. The Town of Albany and others* (1871). However, the court has held that referring only in general terms to the collection and distribution of taxes and failing to mention that the bill affected only Milwaukee County violated this section. *Whitefish Bay v. Milwaukee County* (1937). A title need not necessarily identify purposes that closely relate to the purpose that it does specify. For example, although a title mentioned only reassessments, it implied that the bill also dealt with future assessments and therefore did not violate this section. *Mills.*

In contrast, a title that fails to mention a bill's effect that is not related closely enough to the purpose that the title identifies violates this section. An example of a violation is a title announcing that the bill was about the appointment of a public administrator for the city and county of Milwaukee but failed to announce that the bill also transferred money from the school fund to the Milwaukee Public Schools. *Estate of Bulewicz* (1933). A bill title that mentioned only the creation of a court, although the bill both created one court and abolished another, violated this section. *State ex rel. Richter v. Chadbourne* (1916). The title of a budget adjustment bill, which referred in very general terms to revising the statutes, violated this section because the bill also included a prohibition against building a railroad overpass at a certain location, which was a local law. *Soo Line R. Co.*

When a statute creates a class of cities that in effect applies only to one city, it is a local and private bill unless the classification is germane to the purpose of the law. *Jackson v. Benson* (1998).

Section 19
Origin of bills.

Any bill may originate in either house of the legislature, and a bill passed by one house may be amended by the other.

This section has not been amended. The only case on this section concerns the second phrase, dealing with the requirement that the house in which a bill originates must conclude work on it before the other house begins its work. Cases interpreting Article IV, Section 10 indicate that legislative journals conclusively identify the legislature's actions. However, failure to record in those journals the senate's vote on a bill does not mean that the senate failed to pass the bill and that therefore the assembly had not amended the bill before the house in which it originated passed it; therefore, the legislature had not violated this section and the law in question was valid. *State ex rel. Crucible S. C. Co. v. Wis. Tax Comm.* (1925).

Section 20
Yeas and nays.

The yeas and nays of the members of either house on any question shall, at the request of one-sixth of those present, be entered on the journal.

This section has not been amended or litigated. The current practice is to take a roll call vote if any member requests it.

Section 22
Powers of county boards.

The legislature may confer upon the boards of supervisors of the several counties of the state such powers of a local, legislative and administrative character as they shall from time to time prescribe.

This section has not been amended. Just as Article XI, Section 3 states the fundamental law for cities and villages, this section states the fundamental law for counties (the next section, before its amendment in 1969, stated part of that fundamental law).

Because this section authorizes grants to counties of only local, legislative, and administrative powers, and not all powers, courts have had to decide whether certain grants fit within those parameters. "Local" is opposed to statewide. Just as municipalities may not be granted authority as to matters of statewide concern under Article XI, Section 3, counties may not be granted authority under this section as to matters of statewide concern, nor may they exercise authority granted under this section to create a statewide effect. Allowing a county board to authorize construction of a dam grants statewide power, because the dam would affect navigation (which, under Article IX, Section 1, is a statewide matter), and therefore violates this section. *Muench v. Public Service Comm.* (1952). Making a property tax exemption contingent on approval by the board of the county where the property is located also grants statewide power and therefore violates this section. *La Crosse Foundation, Inc. v. Town of Washington* (1994). However, allowing counties to establish industrial development corporations does not interfere with statewide concerns. *State ex rel. Bowman v. Barczak* (1967). The following subjects may be delegated to counties under this section: zoning, *Quinn v. Town of Dodgeville* (1985); maintaining and erecting dams, which is a "public" function rather than an operation akin to the operation of a private business, *Vaudreuil Lumber Co. v. Eau Claire County* (1942); and establishing the boundaries of towns within the county, *The State ex rel. Hiles v. The Board of Supervisors of Wood County* (1884), *Knight v. The Town of Ashland* (1884). Statutes that grant counties the authority to create civil actions are constitutional, but statutes that grant them the power to create criminal actions are unconstitutional. *State ex rel. Keefe v. Schmiege* (1947). It follows from the authority to grant legislative powers to counties under this section that a county board's membership must conform to the principle of equal representation. *State ex rel. Sonneborn v. Sylvester* (1965).

If a statute constitutionally grants it general authority, a county may enact an ordinance that fills in the details. *Lund v. Chippewa County and others* (1896); *The Supervisors of La Pointe v. O'Malley and another* (1879). That is, if a statute constitutionally grants legislative authority under this section, the county board becomes, in respect to that grant, a legislative body. *Supervisors of La Pointe.* However, if a grant of authority contains a specific detail, the county must conform to that detail. In other words, a county has *only* the authority granted to it. For example, if a statute authorizes a county to change the boundaries of towns only by referendum, a change of boundaries by the county board is unconstitutional. *State ex rel. Graef v. Forest County* (1889). Comparing two cases on the same grant of authority, the right to regulate dance halls, illustrates this requirement of conforming to a grant of authority's details. It is constitutional to regulate dance halls, under a statutory grant of authority, by requiring them to close on Sundays, Monday mornings, Christmas Eve, and Christmas. *Stetzer v. Chippewa County* (1937). In contrast, it is unconstitutional to allow them to be open for only two days each month, because that restriction goes beyond regulation into virtual prohibition. *State ex rel. Pumplin v. Hohle* (1931).

A grant of authority under this section does not divest the legislature of that authority or preclude the legislature from granting the same authority to another entity. For example, the legislature may grant to a private entity a franchise to operate a ferry even if it has granted that authority to counties. *Chapin and another v. Crusen and another* (1872), and if the legislature has granted to counties the authority to establish the boundaries of towns within the counties, the legislature, too, may establish town boundaries. *The Chicago & Northwestern R'y Co. v. Langlade County and others* (1883). On its face, Article IV, Section 31(9) prevents the legislature from incorporating cities, villages, and towns by special law, but courts have been loath to enforce this prohibition. The legislature may grant authority that affects counties to an entity other than the county board, such as an arbitrator or a mediator. *Milwaukee County v. District Council, 48* (1982). It may also grant towns veto power over zoning, even though it has also granted to counties the power to zone. *Quinn v. Town of Dodgeville* (1985). However, the legislature may not grant authority to a county's electors rather than to a county board. *Meade v. Dane County* (1914); *Marshall v. Dane County Board of Supervisors* (1940).

Section 23
Town and county government.

The legislature shall establish but one system of town government, which shall be as nearly uniform as practicable; but the legislature may provide for the election at large once in every 4 years of a chief executive officer in any county with such powers of an administrative character as they may from time to time prescribe.

This section states the most fundamental principle of legislation related to towns and a detail related to county government. It originally required one system of town and county government, which was to be as nearly uniform as practicable. In 1962, it was amended to allow counties that have a population of 500,000 or more (only Milwaukee County) to elect a chief executive officer. A 1969 amendment specified that the requirement of uniformity does not apply to the administrative means of exercising the powers granted under Article IV, Section 22, and it allowed all counties to elect a chief administrative officer. The current version, which the voters ratified in 1972, deleted the two requirements applicable to counties that were stated in the section's original version. Although the 1972 amendment deleted the requirement that county government be uniform, the cases in which that requirement was litigated are relevant to later cases on towns. *State ex rel. Wolf v. Town of Lisbon* (1977). However, the cases that are directly relevant to towns suffice to elucidate this section's current form, so this commentary is limited to cases on towns.

According to this section "the principal organizational features of town government must be the same," but, as the section specifies, only "practical" uniformity is required, so general enactments that make reasonable distinctions among towns are constitutional. *Wolf.* As to reasonable distinctions, this section "provides for the exercise of different powers by the boards of different towns, when there is anything in a town which calls for the exercise of such different or additional powers." *Land, Log & Lumber Co. and others v. Brown and others* (1889). That is, a law that applies throughout the state and makes reasonable distinctions based on differences among towns does not violate this section. *Thompson v. Kenosha County* (1974).

Examining the distinctions that have been validated gives one an idea of the nature of a reasonable distinction and a sense of the degree of generality required to make a statute constitutional. A statute that allowed a county board to appoint a property tax assessor for a newly created town that had no assessor applied statewide and was thus general. *Strange v. Oconto Land Co.* (1908). A statute specifying that, if a county failed to maintain a highway that formed one of its borders, a town adjoining that county may do so and may charge the costs to the towns that were required to maintain the highway was constitutional because it applied to all towns in that situation. *Kewaunee County v. Door County* (1933). A statute that authorized a tax throughout a town for purposes that applied only to an unincorporated village in the town was constitutional, even though it applied only to towns that had at least one unincorporated village with a population of at least 1,000, because of its general nature and the reasonableness of the distinction drawn between towns. *Land, Log & Lumber Co.* Authorizing only towns that border on, or through which runs, a navigable or meandered stream to build bridges does not violate this section because that classification is reasonable. *State ex rel. Owen v. Stevenson* (1917). Providing that towns included in a county property tax assessment system be the only towns that do not have their own assessors is constitutional because the law applies throughout the state and makes reasonable distinctions. *Thompson v. Kenosha County* (1974). Allowing only towns that have a population of more than 2,500 to have five, instead of three, supervisors does not violate this section because the law is general and the distinction reasonable. *Wolf.*

Several other reasons also make distinctions constitutional under this section. The section does not apply to the organization of towns, only to their duties and responsibilities after they are formed. *Scharping v. Johnson* (1966). This exception exists because the section applies only to "the plan or scheme by which the town... [is] to be governed." *The Chicago & Northwestern R'y Co. v. Langlade County and others* (1883). Another exception, for tax laws, *State ex rel. Joint School Dist. v. Becker* (1928), is an anomaly because in no other case has the court considered the validity of tax laws under this section, rather than simply validating them due to their subject matter. Similarly, validating a statute that makes unincorporated villages taxing districts simply because the issue is a "matter of legislative consideration," *Paul v. Greenfield* (1930), which seems to imply that any statutory classification is valid, is an anomaly. In no other case has the court refused to examine the statute that was at issue under this section and the relevant facts.

Local laws, however, violate this section. Examples include a statute that required only one town to pay a bounty for service in the Civil War, *State ex rel. McCurdy v. Tappan, Town Clerk* (1872); a statute that imposed a higher tax on one town in a county than on the others, *State ex rel. The Town of La Valle v. Supervisors of Sauk County* (1885); and a statute that directed the towns in one county to send tax revenue to that county, *McRae v. Hogan* (1876).

Although most of the cases on this section deal with the uniformity requirement, some deal, or also deal, with the requirement that there be only one system of town government. Denying a town the authority to have its own assessor, because the town is part of a county property tax assessment system, is not a distinction great enough to create a new system of town government. *Thompson v. Kenosha County* (1974). Distributing unemployment relief funds to towns on a per capita basis does not alter the system of town government. *Appeal of Van Dyke* (1935). Making town and county officials in only one county responsible for draining swamps and marshes is constitutional because that kind of responsibility is not "a part of the system of government" and because that mandate was made under special authority for a special purpose. *Bryant and others v. Robbins and another* (1887). This last case is problematical, because the duties seem to be governmental. Specifically, they relate to the police power that governmental units inherently have. Also, town government appears to be town government; it is not divided into two categories, a system and something else. The most plausible interpretation of the section's reference to "one system of town government" is that it reiterates the practicable uniformity requirement.

Section 23A
Chief executive officer to approve or veto resolutions or ordinances; proceedings on veto.

Every resolution or ordinance passed by the county board in any county shall, before it becomes effective, be presented to the chief executive officer. If he approves, he shall sign it; if not, he shall return it with his objections, which objections shall be entered at large upon the journal and the board shall proceed to reconsider the matter. Appropriations may be approved in whole or in part by the chief executive officer and the part approved shall become law, and the part objected to shall be returned in the same manner as provided for in other resolutions or ordinances. If, after such reconsideration, two-thirds of the members elect of the county board agree to pass the resolution or ordinance or the part of the resolution or ordinance objected to, it shall become effective on the date prescribed but not earlier than the date of passage following reconsideration. In all such cases, the votes of the members of the county board shall be determined by ayes and noes and the names of the members voting for or against the resolution or ordinance or the part thereof objected to shall be entered on the journal. If any resolution or ordinance is not returned by the chief executive officer to the county board at its first meeting occurring not less than 6 days, Sundays excepted, after it has been presented to him, it shall become effective unless the county board has recessed or adjourned for a period of more than 60 days, in which case it shall not be effective without his approval.

This section specifies the veto power of counties' chief executive officers. It has been amended; originally it gave the veto power only to the chief executive officer of a county that had a population of at least 500,000. At that time, and now, only Milwaukee County has a population that large. A 1969 amendment extended the veto power to the chief executives of all counties. This section's resemblance to Article V, Section 10, which grants the veto power to the governor, is clear. A *de facto* veto is effective under this section. *State ex rel. La Follette v. Board of Supvrs.* (1982). In *La Follette*, the court considered that a county executive's failure either to approve or veto a resolution during the two days between a county board's passage of the resolution, which required the county to issue bonds to acquire revenue to pay its share of the costs of a sewerage district, and the deadline for bidding on the bonds was in effect a veto of the resolution. That is, the county executive's signature was required to enact the resolution, and that enactment was necessary to accept bids on the bonds. The grant of power to a county executive to veto a county board resolution does not make unconstitutional a statute that grants to town boards the authority to veto county zoning ordinances; this section does not exclusively grant to county executives the power to veto ordinances and resolutions. *Quinn v. Town of Dodgeville* (1985).

Section 24
Gambling.

(1) Except as provided in this section, the legislature may not authorize gambling in any form.

(2) Except as otherwise provided by law, the following activities do not constitute consideration as an element of gambling:

(a) To listen to or watch a television or radio program.

(b) To fill out a coupon or entry blank, whether or not proof of purchase is required.

(c) To visit a mercantile establishment or other place without being required to make a purchase or pay an admittance fee.

(3) The legislature may authorize the following bingo games licensed by the state, but all profits shall accrue to the licensed organization and no salaries, fees or profits may be paid to any other organization or person: bingo games operated by religious, charitable, service, fraternal or veterans' organizations or those to which contributions are deductible for federal or state income tax purposes. All moneys received by the state that are attributable to bingo games shall be used for property tax relief for residents of this state as provided by law. The distribution of moneys that are attributable to bingo games may not vary based on the income or age of the person provided the property tax relief. The distribution of moneys that are attributable to bingo games shall not be subject to the uniformity requirement of section 1 of article VIII. In this subsection, the distribution of all moneys attributable to bingo games shall include any earnings on the moneys received by the state that are attributable to bingo games, but

shall not include any moneys used for the regulation of, and enforcement of law relating to, bingo games.

(4) The legislature may authorize the following raffle games licensed by the state, but all profits shall accrue to the licensed local organization and no salaries, fees or profits may be paid to any other organization or person: raffle games operated by local religious, charitable, service, fraternal or veterans' organizations or those to which contributions are deductible for federal or state income tax purposes. The legislature shall limit the number of raffles conducted by any such organization.

(5) This section shall not prohibit pari-mutuel on-track betting as provided by law. The state may not own or operate any facility or enterprise for pari-mutuel betting, or lease any state-owned land to any other owner or operator for such purposes. All moneys received by the state that are attributable to pari-mutuel on-track betting shall be used for property tax relief for residents of this state as provided by law. The distribution of moneys that are attributable to pari-mutuel on-track betting may not vary based on the income or age of the person provided the property tax relief. The distribution of moneys that are attributable to pari-mutuel on-track betting shall not be subject to the uniformity requirement of section 1 of article VIII. In this sub- section, the distribution of all moneys attributable to pari-mutuel on-track betting shall include any earnings on the moneys received by the state that are attributable to pari-mutuel on-track betting, but shall not include any moneys used for the regulation of, and enforcement of law relating to, pari-mutuel on-track betting.

(6) (a) The legislature may authorize the creation of a lottery to be operated by the state as provided by law. The expenditure of public funds or of revenues derived from lottery operations to engage in promotional advertising of the Wisconsin state lottery is prohibited. Any advertising of the state lottery shall indicate the odds of a specific lottery ticket to be selected as the winning ticket for each prize amount offered. The net proceeds of the state lottery shall be deposited in the treasury of the state, to be used for property tax relief for residents of this state as provided by law. The distribution of the net proceeds of the state lottery may not vary based on the income or age of the person provided the property tax relief. The distribution of the net proceeds of the state lottery shall not be subject to the uniformity requirement of section 1 of article VIII. In this paragraph, the distribution of the net proceeds of the state lottery shall include any earnings on the net proceeds of the state lottery.

(b) The lottery authorized under par. (a) shall be an enterprise that entitles the player, by purchasing a ticket, to participate in a game of chance if: 1) the winning tickets are randomly predetermined and the player reveals preprinted numbers or symbols from which it can be immediately determined whether the ticket is a winning ticket entitling the player to win a prize as pre- scribed in the features and procedures for the game, including an opportunity to win a prize in a secondary or subsequent chance drawing or game; or 2) the ticket is evidence of the numbers or symbols selected by the player or, at the player's option, selected by a computer, and the player becomes entitled to a prize as prescribed in the features and procedures for the game, including an opportunity to win a prize in a secondary or subsequent chance drawing or game if some or all of the player's symbols or numbers are selected in a chance drawing or game, if the player's ticket is randomly selected by the computer at the time of purchase or if the ticket is selected in a chance drawing.

(c) Notwithstanding the authorization of a state lottery under par. (a), the following games, or games simulating any of the following games, may not be conducted by the state as a lottery: 1) any game in which winners are selected based on the results of a race or sporting event; 2) any banking card game, including blackjack, baccarat or chemin de fer; 3) poker; 4) roulette; 5) craps or any other game that involves rolling dice; 6) keno; 7) bingo 21, bingo jack, bingolet or bingo craps; 8) any game of chance that is placed on a slot machine or any mechanical, electromechanical or electronic device that is generally available to be played at a gambling casino; 9) any game or device that is commonly known as a video game of chance or a video gaming machine or that is commonly considered to be a video gambling machine, unless such machine is a video device operated by the state in a game authorized under par. (a) to permit the sale of tickets through retail outlets under contract with the state and the device does not determine or indicate whether the player has won a prize, other than by verifying that the player's ticket or some or all of the player's symbols or numbers on the player's ticket have been selected in a chance drawing, or by verifying that the player's ticket has been randomly selected by a central system computer at the time of purchase; 10) any game that is similar to a game listed in this paragraph; or 11) any other game that is commonly considered to be a form of gambling and is not, or is not substantially similar to, a game conducted by the state under par. (a). No game conducted by the state under par. (a) may permit a player of the game to purchase a ticket, or to otherwise participate in the game, from a residence by using a computer, telephone or other form of electronic, telecommunication, video or technological aid.

This section, which deals primarily with gambling, originally consisted of eleven words: "[t]he legislature shall never authorize any lottery, or grant any divorce." It is now the constitution's longest section. It retained its original form until 1965, when the statement about television, radio, filling out coupons, and visiting mercantile establishments and other places was added. That change responded to a case in which the court declared unconstitutional a statute specifying that listening to a radio program and watching and listening to a television program were not consideration for this section, *State v. Laven* (1955), and to a case in which movie theater promotions were held to be unconstitutional, *State ex rel. Cowie v. La Crosse Theaters Co.* (1939). The change was necessary because the attorney general and the courts defined "lottery" as a scheme that included consideration, chance, and a prize rather than as a synonym of "raffle." See, e.g., *State ex rel. Cowie v. La Crosse Theaters Co.* (1939).

In 1974, another amendment authorized bingo games that nonprofit organizations sponsored. An amendment ratified in 1977 authorized nonprofit organizations to conduct raffles. The most significant expansion of gambling occurred in 1987, when the subsections on pari-mutuel betting and the state lottery were added. In 1993, the voters ratified an amendment that changed "lottery" to "gambling" in subsection (1) and described the state lottery in subsection

(6)(b). The intended effect was to indicate that the state "lottery" was merely a raffle. This provision and the Indian Gaming Regulatory Act's requirement that states negotiate gaming compacts that allow American Indian tribes to conduct all kinds of gambling that the state allows do not, in conjunction, open the door to all forms of Indian gaming. That amendment also listed the games of chance that this section did not authorize, and it moved the prohibition on granting divorces to Article IV, Section 31. Article III, Section 6, another section relating to gambling, denies voting rights to anyone who bets on an election.

Although recent amendments to this section moot much of the case law, the current version has not been litigated, and some of the existing cases may shed light on the ways in which courts will interpret it. The court in *Kayden Industries, Inc. v. Murphy* (1967) noted that "[t]he legislature, the courts, and the attorney general of Wisconsin have traditionally taken a restrictive view of games, schemes, and plans involving a prize, chance, and consideration, condemning them as lotteries prohibited by the constitution." This restrictiveness follows from defining "lottery" not as a raffle but as a scheme that involves a prize, chance, and consideration. The presence or absence of a prize and of an element of chance are usually obvious. Thus, litigation about whether an activity is a lottery has turned on whether there was consideration. "Consideration" is "a disadvantage to the one party or an advantage to the other." *State ex rel. Regez v. Blumer* (1940). A classic example is A paying money to B. The instances of consideration in the case law are leaving a coupon at a store, registering at a theater, watching and listening to a television program or listening to a radio program, buying a ticket to a theater, and buying bingo cards. Later amendments to the constitution, which were prompted by the cases in which courts held that those things were consideration, have specified that, unless the legislature provides otherwise, these things are not consideration for the purpose of determining whether an activity is a lottery. Nevertheless, these cases illustrate the restrictive view and courts' propensity to consider minimal transfers of "advantages" to be consideration.

A nonprofit organization's administration of a lottery does not transform it into a non-lottery. *State ex rel. Trampe v. Multerer* (1940). The participation of some contestants who have not furnished consideration does not transform a lottery into a non-lottery. *Stern v. Miner* (1941). Courts that have determined that a lottery is being conducted have usually declared unconstitutional the statute authorizing it, but one court voided a contract between a lottery's administrator and the owner of the premises where it was conducted, *id.*, and another court held that a lower court may issue an injunction against using a premises for gambling, because the gambling made the premises a public nuisance. *State ex rel. Trampe v. Multerer* (1940).

The 1993 amendment clearly distinguished between the state "lottery" and other "gambling" and explicitly prohibited a number of games. The legislature based the amendment on the premise that in this section "lottery" had had a broad meaning.

The 1999 amendment to subsections (3), (5), and (6) reorganized the distribution of lottery proceeds.

The governor has no authority to unilaterally approve American Indian gaming contracts for games that are outlawed by this section, nor can he or she approve contracts with no expiration date or waive the state's sovereign immunity. *Panzer v. Doyle* (2004). Only the legislature can waive the state's sovereign immunity, although it could delegate such authority to the governor. Nor can the governor enter into a perpetual contract with American Indian tribes. *Id.* The 1993 amendment to this subsection that outlawed certain games did not invalidate existing contracts between the state and American Indian tribes that had allowed those games. *Dairyland Greyhound Park, Inc. v. Doyle* (2006). Under federal law, if the state decriminalizes poker machines for tavern owners, it must also decriminalize them for the tribes. *Wisconsin v. Ho-Chunk Nation* (2015).

Section 25
Stationery and printing.

The legislature shall provide by law that all stationery required for the use of the state, and all printing authorized and required by them to be done for their use, or for the state, shall be let by contract to the lowest bidder, but the legislature may establish a maximum price; no member of the legislature or other state officer shall be interested, either directly or indirectly, in any such contract.

This section, which is about the printing of state documents, has not been amended, but, surprisingly, it has been litigated. Printing might seem to be the kind of detail that would be left to statutory law rather than included in the constitution. However, at the time the constitution was drafted, many printers allied with political parties because they usually also published a newspaper. In fact, political parties subsidized some newspapers. Therefore, awarding printing contracts often was political patronage. Requiring that the lowest bidder receive the contract prevented dispensing patronage, and placing that requirement in the constitution made it impossible for a legislature and governor to circumvent it by enacting a statute.

In *Sholes v. The State* (1850), although the plaintiff was much more famous for inventing the typewriter than for bringing this suit, he discovered that the governor had paid him less than the amount authorized for a printing job, so he sued. In response, the state asserted that not only did he have no right to more compensation but also that the contract was invalid because the job had not been let on bid, as the constitution required. The court held that the constitutional provision served to prevent corruption and, because there was none in this instance, the absence of a bid did not preclude payment. Thus, within two years after the constitution was ratified, a court attenuated this provision.

Read literally, this section requires all state printing to be done under contract; it does not allow the state to do its own printing. Probably none of the framers of the constitution foresaw that result. Almost 100 years later, a printing company sought an injunction to prevent the state from printing its own material; in *Democrat Printing Co. v. Zimmerman* (1944), the court recognized that the constitution did not allow such a practice. In a confused passage, it remarked that a statute could permit that practice and, there being no such statute, it could not rule on the matter. The courts have also held that this section does not guarantee that the lowest bidder will get a printing contract; the bid must also be reasonable. *State ex rel. Democrat Printing Co. v. Schmiege* (1963).

Section 26
Extra compensation; salary change.

(1) The legislature may not grant any extra compensation to a public officer, agent, servant or contractor after the services have been rendered or the contract has been entered into.

(2) Except as provided in this subsection, the compensation of a public officer may not be increased or diminished during the term of office:

(a) When any increase or decrease in the compensation of justices of the supreme court or judges of any court of record becomes effective as to any such justice or judge, it shall be effective from such date as to every such justice or judge.

(b) Any increase in the compensation of members of the legislature shall take effect, for all senators and representatives to the assembly, after the next general election beginning with the new assembly term.

(3) Subsection (1) shall not apply to increased benefits for persons who have been or shall be granted benefits of any kind under a retirement system when such increased benefits are provided by a legislative act passed on a call of ayes and noes by a three-fourths vote of all the members elected to both houses of the legislature and such act provides for sufficient state funds to cover the costs of the increased benefits.

This section prevents paying certain kinds of retroactive compensation. Its original version contained the prohibition that now appears in subsection (1) and the prohibition that now appears in the introduction to subsection (2). That is, it included no exceptions. In 1956, it was amended to allow increased retirement benefits for teachers if the act granting them passed with at least a three-fourths vote. That amendment was needed to increase the benefits of retired teachers because of *State ex rel. Thomson v. Giessel* (1952). A 1967 amendment added an exception for the compensation of supreme court justices and circuit court judges. That amendment was made necessary by *State ex rel. Sullivan v. Boos* (1964), which held that the salary of a circuit court judge may not be increased during his or her term of office. A 1974 amendment broadened the retirement exception to include all persons, not just teachers, and required that each act granting increased benefits must fund their costs. In 1977, this section was amended to replace a reference to circuit court judges with a reference to judges of courts of record, which reflected an extensive revision of Article VII that, among other things, created courts of appeals. In 1992, this section was amended to add the current subsection (2)(b). That change reflected the fact that state senators' terms are four years and the terms of representatives to the assembly are two years. Accordingly, before that amendment was ratified increases in the compensation of legislators applied to senators who began their term at the beginning of the legislative session during which the increase became effective, but not to the senators whose term began during the previous session.

The definitions of the most important terms in this section are crucial to understanding it. "Compensation" means "a fixed salary payable out of the public treasury of the state." *Board of Supervisors v. Hackett* (1867); *The State ex rel. Martin v. Kalb, County Treasurer, and another* (1880). "Extra" means more than previously agreed upon. *Department of Administration v. WERC* (1979). "Public officer" means an individual who receives a fixed salary payable from the state treasury. *State ex rel. Sullivan v. Boos* (1964).

Several corollaries follow from those definitions. Because of the definition of "public officer," this section does not apply to local officials who are paid entirely with local funds. That means that this section does not apply to county officers. *Columbia County v. Wisconsin Retirement Fund* (1962); *State ex rel. Singer v. Boos* (1969). It does, however, apply to state legislators. *State ex rel. Zimmerman v. Dammann* (1930). It follows from the definitions of "contractor" and "extra" that paying a printer who has completed his or her work for the state an amount that is commensurate with the value of the work but is more than the amount specified in the contract violates this section. *Carpenter v. The State* (1876). This result also accords with the section's purpose as it relates to contractors: "preventing all legislative tampering with the fixed prices of public contracts," *Id.* It follows from the definition of "extra" that retroactive pay given to union members who have been working without a contract does not violate this section. *WERC.* That is, the back pay is not extra; it is the pay that they earned under their new contract for the period when they worked without a contract.

Much of the litigation about this section involves two types of individuals: retirees and judges. The 1956 and 1974 amendments, by allowing increases in retirement benefits, the former for teachers and the latter for all employees, reduced the relevancy of the cases on retirees, but these cases illustrate the court's reasoning about, and interpretation of, this section. Additions to the pension fund for teachers who are still at work and who have more than twenty-five years of service is not extra compensation but an inducement to teachers to remain in service; that is, it is future compensation. *State ex rel. Dudgeon v. Levitan* (1923). However, unconditionally increasing pensions for retired teachers is extra compensation. *Giessel.* That decision prompted the 1956 amendment. Payments to retired teachers who agree to make themselves available for substitute teaching is not compensation for past services but an inducement to be available for future services. *Id.* Because the benefits were not retirement benefits per se, even though they were paid to retired teachers, the 1956 amendment did not apply to them. State payments to a retirement fund for county employees is not compensation because they would not necessarily receive those payments. *Columbia County v. Wisconsin Retirement Fund* (1962). The reasoning in that case is a bit questionable; the 1974 amendment puts that practice on much firmer ground. Thus, the courts have stretched a bit to allow increased retirement benefits. Without the two amendments, a literal reading of this section would prohibit increasing those benefits, which would be a manifestly unfair result. One may conclude from the cases, with somewhat less confidence, that, to avoid an obviously unfair result, a court will liberally interpret this section, recognizing that its purpose is to prevent windfalls, not, for example, to freeze retirement benefits.

At first county judges did not receive state funds, so this section did not apply to them. *The State ex rel. Martin v. Kalb, County Treasurer, and another* (1880). However, circuit court judges, who were paid at least in part with state funds, were subject to this section. *Boos.* To that point in time the cases on judges make sense; each turns on the question of whether the judge is paid at least in part with state money. However, the court in a case concerning judges' benefits repudiated that test and held that, even though county judges were paid partly by the state and partly by the county, they were exempt from this section. *State ex rel. Sachtjen v. Festge* (1964). In the last of these cases, the court stretched to obtain a result, and the 1967 amendment placed this result (creating an exemption for judges) on a more solid footing.

Several miscellaneous principles also may be found in the cases. A statute that dissolved the terms of certain state officers and increased their pay for their new terms, although it was clearly a ruse to circumvent this section—the court went to great lengths to assert that it would not look into the legislature's motives—did not violate the section. *State ex rel. Reuss v. Giessel* (1952). If an officer dies during his or her term of office and if, during that term, the salary for the office has been increased, the new officeholder may receive the higher salary without violating this section, because the section refers to "officer," not to "office." *State ex rel. Bashford v. Frear* (1909). An income tax enacted during an officer's term does not reduce the officer's compensation; only direct reductions violate this section. *State ex rel. Wickham v. Nygaard* (1915).

A statute authorizing additional payment to highway contractors for increased fuel costs after the contracts were executed violates this section. *Krug v. Zueske* (1996).

Subsection (3) does not require a three-fourths vote of the members in each house of the legislature to increase pension benefits, but requires that the bill pass with the votes of three-fourths of all members of the legislature. *Wisconsin Professional Police Association, Inc. v. Lightbourn* (2001).

Section 27
Suits against state.

The legislature shall direct by law in what manner and in what courts suits may
be brought against the state.

This section has not been amended. It asserts the state's "sovereign immunity": its prerogative to decide the conditions under which it may be sued. Its
roots run far back into the middle ages, to the doctrine that "the king can do no
wrong," and is thus immune from legal challenge.

An entity of the state has sovereign immunity unless the legislature creates
it as an independent going concern. To decide if the entity is a public agency
or an independent entity, the court will consider the character and breadth of
the statutory powers granted to the entity, such as the extent to which statutes
have given it proprietary powers, including the authority to sue and be sued, to
convey real estate, to dispose of personal property, to hold funds outside the
treasury, to pay money without using warrants from the department of administration, to borrow money, and to issue and sell bonds. *Mayhugh v. State* (2015).

This section relates to four other sections. Although Article I, Section 9
guarantees a legal remedy for every wrong, it does not override this section.
Forseth v. Sweet (1968); *Erickson Oil Products, Inc. v. State* (1994). If the state
committed the alleged wrongful act, the victim has no right to sue the state on
that basis unless a statute grants that right. Although Article VII, Section 3(2)
grants, apparently without limits, to the supreme court appellate jurisdiction and
the right to take original jurisdiction and Article VII, Section 8 grants to circuit
courts jurisdiction over all civil and criminal matters, this section does not yield
to those provisions. *Kenosha v. State* (1967). A court has no jurisdiction in a case
brought against the state unless the state has created that jurisdiction. However,
Article I, Section 13, which requires just compensation to be paid when property is taken for public use, is self-executing, so it gives persons the right to sue
the state for compensation in that kind of case. *Zinn v. State* (1983).

This section means that the state may not be sued unless it has given its
consent. *State ex rel. Martin v. Reis* (1939); *Metzger v. Department of Taxation*
(1967). That consent must be in the form of a statute. *The Chicago, Milwaukee
& St. Paul R'y Co. v. The State* (1881). If a statute grants consent, the consent
applies only to the kinds of cases that could have been maintained at the time
that the statute was enacted. *Townsend v. Wisconsin Desert Horse Assoc.* (1969).
Moreover, the statute must explicitly grant consent. *Kegonsa Jt. Sanitary Dist.
v. City of Stoughton* (1979). For example, a statute that provides for the arbitration of disputes about contracts does not grant the right to sue the state. *State
v. P. G. Miron Const. Co., Inc.* (1994). Similarly, neither a statute that requires the
state to indemnify its employees who must pay damages in cases that result from
their official actions nor a statute that requires persons to give notice of claims
grants the right to sue the state directly. *Fiala v. Voight* (1980). One exception

to the requirement of explicit consent exists: a statute allowing suits against the state to quiet title must be interpreted to grant consent for "any equitable action involving land where no judgement for the recovery of money or personal property is sought against the state." *Herro v. Wisconsin Fed. Surp. P. Dev. Corp.* (1969).

The section's reference to "in what manner and in what courts" authorizes any option regarding those two issues that a statute provides. *Dickson v. State of Wisconsin* (1853). For example, the first statute on suits against the state required them to be brought before the state supreme court. Even though that created problems, such as the impossibility of testimony by witnesses, the court was bound by the statute. If a statute specifies the way suits may be brought against the state, a litigant must meticulously follow those procedures. *State ex rel. Martin v. Reis* (1939).

Despite this section's lapidary quality, parties have disputed the meaning of two of its words. The first is "state." The term encompasses state agencies. *Lister v. Board of Regents* (1976); *Lindas v. Cady* (1987). However, the diversity of entities that have some relation to the state, and thus might be state agencies, makes defining this term difficult. If an entity has enough proprietary powers and duties, it is not a state agency, despite its links to the state. *Busse v. Dane County Regional Planning Comm.* (1993). The court will balance the entity's governmental and nongovernmental powers and duties, because no definite boundary exists between state agencies and other entities. Another test is whether the entity is an "independent going concern." *Busse.* For example, an entity that receives its funds from the state and operates under general statutory guidelines is likely to be a state agency. Conversely, an entity that may convey real estate, hold its own funds, borrow money, and sell bonds and that receives no state funds is not a state agency. *Majerus v. Milwaukee County* (1968). A statute decreeing that an entity may sue and be sued does not make that entity something other than a state agency. The Department of Health and Social Services, although it has a statutory right to sue and be sued, is a state agency and thus immune from suit. *Lindas v. Cady* (1987). That is, it may not be sued despite the statutory statement that it may be sued. In at least one case, the court thought that statutory rights to sue and be sued, although they did not dispose of this issue, were one indicator of the degree of the entity's independence and thus of the possibility of suing it. *Bahr v. State Inv. Board* (1994).

Determining whether this section applies to state employees requires a different analysis. If the employee acted within the scope of his or her authority, he or she is immune from suit. *Appel v. Halverson* (1971). If the person did not act within the scope of his or her authority, however, he or she is not immune from suit. For example, a person who acts upon a mistaken interpretation of a statute acts beyond the scope of his or her authority and thereby abnegates the immunity that this section grants. *Wisconsin Fertilizer Asso. v. Karns* (1968). Indeed, a legal action may be brought to obtain a declaratory judgment or an injunction that would prohibit a state employee from acting beyond the scope of his or her authority. *Graney v. Board of Regents* (1979).

There are several cases about waiving sovereign immunity. The University of Wisconsin's agreement to judicial enforcement of arbitration awards, which in effect waived the state's sovereign immunity, was void because no statute granted the right to sue in those cases to begin with. *State ex rel. Teach. Assts. v. Wis.-Madison Univ.* (1980). Participating in a federal case does not waive the state's sovereign immunity against suits in state courts. *Lister v. Board of Regents* (1976). An elected official's failure to assert immunity under this section waives that immunity and makes possible a suit against that official. *Kenosha v. State* (1967). A waiver of immunity is not subject to litigation on the ground that it violated the equal protection of the laws. *Apfelbacher v. State* (1915).

The other word in this section that has required definition is "suit." Here, it means "any proceeding by one person or persons against another or others in a court of law in which the plaintiff pursues, in such court, the remedy which the law affords him for the redress of an injury or the enforcement of a right, whether at law or equity." *State v. P. G. Miron Const. Co., Inc.* (1994). For example, a proceeding in a court to request an injunction and an order of specific performance is a suit. *Erickson Oil Products, Inc. v. State* (1994).

This section limits procedural, not substantive, rights. *Milwaukee County v. Schmidt* (1971); *Holytz v. Milwaukee* (1962). That is, it denies access to the courts unless a statute grants that access. Sovereign immunity, the right that this section creates, needs to be distinguished from governmental immunity. The latter concept derives from the English common law and is substantive: it specifies that units of government are not liable for certain kinds of actions that would subject other entities to legal liability. It follows from this distinction that making the state liable for certain kinds of action does not constitute consent to sue the state. *Forseth v. Sweet* (1968). This distinction was important in a landmark case that explicitly overturned several earlier cases. The state, for more than a century, has had a procedure for making claims against the state. If the claims board determined that the state was liable for damages it would pay those damages, which did not mean that those damages could be sought in court. The court has held that this statute applied only to debts, not to torts. *Houston v. The State* (1893). However, the court in 1962 held that this doctrine of governmental immunity from tort litigation no longer made sense. *Holytz*. It overruled all of the cases to the contrary and applied the new rule to all units of government, including the state. The court cautioned that "a careful distinction must be made between the abrogation of the [governmental tort] immunity doctrine and the right of a private party to sue the state." That court did not negate this section; it maintained that the right to sue the state still depended on the existence of a pertinent statute.

Section 28
Oath of office.

Members of the legislature, and all officers, executive and judicial, except such inferior officers as may be by law exempted, shall before they enter upon the duties of their respective offices, take and subscribe an oath or affirmation to support the constitution of the United States and the constitution of the state of Wisconsin, and faithfully to discharge the duties of their respective offices to the best of their ability.

This section has not been amended. Failure by members of a commission, who were appointed to appraise property that a railroad (under its statutory charter) wished to condemn, to take the oath under this section, as required by a general statute on railroads, invalidated their later actions. *Bohlman v. Green Bay & Minnesota Railway Company* (1876). The commissioners, whom a circuit court had appointed, took an oath that conformed to the railroad's charter but not to this section. Because a statute created the duty to take the oath specified in this section, this case does not illuminate the meaning of "officer" in this section. A few Attorney General's Opinions, 4 Op. Atty. Gen 964 (1915); 1906 Op. Atty. Gen. 628, comment on the meaning of "officer," but the question of this section's scope remains unsettled, even though much could be at stake. If an officer who is required by this section to take an oath fails to do so, his or her actions might be invalid.

Section 29
Militia.

The legislature shall determine what persons shall constitute the militia of the state, and may provide for organizing and disciplining the same in such manner as shall be prescribed by law.

This section has not been amended. It is one of the sections based upon the notion that the state is in a sense a separate sovereign state. Others are Article I, Section 20; Article V, Section 4; Article V, Section 7(2); Article VIII, Section 7(1). Those sections, as well as other considerations, justify the granting of bonuses to World War I veterans. *State ex rel. Atwood v. Johnson* (1919).

Section 30
Elections by legislature.

All elections made by the legislature shall be by roll call vote entered in the journals.

This section originally required elections "viva voce" (orally). In this section, "elections" means elections of certain legislative officers. It was amended in 1982 to validate electronic voting, which the assembly, but not the senate, currently uses. Although this section requires roll calls on elections, many voice votes on bills occur.

Section 31
Special and private laws prohibited.

The legislature is prohibited from enacting any special or private laws in the following cases:

(1) For changing the names of persons, constituting one person the heir at law of another or granting any divorce.

(2) For laying out, opening or altering highways, except in cases of state roads extending into more than one county, and military roads to aid in the construction of which lands may be granted by congress.

(3) For authorizing persons to keep ferries across streams at points wholly within this state.

(4) For authorizing the sale or mortgage of real or personal property of minors or others under disability.

(5) For locating or changing any county seat.

(6) For assessment or collection of taxes or for extending the time for the collection thereof.

(7) For granting corporate powers or privileges, except to cities.

(8) For authorizing the apportionment of any part of the school fund.

(9) For incorporating any city, town or village, or to amend the charter thereof.

This section, which prohibits narrow legislation on certain subjects, became part of the constitution in 1871. In 1892, "any city" was added to the ninth item in the list, and in 1993, "granting any divorce" was added to the first item in the list (and that prohibition was removed from Article IV, Section 24). This section interacts with Article IV, Section 18, which creates requirements for private and local bills, and with Article IV, Section 32, which authorizes general laws on the subjects for which, under this section, private and local laws may not be enacted. Private laws apply only to particular (usually one or a small number of) entities.

This section was added to the constitution because the statute books contained many special and private laws that "broke the uniformity and harmony of law so essential to good government; substituting special for general rules, and rendering a large body of the municipal law fragmentary in character, and different by locality." *Kimball v. Rosendale* (1877). The section ensures that "legislation will promote the general welfare and further statewide interests," as opposed to private concerns. *State ex rel. La Follette v. Reuter* (1967).

Occasionally courts have refused to accept the use of fictions to make special and local laws appear to be general. The court in *State ex rel. Sanderson v. Mann* (1890) held that a tax that applied only in counties the population of which exceeded 150,000 (at the time only Milwaukee County) violated this section and the next section. Also, a reference to cities of certain classes violated this section. *Federal Paving Corp. v. Prudisch* (1940). More frequently, courts have accepted such fictions. Among those they have accepted are references to one or more of the four classes of cities that Wis. Stat. § 62.05(1), establish, *Madison Metropolitan Sewerage Dist. v. Stein* (1970); *Brennan v. Employment Relations Com'n of State* (1983); references to a county that includes a city of one of the classes, *Thielen v. Metropolitan Sewerage Commission* (1922); references to a city that has a population of at least a certain magnitude, *id.*; and references to cities that operate under a special charter, which now applies only to the *City of Milwaukee, Schintgen v. City of La Crosse* (1903).

Some cases concerning this section turn on whether a law is either general or special (or private). In a 1988 case, *Brookfield v. Milwaukee Sewerage* (1988), the court summarized the rules that earlier courts had developed for determining whether a classification makes a law general so that, even though it is about one of the subjects specified in this section, it does not violate this section. Those rules are that the classes created must be truly different from one another, that the classification must be germane to the purposes of the law to which it is relevant, that the classification must allow for other entities to become members of the class, that the law must apply equally to all members of a class, and that treating the classes differently is proper and furthers the public good. However, curative legislation need only fulfill the requirement that the statute applies equally to all of the members of a class. In contrast, a court may make a more perfunctory examination, such as one that resulted in a determination that a law directing the construction of a few specified portions of the interstate highway system was general because the promotion of traffic safety promoted the general welfare. *State ex rel. La Follette v. Reuter* (1967).

Other cases on this section turn on whether the law is about one of the specified subjects. As to the prohibition against special and private laws for the assessment and collection of taxes, "assess" means "the whole operation of raising taxes, from commencement to termination." *Chicago & Northwestern R. Co. v. Forest County and others* (1897). Although taxes and special assessments are distinguished in the statutes and are even based upon different governmental powers (the power to tax versus the police power to enhance the public health, safety, and welfare), this section also applies to special assessments. *Harrison v. The Board of Supervisors of Milwaukee County, imp.* (1881). A tax law that merely "completes" another law, such as one that specifies the method by which property tax revenue should be apportioned between a new county and the county from which it was created, does not violate this section if the law that it completes does not do so. *Cathcart v. Comstock* (1883). A tax law that applies to all counties is general. *State ex rel. Blockwitz v. Diehl* (1929).

The results of some of the cases on the prohibition against special and local laws on taxation depend upon the point in the tax process that is at issue. Even if that point occurs before the process begins, the law might violate this section. Examples are a limit on the amount of taxes that towns in one county may impose, *Chicago & Northwestern R. Co. v. Forest County and others* (1897), and a curative act that validated the construction of a school, because the construction would require a tax, *Nevil and another v. Clifford and others* (1885). A law that deals with a tax itself and that is special or local will violate this section. Examples are a curative act that validated a tax that one municipality imposed to fund bonds, *Kimball v. Rosendale* (1877), and a method for assessing and collecting taxes that applied only to school districts in cities of a certain class, *State ex rel. Thompson v. Beloit City School Dist.* (1934).

In contrast, events that occur after a tax is assessed and collected will not violate this section. Examples are a statute that required the portion of railroad taxes that are attributable to docks, piers, wharves, and grain elevators, if those structures are used to transfer freight or passengers, to be transmitted to municipalities, *State ex rel. Superior v. Donald* (1916), a statute that required the withholding of state aid if that was necessary to fund a pension system because a county's taxes and other funds were insufficient to do so, *Columbia County v. Wisconsin Retirement Fund* (1962), and a statute that governed the return by a county to municipalities in the county of revenue collected from taxpayers who had been delinquent in paying their taxes, *Whitefish Bay v. Milwaukee County* (1937).

For purposes of subsection (7), school districts are not corporations. *State ex rel. Vandenhouten v. Vanhuse* (1903). Although subsection (7) pertains to grants of corporate franchises, it does not pertain to grants of franchises to corporations. *In re Southern Wisconsin Power Co.* (1909); *Linden Land Co. and another v. Milwaukee Electricity & Light Co.* (1900). Merely recognizing, by enacting a law, a religious congregation's organizational system does not grant a corporate power. *St. Hyacinth Congregation v. Borucki* (1910). Making an appropriation to an existing corporation does not grant a corporate power. *State ex rel. Warren v. Reuter* (1969). A law that creates only one insurance company is unconstitutional, *The State ex rel. Church Mutual Ins. Co. v. Cheek* (1890), but a law that creates one building corporation is constitutional because that corporation will participate in state building projects. *State ex rel. Warren v. Nusbaum* (1973). The distinction between the results of these two cases is somewhat obscure.

Over time, subsection (9) became nearly a dead letter as courts have found ways around its prohibition. According to an early case, towns may be created in a county that was formed by dividing an existing county, because the towns were not granted any powers and general laws on towns' powers existed. *Cathcart v. Comstock* (1883). The court has also authorized the same process for counties. *The Chicago & Northwestern R'y Co. v. Langlade County and others* (1883). Similarly, dividing and creating towns does not violate this subsection. *State ex rel. Graef v. Forest County* (1889). Much later the court brushed off, with some general remarks about the constitution's adaptability to new conditions, an attempt to assert that a law creating one village violated this subsection. *In re Village of Chenequa* (1928).

Subsection (9) was brought back to life in 2009, when the court held in *State ex rel. Kuehne v. Burdette* (2009) that a provision in the state budget bill authorizing a single town to bypass general procedures for incorporating into a village violates the subsection.

Section 32
General laws on enumerated subjects.

The legislature may provide by general law for the treatment of any subject for which lawmaking is prohibited by section 31 of this article. Subject to reasonable classifications, such laws shall be uniform in their operation throughout the state.

In 1992, an amendment added the exception for reasonable classification to this section and replaced a reference to "the transaction of any business that may be prohibited by section thirty-one" with the reference to "[t]he treatment of any subject for which lawmaking is prohibited by section 31." That first addition codified several judicial decisions in which statutes that made reasonable classifications were held to be constitutional in spite of the requirement of uniform operation that existed before ratification of the amendment that added this exception. E.g., *White Const. Co. v. City of Beloit* (1926); *Barth v. Village of Shorewood* (1938). The second addition made it clear that general lawmaking authority was indeed general and that it did not apply only to transaction of business.

This section itself indicates its relation to Article IV, Section 31. It also relates to the home-rule section, Article XI, Section 3, which makes an exception to the home-rule power of cities and villages for laws of statewide concern that uniformly affect all cities and villages. In other words, both this section and Article XI, Section 3 refer to laws that operate uniformly throughout the state. The creation of that section did not invalidate this one regarding the authority to organize municipalities. *Bleck v. Monona Village* (1967). Section 31(9) of this article prohibits special laws to incorporate municipalities, so that must be done by general laws under this section, except that courts have not vigorously enforced the prohibition. That is, home-rule authority applies only after cities and villages are organized; it grants power to cities and villages, not to territories the residents of which wish to organize as a city or village. Thus, after the ratification of Article XI, Section 3, this section continues to apply to organizing cities and villages.

The cases on the reasonableness of classification continued to apply after the 1992 amendment that added that concept to this section. E.g., *Brookfield v. Milwaukee Sewerage* (1988). One early case, *Johnson v. The City of Milwaukee* (1894), propounded four tests for the reasonableness of a classification that are still used: it must be based on substantial distinctions that make one class really different from another, the classification must be germane to the purpose of the law that created it, the classification must not be based only upon existing circumstances but must make possible addition of members to the class, and if the law applies to a class, it must apply equally to all members of the class. A fifth rule, that the characteristics of each of the classes created must be so different from the characteristics of the other classes as to suggest that it is proper to enact substantially different legislation for the classes, appeared later. *State ex rel. Risch v. Board of Trustees of Policemen's Pension Fund* (1904).

One type of classification has been important in enacting legislation: it is sometimes necessary to enact laws that apply to only some municipalities or to only some counties. Legislation that applies to only one class of city (the statutes identify four classes of cities, Wis. Stat. § 62.05) is constitutional. *Wisconsin Central R. Co. v. Superior* (1913); *State ex rel. Michael v. McGill* (1953). Similarly, limiting the application of statutes to counties that have no more or no less than a certain population is constitutional. *Michael.* A curative act may apply only to a class, rather than uniformly throughout the state, if it applies equally to all members of that class. *Madison Metropolitan Sewerage Dist. v. Stein* (1970).

The most extreme example of limiting the effect of legislation to fewer than all of the examples of a type of municipality is limiting a law's effects to cities that operate under a special charter. Early in the state's history, municipalities and counties were organized by special charter, but Chapter 242 of the laws of 1921 repealed all municipal special charters except the City of Milwaukee's. That law did not violate this section as to Milwaukee because it did not change the city's charter, so it had no effect on the city. *Zweifel v. Milwaukee* (1925).

Section 33
Auditing of state accounts.

The legislature shall provide for the auditing of state accounts and may establish such offices and prescribe such duties for the same as it shall deem necessary.

This section, which concerns the administrative approval of state expenditures, has not been amended. On its face, it seems to require the state to ensure that its financial books are in order. However, "auditing" in this section means determining whether an expenditure complies with state law and, if it does, authorizing payment of state funds. Unless there is an "audit" in this sense, no state money may be expended, except that the supreme court, due to its supervisory power over the judicial system makes the decisions on spending for administration of the courts. *State ex rel. Moran v. Dept. of Admin.* (1981). Under Article VI, Section 2, before it was amended in 1946, the secretary of state was the state auditor; the person elected to that position, after "auditing" the accounts, issued the warrants that allowed state spending. Several cases from that era make it clear that no state money could be expended unless an audit held the expenditure valid. E.g., *Wadham's Oil Co. v. Tracy* (1909). Since that time, the legislature, acting under this section's authority, has given to the secretary of the Department of Administration the duty of auditing the state's accounts.

Section 34
Continuity of civil government.

The legislature, in order to ensure continuity of state and local governmental operations in periods of emergency resulting from enemy action in the form of an attack, shall (1) forthwith provide for prompt and temporary succession to the powers and duties of public offices, of whatever nature and whether filled by election or appointment, the incumbents of which may become unavailable for carrying on the powers and duties of such offices, and (2) adopt such other measures as may be necessary and proper for attaining the objectives of this section.

This section has not been amended or litigated. It was ratified in 1961, the same year that the legislature enacted a property tax exemption for nuclear shelters. Both this section and that exemption result from the "Red Scare": the belief that many U.S. citizens had during that era that the Soviet Union might attack this country.

Article V

Executive

Section 1
Governor; lieutenant governor; term.

The executive power shall be vested in a governor who shall hold office for 4 years; a lieutenant governor shall be elected at the same time and for the same term.

This section, which specifies the general authority of the governor and sets the term of office for that position and for the lieutenant governor, has been amended once, in 1979, to increase those terms from two to four years. It, along with two other sections, has required the courts to make some difficult decisions. Article IV, Section 1 vests the legislative power in the assembly and senate, and Article VII, Section 2 vests the judicial power of the state in a unified court system. This section and those others together create a separation of powers. Each of those sections (like Article X, Section 1 regarding the State Superintendent of Public Instruction) uses "is vested," as if to suggest that the power conferred is plenary or virtually plenary. Although state government is divided into three parts, the difficulty is that, like the boundaries in the tripartite Gaul that Julius Caesar described, the boundaries between any two of the three domains blur. The separation of powers doctrine is violated if the actions of one branch of government usurp the powers of another branch. *J. F. Ahern Co. v. Building Comm'n* (1983). However, separation does not mean absolute division. *Layton School of Art & Design v. WERC* (1978). The court has had difficulty drawing the boundaries between the judiciary and the executive branch—that is, in establishing the proper relationship between this section and Article VII, Section 2.

Three of the cases concerning this section resolved constitutional crises of varying degrees of intensity, because in each the governor was a party. In all three the court declined to concede that the governor had plenary executive power and that the court therefore could not rule on his or her actions. The court then confronted the problem of establishing a different kind of boundary: one between the kind of actions by the governor that it had to accept because of the governor's executive power, and the kind over which it had jurisdiction and could thus choose to validate or invalidate. In three of the cases it drew the boundary at roughly the same place. In one of them it contrasted powers vested in the governor and powers vested elsewhere. *The Attorney General ex rel. Taylor v. Brown* (1853). Similarly, in a case involving a dispute over the person who had the right to the office and the refusal of the incumbent to vacate the office, the court distinguished between powers that were entrusted to the governor, to which the court's jurisdiction did not extend, and powers that were entrusted to another, to which the court's jurisdiction did extend. *The Attorney General ex rel. Bashford v. Barstow* (1856). The authority to determine the person who should fill an elective office lies with the people; when former Governor Williams A. Barstow ventured beyond his authority, he could be restrained by the court. A later case involved a governor's authorization of the forcible ejection of the Commissioner of Insurance from his office. *Ekern v. McGovern* (1913). This case illustrates not only the court's difficulties with cases in which a governor is a party, but the disintegration of the Progressive alliance into warring factions. In *Ekern*, the court distinguished between actions that were within the governor's authority and those that were outside that authority. Although the governor had the power to appoint, and therefore to remove, the Commissioner of Insurance, by authorizing the forcible ejection of that official, he acted beyond his authority.

Another court drew a different boundary between those gubernatorial actions subject to judicial review and those that were not. A governor had refused to issue stock certificates that had been authorized by law and to which claimants had a valid right. *State ex rel. Resley and others v. Farwell, Gov., etc.* (1852). In a philosophical opinion, the court distinguished between the office of governor and the individual who held the office. It went on to distinguish between actions about which the governor had discretion (regarding them, the court could not interfere) and those about which the governor had a duty (regarding them, the court could interfere). The court later decided that a governor exercising discretion was beyond its reach. *State ex rel. Pierce v. Board of Trustees* (1914). The cases present conflicting methods of determining the court's authority to interfere with a governor's actions. One is to determine first whether the governor was acting within the authority of the office. The other is to determine first whether the governor was performing a discretionary act.

This section's grant of executive power to the governor does not mean that that official and his subordinates have the exclusive authority to appoint employees of the state government. *In re Appointment of Revisor* (1910). The office at stake there was the Revisor of Statutes, who compiled enacted bills into the statutes and performed other duties. The court reasoned that the functions to be performed most closely related to the judicial branch of government, so the supreme court could make the appointment. Today, that function belongs to the legislative branch.

Section 2
Eligibility.

No person except a citizen of the United States and a qualified elector of the state shall be eligible to the office of governor or lieutenant governor.

This section has not been amended or litigated.

Section 3
Election.

The governor and lieutenant governor shall be elected by the qualified electors of the state at the times and places of choosing members of the legislature. They shall be chosen jointly, by the casting by each voter of a single vote applicable to both offices beginning with the general election in 1970. The persons respectively having the highest number of votes cast jointly for them for governor and lieutenant governor shall be elected; but in case two or more slates shall have an equal and the highest number of votes for governor and lieutenant governor, the two houses of the legislature, at its next annual session shall forthwith, by joint ballot, choose one of the slates so having an equal and the highest number of votes for governor and lieutenant governor. The returns of election for governor and lieutenant governor shall be made in such manner as shall be provided by law.

This section prescribes the method of electing the governor and lieutenant governor. It was amended in 1967 to add the second sentence, so that the governor and lieutenant governor, having been running mates, will be of the same political party. Certification of the person who has the highest number of votes is not conclusive; a court may determine whether the voting and the counting of the ballots were proper. *The Attorney General ex rel. Bashford v. Barstow* (1856). Within limits, laws—for example, a law providing that violation of spending limits in the primary make a candidate ineligible for office—may be enacted to add qualifications for election to the office of governor beyond receiving the most votes. *State ex rel. La Follette v. Kohler* (1930).

Section 4
Powers and duties.

The governor shall be commander in chief of the military and naval forces of the state. He shall have power to convene the legislature on extraordinary occasions, and in case of invasion, or danger from the prevalence of contagious disease at the seat of government, he may convene them at any other suitable place within the state. He shall communicate to the legislature, at every session, the condition of the state, and recommend such matters to them for their consideration as he may deem expedient. He shall transact all necessary business with the officers of the government, civil and military. He shall expedite all such measures as may be resolved upon by the legislature, and shall take care that the laws be faithfully executed.

This section is one of a number that are based on the notion that the state is in some sense a separate sovereign state. Other such sections are Article I, Section 20; Article IV, Section 29; Article V, Section 7(2); and Article VIII, Section 7(1). Those sections, along with other considerations, justify granting bonuses to World War I veterans. *State ex rel. Atwood v. Johnson* (1919).

A court might read literally the last phrase and not allow the governor to perform actions that the relevant statute does not authorize; for example, if a statute that gives the governor the power to remove officers for misconduct does not authorize the appointment of commissioners to take testimony about the alleged misconduct, a court may presume that the governor may not do so. *Randall v. The State* (1863). A statute that requires the governor to include in his or her state budget bill the amount necessary for a certain purpose encroaches on the governor's power to recommend matters for the legislature to consider. *State ex rel. Warren v. Nusbaum* (1973). It is thus unconstitutional and is to be considered a request rather than an order. When negotiating tribal gaming compacts, the governor cannot authorize forms of gambling that the constitution, Article IV, Section 24, and the statutes prohibit. *Panzer v. Doyle* (2004).

Section 6
Pardoning power.

The governor shall have power to grant reprieves, commutations and pardons, after conviction, for all offenses, except treason and cases of impeachment, upon such conditions and with such restrictions and limitations as he may think proper, subject to such regulations as may be provided by law relative to the manner of applying for pardons. Upon conviction for treason he shall have the power to suspend the execution of the sentence until the case shall be reported to the legislature at its next meeting, when the legislature shall either pardon, or commute the sentence, direct the execution of the sentence, or grant a further reprieve. He shall annually communicate to the legislature each case of reprieve, commutation or pardon granted, stating the name of the convict, the crime of which he was convicted, the sentence and its date, and the date of the commutation, pardon or reprieve, with his reasons for granting the same.

This section has not been amended. The power to pardon is the power to stop the further imposition of a criminal sentence, and the governor may exercise the pardon for reasons that are unrelated to the proceedings in which a court imposed the sentence. *Drewniak v. State ex rel. Jacquest* (1942). In contrast, courts have the power to stop, either temporarily or permanently, the imposition of a criminal sentence, but they may do so only for reasons related to the proceedings in which the sentence was first imposed. Because this section limits the power to pardon to relief of the sentences of persons who have been convicted of a crime, the governor may not pardon persons who are incarcerated for contempt of court. *State ex rel. Rodd v. Verage* (1922). A reprieve postpones a sentence, and it most frequently occurs regarding a death sentence; Wisconsin at this writing has no death penalty. A commutation substitutes a less severe penalty for a more severe penalty. If it makes a sentence equal to or less than the length of time served, it in effect releases the prisoner whose sentence has been reduced.

Section 7
Lieutenant governor, when governor.

(1) Upon the governor's death, resignation or removal from office, the lieutenant governor shall become governor for the balance of the unexpired term.

(2) If the governor is absent from this state, impeached, or from mental or physical disease, becomes incapable of performing the duties of the office, the lieutenant governor shall serve as acting governor for the balance of the unexpired term or until the governor returns, the disability ceases or the impeachment is vacated. But when the governor, with the consent of the legislature, shall be out of this state in time of war at the head of the state's military force, the governor shall continue as commander in chief of the military force.

This section specifies the succession to the governorship. Subsection (2) is one of several provisions that are based on the notion that the state is in some sense a separate sovereign state. Others are Article I, Section 20; Article IV, Section 29; Article V, Section 4; and Article VIII, Section 7(1). Those sections, along with other considerations, justify granting bonuses to World War I veterans. *State ex rel. Atwood v. Johnson* (1919).

This section's original version provided that, if the governor was impeached, removed from office, dies, could not continue to hold office, resigned, or was absent from the state, the governor's duties would be assumed by the lieutenant governor. In those instances, the lieutenant governor became the acting governor, not the governor. It also provided that, when the governor returns or his or her disability ceases, he or she again assumed the duties of the office. The current version was ratified during 1979.

If a governor-elect dies before taking office, a vacancy exists and the rules under this section that mandate replacement by the lieutenant governor apply. *State ex rel. Martin v. Heil* (1942). Under the section's current version, in this situation the person who was elected lieutenant governor is governor for the full term. A lieutenant governor who is acting as governor (and, presumably, a former lieutenant governor who becomes governor) may represent a client before a state commission. *Boles v. Industrial Comm.* (1958).

Section 8
Secretary of state, when governor.

(1) If there is a vacancy in the office of lieutenant governor and the governor dies, resigns or is removed from office, the secretary of state shall become governor for the balance of the unexpired term.

(2) If there is a vacancy in the office of lieutenant governor and the governor is absent from this state, impeached, or from mental or physical disease becomes incapable of performing the duties of the office, the secretary of state shall serve as acting governor for the balance of the unexpired term or until the governor returns, the disability ceases or the impeachment is vacated.

This section now states the remainder of the state's fundamental law on the succession to the governorship. It originally called for the lieutenant governor to preside over the senate and to have the right to vote if the senate deadlocked. It also specified that if the governorship is vacant and the lieutenant governor (upon whom the duties of the office had devolved under the original version of the previous section) is impeached, displaced, resigns, dies, becomes incapable of serving, or is absent from the state, the secretary of state acts as governor until the vacancy is filled or the disability ceases. The present version of this section was ratified during 1979. It has not been litigated.

Section 10
Governor to approve or veto bills; proceedings on veto.

(1) (a) Every bill which shall have passed the legislature shall, before it becomes a law, be presented to the governor.

(b) If the governor approves and signs the bill, the bill shall become law. Appropriation bills may be approved in whole or in part by the governor, and the part approved shall become law.

(c) In approving an appropriation bill in part, the governor may not create a new word by rejecting individual letters in the words of the enrolled bill, and may not create a new sentence by combining parts of 2 or more sentences of the enrolled bill.

(2) (a) If the governor rejects the bill, the governor shall return the bill, together with the objections in writing, to the house in which the bill originated. The house of origin shall enter the objections at large upon the journal and proceed to reconsider the bill. If, after such reconsideration, two-thirds of the members present agree to pass the bill notwithstanding the objections of the governor, it shall be sent, together with the objections, to the other house, by which it shall likewise be reconsidered, and if approved by two-thirds of the members present it shall become law.

(b) The rejected part of an appropriation bill, together with the governor's objections in writing, shall be returned to the house in which the bill originated. The house of origin shall enter the objections at large upon the journal and proceed to reconsider the rejected part of the appropriation bill. If, after such reconsideration, two-thirds of the members present agree to approve the rejected part notwithstanding the objections of the governor, it shall be sent, together with the objections, to the other house, by which it shall likewise be reconsidered, and if approved by two-thirds of the members present the rejected part shall become law.

(c) In all such cases the votes of both houses shall be determined by ayes and noes, and the names of the members voting for or against passage of the bill or the rejected part of the bill notwithstanding the objections of the governor shall be entered on the journal of each house respectively.

(3) Any bill not returned by the governor within 6 days (Sundays excepted) after it shall have been presented to the governor shall be law unless the legislature, by final adjournment, prevents the bill's return, in which case it shall not be law.

A 2008 amendment added the phrase "and may not create a new sentence by combining parts of 2 or more sentences of the enrolled bill" to Section 10(1)(c).

This is one of the constitution's more important sections because, as the courts have interpreted it, it grants to Wisconsin's governor greater veto power than that possessed by any other governor. Its original form bestowed the authority to veto only entire bills. It also specified the procedures for presenting bills to the governor, for the governor's action on them and for the legislature's action upon vetoes. For example, it decreed that if the governor failed to return a bill to the legislature within three days after presentation of it to him or her, that bill became law unless the legislature, by adjournment, prevented its return. That period was extended to six days by a 1908 amendment. The crucial amendment, allowing vetoes of less than complete bills, occurred during 1930. The drafter worded that provision thus: "[a]ppropriation bills may be approved in whole or in part by the governor, and the part approved shall become law, and the part objected to shall be returned in the same manner as provided for other bills." The drafter opted later made it clear that he considered "part" and "item" to be synonyms, the supreme court has consistently disagreed, in one opinion explicitly declaring the drafter's statement irrelevant. *State ex rel. Wis. Senate v. Thompson* (1988). Courts have approved steady expansion of the veto power to include striking of words, letters, and digits and of writing in lower numbers to replace numbers in appropriations. In 1990, the voters ratified an amendment that disallowed the creation of new words by striking letters.

In deciding a veto case, the most basic issue is whether the veto affected an "appropriation bill." That was the central issue in the second veto case, *State ex rel. Finnegan v. Dammann* (1936). There, the court proposed three definitions of "appropriation," one from a dictionary and two from legal opinions that courts in other states had rendered. Of those definitions, later courts chose Arizona's: "the setting aside from the public revenue of a certain sum of money for a specified object." The governor had vetoed an increase in the fees assessed against motor carriers. The bill contained no appropriation per se, but the increase in the fees would have increased the money that flowed through "continuing revolving fund appropriations." Today this kind of appropriation is called a program revenue appropriation, disbursing for a specified purpose, revenue generated from a specified source. A mere increase in the magnitude of the flow of money did not make the bill an appropriation bill. The *Dammann* court voided the entire bill, despite the directive in this section that the part of the bill that the governor approved is to become law. This is the only case in which a Wisconsin court has invalidated a veto.

In the other case, *State ex rel. Kleczka v. Contac* (1978), the plaintiff argued that a non-appropriation bill had been vetoed, the bill was quite different from the bill that was at issue in *Dammann*. The legislature had allowed individuals to designate that the income tax that they owed be increased by $1, the money to be deposited in the campaign finance fund, and it had created two appropriations and amended another in accomplishing the latter end. The court held that the bill did set aside public money for a specified purpose and therefore was an appropriation bill. After *Kleczka*, the law on the meaning of "appropriation bill" for purposes of the veto power was clear: a bill that sets aside money for a public purpose is an appropriation bill; a bill that merely increases or decreases the flow of money through a program revenue appropriation is not.

The other issue is whether certain kinds of vetoes are constitutional. Because the history of the decisions on this issue indicates an uninterrupted increase in the veto power, as determined by the court, it makes the most sense to treat the cases in chronological order. In the first, the court noted that the constitution referred to "part," not "item." *State ex rel. Wisconsin Tel. Co. v. Henry* (1935). It then turned to a dictionary for a definition of "part" and discovered that it meant *any* portion. The die was cast. The court next noted that the veto left "a complete, entire and workable law." Later cases transformed this observation into a requirement. To emphasize the magnitude of the power that it thought resulted from the use of "part," the court stated that the governor's veto power was "coextensive as the legislature's power to join and enact separable pieces of legislation in an appropriation bill." Having determined that the governor's veto powers were broad, the court naturally approved the veto, which had struck from the bill a condition related to an appropriation. The facts of the case allowed the court to take two very different directions than the one that it took. The Wisconsin court could have held that "item" and "part" are synonyms and, following the lead of courts in other states, invalidated the veto because it excised less than an item. Courts in other states had also allowed vetoes only of appropriations and of conditions attached to them. The Wisconsin court could have followed the lead of those courts, validated the veto and held that only those two kinds of veto would be valid. If the court had proceeded in either of those ways, its decision would have produced a very different balance of power between the executive and legislative branches.

Five years later, the court decided that the veto power existed even if the legislature had adjourned without setting a time for its return and the veto at issue was proper. *State ex rel. Martin v. Zimmerman* (1940). It very tersely approved the veto, noting that the veto left an "effective and enforceable law." Because most of the issues in this case involved procedure and because the portion of the opinion on the veto power's substance was very brief, the decision did little to clarify the veto power.

By the middle 1970s, one Wisconsin governor, probably encouraged by the existing veto cases, exercised the power more boldly. The governor vetoed not a complete section of a bill or a complete statutory unit that a bill created, but parts of a sentence. Moreover, the veto reversed the statute's meaning. The bill that the legislature passed allowed voters to petition for a referendum on whether a local unit of government may exceed the limit on its property tax levy. After the veto, the referendum was mandatory, not optional. In the litigation on this veto the court followed *Wisconsin Tel. Co.* and *Martin*, which it viewed as establishing that a governor may veto any portion of an appropriation bill if the remainder of the bill is a complete and workable law. *State ex rel. Sundby v. Adamany* (1975).

In the next case, a veto was attacked on three grounds: that the bill was not an appropriation bill, that the return of the bill to the legislature was improper, and that the veto itself was unconstitutional. *State ex rel. Kleczka v. Conta* (1978). The bill at issue in this case was, indeed, an appropriation bill. Although this section requires the governor to return to the legislature the part of a bill that he or she disapproves, the court held that submitting objections and a veto message was close enough. Because the veto made the income tax check off for campaign finance affect money that was already owed rather, as under the bill, affect additional money, the veto affected a condition of an appropriation. The court held that the test of validity was severability—whether a complete and workable law remained after the veto—and it held that requirement fulfilled.

The next step was to veto letters (which the 1990 amendment later forbade) and digits. Most of the vetoes of digits reduced the amounts of appropriations. In the ensuing litigation, the court approved both types of vetoes. *State ex rel. Wis. Senate v. Thompson* (1988). The main foundation of the opinion was the principle, which by that time was firmly established, that a partial-veto authority is broader than an item-veto authority. The court recognized only two limits on the authority. One was familiar from previous cases: that the remaining part of the bill be a complete and workable law. The other was that the practice of limiting vetoes to those that left a law that was germane to the portion of the bill that was vetoed was of such long standing that it had attained the force of law. This requirement of germaneness is the second limit on the veto power. A footnote in *Thompson* expressed no opinion on whether the governor could replace an amount in an appropriation not with an amount constructed with a veto, but with an amount written in. This seemed to be an invitation to a governor to attempt that kind of "veto."

A governor soon accepted the invitation, using this kind of veto several times in a budget bill. In the instance that was litigated the governor lined out "$350,000" in an entry in the appropriation schedule—the portion of a budget bill that lists the amount of each appropriation for each of the two fiscal years that the budget covers—and wrote in "$250,000." *Citizens Utility Board v. Klauser* (1995). The court concluded that $250,000 was part of $350,000, and that the governor had violated none of the principles specified in the previous veto cases. The dissenters argued that the governor's actions went beyond those approved in earlier cases and that it makes no sense to allow a governor to write in a lower number in the appropriation schedule, but not to write in a lower number elsewhere in a bill or to write in a concept that is narrower than the concept that is expressed in the bill (e.g., replacing "animal" with "bovine"). Despite the force of the dissent's arguments, the court had again expanded the governor's veto power.

Two years later, the supreme court took original jurisdiction in *Risser v. Klauser* (1997). The governor had used a partial veto to reduce the amount of revenue bonds authorized to be sold in a bill. He wrote in a number that was $40 million less than the legislature had passed. The court rejected this expansion of the partial veto power, finding that the language which set the limits for the sale of revenue bonds was not an appropriation. While acknowledging that the governor and the partial veto have a valid place in creating legislation, the court found that the constitutional doctrine of separation of powers does set some limits on the governor's power. Bonding limits are not appropriations and the governor does not have the power to write in numbers in non-appropriation parts of a bill. Reviewing the complete line of veto cases, the court listed the rules for the partial veto:

1. The governor may only veto parts of bills that contain an appropriation,
2. After the veto, the part remaining must constitute a complete, entire, and workable law,
3. The use of the veto must not result in a provision that is totally new, unrelated, or non-germane to the original bill,
4. The partial veto extends to any part of an appropriation bill, not just the appropriations,
5. The governor may strike words or digits from an appropriation bill but may not create a new word by striking individual letters in the words of the enrolled bill, and
6. The governor may write in a smaller number for an appropriation amount.

Article VI

Administrative

Section 1
Election of secretary of state, treasurer and attorney general; term.

The qualified electors of this state, at the times and places of choosing the members of the legislature, shall in 1970 and every 4 years thereafter elect a secretary of state, treasurer and attorney general who shall hold their offices for 4 years.

This section was amended in 1979 to conform to the change in the terms of office of the secretary of state, the treasurer, and the attorney general from two to four years, which had been changed by amendment in 1967. The reference to 1970 is not an error: because each amendment to the constitution must be submitted separately to the voters (see the commentary on Article XII, Section 1), the voters were presented with a separate question for each of the three state officers. It was thus impossible to know which of the three amendments would be ratified. In 1979, the three sections that extended the terms (Sections 1m, 1n, and 1p) were repealed, and this section was amended to indicate that the change from two-year terms to four-year terms happened because of the 1967 amendment and took effect in 1970. This section has not been litigated.

Section 2
Secretary of state; duties, compensation.

The secretary of state shall keep a fair record of the official acts of the legislature and executive department of the state, and shall, when required, lay the same and all matters relative thereto before either branch of the legislature. He shall perform such other duties as shall be assigned him by law. He shall receive as a compensation for his services yearly such sum as shall be provided by law, and shall keep his office at the seat of government.

This section was amended in 1979 to delete the designation of the secretary of state as the state auditor. (See the discussion of Article IV, Section 33 for an explanation of the meaning of "audit" in this context and for a discussion of the cases on that subject from the era when the secretary of state performed that function.) The secretary of state has only the powers that the section explicitly grants. In other words, he or she is "a mere ministerial officer" and, for example, does not have the authority to compel a corporation to forfeit its charter, although he or she may declare that there are grounds for forfeiture so that the attorney general may attempt to effect the actual forfeiture. *West Park Realty Co. v. Porth* (1927). Conversely, the secretary of state is required to perform all the duties required of him or her "by law," including the duty to publish a law that he or she thinks is invalid because it is unconstitutional. *State ex rel. Martin v. Zimmerman* (1939).

Section 3
Treasurer and attorney general; duties, compensation.

The powers, duties and compensation of the treasurer and attorney general shall be prescribed by law.

This section has not been amended. This section's wording indicates that the powers and duties of the treasurer and attorney general derive from the statutes. In contrast, Article X, Section 1 *vests* the superintendency of public instruction in another state elected official, the state superintendent of public instruction. The difference suggests that the latter official has considerable inherent power. This section's limitation of the attorney general's powers and duties to those specified by statute is unusual. However, the limitation is not quite as severe as the literal meaning of this section suggests. For example, Article X, Section 7 makes the attorney general one of the commissioners of public land.

Most often courts narrowly interpret the statutes that attorneys general have asserted as the basis of their power or responsibilities. For example, the attorney general may not authorize an expenditure for security for the costs in a federal case. *State ex rel. Reynolds v. Smith* (1963). A statute that allows the attorney general to litigate to restrain corporations from performing acts that were outside the authority that their charter grants, or to restrain individuals from exercising corporate rights, privileges, or franchises not authorized by law, does not allow the attorney general to seek an injunction to prevent recounting the votes in a referendum because the board of canvassers was improperly constituted. *State ex rel. Haven v. Sayle* (1918). Municipalities are corporations, so the statute had some relevance, but the municipality had the right to canvass votes, so the first part of the statute did not apply. Although it might be argued that the individuals who wrongfully performed the canvassing had improperly exercised a corporation's privilege, the court held that the statute was too narrow to allow the attorney general to intervene in the case.

Although the attorney general has statutory authority to enforce public trusts, he or she does not have the authority to intervene in a probate proceeding in order to exercise that authority. *Estate of Sharp* (1974). Occasionally, the court has more broadly interpreted the attorney general's powers. An example is allowing press releases, if they do not interfere with the defendant's rights, based upon the statutory authority to investigate crime. *State v. Woodington* (1966). The other side of the coin is that, if a statute requires the attorney general to perform a duty, the holder of that office has no quasi-judicial authority to weigh the merits of the situation and decline to perform that duty. *State v. Coubal* (1946).

The attorney general's powers and duties are not quite as limited as a literal reading of this section suggests. Many statutes grant powers or impose duties about particular kinds of cases or activities. Under the authority of a statute, Wis. Stat. § 165.25(3), the attorney general, or much more often, one of the assistant attorneys general, appears in circuit court (the lowest Wisconsin court) if a district attorney asks for assistance. Also, a general statute requires the attorney general to represent the state if the governor or either house of the legislature so requests, Wis. Stat. § 165.25(1). Although this statute is framed in mandatory terms, occasionally an attorney general has declined to defend a statute that he or she thinks is unconstitutional. Moreover, in a few cases, the court expanded the attorney general's powers beyond those that can be asserted based upon a literal reading of this section. An example is allowing the attorney general to represent the state on his or her own initiative in a case in which the supreme court exercises its original jurisdiction. See *State ex rel. Warren v. Reuter* (1969). Still, more recently, in *State v. City of Oak Creek* (2000), when the attorney general initiated a lawsuit to declare a statute unconstitutional, the court held that the attorney general has no inherent constitutional authority to initiate a lawsuit; his or her powers are only those prescribed by statute.

Section 4
County officers; election; terms; removal; vacancies.

(1) (a) Except as provided in pars. (b) and (c) and sub. (2), coroners, registers of deeds, district attorneys, and all other elected county officers, except judicial officers, sheriffs, and chief executive officers, shall be chosen by the electors of the respective counties once in every 2 years.

(b) Beginning with the first general election at which the governor is elected which occurs after the ratification of this paragraph, sheriffs shall be chosen by the electors of the respective counties, or by the electors of all of the respective counties comprising each combination of counties combined by the legislature for that purpose, for the term of 4 years and coroners in counties in which there is a coroner shall be chosen by the electors of the respective counties, or by the electors of all of the respective counties comprising each combination of counties combined by the legislature for that purpose, for the term of 4 years.

(c) Beginning with the first general election at which the president is elected which occurs after the ratification of this paragraph, district attorneys, registers of deeds, county clerks, and treasurers shall be chosen by the electors of the respective counties, or by the electors of all of the respective counties comprising each combination of counties combined by the legislature for that purpose, for the term of 4 years and surveyors in counties in which the office of surveyor is filled by election shall be chosen by the electors of the respective counties, or by the electors of all of the respective counties comprising each combination of counties combined by the legislature for that purpose, for the term of 4 years.

(2) The offices of coroner and surveyor in counties having a population of 500,000 or more are abolished. Counties not having a population of 500,000 shall have the option of retaining the elective office of coroner or instituting a medical examiner system. Two or more counties may institute a joint medical examiner system.

(3) (a) Sheriffs may not hold any other partisan office.

(b) Sheriffs may be required by law to renew their security from time to time, and in default of giving such new security their office shall be deemed vacant.

(4) The governor may remove any elected county officer mentioned in this section except a county clerk, treasurer, or surveyor, giving to the officer a copy of the charges and an opportunity of being heard.

(5) All vacancies in the offices of coroner, register of deeds or district attorney shall be filled by appointment. The person appointed to fill a vacancy shall hold office only for the unexpired portion of the term to which appointed and until a successor shall be elected and qualified.

(6) When a vacancy occurs in the office of sheriff, the vacancy shall be filled by appointment of the governor, and the person appointed shall serve until his or her successor is elected and qualified.

This section has been amended nine times. Several of the amendments make some of the case law irrelevant. In its original form, this section established two-year terms for sheriffs, coroners, registers of deeds, and district attorneys; forbade sheriffs from holding other offices and forbade them from holding the office of sheriff again within two years after their term expired and required them to renew their security; absolved counties from responsibility for their sheriffs' acts; and allowed the governor to remove any of the officers listed in this section. In 1882, this section was amended to establish two-year terms for all county officers except judicial officers and specified that all vacancies were to be filled by appointment (presumably by the governor). At that time, a statute allowed the governor to fill vacancies in the office of sheriff by appointment, and it was held to be constitutional. *Sprague and others v. Brown* (1876). A 1929 amendment deleted the prohibition against sheriffs succeeding themselves and replaced it with a two-term limit. An amendment that was ratified in 1962 exempted chief executive officers from the two-term limit. A 1965 amendment abolished the offices of coroner and surveyor in counties with a population of 500,000 or more (then and now only Milwaukee County). In 1967, the two-term limit that applied to sheriffs was eliminated. In 1972 counties that had a population of less than 500,000 were given the option of electing a coroner, hiring a medical examiner, or, with one or more other counties, appointing a joint medical examiner. The current version is the product of an amendment that was ratified in 1982 and limits the governor's power to remove officers to elected officers, and limits the offices that are to be filled by appointment to: sheriff, coroner, register of deeds, and district attorney. In addition to subsection 4(4) of this article, Article IV, Section 8; Article VII, Sections 1, 11, and 13; and Article XIII, Section 12, provide for removal of officials. This section was amended in 1995 to allow sheriffs to serve four-year terms, and in 2005 to allow county clerks to serve four-year terms.

Nearly all of the cases dealing with the sheriff's powers involve labor disputes with deputy sheriffs' unions. Although most of the relevant cases are on sheriffs' powers, two of them clarify other issues. The governor's power to appoint officials under subsection (5) does not apply to vacancies that occur because the winner of an election has died before his or her term begins, because that appointment would be for a full term, not for the "unexpired portion of the term." *State v. Roden* (1935). The governor, under subsection (4), may remove officers only for cause; otherwise the will of the voters could be foiled and the requirements of giving to the officer a copy of the charges and affording the officer an opportunity to be heard would make no sense. *State ex rel. Rodd v. Verage* (1922).

This section says nothing about the duties of sheriffs or of any of the other officers that it mentions. However, courts have held not only that sheriffs have certain duties that may not be taken from them, but that those duties have a constitutional status. The best way to elucidate this doctrine is to trace its development chronologically. Custody of the jail and its prisoners may not be taken from the sheriff, because "there can be no doubt that the framers of the constitution had reference to the office with those generally recognized legal duties and functions belonging to it in this country, and in the territory, when the constitution was adopted," so to strip the sheriff of those duties would be to deprive the voters of their right to elect a sheriff. *State ex rel. Kennedy v. Brunst* (1870). However, among the sheriff's common-law duties, only "those immemorial principal and important duties that characterized and distinguished the office" have constitutional protection, and, although "at common law the sheriff possessed the power to appoint deputies, it was not a power or authority that gave character and distinction to the office," so a civil service law prevailed over a sheriff's appointment authority. *State ex rel. Milwaukee County v. Buech* (1920).

The issue of the sheriff's duties lay dormant for several decades. Then the supreme court held that a sheriff had a special relationship with the courts under the common law, and it sent a case back to the trial court to identify the duties of the sheriff's deputy who was appointed to be the "court officer" so that that court could determine whether the special relationship authorized the sheriff to appoint that officer without regard to civil service laws. *Professional Police Ass'n v. Dane County* (1989). A sheriff may contract with the U.S. Marshals Service for transportation of prisoners to the state, despite a collective bargaining agreement, because attendance upon the court is one of the sheriff's constitutional duties. *Professional Police Ass'n v. Dane County* (1989). By the time it decided *Professional Police Ass'n*, the court had gone well beyond this section's literal meaning—it had created constitutionally protected duties of sheriffs and had specified a test—albeit a somewhat vague one—for determining which duties enjoy that protection.

In the next case concerning this section the court held that the appointment of an undercover agent, notwithstanding a collective bargaining agreement, was unconstitutional because that agent would assist the sheriff in enforcing the law, preserving the peace, and investigating crimes, which are not constitutional prerogatives of a sheriff, as they were duties that, under the common law, were not exclusively those of the sheriff. *Manitowoc County v. Local 986B* (1992). That case further obscured the interpretation of this section by introducing the test of exclusivity.

Notwithstanding *Manitowoc County*, a sheriff may enter into a contract with law enforcement personnel from outside the county to augment the sheriff's department in an emergency, notwithstanding a collective bargaining agreement, because maintaining law and order are among the sheriff's constitutionally protected duties. *Washington County v. Deputy Sheriffs' Ass'n* (1995). In the next case, the court doubled back to a more restrictive view of sheriffs' authority in personnel matters, a view congruent with that of *State ex rel. Milwaukee County v. Buech* (1920), holding that a sheriff may not refuse to reappoint a deputy contrary to the civil service laws, because that refusal had no constitutional basis. *Heitkemper v. Wirsig* (1995). An arbitrator's award of reinstatement of a sheriff's employee does not conflict with a sheriff's constitutional duties. *Brown Cty. Sheriff's Dept. v. Employees Ass'n* (1995).

The court has settled on the test in *Buech*. In a case involving the provision of food service to jail inmates by a private contractor, the court stated that the test of whether a duty is constitutionally protected (and thus beyond the reach of collective bargaining) is simple to state but difficult to apply: "certain immemorial, principal, and important duties of the sheriff at common law that are peculiar to the office of sheriff and that characterize and distinguish the office" cannot be altered by the legislature or made subject to collective bargaining agreements. The court decided that provision of food to inmates is not such a constitutional duty, allowing the job action to go forward. *Kocken v. Wisconsin Council 40* (2007).

The same sheriff later contracted for the interstate transportation of prisoners, mental patients, and juveniles, again giving rise to a labor dispute. The union argued that the contract was for "mundane and commonplace" services that are not constitutionally protected. The court of appeals held that interstate transportation of prisoners fell within the constitutionally protected duty of attending to the court, granting declaratory judgment to the sheriff and the county. *Brown County Sheriff's Department Non-Supervisory Labor Association v. Brown County* (2009).

When Washington County built a new justice center, the county board asked the sheriff to supply two deputies to staff X-ray and metal detector machines at the entrance. Due to the board's budget concerns, the sheriff reduced his proposal from hiring two full-time deputies to hiring two part-time special deputies, who would not be union members. The deputies association filed a grievance. The court of appeals held that appointing special deputies to staff a metal detector is not one of the sheriff's immemorial, principal, and important duties and therefore the hiring was a grievable issue. *Washington County v. Washington County Deputy Sheriff's Association* (2009).

A sheriff does not have constitutional authority to hire as many deputies as he or she sees fit as long as he or she is able to perform the constitutional duties of the office by using overtime. *Milwaukee Deputy Sheriff's Ass'n. v. Milwaukee County* (2016).

Article VII

Judiciary

Section 1
Impeachment; trial.

The court for the trial of impeachments shall be composed of the senate. The assembly shall have the power of impeaching all civil officers of this state for corrupt conduct in office, or for crimes and misdemeanors; but a majority of all the members elected shall concur in an impeachment. On the trial of an impeachment against the governor, the lieutenant governor shall not act as a member of the court. No judicial officer shall exercise his office, after he shall have been impeached, until his acquittal. Before the trial of an impeachment the members of the court shall take an oath or affirmation truly and impartially to try the impeachment according to evidence; and no person shall be convicted without the concurrence of two-thirds of the members present. Judgment in cases of impeachment shall not extend further than to removal from office, or removal from office and disqualification to hold any office of honor, profit or trust under the state; but the party impeached shall be liable to indictment, trial and punishment according to law.

Although this section applies to the impeachment of all civil officers, it appears in the article on the judiciary. Article VII, Section 11 provides for removal of judges and justices, and Section 13 creates a less formal method for removing judges and justices; Article IV, Section 8 authorizes expulsion of legislators; Article VI, Section 4(4) authorizes the governor to remove county officers; and Article XIII, Section 12, specifies the procedures for recalling state, congressional, judicial, legislative, and county officers. This section's only amendment, in 1932, changed "house of representatives" to "assembly" at the beginning of the second sentence. This change merely corrected an error: Article IV, Section 1 has always vested the legislative power in a senate and assembly. This section's grant of the power to remove an official does not preclude imposing less severe sanctions. *In re Honorable Charles E. Kading* (1975).

The supreme court has the inherent power to ensure that the judiciary has funds to maintain the state court system, and it will exercise this power only upon the highest standard of proof of an articulated and compelling need. *Flynn v. Department of Administration* (1998).

Section 2
Court system.

The judicial power of this state shall be vested in a unified court system consisting of one Supreme Court, a court of appeals, a circuit court, such trial courts of general uniform statewide jurisdiction as the legislature may create by law, and a municipal court if authorized by the legislature under section 14.

This section establishes the third of the three branches of government. Its original version required the creation of, and vested the judicial power of the state in, a supreme court, circuit courts, courts of probate, and justices of the peace, and allowed the legislature to create municipal courts and inferior (lower) county courts. A 1966 amendment allowed inferior courts to be formed also in cities, towns, and villages. The current version was added as part of the 1977 revision of this article.

By vesting the judicial power in a system of courts, this section implicitly grants certain powers to the courts. The connection between a court's existence and its possession of certain basic powers is both ancient and logical:

from time immemorial certain powers have been conceded to courts because they are courts. Such powers have been conceded because without them they could neither maintain their dignity, transact their business, nor accomplish the purpose of their existence. These powers are called inherent powers. *In re Court Room* (1912).

These powers are also sometimes called "incidental," "implied," or "inherent," all of which have the same meaning. *State v. Cannon* (1928). A court inherently has these powers "to protect itself against any action that would unreasonably curtail its powers or materially impair its efficiency." *In re Court Room.*

Although courts do not always refer to this section when they exercise their inherent powers, this section is the basis of those powers. Among the powers are: appointing special prosecutors, *State v. Lloyd* (1981); determining the compensation of court-appointed attorneys, *State ex rel. Friedrich v. Circuit Court for*

Dane County (1995); disbarring attorneys, *State v. Cannon* (1928); appointing employees, *In re Janitor of Supreme Court* (1874), *Stevenson v. Milwaukee County* (1909); deciding on the location of a courtroom, *In re Court Room* (1912); punishing for contempt of court to preserve order, *State ex rel. Rodd v. Verage* (1922); inquiring into attorneys' professional conduct, *Rubin v. State* (1927); ordering installation of air conditioning in a courtroom, *State ex rel. Reynolds v. County Court* (1960); and demanding funds for a computerized research system, *State ex rel. Moran v. Dept. of Admin.* (1981). These inherent powers are subject to the limits of the constitution. *In re Cannon* (1932); *Jacobson v. Avestruz* (1977). In exercising them, a court may not extend its jurisdiction. *Jacobson.* Statutes may regulate some of the courts' inherent powers. *Kenosha Unified School District v. Kenosha Education Association* (1975). A court may decline to exercise an inherent power. *Moran.*

The following powers are not inherent: dismissing a criminal case before jeopardy attaches, *State v. Braunsdorf* (1980); ordering that the records in juvenile proceedings be expunged, *In Interest of E. C.* (1986); imposing regulations, in addition to those that statutes impose, on the privilege of operating a motor vehicle, *State v. Darling* (1988); and requiring the parties in a case to pay a penalty to the court if they fail to settle a case before a trial begins, *State ex rel. Collins v. American Family Mut. Ins. Co.* (1990).

The three branches of state government are not hermetically sealed but frequently interact. These interactions create difficult cases in which courts must determine whether one branch has unconstitutionally intruded into another branch's territory. Revocation of probation is one example. By assigning revocation of probation hearings to the executive branch, the legislature did not intrude upon the judiciary's core function and therefore did not violate this section. *State v. Horn* (1999). Issuance of a search warrant is not an exercise of the judicial power under this section. *State v. Williams* (2012).

A court does not have the inherent power to order a default judgment against a party who is represented by counsel but who fails to appear personally in court. *City of Sun Prairie v. Davis* (1999). But a court has the inherent power to determine if a party to a lawsuit is trying to defraud the court by coaching a witness to lie, and the court has the power to hold a hearing on the issue, to sanction the offending party, and even to dismiss the case. *Schultz v. Sykes* (2001).

The judicial branch has exclusive authority over some issues, although a court may choose not to assert its authority and to abide by a statute. *State ex rel. Reynolds v. Dinger* (1961). Conversely, the judicial branch will not interfere with certain kinds of legislative actions or with certain kinds of decisions that ought to be addressed by the legislature. Federal courts often refer to the latter kind of issues as "political questions," and the federal case law on this issue is quite extensive. The case law in Wisconsin, however, is meager. One of the few Wisconsin cases on this issue cogently summarizes the court's position:

> [T]his court will not interfere with the conduct of legislative affairs in the absence of a constitutional mandate to do so or unless either its procedure or end result constitutes a deprivation of constitutionally guaranteed rights. Short of such deprivations which give this court jurisdiction, recourse against legislative errors, nonfeasance, or questionable procedure is by political action only. (*Outagamie County v. Smith* (1968))

More problematical are issues that lie in the "great borderlands of power which may be said to approach nearer and nearer until they merge gradually into each other." *In re Appointment of Revisor* (1910). By far the majority of conflicts are between the judicial and legislative branches. In this area of shared responsibility, statutory regulation is "subject to [the] court's authority to preserve the integrity of the judicial system and to preserve the integrity of the doctrine of the separation of powers." *State v. Holmes* (1982). That is, legislation may not unreasonably or substantially interfere with the judicial system. *State v. Unnamed Defendant* (1989). An interference of this type must be proved beyond a reasonable doubt, the standard that applies to most challenges to statutes' constitutionality. *Holmes.*

One can get some idea of these principles by analyzing examples. A rule of the Real Estate Brokers' Board that allowed brokers to give legal advice and to provide certain legal services unconstitutionally intruded on the judicial branch's authority to regulate the practice of law, but the court acquiesced because the practice was salutary. *State ex rel. Reynolds v. Dinger* (1961). A statute establishing time limits within which judges must decide cases and requiring judges to supply affidavits about the handling of their caseloads was a constitutional exercise of the legislature's authority to ensure that the courts operate efficiently and effectively, but a statute that authorizes withholding of a judge's salary for failing to decide cases within a specified time period is unconstitutional. *In Matter of Complaint Against Grady* (1984). The power to appoint the Revisor of Statutes, a position that at the time was within the judicial branch, may be shared. *In re Appointment of Revisor* (1910). Criminal sentencing is a shared responsibility, so the legislature may delegate to the courts the power to decide eligibility for parole. *State v. Borrell* (1992). Regulation of bail is a shared responsibility—the legislature's interest in ensuring a fair judicial system gives it some authority in this area—so the Wisconsin Judicial Conference's bail schedule is unconstitutional because it does not conform to the statute that authorized the commission to write the schedule. *Demmith v. Wisconsin Judicial Conference* (1992). A statute that allows the Patients' Compensation Board to determine damages in medical malpractice cases does not unconstitutionally intrude on the judicial branch because its awards are subject to judicial review. *State ex rel. Strykowski v. Wilkie* (1978). A statute that requires jury instructions to be written is constitutional, but the statute is not to be interpreted to require dismissal of a case because of the nonfulfillment of this requirement; that would be an unconstitutional intrusion into the judiciary's domain. *In Matter of E. B.* (1983). A statute may regulate a court's power to enforce its orders. *Upper Great Lakes Shipping v. Seafarers' I. Union* (1963).

The court held in *State ex rel. Two Unnamed Petitioners v. Peterson* (2015) that a judge can only appoint a special prosecutor in a John Doe investigation if certain statutory conditions are met. A John Doe investigation, which is defined by statute, functions like a grand jury, but is administered by a judge. The dissent noted that judges have the inherent power to appoint a special prosecutor and under the separation of powers doctrine, this power cannot be limited by the legislature. The court held in *Gabler v. Crime Victims Rights Board* (2016) that the legislature cannot create an executive-branch board with the authority to discipline judges. Citing to its authority under this section, the court in *Tetra Tech EC v. Wisconsin D.O.R.* (2018) ended its practice of deferring to administrative agencies' conclusions of law.

Section 3
Supreme court: jurisdiction.

(1) The supreme court shall have superintending and administrative authority over all courts.

(2) The supreme court has appellate jurisdiction over all courts and may hear original actions and proceedings, the supreme court may issue all writs necessary in aid of its jurisdiction.

(3) The supreme court may review judgments and orders of the court of appeals, may remove cases from the court of appeals and may accept cases on certification by the court of appeals.

This section's original version gave the supreme court appellate jurisdiction only, superintending control over other courts, and the authority to issue the writs of *habeas corpus, mandamus, injunction, quo warranto,* and *certiorari* and other original and remedial writs. As part of the revision of this article in 1977, this section was amended to give the supreme court administrative authority over other courts (in addition to superintending authority); to give it, in addition to its appellate jurisdiction, original jurisdiction; authorized it to issue all writs; and added the current subsection (3), which reflects that revision's creation of courts of appeals.

Its superintending authority allows the supreme court to limit lower courts' freedom of action. It is based upon the superintending power of the King's Bench in England. *State ex rel. Fourth Nat. Bank v. Johnson* (1899). It is not be used lightly or when other remedies exist; rather, it will be used to prevent irreparable mischief or great hardship. *Petition of Phelan* (1937). Its purpose is "to protect the legal rights of litigants when the ordinary processes of action, appeal and review are inadequate," and in order for the supreme court to exercise this power there must be a clear legal right at stake, the lower court must have a duty to act, the rights to appeal and to petition for a writ of error must be inadequate, the situation must be exigent, and the litigant must be at risk of grave hardship. *State ex rel. Department of Agriculture v. Aarons* (1946). The supreme court has superintending authority over the lower courts but not over quasi-judicial officers who are part of the executive branch of government. *Guthrie v. WERC* (1983).

The supreme court may use its superintending authority to "control the course of litigation in all of the other courts of this state." *State ex rel. Hustisford L., P. & M. Co. v. Grimm* (1932). For example, the supreme court may order a lower court to refrain from conducting further proceedings in a case that is also being heard in a federal court in another state. *Petition of Phelan* (1937). Under this authority, the supreme court may promulgate and enforce a Code of Judicial Ethics. *In re Honorable Charles E. Kading* (1975); *State ex rel. Lynch v. Dancey* (1976). Despite a statute that makes a particular order nonappealable, the supreme court may use this authority to hear a case in which a lower court has issued that kind of order. *McEwen v. Pierce County* (1979). Although circuit courts have under Article VII, Section 8 "original jurisdiction in all matters civil and criminal," the supreme court may use its superintending authority to direct circuit courts not to take jurisdiction to order sterilization of persons who are incapable of giving informed consent to that procedure. *In Matter of Guardianship of Eberhardy* (1981). The supreme court has refrained from using this authority to impose felony sentencing guidelines on trial courts, *In re Felony Sentencing Guidelines* (1983), and to create a recourse for a litigant who has no right to appeal a refusal to appoint condemnation commissioners, *Aarons*.

The supreme court exercised its supervisory authority under subsection 3(1) to prohibit circuit courts from issuing orders of reference—referring issues in a case to a referee—that are subject to only an "erroneous-exercise-of-discretion" review by the circuit court, because such orders delegate judicial power to a nonjudicial officer in violation of subsection 3(2). *State ex rel. Universal Processing Servs. of Wis. LLC v. Circuit Court of Milwaukee Cty.* (2017).

The court has the power to remove a justice permanently but cannot prevent a justice from hearing an individual proceeding on a case-by-case basis. *State v. Henley* (2011).

The supreme court's administrative authority differs from its superintending authority. The former power relates to workload and funding; the latter power has to do with substantive legal issues. Because the supreme court has administrative authority, circuit courts may not purport to exercise such authority to dismiss claims in order to alleviate their case load. *State v. Halverson* (1986). Similarly, a circuit court may not refuse to accept a case the venue of which had been changed to it. *Schroeder v. Register Pub. Corp.* (1985). The court's administrative authority includes the authority to approve a budget for the use of its funds; therefore, the refusal of the Secretary of Administration to issue a warrant under Article IV, Section 33 for one of its expenses violated this section, although because of certain circumstances the supreme court did not order the warrant to be issued. *State ex rel. Moran v. Dept. of Admin.* (1981). A statute that denies payment of the salary of a judge who fails to decide cases within the statutory time limits violates this section because it intrudes upon the supreme court's administrative authority. *In Matter of Complaint Against Grady* (1984).

Jurisdiction "includes not only jurisdiction over persons and subject matter but power to render a particular form of judgment." *Reburg v. Lang* (1942). The 1977 amendment that granted original jurisdiction to the supreme court mooted many early decisions about that court's ability to assert that kind of jurisdiction. The nature and scope of the supreme court's appellate jurisdiction is still a live issue. Regarding both kinds of jurisdiction, the court may either take or decline to take jurisdiction. One concern in deciding whether to take original jurisdiction is whether the case pertains to the people of the state as a whole. *State ex rel. Wisconsin Senate v. Thompson* (1988). If facts need to be established to decide the case, the court probably will not take original jurisdiction because of its limited capacity to determine facts.

Upon appeal to it, the supreme court assumes virtually total control over the case:

> In order to ensure the orderly administration of justice and to prevent the trial court from doing anything that might adversely affect the rights and interests of the parties to the appeal, the general rule is that an appeal from a judgment or order strips the trial court of jurisdiction with respect to the subject matter of the judgment or order, except as to certain unsubstantial and trivial matters, and the supreme court then has jurisdiction until the determination of the appeal. However, in matters not directly concerned with the appeal but still a part of the case, the trial court may properly retain its jurisdiction. (*Hunter v. Hunter* (1969))

In exercising its appellate jurisdiction, the supreme court usually will not consider factual matters that the parties did not raise in the pleadings or during the trial. *Chrome Plating Co. v. Wisconsin Electric Power Co.* (1942). The supreme court, however, will take judicial notice of facts, which is "informing itself in regard to the pertinent facts which are matters of common knowledge." *Ritholz v. Johnson* (1944). In general, the supreme court's review of factual issues is narrow. In exercising its appellate jurisdiction, the supreme court decides whether the lower court judge made errors or misinterpreted the applicable law. In exercising this jurisdiction, the court may not make findings or issue orders or judgments based on them. *Estate of Bray* (1950). On appeal, the court may review issues that are moot if those issues are of great public importance, the constitutionality of a statute is challenged, or the situation arises frequently. *Ziemann v. Village of North Hudson* (1981).

The other main issue concerning this section is the supreme court's authority to issue writs. Two writs are pertinent to this section because they have special applicability to the supreme court. One is a means by which the supreme court may acquire jurisdiction over a matter. The writ of *certiorari* is an order directing a lower court or another entity that has made a quasi-judicial decision to send the record to the court that issued the writ so that the latter court may act on the case. In addition to decisions of lower courts, decisions of local officials, *State ex rel. Oelke v. Doepke* (1952), and of administrative agencies, *State ex rel. Beierle v. Civil Service Comm.* (1969), are reviewable by *certiorari*. A court may issue this writ if there is no statutory mechanism for judicial review. *Marquette Savings & Loan Asso. v. Twin Lakes* (1968); *State ex rel. Oelke v. Doepke* (1952).

Wisconsin courts have disagreed about the scope of appellate review when the issue is an administrative body's decision. Issues have included whether the order or decision under review was within the jurisdiction of the body that issued it; whether it was according to law; whether it was arbitrary, oppressive, or unreasonable and therefore represented the body's will rather than its judgment; and whether there is sufficient evidence to make the order or determination questionable. *State ex rel. Wasilewski v. Board of School Directors* (1961); *State ex rel. Ball v. McPhee* (1959). As well there are the questions whether the body had jurisdiction and the power to make the order or determination, *State ex rel. Badtke v. Civil Service Comm.* (1969), or whether there is sufficient evidence to demonstrate that the order or determination could reasonably have been made, *State ex rel. Beierle v. Civil Service Comm.* (1969).

The writ of prohibition—an order directing a lower court to refrain from acting—is the other writ that is pertinent to this section, because the supreme court uses it in exercising its superintending and administrative powers over the courts. *Petition of Phelan* (1937). The court will issue this writ if a lower court has exceeded its jurisdiction or inflicted extraordinary or exceptional hardship on a party. *Id.* The supreme court also may issue a writ of prohibition if a lower court has jurisdiction to proceed but should not do so; for example, if the case should be tried in another state. *State ex rel. Goldwyn D. Corp. v. Gehrz* (1923). Conversely, the supreme court will not issue a writ of prohibition if the lower court acted within its jurisdiction, violated no rights, and did not abuse its discretion. *State ex rel. Kowaleski v. District Court* (1949). The court may also refrain from issuing this writ if the party who requests it has another remedy, such as an appeal. *State ex rel. Pardeeville Electric Light Co. v. Sachtjen* (1944). The supreme court issued this writ after a trial court imposed a time limit to serve a summons and a complaint even though the pertinent statute did not provide for one. *State ex rel. Conners v. Zimmerman* (1930). It also issued this writ after a trial judge overruled objections to the service of summons and the party aggrieved by the summons could not appear to object because that would constitute a waiver of the trial court's lack of jurisdiction. *State ex rel. Oak Park Country Club v. Goodland* (1943).

As a superintending court, the supreme court has ruled that it has the power to require the court of appeals to certify a question to the supreme court when confronted by a precedent in Wisconsin law that conflicts with subsequent U.S.

Supreme Court precedent. But the court declined to promulgate such a rule, noting that the court of appeals is required by the Supremacy Clause to follow the federal precedent anyway, and it still may certify questions as it sees fit. *State v. Jennings* (2002).

Citing subsection (3), the court announced in *In re Jerrell C.J.* (2005) that custodial interrogations of juveniles may not be introduced in evidence unless they are tape-recorded. Exercising its superintending authority, the court held in *Koschkee v. Evers* (2018) that the superintendent of public instruction is not required to be represented by the department of justice, but is entitled to choose his or her own legal counsel.

Section 4
Supreme court: election, chief justice, court system administration.

(1) The supreme court shall have 7 members who shall be known as justices of the supreme court. Justices shall be elected for 10-year terms of office commencing with the August 1 next succeeding the election. Only one justice may be elected in any year. Any 4 justices shall constitute a quorum for the conduct of the court's business.

(2) The chief justice of the supreme court shall be elected for a term of 2 years by a majority of the justices then serving on the court. The justice so designated as chief justice may, irrevocably, decline to serve as chief justice or resign as chief justice but continue to serve as a justice of the supreme court.

(3) The chief justice of the supreme court shall be the administrative head of the judicial system and shall exercise this administrative authority pursuant to procedures adopted by the supreme court. The chief justice may assign any judge of a court of record to aid in the proper disposition of judicial business in any court of record except the supreme court.

The original version of this section provided that the circuit court judges also constituted the supreme court for at least five years. After that period elapsed, the legislature could provide otherwise and, specifically, could create a separate supreme court that consisted of three justices. If the legislature created a separate supreme court, it could not change or dissolve it later, and it could reduce the number of circuit courts, but in so doing could not shorten any circuit court judge's term of office. In 1877, an amendment increasing the size of the supreme court to five and setting its members' term of office at ten years was ratified (by that time the legislature had established a separate supreme court). An 1889 amendment deleted a transitional provision in the 1877 amendment and specified that the supreme court justices had the same terms of office as they then had. That amendment also renumbered this section. In 1963, the ten-year term was explicitly specified by an amendment that also increased the number of justices to seven and provided that no more than one may be elected during any year. During 1977, as part of a substantial rewriting of this article to reform the court system, this section was renumbered back to 4, and added provisions stating that the term of office begins on August 1, and a justice who was eligible to be the chief justice might decline the position. The most important part of the amendment created subsection (3), which makes the chief justice the administrative head of the judicial system. This section was amended in 2015 to provide that the chief justice shall be elected by the members of the court. Previously, this section designated the senior member of the court as chief justice.

In only one case has this section been litigated directly. In *State ex rel. Moran v. Dept. of Admin.* (1981), the court determined that the Director of State Courts, an agent of the supreme court and thus an official to whom had been delegated some of the supreme court's authority to administer the judicial system, was entitled to a warrant (see the discussion of Art. IV, Sec. 33) to spend funds that had been set aside for the court system. In earlier cases the courts' inherent judicial authority under Article VII, Section 2 had been held to include the right to receive adequate funding. E.g., *In re Janitor of Supreme Court* (1874); *In re Court of Appeals of Wisconsin* (1978). Ratification of the amendment that added subsection (3) more definitely established the judiciary's entitlement to adequate funding.

Section 5
Court of appeals.

(1) The legislature shall by law combine the judicial circuits of the state into one or more districts for the court of appeals and shall designate in each district the locations where the appeals court shall sit for the convenience of litigants.

(2) For each district of the appeals court there shall be chosen by the qualified electors of the district one or more appeals judges as prescribed by law, who shall sit as prescribed by law. Appeals judges shall be elected for 6-year terms and shall reside in the district from which elected. No alteration of district or circuit boundaries shall have the effect of removing an appeals judge from office during the judge's term. In case of an increase in the number of appeals judges, the first judge or judges shall be elected for full terms unless the legislature prescribes a shorter initial term for staggering of terms.

(3) The appeals court shall have such appellate jurisdiction in the district, including jurisdiction to review administrative proceedings, as the legislature may provide by law, but shall have no original jurisdiction other than by prerogative writ. The appeals court may issue all writs necessary in aid of its jurisdiction and shall have supervisory authority over all actions and proceedings in the courts in the district.

This section, which authorizes the creation of a court of appeals, like much of the current version of Article VII, was ratified in 1977 as a prelude to reform of the judicial system. Subsection (1) interposes another level between the circuit courts and the Wisconsin Supreme Court, thus reducing the supreme court's workload. Prerogative writs (orders) include the writ of *procedendo* (an order by a higher court sending a case back to a lower court that is to begin proceedings on it), the writ of *mandamus* (an order addressed to an official requiring the performance of an action), the writ of *prohibition* (an order to a lower court to refrain from exercising its jurisdiction; the court of appeals' right to supervise the lower courts in their districts justifies issuing this writ), the writ of *quo warranto* (an order to demonstrate a person's, including a corporation's, right to a franchise, power, or office), the writ of *habeas corpus* (an order to show the reason why someone is held in custody), and the writ of *certiorari* (an order to a lower court or other tribunal to turn over the record of a case so that a higher court can begin proceedings on it).

The court of appeals may issue only the writs that the court's appellate or supervisory jurisdiction justifies. *State ex rel. Swan v. Elections Bd.* (1986). It may issue an injunction only if it has original jurisdiction or if it has supervisory jurisdiction over another decision-making body, and it does not have supervisory jurisdiction over an administrative agency *Swan*. It may issue a writ of *mandamus* to a circuit court, because of its supervisory authority over that court, to require that court to permit inspection of its records. *State ex rel. Journal v. Jennings* (1987).

The court of appeals has supervisory authority over juvenile courts, which are branches of the circuit courts. *In Interest of Peter B.* (1994). The court of appeals' authority over the assignment of cases by the chief judges of circuit courts is unclear because of conflicting decisions. In one case the court of appeals ordered a chief judge to assign companion cases to the same circuit court judge. *United Pac. Ins. Co. v. Met. Sewerage Comm.* (1983). And, in another case, the court of appeals held that it had no authority to issue a writ of *mandamus* to effect a substitution of judges, that decision being administrative rather than related to the "actions and proceedings" over which the court of appeals has supervisory power. *State ex rel. Gilboy v. Waukesha Circuit Ct.* (1984).

A party in circuit court may petition the court of appeals for a supervisory writ, which gives the court of appeals control over the case. However, supervisory writs may only be used in extraordinary cases and cannot be used as a substitute for the normal appeals process. The court of appeals may issue a supervisory writ only if "(1) an appeal is an inadequate remedy; (2) grave hardship or irreparable harm will result; (3) the duty of the trial court is plain and it must have acted or intends to act in violation of that duty; and (4) the request for relief is made promptly and speedily." *State ex rel. Kalal v. Circuit Court* (2004).

Section 6
Circuit court: boundaries.

The legislature shall prescribe by law the number of judicial circuits, making them as compact and convenient as practicable, and bounding them by county lines. No alteration of circuit boundaries shall have the effect of removing a circuit judge from office during the judge's term. In case of an increase of circuits, the first judge or judges shall be elected.

This section was amended once, in 1977, as part of the rewriting of this article to effect court reform. Most of the changes were stylistic, but the amendment also deleted a provision guaranteeing that judges in newly formed circuits would receive a salary at least as high as that of the other circuit court judges. Only a few cases pertain to this section. In the most important, *State ex rel. Pierce v. Kundert* (1958), the court held unconstitutional a statute that provided that one person be the circuit court judge, county judge, small claims court judge, and juvenile judge for a county that was removed from its circuit, and that the individual receive a lower salary and have a shorter term of office than other circuit court judges. This case illustrates the fact that phrases such as "the legislature shall provide by law," which appears in this section, do not grant absolute power to the legislature to do as it pleases regarding the subject matter to which they refer.

Section 7
Circuit court: election.

For each circuit there shall be chosen by qualified electors thereof one or more circuit judges as prescribed by law. Circuit judges shall be elected for 6-year terms and shall reside in the circuit from which elected.

This section originally required that circuit court judges be elected and reside in the district where they served, required designation of one circuit court judge as chief judge (originally the circuit court judges also constituted the supreme court); provided for staggered terms and then specified that, when the first set of the staggered terms was completed, the terms were to be six years. An amendment ratified in 1897 allowed the legislature to authorize additional circuit court judges in circuits composed of only one county if that county has a population of at least 100,000. That amendment also allowed the legislature to set the circuit court judges' term of office. A 1924 amendment allowed the legislature to provide for more than one circuit court judge in a circuit composed of only one county if that county had a population of more than 85,000. The 1977 revision of this article sets the term of office, but the legislature, not the constitution, now sets the number of judges in each circuit.

The requirement that each circuit court judge reside in the circuit for which he or she was elected, which has been in this section since 1848, also means that each of them must reside, at the time of his or her election, in the circuit for which he or she is to serve. *State v. Messmore* (1861).

Section 8
Circuit court: jurisdiction.

Except as otherwise provided by law, the circuit court shall have original jurisdiction in all matters civil and criminal within this state and such appellate jurisdiction in the circuit as the legislature may prescribe by law. The circuit court may issue all writs necessary in aid of its jurisdiction.

This section's original version allowed the jurisdiction of circuit courts to be reduced by statute, and it gave the circuit courts supervisory authority over lower courts. It also bestowed on the circuit courts the power to issue the writs of *habeas corpus* (ordering a person to be brought before the court in order to determine whether he or she was being lawfully detained), *mandamus* (ordering an official to perform an act), *certiorari* (ordering a lower court to send the record of its proceedings in a case to a higher court so that the latter may decide the case), and all other writs that were necessary for circuit courts to "effect their orders, judgments and decrees, and give them a general control over inferior courts and jurisdictions." The 1977 amendment that extensively revised this article deleted the authority of the legislature and the governor to limit circuit court jurisdiction, stripped the circuit courts of their supervisory power, and inserted the present reference to the circuit courts' authority to issue writs.

Although this section appears to give circuit courts complete jurisdiction over cases, a circuit court may still be prevented from proceeding on this basis. That is, one must distinguish between jurisdiction, which is the authority to hear and decide a particular case at some time and under some circumstances, and the authority to hear and decide a particular case at a particular time and in the circumstances that then exist. E.g., *Kotecki & Radtke, S. C. v. Johnson* (1995); *Michael J. L. v. State* (1993); *Miller Brewing Co. v. LIRC* (1993); *State ex rel. Parker v. Sullivan* (1994). The latter is sometimes called competency, the power to "proceed to judgment." *Mueller v. Brunn* (1982). If an administrative agency is better able to determine facts, a court, rather than exercising its competency, may allow that agency to do so. *State v. Dairyland Power Cooperative* (1971).

Several conditions may result in a circuit court having jurisdiction but not competency. One, of course, is that a party has not followed the procedures needed to activate the court's competency. For example, if a party is required to exhaust his or her administrative remedies (to exercise all available rights of appeal to state administrative agencies) and has failed to do so, a circuit court lacks competency. *Dairyland Power Cooperative*. A party's failure to comply with the statutory requirements for a particular type of lawsuit may deprive the court of competence unless the error was not "central to the statutory scheme." *Xcel Energy Services, Inc. v. Labor and Industry Review Commission* (2013). A court will lose its competency if it fails to perform an act within a prescribed time limit. *In Matter of Guardianship of N. N.* (1987). A court will lose its competency if an appeal has begun in another court. *In re Marriage of Hengel v. Hengel* (1984). A circuit court is not competent to hear a case if that court is the wrong venue for the trial. *Shopper Advertiser v. Department of Rev.* (1984); *Mueller v. Brunn* (1982). The question of a circuit court's competency must be raised during the trial and cannot be first raised on appeal. *Village of Trempealeau v. Mikrut* (2004).

Even if a circuit court has jurisdiction over a case and is competent to hear and decide it, other reasons may preclude it from doing so. The supreme court, exercising its authority under Article VII, Section 3(1) to supervise other courts,

has ordered lower courts not to exercise their jurisdiction to order the sterilization of persons who are incapable of giving informed consent to that procedure.
In Matter of Guardianship of Eberhardy (1981). A circuit court may proceed in a
criminal case in which the defendant was an American Indian, if the alleged act
did not occur on a reservation; but if the act had occurred on a reservation, the
circuit court may not hear the case, due to federal laws and treaties. *Sturdevant
v. State* (1977). Unless there is a statute to the contrary, a court's territorial reach
is the county in which it is located. *Kentzler v. The C., M. & St. P. R'y Co., Garnishee*
(1879). Also, despite the deletion of the legislature's authority to limit circuit
courts' jurisdiction and strong statements about the plenary nature of their jurisdiction in the 1977 amendment, a statute that circumscribes their jurisdiction in
divorce actions is constitutional. *In re Marriage of Stasey v. Stasey* (1992).

Courts have also decided a few miscellaneous issues concerning this section. A judge is legally liable for wrongly exercising jurisdiction only if there was
"clearly an utter lack of jurisdiction and [if] the facts presented have no legal
value or color [appearance] of legal value." *Langen v. Borkowski* (1925). Review
of decisions by administrative agencies is a civil matter and therefore subject
to this section. *Clintonville Transfer Line v. Public Service Comm.* (1945). This
section's grant of jurisdiction is not negated by the absence of one of the parties
in a case, *Comstock v. Boyle* (1908), or by another tribunal's possession of jurisdiction over the matter, *Dairyland Cooperative.* This section's broad grant of
jurisdiction implicitly grants other authority; for example, that grant of jurisdiction authorizes circuit court judges to appoint court officers, such as bailiffs.
Stevenson v. Milwaukee County (1909), and to decide, over the objections of the
county board, where its courtroom will be. *In re Court Room* (1912).

The 1977 amendment, by deleting the grant of authority to circuit courts to
supervise lower courts and the references to particular writs, made irrelevant
much of the case law about writs under this section. The major relevant issue
now is the relationship between circuit courts' authority to issue writs and statutory statements of the right to appeal the decisions of governmental and quasi-
governmental agencies. Unfortunately, the law on this subject covers a broad
spectrum of positions on this issue. At one end is a case holding that if a statute
provides only one means of appeal, that means is exclusive and a circuit court
may not issue a writ that would create another means. *Superior v. Committee on
Water Pollution* (1953). The middle of the spectrum is occupied by two cases in
which an appellate court allowed a little flexibility but created a high standard
that must be met to issue a writ that would grant an appeal other than the one
that a statute creates, and then decided that the circuit court may not issue the
writ. One of these standards is that a circuit court may not issue a writ unless the
right to due process of law has been violated, and the statutory means of appeal
would not provide an adequate remedy for that violation. *State ex rel. Thompson
v. Nash* (1965).

Another such standard is that the statutory review is inadequate. *Perkins v. Peacock* (1953). The court in *Perkins*, a case about school district boundaries, tried, with less than overwhelming success, to harmonize its opinion with several previous cases. The other end of the spectrum includes cases in which, despite a statutory means of appeal, an appellate court held that a writ should be issued to create a different means of appeal. In one, *State ex rel. Bidgood v. Clifton* (1902), which also involved school district boundaries, the court used the available adequate remedies test but allowed the writ because the original decision was void, making an appeal to the State Superintendent of Public Instruction inadequate. Another court used both the available adequate remedy test and the hardship test and held that a writ of prohibition (an order preventing another judicial or quasi-judicial body from hearing a case) should be issued to stop the statutorily specified administrative hearing. *Dept. of Pub. Instruction v. ILHR* (1975). The debatability of an administrative agency's jurisdiction does not preclude issuing a writ of prohibition to prevent that agency from holding administrative hearings in the manner that a statute provides. *St. Michael's Church v. Admin. Dept.* (1987). Although the court in several cases used the available adequate remedy test, it was applied with varying degrees of rigor, and that the only common theme among the cases. There may be no convincing way to harmonize all of the decisions on this issue.

Section 9
Judicial elections; vacancies.

When a vacancy occurs in the office of justice of the supreme court or judge of any court of record, the vacancy shall be filled by appointment by the governor, which shall continue until a successor is elected and qualified. There shall be no election for a justice or judge at the partisan general election for state or county officers, nor within 30 days either before or after such election.

The original version of this section applied to vacancies in the office of judge of the supreme court (the original term for members of that court) or of a circuit court and stated that the successor is to fill the balance of the unexpired term. A 1953 amendment provided that the successor's term is ten years for supreme court justices. A 1977 amendment made the section apply to judges of any courts of record. That amendment recognized the creation of the court of appeals.

Only three cases pertain to this section, two of them quite significant. One was the first in which the court rigorously interpreted the constitution. *State ex rel. Bond v. French* (1849). The court held that the prohibition against electing judges at, or within thirty days of, a general election, did not apply to probate judges. In the other major case, the court held that the governor's power to make appointments to fill judicial vacancies did not extend to newly created judgeships because regarding them there was no vacancy. *State v. Messmore* (1861).

Section 10
Judges: eligibility to office.

(1) No justice of the supreme court or judge of any court of record shall hold any other office of public trust, except a judicial office, during the term for which elected. No person shall be eligible to the office of judge who shall not, at the time of election or appointment, be a qualified elector within the jurisdiction for which chosen.

(2) Justices of the supreme court and judges of the courts of record shall receive such compensation as the legislature may authorize by law, but may not receive fees of office.

This section's original version set the salary of the supreme court judges (the original term for the members of that court) and the circuit court judges at $1,500 annually; prohibited those judges from accepting other compensation or holding any public office except judicial offices; and required them, at the time of their election, to be citizens, at least twenty-five years old, and an elector in the jurisdiction for which they were chosen to serve. An amendment that was ratified during 1912 changed the payment of the judges' salaries from quarterly to a schedule that the legislature determined. The final version is yet another result of the reworking of this article in 1977. Article VII, Section 7 also requires certain judges to reside within the jurisdiction that they serve. Article XIII, Section 3 prohibits a broader range of officials from holding certain other positions.

The requirement that judges be at least twenty-five years old applies not only at the time when service in the position begins but also at the time of election. *State ex rel. Sullivan v. Hauerwas* (1949). This may indicate that the requirement of residence within the jurisdiction served also applies at that time, as that interpretation would be consistent with the result in a case on that requirement as it appears in Article VII, Section 7. *State v. Messmore* (1861).

The prohibition against holding nonjudicial offices does not extend to membership on the board of trustees of the state law library, which is a judicial office. *In re Appointment of Revisor* (1910). However, it does extend to membership in the U.S. Senate, although a state court is powerless to stop a circuit court judge who violates that provision from taking office, because Article I, Section 3 of the U.S. Constitution, not a state constitutional provision, specifies the eligibility requirements for that office. *State ex rel. Wettengel v. Zimmerman* (1946). Although a violation of this section is a violation of the oath of office of circuit court judges, who swear to uphold the state constitution, it is not an act of moral turpitude that justifies revocation of the judge's license to practice law. *State v. McCarthy* (1949). Both of these cases involved the same judge; if the first had been decided the other way, the history of this country would be significantly different, because the judge was Joseph R. McCarthy, who, while in the U.S. Senate, stirred up considerable controversy by alleging that Communists had infiltrated the State Department, the movie industry, and other groups.

As to the meaning of the requirement that the legislature set the compensation for circuit court judges, a statute allowing Milwaukee County to supplement its circuit court judges' compensation was constitutional. *Petition of Breidenbach* (1934). This section prohibits a circuit judge who has resigned from running for another office during the term for which he or she was elected. The "term for which elected" does not end simply because the judge resigns. *Wagner v. Milwaukee County Election Commission* (2003).

Section 11
Disciplinary proceedings.

Each justice or judge shall be subject to reprimand, censure, suspension, removal for cause or for disability, by the supreme court pursuant to procedures established by the legislature by law. No justice or judge removed for cause shall be eligible for reappointment or temporary service. This section is alternative to, and cumulative with, the methods of removal provided in sections 1 and 13 of this article and section 12 of article XIII.

This section, too, was created as part of the amendment of this article ratified in 1977. The disciplinary procedures are issuance of a complaint by the Judicial Commission after the judge has an opportunity to be heard, a hearing by the judicial conduct panel (or, if the Judicial Commission chooses, by a jury), and review by the supreme court. The four types of sanction are listed in the ascending order of their severity. This section's assignment to the legislature of the duty to establish the procedures to be used does not violate the principle of separation of powers. *In Matter of Complaint Against Seraphim* (1980). Violation of the Code of Judicial Ethics, which the supreme court promulgates by rule, is grounds for imposing a sanction under this section. *In Matter of Complaint Against Raineri* (1981); *Disciplinary Proc. Against Aulik* (1988). Sections 1 and 13 of this article and Article IV, Section 8; Article VI, Section 4; and Article XIII, Section 12 also provide for removal of officers.

The court has the power to remove a justice permanently but cannot prevent a justice from hearing an individual proceeding on a case-by-case basis. *State v. Henley* (2011).

Section 12
Clerks of circuit and supreme courts.

There shall be a clerk of the circuit court chosen in each county organized for judicial purposes by the qualified electors thereof, who shall hold his office for two years, subject to removal as shall be provided by law; in case of a vacancy, the judge of the circuit court shall have power to appoint a clerk until the vacancy shall be filled by an election; the clerk thus elected or appointed shall give such security as the legislature may require the supreme court shall appoint its own clerk, and a clerk of the circuit court may be appointed a clerk of the supreme court.

This section originally stated that a clerk of court who was elected shall hold office for a full term. An 1882 amendment deleted that provision, which was the subject of the only case concerning this section.

Section 13
Justices and judges: removal by address.

Any justice or judge may be removed from office by address of both houses of the legislature, if two-thirds of all the members elected to each house concur therein, but no removal shall be made by virtue of this section unless the justice or judge complained of is served with a copy of the charges, as the ground of address, and has had an opportunity of being heard. On the question of removal, the ayes and noes shall be entered on the journals.

This section's original version applied to judges of the supreme court (the original term for members of that court) and of the circuit courts. A 1974 amendment changed the application to judges of the supreme, circuit, county, and municipal courts. A 1977 amendment, which was one of the court reorganization amendments, changed the application to justices of the supreme court and judges. That amendment corrected the reference to the title of members of the supreme court and reflected the fact that other amendments made to this article at that time changed the types of courts for which the constitution provides (the court of appeals was added, and statutory implementation of the constitutional changes eliminated county courts). The existence of this section does not preclude less severe sanctions. *In re Honorable Charles E. Kading* (1975). In fact, Section 11 authorizes less severe sanctions. Section 1 of this article also provides a way to remove justices and judges. The procedure under this section is more informal, less like a trial, than the procedure under Section 1. "Address" means requesting that the governor to remove the justice or judge. Section 11 also provides for removal of justices and judges. Article IV, Section 8 authorizes expulsion of legislators; Article VI, Section 4(4) authorizes the governor to remove county officers; and Article XIII, Section 12 authorizes the recall of state, congressional, judicial, legislative, and county officers.

Section 14
Municipal court.

The legislature by law may authorize each city, village and town to establish a municipal court. All municipal courts shall have uniform jurisdiction limited to actions and proceedings arising under ordinances of the municipality in which established. Judges of municipal courts may receive such compensation as provided by the municipality in which established, but may not receive fees of office.

This section originally required the electors of each county to choose a judge of probate, whose duty was not to decide probate cases but to recommend to the legislature rules of procedure for those cases, and it allowed the legislature to abolish the office in any county and to transfer that duty to other judges. The current version of this section was created in 1977 as part of the court reform initiative. This section implicitly grants certain inherent powers to municipal courts, as other sections of this article implicitly grant certain inherent powers to other courts. For example, municipal courts may determine whether ordinances are constitutional. *Milwaukee v. Wroten* (1991).

Section 24
Justices and judges: eligibility for office; retirement.

(1) To be eligible for the office of Supreme Court justice or judge of any court of record, a person must be an attorney licensed to practice law in this state and have been so licensed for 5 years immediately prior to election or appointment.

(2) Unless assigned temporary service under subsection (3), no person may serve as a Supreme Court justice or judge of a court of record beyond the July 31 following the date on which such person attains that age, of not less than 70 years, which the legislature shall prescribe by law.

(3) A person who has served as a Supreme Court justice or judge of a court of record may, as provided by law, serve as a judge of any court of record except the supreme court on a temporary basis if assigned by the chief justice of the supreme court.

This section's original version became effective only after the voters approved it in a referendum. Under that version no person who was seventy years old or older or who had not practiced law for at least five years could take office as a judge, and all judges, except those who were serving when the amendment became effective, had to retire at the end of the month in which they turned seventy. Retired judges could be appointed to serve temporarily as circuit court judges, and were to receive the compensation that the legislature provided. An amendment ratified in 1968 forced judges to retire on the July 31 (the end of the judicial year) of the year in which they turned seventy, required eight years of experience as a judge for appointment as a temporary circuit court judge, and specified that general laws were to govern these appointments, thus making it impossible, for example, for the legislature to establish different levels of compensation for different temporary judges. A 1977 amendment (as part of the redrafting of this article) extended the provisions on retirement to all judges of courts of record to reflect the addition of courts of appeals, deleted the requirement that only retired judges who had been judges for eight years could be appointed temporary judges, and allowed the legislature to set a mandatory retirement age, which had to be at least seventy years of age.

The requirements for circuit court judges under this section are not exclusive; for example, judges must adhere to the Code of Judicial Ethics. *In re Honorable*

Charles E. Kading. Appointments under subsection (3) are to the *duties*, not to the *office*, of judge, so that an appointee need not fulfill the requirement of being less than seventy years of age. *State ex rel. Godfrey v. Gollmar* (1977). That is, an appointee does not become a court's new judge but merely performs the duties of that court's judge—a subtle distinction.

Article VIII

Finance

Section 1
Rule of taxation uniform; income, privilege and occupation taxes.

The rule of taxation shall be uniform but the legislature may empower cities, villages or towns to collect and return taxes on real estate located therein by optional methods. Taxes shall be levied upon such property with such classifications as to forests and minerals including or separate or severed from the land, as the legislature shall prescribe. Taxation of agricultural land and undeveloped land, both as defined by law, need not be uniform with the taxation of each other nor with the taxation of other real property. Taxation of merchants' stock-in-trade, manufacturers' materials and finished products, and livestock need not be uniform with the taxation of real property and other personal property, but the taxation of all such merchants' stock-in-trade, manufacturers' materials and finished products and livestock shall be uniform, except that the legislature may provide that the value thereof shall be determined on an average basis. Taxes may also be imposed on incomes, privileges and occupations, which taxes may be graduated and progressive, and reasonable exemptions may be provided.

This section, the foundation of the state's tax policy, is often called the uniformity clause, although only the first seven words mandate uniform taxation. That term harks back to the original version, which included those words, a comma, and "and taxes shall be levied upon such property as the legislature shall prescribe." The first amendment to this section, in 1908, authorized income, privilege and occupational taxes, and reasonable exemptions. The second amendment, in 1927, allowed classification of forests and minerals for tax purposes. The third amendment, in 1941, allowed collection of taxes by optional methods; that is, it authorized nonuniform tax collection. The fourth amendment, in 1961, allowed nonuniform taxation of merchants' stock-in-trade, livestock, and manufacturers' materials and finished products. The most recent amendment, in 1974, allowed nonuniform taxation of agricultural and undeveloped land. Article II, Section 2 forbids imposing higher taxes on nonresident proprietors.

This section is among the more important in the constitution. For example, it limits the legislature's authority to tax property, to institute property tax relief, and to aid local units of government financially. Wisconsin allows fewer kinds of local taxes than do most states, so the property tax plays a vital role in the finances of municipalities, school districts, and the technical college system. For this and other reasons, this section is also among the more heavily litigated.

The issue of which taxes and other charges must be uniform has frequently been litigated. In the first such case, *Weeks v. City of Milwaukee* (1860), the court held that special assessments—charges for improvements, such as sewers and sidewalks, that benefit only certain properties—need not be uniform and, oddly, based that conclusion upon the appearance of both "tax" and "assess" in the original version of Article XI, Section 3 (the home rule section). More logically, a later court held that units of government impose special assessments under the police power, rather than under the taxing power, and that special assessments were, therefore, not subject to the uniformity requirement. *Donnelly v. Decker* (1883). The court in a long series of cases adhered to this position.

The test case on the first income tax law, *Income Tax Cases* (1912), demonstrated that income taxes need not be uniform. The requirement of uniformity also does not apply to other taxes: the inheritance tax, e.g., *Black v. State* (1902); a capital stock tax, *State ex rel. Reedsburg Bank v. Hastings* (1860); a premium tax, e.g., *Fire Department v. Helfenstein* (1862); the occupational taxes and privilege taxes that the 1908 amendment authorized, e.g., *State ex rel. Bernhard Stern & Sons v. Bodden* (1917); *State ex rel. Froedert Grain & Malting Co. v. Tax Commission* (1936); the franchise tax that is imposed on corporations and is virtually an income tax, *Mobil Oil Corp. v. Ley* (1987); the sales tax, *Ramrod Insurance v. Department of Revenue* (1974); and fees, *Wadham's Oil Co. v. Tracy* (1909). These cases, considered together, make it clear that only the property tax must be uniform.

Courts have read much into the uniformity requirement. For example, beginning with the first recorded uniformity clause case, *Knowlton v. Board of Supervisors* (1859), the court has consistently held that partial exemptions of property violate the uniformity clause. In other words, property must be either fully taxed or fully exempt. That is true even if a municipality indirectly achieves the partial exemption. In *Ehrlich v. Racine* (1965), the issue was an agreement between the city and a property owner under which the city would, for ten years, rebate property taxes in excess of $500 per acre in return for permission to build a storm sewer across the property. That case is significant because it indicates that courts will look at the ultimate economic effect of an agreement, and presumably of a statute, in determining whether it violates the uniformity clause. This is an important consideration, for example, in determining whether various kinds of property tax relief will be found to be unconstitutional, because some kinds of relief ultimately reduce property taxes.

Courts have found various methods to attenuate the uniformity requirement. One is to hold that the part of the property tax process at issue is a mere detail. Examples of this approach are cases involving the time of assessment, *Wisconsin Central Railroad v. Lincoln County* (1883), and the possible creation of a lien because of nonpayment of property taxes, *State ex rel. Hammermill Paper Co. v. La Plante* (1973). Another method is to determine that the statute at issue is a welfare statute, not a tax statute, so that, even though the statute relates in part to the property tax, the uniformity clause does not apply. Using this line of reasoning, the court approved the homestead credit, which is a credit against the individual income tax and is calculated in part on the basis of property taxes paid or rent constituting property taxes paid. *State ex rel. Harvey v. Morgan* (1966). Later the court decided that if this reasoning applied to the homestead credit, it also applied to the farmland preservation credit, which gives property tax relief to owners whose agricultural land is subject to prohibitions against nonagricultural uses. *McManus v. Department of Revenue* (1990).

Courts have had difficulty determining whether a particular use of property tax revenue violates the uniformity clause. Some cases on this subject conflict with one another. In a case challenging the use of only one municipality's property tax revenue to pay a bounty to a Civil War veteran, the court held that the differential treatment of municipalities and the absence of a local benefit violated the uniformity clause. *State ex rel. McCurdy v. Tappan* (1872). However, in three cases concerning taxing property to produce revenue to build a bridge outside the area that was being taxed, the court found nonuniformity. *State ex rel. Town of Baraboo v. Board of Supervisors* (1888); *Rinder v. City of Madison* (1916); *State ex rel. Owen v. Stevenson* (1917). The court resolved some cases on this issue by determining whether uniformity of taxation pertained within the taxing jurisdiction (a unit of government that has the power to impose taxes). For example, it approved a county levy to pay a sum to the state. *Lund v. Chippewa County and others* (1896).

In 1962, the court finally seemed to have arrived at a way to resolve these cases. It held in *Columbia County v. Wisconsin Retirement Fund* (1962) that the use of property tax revenue was not subject to the uniformity requirement. However, a few years later the state enacted a law that required school districts that had high property tax values per pupil to collect revenue that would be distributed to school districts that had low property tax values per pupil. After a less than convincing analysis, the court held that this use of revenue violated the uniformity clause. *Buse v. Smith* (1962). That scheme, however, was at best questionable on the ground that one unit of government was taxing and another was spending the revenue from the tax. Also, the uniformity clause applies to the use of any revenue directly or indirectly to reduce someone's property taxes. An example is a statute that allowed income tax credits to offset increases in property taxes resulting from improvements to houses and garages and that was held to be unconstitutional. *State ex rel. La Follette v. Torphy* (1978).

Courts have also had difficulty deciding uniformity clause cases that involve classification of property. In *Knowlton v. Board of Supervisors* (1859), the court held that classification established different "rules" of taxation and thus violated the requirement that the rule of taxation must be uniform. On the other hand, courts have approved classifications that resulted in classes consisting of only a few entities. See *Green Bay & Mississippi Canal Co. v. Outagamie County* (1890). Later, however, the court invalidated a statute that granted a total exemption to one institution of higher learning; whereas, other such institutions had an exemption for only forty acres. *Board of Trustees of Lawrence University v. Outagamie County* (1912). The court stated that "persons of the same class owning property of the same general description" must be taxed alike. *Id.* The trend recently has been to require uniform taxation of all of the members of a class. The difficulty, then, is determining the composition of a class. In some instances, such as the *Lawrence University* case, the answer is easy: institutions of higher learning are a class. Other cases, like *Green Bay & Mississippi Canal Co.*, are not so easily explained.

The geographical area over which uniformity is to be imposed has occasionally been an issue. In the *Knowlton* case, the test was applied over the area that levied the tax. A few years later a court made obvious that rule's wisdom. *Jensen v. Board of Supervisors* (1879) involved a statutory requirement that counties tax in order to build roads. The court recognized that, if it focused on the amount of tax revenue collected, and if it required statewide uniformity, no tax would survive scrutiny. A few years later the court explicitly stated that the taxing jurisdiction—the unit of government that may impose a tax—is the geographical area over which uniform taxation must apply. *Lund v. Chippewa County* (1896). Notwithstanding outlier cases, see *State ex rel. Town of Baraboo v. Board of Supervisors* (1888), the great weight of opinion is that uniformity must apply throughout the taxing jurisdiction.

The portion of this section that authorizes income, privilege, and occupational taxes has only occasionally been litigated. In the first case on the income tax, the court held that that tax need not be uniform but that classification of taxpayers must be based on "substantial difference of situation." *Income Tax Cases* (1912). The definition of "income," the object of the taxation, has sometimes been at issue. One court rejected the argument that dividends could not be fully taxed because part of them was a return of capital. *Van Dyke v. City of Milwaukee* (1915). Three other cases on dividends followed, each of which had the same result. There has been only one case on the portion of the section that requires income tax, privilege tax, and occupational tax exemptions to be reasonable, *State ex rel. Warren v. Nusbaum* (1973). The court held that an exemption for the income earned on notes and bonds issued by the Wisconsin Housing Finance Authority was reasonable.

Unsurprisingly, the case law on this section is voluminous and on some issues inconsistent. In *Gottlieb v. City of Milwaukee* (1967), the court enunciated the legal rules that had emerged from the cases at that time:

1. For direct taxation of property, under the uniformity rule there can be but one constitutional class.

2. All within that class must be taxed on a basis of equality so far as practicable, and all property taxed must bear its burden equally on an *ad valorem* [according to value] basis.

3. All property not included in that class must be absolutely exempt from property taxation.

4. Privilege taxes are not direct taxes on property and are not subject to the uniformity rule.

5. While there can be no classification of property for different rules or rates of property taxation, the legislature can classify as between property that is to be taxed and that which is to be wholly exempt, and the test of such classification is reasonableness.

6. There can be variations in the mechanics of property assessment or tax imposition so long as the resulting taxation shall be borne with as nearly as practicable equality on an *ad valorem* basis with other taxable property.

One can find cases that contradict each of these rules. Also, income taxes and occupational taxes should be added to the exception stated in number four. One could also add three more rules: the geographical area over which uniformity is tested is the taxing jurisdiction that imposed the tax; a law's ultimate effects, not only its immediate effects, are pertinent in determining whether it violates this section; and the requirement of uniformity does not apply to the use of tax revenue unless the use either directly or indirectly reduces property tax liability.

The tax assessor must have either the owner's permission or a warrant to enter the property. The property owner has a due process right to challenge an assessment even though he or she has refused to let the assessor view the property. A statute that requires a homeowner to surrender this due process right in order to challenge the assessment violates this section. *Milewski v. Town of Dover* (2017). The assessor's role figures prominently in the uniformity clause cases. In a resort area (the Wisconsin Dells), the assessor re-valued one resort property after it was sold but did not re-value similar properties that had recently sold well above their tax appraisals. The court held that this violated the uniformity clause—the assessor must consider the actual value of all property in the class without singling out one property, *Noah's Ark Family Park v. Board of*

Review (1998), or by assessing only a few properties, *State ex rel. Levine v. Board of Review* (1995).

To achieve uniformity, statutes require assessors to use the "three tier" method of assessment to establish value. In order of preference, the three tiers are: (1) establish value by a recent arm's-length sale of the subject property; (2) calculate the value by using sales of reasonably comparable properties; (3) use a combination of cost, depreciation, replacement value, income, industrial conditions, location and occupancy, sales of like property, book value, amount of insurance carried, value asserted in a prospectus, and appraisals produced by the owner to establish value. The income that a property may produce is an element of its value. *Allright Properties, Inc. v. City of Milwaukee* (2009).

In a school district covering parts of two counties, one assessor valued idle farm land as residential land and another assessor valued it as agricultural, resulting in differing tax burdens after the state equalized the assessments. The state then adopted these valuations without further review, which resulted in a violation of the uniformity clause. The court of appeals reversed a summary judgment in favor of the state and remanded the case to trial. *Town of Eagle v. Christiansen* (1995).

The court of appeals held that an exemption from a recycling surcharge on privilege taxes for noncorporate farmers rationally furthers the legitimate state purpose of promoting farming, surviving a uniformity clause challenge. *Love, Voss, and Murray v. D.O.R.* (1995). Similarly, a "hub exemption" for airlines that maintain an airport hub in the state bears a rational relationship to the legitimate state purpose of aiding the local economy. *N.W. Airlines v. D.O.R.* (2006).

Section 2
Appropriations; limitation.

No money shall be paid out of the treasury except in pursuance of an appropriation by law. No appropriation shall be made for the payment of any claim against the state except claims of the United States and judgments, unless filed within six years after the claim accrued.

This section establishes a requirement for the expenditure of state funds and a requirement for making claims against the state. Its original version included only the first sentence. An amendment ratified in 1877 added the second. This section has been cited as a source of the public purpose doctrine, and courts have analyzed expenditures according to that doctrine under the authority of this section. E.g., *Chicago & N. W. R. Co. v. The State* (1906); *State ex rel. La Follette v. Reuter* (1967). Courts will give "very wide discretion" to the legislature's declarations of public purpose, but ultimately the court decides if an appropriation serves a public purpose. *Town of Beloit v. County of Rock* (2003).

The public purpose doctrine is discussed at length in the history section of this book. Appropriations of indefinite amounts (now called sum sufficient appropriations, signifying that the appropriation is for whatever amount is needed to fulfill the appropriation's purpose) are constitutional. *State ex rel. Board of Regents v. Zimmerman* (1924). An appropriation to the Industrial Commission that is made by employers, to be used to pay workers' compensation claims, is constitutional even though the statute unconventionally authorized the payment of money. *B. F. Sturtevant Co. v. Industrial Comm.* (1925). It probably follows that program revenue appropriations—appropriations for specified purposes of funds from particular sources—and a state agency's administration of payments from an appropriation are constitutional. A payment to a school district that, because it was improperly formed, had no legal basis for its existence, is not an appropriation "by law" and is therefore unconstitutional. *Joint School Dist. v. Security State Bank* (1958).

In this section "claim" means "a legal claim, a demand as of right," and generally includes only those "arising out of a contract, where the relation of debtor and creditor exists." *Will of Heinemann* (1930). Thus, neither a request for a refund of inheritance taxes, *id.*, nor a request for payment of Aid to Families of Dependent Children, *Burton v. Department of Health & Social Serv.* (1981), is a claim. The six-year limit for presenting claims does not affect statutes of limitations. *New York Life Ins. Co. v. State* (1927).

Section 3
Credit of state.

Except as provided in s. 7(2)(a), the credit of the state shall never be given, or loaned, in aid of any individual, association or corporation.

This section was amended in 1975 to reflect the exception in Section 7(2)(a). Giving or loaning the state's credit means the state's assumption of the responsibility for paying a debt.

The most clear-cut instances to which this section does not apply are assumptions by an entity other than the state of an obligation to pay a debt. This seems perfectly obvious and thus hardly the material of litigation, but during the nineteenth century municipalities were much more creatures of the state than they are now. The legislature had created many of them by enacting a charter, which also specified, at least generally, their structure, rights, and duties. Granting to cities and villages the power to manage their own affairs regarding matters that are not of statewide concern ("home rule") by means of a 1924 amendment to Article XI, Section 3, more definitively distinguished the two kinds of local governments from the state. Other developments had had the same effect, not only on cities and villages, but on other units of government. Two early cases in which this exception applied involved the most frequent reason why municipalities incurred debt during the middle of the nineteenth century: to subsidize railroads. *Clark v. City of Janesville* (1860); *Bushnell v. Town of Beloit* (1860). Two later cases also make the point that this section does not apply to assumptions by local governmental units of obligations to pay debts. *State ex rel. Hammermill Paper Co. v. La Plante* (1973); *Libertarian Party v. State* (1996). Another case could have been decided this way, because the obligation in question was a city's, but the court instead validated the arrangement because the obligation served a public purpose, thus confusing the public purpose doctrine with this section. *David Jeffrey Co. v. Milwaukee* (1954).

A less obvious kind of exception is an assumption of an obligation to pay not by an entity that is obviously distinct from the state, as is a municipality, but by an entity that has some relation to the state, as when the state, by statute, has created the entity and has some control over it. For example, authorities—quasi-public entities—are not the state, so this section does not apply to their assumption of obligations to pay debts. Examples are a housing finance authority, *State ex rel. Warren v. Nusbaum* (1973); a solid waste recycling authority, *Wisconsin Solid Waste Recycling Auth. v. Earl* (1975); and a development authority, *State ex rel. Wisconsin Dev. Authority v. Dammann* (1938). Similarly, shell corporations are not the state. *State ex rel. La Follette v. Reuter* (1967). Some of the shell corporations that the state has used are listed in Section 7(2)(d). By means of elaborate arrangements with these corporations of leases and subleases or sales and leases back to the seller, the state kept control of property without violating this section. Enacting statutes that create this kind of entity requires a balancing act: the entity must be given enough power and the state must have such a minimal relation to it that this section is not violated, but the state must retain sufficient power over the entity so that it does not become a renegade.

Even if the state has assumed some sort of obligation to pay money, there are several reasons why this section does not apply. The most common is that the state has assumed no legally enforceable obligation. E.g., *State ex rel. Warren v. Nusbaum* (1973); *Wisconsin Solid Waste Recycling Auth. v. Earl* (1975); *Libertarian Party v. State* (1996). Most often this occurs when the state has assumed only a "moral obligation" to pay the interest and principal on bonds that another entity has issued if the other entity fails to do so. Such an obligation is not legally enforceable, so it does not constitute loaning or giving the state's credit, but failure to fulfill the obligation would have a serious negative effect on the state's credit and bond ratings.

This section is also avoided if the state's action is not loaning or giving credit. A grant, such as paying some of the expenses of highway construction, is distinct from giving or loaning credit. *Libertarian Party*. Payments of money, such as a security deposit, do not violate this section. *State ex rel. American Legion 1941 Con v. Corp. v. Smith* (1940). Gifts, too, even if the payment differs from conventional kinds of gifts, are exempt from this section's requirements. *State ex rel. Atwood v. Johnson* (1919) (a soldiers' educational bonus); *Appeal of Van Dyke* (1935) (unemployment relief). Finally, if the obligation is paid entirely from money that other entities have made available—for example, banks that have turned over their dormant accounts to the state along with the obligation to refund the deposit of anyone who properly claims the deposit—this section is not violated. *Marine Nat. Exchange Bank v. State* (1946).

Section 4
Contracting state debts.

The state shall never contract any public debt except in the cases and manner herein provided.

This section has not been amended. It makes clear that the state has no inherent, plenary power to incur debt, but may do so only in the ways that other sections specify. Accordingly, if a plaintiff challenges an action by the state under this section, almost invariably other sections, most frequently Article VIII, Section 3, also are grounds for challenge. In fact, virtually the same analysis applies to this section and Section 3. This section does not affect obligations that entities other than the state incur. Examples of other entities are municipal authorities, *Redevelopment Authority v. Canepa* (1959); counties, *State ex rel. Bowman v. Barczak* (1967); state authorities, *State ex rel. Warren v. Nusbaum* (1973); *Wisconsin Solid Waste Recycling Auth. v. Earl* (1975); *State ex rel. Wisconsin Dev. Authority v. Dammann* (1938); and dummy corporations, *State ex rel. Thomson v. Geissel* (1953); *State ex rel. La Follette v. Reuter* (1967). There is no debt if there is no legally enforceable obligation to pay, *Warren; Wisconsin Solid Waste Recycling Auth.; Dammann, Bowman.* This section does not apply to soldiers' educational bonuses. *State ex rel. Atwood v. Johnson* (1919). It also does not apply if the money to pay the obligation has been provided by another entity to the state and is on hand. *Marine Nat. Exchange Bank v. State* (1946).

The classic definition of "debt," as the term is used in the constitution, includes another requirement besides the existence of a legally enforceable obligation to pay, which has been cited in the analyses of Sections 3, 7, and 10 and this section: a debt "includes all absolute obligations to pay money, or its equivalent, from funds to be provided, as distinguished from money presently available or in process of collection and so treatable as in hand." *Earles v. Wells and others* (1896). Because an obligation that will be paid with money that is in the process of collection is not debt, it was constitutional to issue $750,000,000 in "operating notes" (short-term bonds) to keep the state solvent when it had cash flow problems lasting no longer than the current biennium and that were to be paid off during that biennium from the state's general fund when tax collections and other revenue were sufficient to do so. *State ex rel. La Follette v. Stitt* (1983).

Section 5
Annual tax levy to equal expenses.

The legislature shall provide for an annual tax sufficient to defray the estimated expenses of the state for each year; and whenever the expenses of any year shall exceed the income, the legislature shall provide for levying a tax for the ensuing year, sufficient, with other sources of income, to pay the deficiency as well as the estimated expenses of such ensuing year.

This section has not been amended. Wisconsin has always had a balanced budget requirement.

The statement that the annual tax is "to defray the estimated expenses of the state" has occasionally been cited as a source of the public purpose doctrine, which is discussed in the history section of this book. This section requires that taxes be imposed only for *state*, not for *private*, expenses. Neither the reference to the expenses of the *state* nor any other part of this section limits the state to statewide taxation, as opposed to taxation of a particular area within the state, to support the area's vocational, technical, and adult education system, which is now called the technical college system. *West Milwaukee v. Area Bd. Vocational, T. & A. Ed.* (1971). In this section, "tax" means any tax or combination of taxes, not only the property tax. *Nunnemacher v. State* (1906). By linking "tax" to "expenses of the state," this section distinguishes taxes from fees. *State ex rel. Atty. Gen. v. Wisconsin Constructors* (1936). That is, taxes raise revenue for general purposes; whereas, fees raise revenue for narrow, usually regulatory or administrative, purposes. In other words, the state has two kinds of power under which it raises revenue: the taxing power (by which it collects revenue for general purposes) and the police power (by which it collects money for the purposes of health, welfare, or safety, often that of the persons from whom it collects the revenue). The requirement of a congruence between the amount of money raised during a year and the amount of money spent during that year need not be exact; the legislature has considerable discretion and may make rough estimates. *Chicago & N. W. R. Co. v. The State* (1906).

Section 6
Public debt for extraordinary expense; taxation.

For the purpose of defraying extraordinary expenditures, the state may contract public debts (but such debts shall never in the aggregate exceed one hundred thousand dollars). Every such debt shall be authorized by law, for some purpose or purposes to be distinctly specified therein; and the vote of a majority of all the members elected to each house, to be taken by yeas and nays, shall be necessary to the passage of such law; and every such law shall provide for levying an annual tax sufficient to pay the annual interest of such debt and the principal within five years from the passage of such law, and shall specially appropriate the proceeds of such taxes to the payment of such principal and interest; and such appropriation shall not be repealed, nor the taxes be postponed or diminished, until the principal and interest of such debt shall have been wholly paid.

This section, which imposes requirements for incurring state debt, has not been amended. As the $100,000 limit on debt indicates, this section is obsolete. The primary section governing state debt is the next one. The amendment of that section in 1965 broadened the state's authority to borrow. Between the time when the $100,000 limit under this section became too restrictive and the time when Section 7 was substantially amended in 1969, the state established shell corporations that borrowed, for example, to construct state buildings that they "leased" to the state. The courts held that such arrangements did not violate this section. E.g., *State ex rel. Thomson v. Giessel* (1955). One case, *State of Wisconsin ex rel. Dean v. Common Council of Madison* (1859), in which the court held that the state debt mentioned in this section is the debt of the state itself, not the total debt of all the units of government in the state, is doubly obsolete: because of the amendment of Section 7 and because the amendment of Article XI, Section 3 in 1874 established a municipal debt limit. Another case that deals in part with this section might still have some pertinence because it defines "debt" to include the amount owed on a land contract. *State ex rel. Owen v. Donald* (1915).

Section 7
Public debt for public defense; bonding for public purposes.

(1) The legislature may also borrow money to repel invasion, suppress insurrection, or defend the state in time of war; but the money thus raised shall be applied exclusively to the object for which the loan was authorized, or to the repayment of the debt thereby created.

(2) Any other provision of this constitution to the contrary notwithstanding:

(a) The state may contract public debt and pledges to the payment thereof its full faith, credit and taxing power:

1. To acquire, construct, develop, extend, enlarge or improve land, waters, property, highways, railways, buildings, equipment or facilities for public purposes.

2. To make funds available for veterans' housing loans.

(b) The aggregate public debt contracted by the state in any calendar year pursuant to paragraph (a) shall not exceed an amount equal to the lesser of:

1. Three-fourths of one per centum of the aggregate value of all taxable property in the state; or

2. Five per centum of the aggregate value of all taxable property in the state less the sum of: a the aggregate public debt of the state contracted pursuant to this section outstanding as of January 1 of such calendar year after subtracting therefrom the amount of sinking funds on hand on January 1 of such calendar year which are applicable exclusively to repayment of such outstanding public debt and, b. the outstanding indebtedness as of January 1 of such calendar year of any entity of the type described in paragraph (d) to the extent that such indebtedness is supported by or payable from payments out of the treasury of the state.

(c) The state may contract public debt, without limit, to fund or refund the whole or any part of any public debt contracted pursuant to paragraph (a), including any premium payable with respect thereto and any interest to accrue thereon, or to fund or refund the whole or any part of any indebtedness incurred prior to January 1, 1972, by any entity of the type described in paragraph (d), including any premium payable with respect thereto and any interest to accrue thereon.

(d) No money shall be paid out of the treasury, with respect to any lease, sublease or other agreement entered into after January 1,1971, to the Wisconsin State Agencies Building Corporation, Wisconsin State Colleges Building Corporation, Wisconsin State Public Building Corporation, Wisconsin University Building Corporation or any similar entity existing or operating for similar purposes pursuant to which such nonprofit corporation or such other entity undertakes to finance or provide a facility for use or occupancy by the state or an agency, department or instrumentality thereof.

(e) The legislature shall prescribe all matters relating to the contracting of public debt pursuant to paragraph (a), including: the public purposes for which public debt may be contracted; by vote of a majority of the members elected to each of the 2 houses of the legislature, the amount of public debt which may be contracted for any class of such purposes; the public debt or other indebtedness which may be funded or refunded; the kinds of notes, bonds or other evidence of public debt which may be issued by the state; and the manner in which the aggregate value of all taxable property in the state shall be determined.

(f) The full faith, credit and taxing power of the state are pledged to the payment of all public debt created on behalf of the state pursuant to this section and the legislature shall provide by appropriation for the payment of the interest upon and instalments of principal of all such public debt as the same falls due, but, in any event, suit may be brought against the state to compel such payment.

(g) At any time after January 1,1972, by vote of a majority of the members elected to each of the 2 houses of the legislature, the legislature may declare that an emergency exists and submit to the people a proposal to authorize the state to contract a specific amount of public debt for a purpose specified in such proposal, without regard to the limit provided in paragraph (b). Any such authorization shall be effective if approved by a majority of the electors voting thereon. Public debt contracted pursuant to such authorization shall thereafter be deemed to have been contracted pursuant to paragraph (a), but neither such public debt nor any public debt contracted to fund or refund such public debt shall be considered in computing the debt limit provided in paragraph (b). Not more than one such authorization shall be thus made in any 2-year period.

This section sets the rules for incurring state debt. Subsection (1) is one of a few provisions based upon the notion that the state is in some sense a separate sovereign entity. Other such provisions are Article I, Section 20; Article IV, Section 29; Article V, Section 4; and Article V, Section 7(2). Those sections, along with other considerations, justify paying bonuses to World War I veterans. *State ex rel. Atwood v. Johnson* (1919).

This section originally contained only the material that is now subsection (1). In 1969, the voters ratified an amendment that substantially increased the section's length and scope. That amendment allowed contracting debt for land, waters, property, highways, and buildings and for equipment or facilities for public purposes, and it directed the legislature to prescribe the public purposes for which the state issued debt. Thus, the concept of public purpose finally appeared in the constitution, but it did so much later than the time when that concept was first accorded constitutional status (see General Topics, I). That amendment added the debt limit that now appears in subsection (2)(b). Current subsection (2)(e), which specifies some of the shell corporations that had been used to circumvent the constitutional limits on incurring state debt, was also added at that time. The same amendment added subsection (2)(f), which pledged the full faith and credit of the state to the payment of the debt that was created under this section. This pledge contrasts with a moral obligation pledge, which is merely the state's acknowledgment that it has a moral obligation to pay a debt and which is often made when another unit of government or a quasi-public entity incurs the debt. The 1969 amendment also added subsection (2)(g) on referendums in the case of fiscal emergencies. A 1975 amendment authorized issuing debt for veterans' housing and a 1992 amendment authorized issuing debt for railways. "Issuing debt" means issuing bonds, the obligation to pay the principal and interest on which is a debt.

Although this section has often been amended and specifies the restrictions that apply to the state's bonding, it rarely has been litigated. It does not apply to entities other than the state, such as shell corporations, *State ex rel. Thomson v. Giessel* (1955), and authorities, *State ex rel. Warren v. Nusbaum* (1973); *Wisconsin Solid Waste Recycling Auth. v. Earl* (1975). It does not apply if there is no legally enforceable obligation to pay. *Giessel; Warren; Earl.* It also does not apply if another entity has provided property that was converted into cash that could be used to pay the obligations. *State ex rel. Resley and others v. Farwell, Gov., etc.* (1852).

Section 8
Vote on fiscal bills; quorum.

On the passage in either house of the legislature of any law which imposes, continues or renews a tax, or creates a debt or charge, or makes, continues or renews an appropriation of public or trust money, or releases, discharges or commutes a claim or demand of the state, the question shall be taken by yeas and nays, which shall be duly entered on the journal; and three-fifths of all the members elected to such house shall in all such cases be required to constitute a quorum therein.

This section has not been amended. Although it, like many of the constitution's original provisions, was borrowed from New York's constitution, and the courts of that state have held their state's version of this section to be directory, the obligation that this section creates is mandatory. *B. F. Sturtevant Co. v. Industrial Comm.* (1925). The house of the legislature taking up a bill not introduced in it before the house in which it was introduced concludes action on it does not violate this section. *State ex rel. Crucible S. C. Co. v. Wis. Tax Comm.* (1925).

Most of the cases concerning this section turn on the definitions of the key words and phrases in it. "Imposes" includes extending, such as extending an existing tax to apply to additional property. *State ex rel. General Motors Corp. v. Oak Creek* (1971). "Debt" means "contracting of a public debt for extraordinary expenditures." *McDonald and another v. The State* (1891). "Debt" does not include incurring an obligation to pay salaries, *id.;* incurring costs for an investigation by the legislature, *State ex rel. Rosenhein v. Frear* (1909); issuing scrip, *State ex rel. Resley and others v. Farwell, Gov., etc.* (1852); or a local unit of government's issuing stock, *Bushnell v. Town of Beloit* (1860). "Public or trust money" does not include the workers' compensation fund, because that fund is not money in which the public has an interest, and this section is designed to protect the public interest. *B. F. Sturtevant Co. v. Industrial Comm.* (1925). "Tax" means a state, not a local, tax, but the imposition by the state of a tax on the residents of only one municipality, which was done when the state controlled local governments to a much greater extent than it has done since the home rule amendment (Article XI, Section 3) was ratified in 1924, is a state tax. *City of Watertown v. Cady* (1866); *Whitaker v. The City of Janesville and its Treasurer* (1873). "Imposes, continues or renews a tax" does not include creating the "necessary machinery" for administering a tax, for apportioning it, and for providing for its collection. *Whitaker.*

Section 9
Evidences of public debt.

No scrip, certificate, or other evidence of state debt, whatsoever, shall be issued, except for such debts as are authorized by the sixth and seventh sections of this article.

This section has not been amended. A written contract that includes a promise to pay is an "evidence of debt" and therefore is invalid unless the debt is authorized by Sections 6 or 7 of this article. *State ex rel. Owen v. Donald* (1915).

Section 10
Internal improvements.

Except as further provided in this section, the state may never contract any debt for works of internal improvement, or be a party in carrying on such works.

(1) Whenever grants of land or other property shall have been made to the state, especially dedicated by the grant to particular works of internal improvement, the state may carry on such particular works and shall devote thereto the avails of such grants, and may pledge or appropriate the revenues derived from such works in aid of their completion.

(2) The state may appropriate money in the treasury or to be thereafter raised by taxation for:

(a)The construction or improvement of public highways.

(b) The development, improvement and construction of airports or other aeronautical projects.

(c) The acquisition, improvement or construction of veterans' housing.

(d) The improvement of port facilities.

(e) The acquisition, development, improvement or construction of railways and other railroad facilities.

(3) The state may appropriate moneys for the purpose of acquiring, preserving and developing the forests of the state. Of the moneys appropriated under the authority of this subsection in any one year an amount not to exceed two-tenths of one mill of the taxable property of the state as determined by the last preceding state assessment may be raised by a tax on property.

This section restricts the state's building program and the state's participation in other entities' building programs. Its original version prohibited the state from incurring debt for works of internal improvement, or engaging in such works, unless the state received a grant of land or other property and used the revenue from the land or property to retire the debt. A 1908 amendment allowed appropriations for public highways. Two years later an amendment authorizing a state property tax and the use of the revenue that it generated for forests was attempted, but the procedure violated the requirements under Article XII, Section 1, so the amendment was deemed invalid. *State ex rel. Owen v. Donald* (1915). Another version of that amendment was made to this section, using the proper procedures, in 1924. Unfortunately, if this section were read literally after that amendment, the limitation on expenditures would apply to the combined appropriations for highways and forests. However, it was not read literally, so appropriations for highways had no limit. *State ex rel. Ekern v. Zimmerman* (1925). In 1945, appropriations for airports and other aeronautical projects were authorized by an amendment, and the problem with the wording about the appropriation limit's applicability to highways was remedied. A 1949 amendment added veterans' housing to the kinds of authorized projects. Port facilities were added to the list during 1960. A 1968 amendment changed the part of the section on expenditures for forestry to allow appropriation of money for forestry in an amount greater than the amount calculated on the basis of the value of the state's property. Finally, in 1992, the section was amended to allow appropriations for railroad purposes (subsection (2)(e)).

If in the future courts follow the portion of the opinion concerning this section in *Libertarian Party v. State* (1996), the section may no longer have an effect, because the court in that case interpreted very broadly the exception for building projects that fulfill governmental purposes. Nevertheless, because future courts may choose to ignore or work around that case, it is worth looking at the extensive case law on this section.

The wording of subsection (3) has twice been an issue. The three purposes for which forests may be used are not exclusive, so part of a forest may be converted into a facility for delinquents. *Cutts v. Department of Public Welfare* (1957).

Payments to towns based upon the forest croplands—lands that receive property tax advantages because they are subject to a contract that prevents their conversion to nonforestry uses—in them are not payments "for forestry," so they are not subject to the spending limit of 0.2 mills times the equalized value of the state's property. *State ex rel. Thomson v. Giessel* (1953).

The section's crucial part is of course not the passage on forests but the restrictions that it imposes on internal improvements. There are two prohibitions in this section that apply to the state: contracting debt to pay for works of internal improvement and being a party in carrying on works of internal improvement. In many cases courts have not clearly distinguished between the two prohibitions. Sometimes they have considered whether the state has incurred debt and ignored the prohibition against being a party in carrying on works of internal improvement, even though that prohibition seemed to be relevant. An example is conveying highways, other improvements, and rights of way to a nonprofit corporation for use in constructing part of an interstate highway system. One court held that the corporation was not the state, so the state had not incurred debt to create a work of internal improvement, but the state seemed, because it rendered assistance, to be a party in carrying on works of internal improvement. *State ex rel. Thomson v. Giessel* (1953). However, the state making loans directly to developers, despite the public purpose that those loans served, violated this section. *Development Dept. v. Bldg. Comm'n.* (1987). Also, paying a housing authority 10 percent of the value of a home and the land on which it was located so that veterans could obtain the property more cheaply, despite the existence of a housing emergency, was deemed being a party to carrying on works of internal improvement. *Giessel*. That case resulted in the 1949 amendment that authorized appropriations for veterans' housing.

This section's purpose becomes clearer if one considers in historical perspective its original form. By 1848 many states had ventured into financial trouble because they overreached to develop themselves by embarking on huge public works projects, both those that they built themselves and those that they aided, financially or otherwise. The construction of the Erie Canal, completed in 1825, is an early, dramatic example of this propensity. The framers of Wisconsin's constitution, many of whom had lived in Eastern states that had run amok fiscally on such projects, recognized this danger, even though they also recognized the need for development. A nineteenth-century justice remarked on this situation:

> When our constitution was adopted, the subject of state indebtedness, particularly for works of internal improvement, was prominent in the public mind. Some of the states had theretofore contracted large debts in the prosecution of such works, and the weight thereof pressed heavily upon the people. . . . [T]he framers

of the constitution were solicitous that no such evil should ever afflict this state. (*Sloan, Stevens & Morris v. State* (1881))

The definition of "works of internal improvement" is a crucial issue. In a 1915 case, the court framed a definition that has generally been accepted ever since:

"Works of internal improvement," as used in the constitution, means, not merely the construction or improvement of channels of trade and commerce, but any kind of public works, except those used by and for the state in performance of its governmental functions, such as a state capitol, state university, penitentiaries, reformatories, asylums, quarantine buildings, and the like, for the purposes of education, the prevention of crime, charity, the preservation of public health, furnishing accommodations for the transaction of public business by state officers, and other like recognized functions of state government. (*State ex rel. Owen v. Donald* (1915))

This definition identifies very well projects that are not works of internal improvement. It does less well in identifying projects that are works of internal improvement.

As one would expect, there are ways to escape this section's claws. The most obvious and clear-cut is to demonstrate that an entity that is not the state is building the project and that the state is not a party. Cities, villages, and towns and their instrumentalities may incur debt to build works of internal improvement. *Clark v. City of Janesville* (1860); *Bushnell v. Town of Beloit* (1860); *State ex rel. Hammermill Paper Co. v. La Plante* (1973); *Bloomer v. Bloomer* (1906); *Redevelopment Authority v. Canepa* (1959). Counties, too, are exempt from this section. *State ex rel. Bowman v. Barczak* (1967); *Jensen v. The Board of Supervisors* (1879). Special districts—units of government that serve limited purposes and generally are not coterminous with municipalities or counties—are also exempt from this section. *Libertarian Party v. State*. Although these governmental units are political subdivisions of the state and during the nineteenth century the state, by enacting their charters, created them, and to a significant extent restricted them, one can easily distinguish them from the state.

Less easy to distinguish from the state—and therefore riskier to use to circumvent this section—are two creatures that were invented much later than were municipalities. The first to be used was the shell corporation—a corporation that was just enough of an entity to be separate from the state and, in a sense, to construct works of internal improvement. By means of intricate patterns of leases and of sales followed by leases of the property back to the seller, the state maintained control over the projects that shell corporations ostensibly built. Section 7(2)(d) lists some of the shell corporations that the state used. Courts have generally been lenient in accepting this fiction. E.g., *Herro v. Wisconsin Fed. Surp. P. Dev. Corp.* (1969). Unfortunately, in some of the cases involving shell corporations, the court, rather than simply stating that the shell, not the state, was building a work of internal improvement, muddied the waters by also analyzing the building project from another perspective. For example, in one of the cases, the court stated that the projects were buildings for the University of Wisconsin and, therefore, their educational purpose made building them a governmental function. *State ex rel. Thomson v. Geissel* (1955). For that reason, the court, using the accepted definition of "works of internal improvement," exempted the projects from the reach of this section.

Creating authorities, a means that the state used later to work its way around this section, was trickier. They are quasi-public and are created by enacting a law and, therefore, more difficult to differentiate from the state. It is also more difficult to walk the narrow line between giving them too much power so that they cannot be controlled and giving them too little power so that they are not distinct from the state. Courts also have been lenient regarding authorities. *State ex rel. Warren v. Nusbaum* (1973); *Wisconsin Solid Waste Recycling Authority v. Earl* (1975). As they did in cases about shell corporations, courts often went beyond merely stating that an authority, not the state, was constructing the work of internal improvement. In *Nusbaum*, the court also analyzed whether the project's dominant purpose was a governmental function and whether private capital was unable to accomplish that purpose. The status of the two-part test that the court used in that case is in doubt. Did the court mean that the test had to be passed even if an authority was building the project, or when it stated the test was the court merely making comments that were inessential to the decision and thus not a precedent for later cases?

Subsection (1) creates an exception for projects for which a grant of land has been made, although the grant by itself is not sufficient to activate the exception: the land must be dedicated to (donated for) the project, and its "avails" (the revenues that it produces) must be used for the project. The federal government's grant of land that was dedicated for the improvement of a river, the state's sale of that land, and the state's use of the proceeds of the sale to build the work, qualified for this exception. *State ex rel. Resley and others v. Farwell, Gov., etc.* (1852). Similarly, a federal grant of land to the state for railroad construction and the state's use of part of the proceeds of the sale of that land to pay for prosecution of trespassers on the remaining land was constitutional. *Sloan, Stevens & Morris v. The State* (1881).

The state, if it is not a party to a work of internal improvement, may escape this section's prohibitions if it demonstrates that it has incurred no debt regarding a building project. For example, if the proceeds from the sale of land that the federal government has given it cover the construction expenses, the state has incurred no debt. *Resley.* Revenue bonds—bonds the principal and interest on which are paid to the bondholders from the revenue that the project generates— are not debt. *Development Dept. v. Bldg. Comm'n* (1987). The status of the last of these rules is somewhat in doubt; because the housing in *Development Dept.* violated this section, the statement about revenue bonds was not necessary to the decision. Moreover, neither party argued that revenue bonds were debt, so the court did not need to decide that issue.

The generally accepted definition of a "work of internal improvement" follows one of Aristotle's suggestions for constructing definitions: stating the general category to which the term belongs and then distinguishing the things that belong to the subcategory that is to be defined from the other entities that belong to the general category. The general category is "public works." Thus, if the state does not build a work, certainly it builds no work of internal improvement. For example, if no physical structure is built, no work is built. *State ex rel. Wisconsin Dev. Authority v. Dammann* (1938). Operating expenses, even if they are incurred to operate a work of internal improvement, are not in themselves a work. *State ex rel. Warren v. Reuter* (1969).

A significant subcategory of works that are not internal improvements is included in the general category of public works. Because the accepted definition of "work of internal improvement" excludes works that have a governmental purpose, one way to escape this section is to demonstrate that the work in question has that kind of purpose. Among the purposes that have been approved because they are governmental are education, in regard to constructing buildings on the campus of the University of Wisconsin, *State ex rel. Thomson v. Giessel* (1953); to constructing off-campus dormitories, *State ex rel. Thomson v. Giessel* (1954); pollution abatement, *Reuter*; supervision of delinquents, *Cutts v. Department of Public Welfare* (1957); reducing unemployment and promoting tourism, industry, and recreation, *Libertarian Party v. State*; providing work space for the state's employees, *Giessel* (1954); and recycling solid waste, because it preserves the health, safety, and welfare of the state's people, *Earl*.

In contrast, certain functions are not governmental, and this section might preclude erecting structures in which they are to be performed. In a case that was decided before the one that produced the generally accepted definition of "work of internal improvement," the court employed a different definition. It distinguished between projects that were "expected to be undertaken for profit," which were works of internal improvement, and projects that "primarily and predominately merely facilitate the essential functions of government." *State ex rel. Jones v. Froehlich* (1902). One could conclude from that definition that this section's purpose is to prevent the state from competing with private developers. At issue in that case were levees. Of their purposes the court wrote that promotion of navigability, creation of water power, and reclamation of land produce pecuniary benefits, so private parties might undertake them. Therefore, levees are works of internal improvement and the state's participation in carrying on their construction was unconstitutional. The case presents two problems. One is that the court used a new definition of "works of internal improvement," but later courts have not adopted that definition. The other is that the three functions seem governmental. The age of the case explains the latter feature. Justices early in the twentieth century were more wary of the dangers of internal improvements and therefore were less willing to declare building projects unconstitutional. As the years passed, courts became much more lenient, accepting, for example, obvious fictions such as shell corporations and other reasons for holding that this section did not preclude building, or participating in the building of, a work of internal improvement. The court that proposed the accepted definition of "works of internal improvement" also declared that dams are such works because their purposes are not sufficiently governmental. *Donald.* Homes are also works of internal improvement. *Development Dept. v. Bldg. Comm'n* (1987).

Two variations on the theme of a governmental purpose appear in the cases. As already noted, one test that is used to determine whether a public work is an internal improvement has two parts: is the dominant purpose governmental, and is private capital unable to serve that purpose? *Nusbaum.* The other variation makes the governmental function requirement less stringent. Under it, building, or participating in the carrying on of, projects that would otherwise be works of internal improvement does not violate this section if the project's purpose is incidental to a primary purpose that is governmental. One example is the state's reimbursement of municipalities for part of the labor costs for building projects, the primary purpose of which is to aid the unemployed. *Appeal of Van Dyke* (1935). Another variation is the state's construction of a fur farm, dams, and a fish hatchery, because they served the primary purpose of creating a park (actually a wildlife refuge). *State ex rel. Hammann v. Levitan* (1929). In contrast, dams that are incidental to conservation of forests, which seems to be a governmental function, are unconstitutional. *Donald.* In short, relying on this latter variation is risky, because the cases are not entirely consistent.

Another way to escape this section's grasp is to demonstrate that the state is not a party to carrying on a work of internal improvement but is merely encouraging the construction of that work. The line between the two actions is exceedingly fine, and the distinction appears to have been devised as part of the courts' growing leniency in internal improvement cases. The state's appropriation of $250,000 to an authority for initial expenses is mere encouragement. *Nusbaum.* An appropriation for double that amount to an authority for initial planning, operations, and administration is also mere encouragement. *Earl.* Making an appropriation, along with providing assistance and advice, is mere encouragement. *Dammann.* An appropriation for $250,000 to investigate a project's feasibility is mere encouragement. *State ex rel. Thomson v. Giessel* (1953).

The protections against the state's imprudently incurring debt for works of internal improvements and its improperly being a party to carrying on those works have certainly been attenuated. As noted previously, the court might have gone even further and eviscerated this section in *Libertarian Party v. State*, which involved a plan to build a stadium for a professional baseball team. To buttress its argument that the statutes in question do not violate this section, the court cited two cases that are not about this section, *State v. Milwaukee*

Braves, Inc. (1966) and *State v. Village of Lake Delton* (1979). It also cited *State ex rel. Hammann v. Levitan* (1929) for the proposition that recreation is a governmental function, but in that case the state built the internal improvements; their cost was minimal; the recreational purposes were secondary, not primary; and the public would probably have been able to use the recreational area free of charge. In this instance, by contrast, a special district would build the stadium according to the baseball team's specifications, and the team and the special district would own the stadium, attending games would be far from free of charge, and the cost, including interest payments, would be in the hundreds of millions of dollars. The distinction that is drawn in *State ex rel. Jones v. Froehlich* (1902) between, on the one hand, functions that are governmental and thus not internal improvements and, on the other hand, functions that are profit-making and thus usually undertaken by private business has obviously been superceded. Here, not only has a provision that was designed in part to prohibit the state from aiding individual private interests at the expense of other private interests, at the expense of the people in general, or at the expense of both, been negated so that a private interest can benefit, but that negation has been justified on the grounds that the aid itself, strengthening the individual private interest's finances—that is the basic effect, of which the three nonrecreational purposes are manifestations—is a *governmental* purpose that makes the project something other than a work of internal improvement. In short, this case calls into question the validity of all the previous cases on works of internal improvements.

Section 11
Transportation fund.

All funds collected by the state from any taxes or fees levied or imposed for the licensing of motor vehicle operators, for the titling, licensing, or registration of motor vehicles, for motor vehicle fuel, or for the use of roadways, highways, or bridges, and from taxes and fees levied or imposed for aircraft, airline property, or aviation fuel or for railroads or railroad property shall be deposited only into the transportation fund or with a trustee for the benefit of the department of transportation or the holders of transportation-related revenue bonds, except for collections from taxes or fees in existence on December 31, 2010, that were not being deposited in the transportation fund on that date. None of the funds collected or received by the state from any source and deposited into the transportation fund shall be lapsed, further transferred, or appropriated to any program that is not directly administered by the department of transportation in furtherance of the department's responsibility for the planning, promotion, and protection of all transportation systems in the state except for programs for which there was an appropriation from the transportation fund on December 31, 2010. In this section, the term "motor vehicle" does not include any all-terrain vehicles, snowmobiles, or watercraft.

This section was added in 2014. It has not since been amended or litigated.

Article IX

Eminent Domain and Property of the State

Section 1
Section 1
Jurisdiction on rivers and lakes; navigable waters.

The state shall have concurrent jurisdiction on all rivers and lakes bordering on this state so far as such rivers or lakes shall form a common boundary to the state and any other state or territory now or hereafter to be formed, and bounded by the same; and the river Mississippi and the navigable waters leading into the Mississippi and St. Lawrence, and the carrying places between the same, shall be common highways and forever free, as well to the inhabitants of the state as to the citizens of the United States, without any tax, impost or duty therefor.

This section, which establishes water rights, has not been amended. Article II, Section 1 establishes the state's boundaries, including those that pass over bodies of water. This section creates a public trust in the waters of the state, which requires the state to protect them:

The wisdom of the policy which, in the organic laws of our state, steadfastly and carefully preserved to the people the full and free use of public waters, cannot be questioned. Nor should it be limited or curtailed by narrow constructions. It should be interpreted in the broad and beneficent spirit that gave rise to it in order that the people may fully enjoy the intended benefits. Navigable waters are public waters and as such they should inure to the benefit of the people. . . . This grant was made to them before the state had any title to convey to private parties, and it became a trustee of the people charged with the faithful execution of the trust created for their benefit. (*Diana Shooting Club v. Husting* (1914))

The emphasis has not only been on "trust," indicating that the state has a duty, but also on "public," indicating that the duty is to protect public, not private, interests. *Priewe v. Wisconsin State Land & Improvement Co.* (1896); *Rossmiller v. State* (1902).

One can trace this section to the Northwest Ordinance (1787). The phrasing that begins with the reference to the navigable waters is identical to the equivalent part of the Ordinance, except "state" has replaced "territory." The federal law that authorized the Territory of Wisconsin to organize as a state, the Wisconsin Enabling Act, included a passage almost identical to this section of the constitution. In fact, this section's principles might have been in effect, because of the Northwest Ordinance and the Wisconsin Enabling Act, even if it had not been included in the constitution. *Flambeau River L. Co. v. Railroad Comm.* (1931); *Lundberg v. University of Notre Dame* (1939); *Wisconsin River Improvement Co. v. Manson* (1877); *Wisconsin River Improvement Co. v. Lyons* (1872); *In re Crawford County L. & D. Dist.* (1924).

Although the state is the trustee of the public waters, it may delegate its trusteeship in certain circumstances, with appropriate controls and so as not to significantly impair the rights of navigation. *Wisconsin's Environmental Decade, Inc. v. Department of Natural Resources* (1978). The delegations in those cases were to state agencies. Delegation of the trusteeship to a local unit of government, however, is unconstitutional. *Muench v. Public Service Commission* (1952).

The public trust doctrine applies not only to the bodies of water that the section lists but to all navigable lakes and streams. *Angelo v. Railroad Commission* (1928). The definition of "navigable" thus becomes a vital issue. The first definition was "could the water float a saw log?" E.g., *Olson v. Merrill* (1877). The court did not randomly choose this test; at the time, the primary commercial use of the state's waterways was floating logs to railheads so that the products of the state's lumbering industry could be transported to a market. As the devastation of the state's forests and the resulting precipitous decline in the state's lumbering industry proceeded, other uses of the waterways became important, and the definition of "navigable" changed to reflect those developments. A statute enacted in 1911 defined "navigable" as able to float any boat, skiff, or canoe; it had become clear that the waterways by that time were both commercial and recreational resources. Courts began to recognize that the definition of "navigable" must reflect recreational uses and that such uses, too, must, under the public trust doctrine, be protected. *Muench; Nekoosa-Edwards Paper Co. v. Railroad Comm.* (1930); *R.W. Docks & Slips v. State* (2001). Despite the change to the test of navigability, the term has always meant navigability *in fact*. *Diana Shooting Club v. Husting* (1914). That is, a stream or lake must be actually navigable to qualify for protection; a statute declaring it to be navigable is neither necessary nor conclusive.

This section creates various forms of protection that apply to navigable waterways. The most obvious is that of the right to navigate. A bridge may not "materially or unnecessarily obstruct" navigation. *Sweeney v. The Chicago, Milwaukee & St. Paul R'y Co.* (1884). A gas company may not lay its lines under a riverbed, impeding boat traffic on the river. *Milwaukee G. C. Co. v. Schooner "Gamecock"* (1868). Filling for a breakwater might violate this section. *Hixon v. Public Service Comm.* (1960). Even a temporary disruption of navigation, such as the mooring of a raft that impeded access to a wharf, might be unconstitutional under this section. *Harrington v. Edwards* (1863). Dams that impede navigation violate this section. *Attorney General v. Eau Claire* (1875); *Wisconsin River Improvement Company v. Lyons* (1872). In the first of the cases on dams, the structure was held to violate this section even though it facilitated the transportation of logs; even in the 1870s, courts did not always defer to logging interests.

This section and the public trust doctrine that derives from it protect not only navigation but also the free use of lakes and rivers. *Nekoosa-Edwards Paper Co.; Muench.* This protection takes precedence even over the rights of riparian owners: the owners of shore land. *Willow River Club v. Wade* (1898).

The public trust doctrine protects many other rights regarding navigable water as well as many activities carried out on navigable water. The most fundamental is the right to the body of water itself. For example, the state may not drain a navigable lake. *Priewe v. Wisconsin Land & Improvement Co.* (1899). The waters must also be kept pure and free from pollution *Winchell v. The City of Waukesha* (1901). The doctrine also protects the following activities: fishing, *Willow River Club v. Wade* (1898); floating logs, even if that activity involves occasional trespass to shore land, *Olson v. Merrill* (1877); preserving wetlands and controlling pollution, *Just v. Marinette County* (1972); cutting ice from lakes if the state owns the lakebed, *Rossmiller v. State* (1902); but not if the lakebed is privately owned, *Haase v. Kingston Co-operative Creamery Ass'n* (1933); constructing piers that aid, rather than obstruct, navigation, *Milwaukee v. State* (1927); hunting, *Diana Shooting Club v. Husting* (1914); *Merwin v. Houghton* (1911) (although the court in another case, *Krenz v. Nichols* (1928), held to the contrary); and viewing scenic beauty, *Madison v. State* (1957). In addition, the broad purpose of recreation is protected, *Muench v. Public Service Comm.* (1952), as is the combination of several recreational uses: hunting, fishing, swimming, skating, and viewing scenic beauty, *Madison v. Tolzmann* (1958).

This section also implicates activities that might be considered to be obstructions of navigation or abridgments of the rights related to it, such as the rights enumerated in the previous paragraph. Many of these questionable activities have been held to be constitutional. Among them are enacting an ordinance that prohibits operating motor boats at certain times, *Menzer v. Elkhart Lake* (1971); building a bridge, *Captain Soma Boat Line v. Wisconsin Dells* (1977); *Sweeney v. Chicago, Milwaukee & St. Paul Ry. Co.* (1884); allowing logs to jam a boom that holds them, *J. S. Keator Lumber Co. and others v. The St. Croix Boom*

Corp. (1888); filling a navigable waterway's bed to construct a municipal harbor, *Milwaukee v. State* (1927); building a waterski jump, *State v. Bleck* (1983); operating a ferry, *Chapin and another v. Crusen and another* (1872); dredging, *Angelo v. Railroad Comm.* (1928); draining, *Merwin v. Houghton* (1911); *In re Horicon D. Dist.* (1905); and building a dam, *Wisconsin River Improvement Co. v. Manson* (1877); *Flambeau River Lumber Co. v. Railroad Comm.* (1931).

A case decided by the court of appeals, *State v. Village of Lake Delton* (1979), might have vastly extended the permissible kinds of obstruction to navigation. There, an ordinance that allowed a municipality to grant exclusive use of part of a lake to a waterski show business in return for payment of a license fee was held to be constitutional. The court, after arguing that the prior cases on this section were not as restrictive as they first appeared, held that the arrangement preserved safety, order, the tourist economy, and recreation. In the earlier cases courts had first examined the obstruction to navigation and the rights related to it. If they found that there was a significant obstruction, they examined the benefits that resulted from it, and, if the obstruction was minimal and the benefits substantial, they were likely to uphold the obstruction's constitutionality. *Village of Lake Delton*, in contrast, focuses on the obstruction's benefits, in particular its economic benefits. Like courts in recent cases on other constitutional provisions, such as the public purpose doctrine and the internal improvements section (Article VIII, Section 10), the court in this case essentially turned a constitutional provision on its head: in litigation involving a section of the constitution that was designed to prevent giving advantages to one business or to a small number of them at the expense of other businesses or of the general public, it held that giving such an advantage not only is constitutional but also that it is constitutional *because of* the advantage.

The ownership of land under or adjacent to a body of water is an important issue in many cases on this section. The state owns the beds of lakes. *State v. Bleck* (1983). The state, however, may grant parts of lakebeds. *Milwaukee v. State* (1927). In fact, this has been a common means of facilitating municipal public works like piers, wharves, and marinas. The state may also authorize filling the lakebeds it has granted. *Id.* In contrast, the riparian owners own one-half of the bed of a river that adjoins their other property. *Jones v. Pettibone and another* (1854); *Walker v. Shepardson* (1856); *Arnold v. Elmore* (1863). The same principle applies to canals. *Lawson v. Mowrey* (1881). Their ownership of part of the riverbed and their status as riparian owners bestow certain rights on those persons.

However, all these rights are subordinate to the duty of allowing navigation and the rights that are related to it. *Wisconsin River Improvement Company v. Lyons* (1872); *Cohn v. The Wausau Boom Co.* (1879). Among the acts and rights of riparian owners that this section protects are: bathing, swimming, and boating, *Bino v. Hurley* (1956); access to a lake, *Boorman v. Sunnuchs* (1877); operating a muskrat farm, *Munninghoff v. Wisconsin Conservation Comm.* (1949); and building dams that materially affect the use of a stream, *A. C. Conn Co. v. Little Suamico Lumber Mfg. Co. and another* (1889).

Where the shoreline of a man-made body of water forms a property line, the upland owner does not have full riparian rights and may not keep a pier over the privately owned submerged property, although the upland owner may enter the water directly from his or her property. *Movrich v. Lobermeier* (2018).

The physical extent of the state's ownership of lakebeds has been an issue in a few cases. Ownership extends to the ordinary high-water mark (a distinct mark on the adjoining land caused by the action of the lake's water), so building or conducting other activities between that line and the lake intrudes on the state's property. *State v. Trudeau* (1987). Despite the state's ownership of lakebeds, land added to the shore by accretion, if it has natural causes or if a third party did it, belongs to the riparian owner, subject to the prohibition against interfering with navigation and the rights related to it. *DeSimone v. Kramer* (1977); *W. H. Pugh Coal Co. v. State* (1981); *Heise v. Village of Pewaukee* (1979). Another boundary is the bulkhead line, which municipalities establish, with the approval of the state, and which runs along the bed of a body of water roughly parallel to the shore. Private development into the body of water beyond the bulkhead line is prohibited. *Ashwaubenon v. Public Service Commission* (1963).

Litigation has also clarified two other phrases in this section. The prohibition against imposing any "tax, impost or duty" does not make it unconstitutional to charge tolls to pass over waters that have been made navigable. *Wisconsin River Improvement Company v. Manson* (1877). In one case, the court held that imposing a fee on the owners of boats was unconstitutional because the "fee was for use of navigable waters." *Madison v. Tolzmann* (1958). Later, the court specifically disavowed that statement and held that such a charge was a fee, not a tax, and therefore was constitutional. *State v. Jackman* (1973). The license fee imposed on the business that was permitted to present a waterski show on navigable water did not violate this section because it was a fee for the legitimate public purpose of administering the ordinance that limited the use of part of the lake. *Village of Lake Delton.* In short, courts have not rigorously enforced this prohibition.

The other phrase that has been explained is "carrying places." In general, the term means portages, but the section does not clarify its scope. Its context—"the navigable waters leading into the Mississippi and St. Lawrence, and the carrying places between the same"—implies that only one portage was meant—the one near the present city of Portage, where a narrow strip of land separates the Wisconsin River, which flows into the Mississippi, from the Fox River, which flows into Lake Michigan and begins a route leading to the St. Lawrence River. This spot was a vital nexus in the era before Wisconsin became a state. However, "carrying places" means those that existed at the time the Northwest Ordinance went into effect (1787) and have not been abandoned; although new carrying places, caused, for example, by the meandering of streams, are included if they serve trails of commerce that existed at that time. *Lundberg v. University of Notre Dame* (1939).

The court of appeals in *Citizens for U, Inc. v. D.N.R.* (2010) held that the Department of Natural Resources did not violate the Public Trust Doctrine when it approved the closure of a public road along the Wisconsin River to permit riverfront development, and approved replacement public access even though the replacement road was not close to the shoreline, making it less desirable.

The state holds the navigable waters in trust for the public—not only for navigation but for use in fishing, hunting, recreation, and the enjoyment of scenic beauty. The state delegates its Public Trust duties to the Department of Natural Resources through the statutes, giving the department a general duty to protect the waters. The legislature may assign additional duties to the Department under the state's general police powers. In a case involving a high-capacity well, the court held that the Department had authority to regulate use of groundwater based on both the constitution and the statutes, but it did not explicitly hold that the constitution protects groundwater. *Lake Beulah Management District v. Lake Beulah Protective and Improvement Assoc.* (2011). While *Lake Beulah* was pending in the supreme court, the legislature passed 2011 Wisconsin Act 21, making it clear that the constitutional authority delegated to the Department does not include groundwater protection.

Two years after *Lake Beulah*, the supreme court held that the Public Trust Doctrine does not pertain to non-navigable land and non-navigable wetlands adjacent to navigable waters. The doctrine applies to the ordinary high-water mark of navigable water. Where a dam affects the water level of a navigable upstream lake, the Department properly determines the outflow of the dam. However, it cannot take into consideration the effect of the lake's level on adjacent, non-navigable wetlands. Some of the Department's statutory duties to protect wetlands are not grounded in the Public Trust Doctrine but in the police powers of the state. Because the court found that the Department had misinterpreted its role, it gave no weight to the Department's interpretation of the law. *Rock-Koshkonong Lake District v. D.N.R.* (2013).

Section 2
Territorial property.

The title to all lands and other property which have accrued to the territory of Wisconsin by grant, gift, purchase, forfeiture, escheat or otherwise shall vest in the state of Wisconsin.

This section has not been amended or litigated.

Section 3
Ultimate property in lands; escheats.

The people of the state, in their right of sovereignty, are declared to possess the ultimate property in and to all lands within the jurisdiction of the state; and all lands the title to which shall fail from a defect of heirs shall revert or escheat to the people.

This section has not been amended. "Escheat" usually means to become the property of the state, although this section designates the people as the owners of land that escheats. Underlying this section's rule about the ownership of land that no one is authorized to inherit is the view that the people of the state are the ultimate owners of the land within the state's jurisdiction and that the individual owners of land thus hold their title to it at the people's sufferance.

In the only case in which this section was cited, the court declined to read the section literally, holding, rather, that the *state* has the ultimate authority over lands covered by navigable waters. *Angelo v. Railroad Commission* (1928). Section 1 of this article deals with navigable waters.

Article X

Education

Section 1
Superintendent of public instruction.

The supervision of public instruction shall be vested in a state superintendent and such other officers as the legislature shall direct; and their qualifications, powers, duties and compensation shall be prescribed by law. The state superintendent shall be chosen by the qualified electors of the state at the same time and in the same manner as members of the supreme court, and shall hold office for 4 years from the succeeding first Monday in July. The term of office, time and manner of electing or appointing all other officers of supervision of public instruction shall be fixed by law.

This section, which creates the constitutional office of state superintendent of public instruction, has been amended twice. The original version, like the current version, vested the supervision of public instruction (kindergarten through grade twelve education) in a state superintendent and "such other officers as the legislature shall direct." It also specified that the state superintendent be elected and limited the superintendent's salary to $1,200. A 1902 amendment required election in the same manner as members of the supreme court; that is, the election was to be held during the spring. At that election voters choose among candidates for nonpartisan offices, and the state superintendent candidates run without party labels. The 1902 amendment also provided for a four-year term of office. The other elected officials in the executive branch of the state government were not granted four-year terms by constitutional amendment until 1967.

A 1982 amendment deleted an obsolete provision about the conclusion of the term of office of the state superintendent who was elected in 1902.

The section has generated little litigation, but the short list of cases on it includes one of the more important cases in the state's history. In an early, fairly insignificant case about the compensation limit that appeared in the original version of this section, the court remarked that the reference to "such other officers as the legislature shall direct" "left the legislature free to prescribe such assistants and clerks as may be deemed essential." *State ex rel. Raymer v. Cunningham* (1892). Those words would become important more than 100 years later. Before 1996 only two other, minor cases on this section were decided. In one, the court held that the state superintendent's supervisory power includes the power to alter school district boundaries. *School Dist. v. Callahan* (1941). In the other, the court held that members of committees that drew school boundaries are officers, so that they derive their authority from this section. *Burton v. State Appeal Board* (1968).

Despite two opinions of the attorney general, 37 Op. Att'y Gen. 8 (1948); 37 Op. Att'y Gen. 347 (1948), that appointment of a state board of education to make policy decisions would violate this section if the state superintendent did not direct such a board, the state budget bill that was enacted during the 1995–1996 legislative session included a number of provisions that created an Education Commission to establish educational policy and that vastly diminished the state superintendent's authority and staff. In essence, the act transformed the Department of Public Instruction into a cabinet agency by transferring most of its resources and functions to the new Department of Education, the secretary of which the governor was to appoint. Litigation ensued and, the governor and the state superintendent being two of the five executive branch elected officials that the constitution specifically mentions, so did a constitutional crisis. *Thompson v. Craney* (1996).

The court decided that this section was ambiguous. It then turned to the debates on the pertinent section during the 1846 and 1848 constitutional conventions and found that the delegates understood that the state superintendent would have sole supervisory authority over the schools and would be elected, not appointed. The court, using as an aid to interpretation some letters that the drafter of the 1902 amendment wrote, determined that the other officers mentioned in that amendment were local officials and were to be supervised by the state superintendent. The next phase of the court's analysis, examining the first relevant acts that were passed after both the ratification of the 1848 constitution and the 1902 amendment to this section, confirmed the court's opinion that all state educational officers must be directed by the state superintendent. The court, therefore, declared void all the provisions in the budget bill that shifted power from the state superintendent and that altered the governance of public instruction.

In 2011, the legislature passed Act 27 requiring all state agencies, including the superintendent of public instruction and the department of public instruction, to seek the prior approval of the governor and the secretary of administration before drafting and promulgating of all administrative rules. In effect, the statute gave the governor and the secretary veto power over any change in the rules. Following *Thompson v. Craney*, the court concluded in *Coyne v. Walker* (2016) that rulemaking is a supervisory power because the constitution requires a uniform system of education, the superintendent is required to implement such a system, and rulemaking is one of the tools used for implementation. Vesting rulemaking in officers who are not subordinate to the superintendent violates this section.

Section 2
School fund created; income applied.

The proceeds of all lands that have been or hereafter may be granted by the United States to this state for educational purposes (except the lands heretofore granted for the purposes of a university) and all moneys and the clear proceeds of all property that may accrue to the state by forfeiture or escheat; and the clear proceeds of all fines collected in the several counties for any breach of the penal laws, and all moneys arising from any grant to the state where the purposes of such grant are not specified, and the 500,000 acres of land to which the state is entitled by the provisions of an act of congress, entitled "An act to appropriate the proceeds of the sales of the public lands and to grant pre-emption rights," approved September 4, 1841; and also the 5 percent of the net proceeds of the public lands to which the state shall become entitled on admission into the union (if congress shall consent to such appropriation of the 2 grants last mentioned) shall be set apart as a separate fund to be called "the school fund," the interest of which and all other revenues derived from the school lands shall be exclusively applied to the following objects, to wit:

(1) To the support and maintenance of common schools, in each school district, and the purchase of suitable libraries and apparatus therefor.

(2) The residue shall be appropriated to the support and maintenance of academies and normal schools, and suitable libraries and apparatus therefor.

This section originally included a reference to all moneys paid for exemption from military service in the list of the school fund's sources. An amendment that voters ratified in 1982 deleted that source. "Escheat" means to become the state's property, usually because there are no heirs to inherit the property or because the owner cannot be found. The theory is that the state is the ultimate owner of all property in the state and that, therefore, the holders of title to any property do so at the state's sufferance. At one time this was an important section because it dealt with one of the major sources of funding for the state's schools. Now the state provides, from its general fund, massive amounts of school aid. A statute requires that school districts must spend all the money that they receive from the school fund on library books and other instructional materials for school libraries, Wis. Stat. § 43.70(3). Because money is fungible, one cannot trace the dollars that schools receive from the school fund to determine whether they are used for that purpose, but § 43.70(3) does indirectly establish a lower limit for money that each school district must spend for the named purposes.

Much of the litigation concerning this section hinges on defining its words and phrases. "Penalty" means "penalties or fines for breaches of penal statutes, collected by ordinary judicial proceedings in the courts of the state." *The Village of Platteville v. Bell* (1878). The reference to the "clear proceeds" indicates that certain deductions may be made. *The State v. De Lano* (1891). The problem then becomes identifying the permissible deductions. The legislature has the authority to resolve that issue. *De Lano; The State ex rel. Guenther, State Treasurer v. Miles, County Treasurer* (1881); *State ex rel. Commrs. of Public Lands v. Anderson* (1973). Thus, counties have no right to determine the proceeds that they will withhold. *Guenther.*

However, the legislature does not have unbridled power in this area. *State ex rel. Commrs. of Pub. Lands v. Anderson* (1973). As the following sequence of cases indicates, the propriety of deductions is a matter of degree and thus of judgment. Giving half of the proceeds to an informer is acceptable. *Lynch v. the Steamer "Economy"* (1870). Giving two-thirds of the proceeds to an informer is acceptable. *De Lano.* However, giving all the proceeds to an informer and leaving none for the school fund is not acceptable. *Dutton v. Fowler* (1871). A statute allowing counties to retain 2 percent of the proceeds for the costs of prosecution is acceptable. *Guenther.* Allowing the counties to retain one-third of the proceeds is not acceptable, if that portion pays for future prosecutions, not for the prosecutions that generated the proceeds. *State ex rel. Johnson v. Mauer* (1915). However, allowing counties to retain half of the proceeds in motor vehicle cases is acceptable. *Anderson. Anderson* seems to have implicitly overruled the prior case cited, *Mauer,* although it does not explicitly do so. Because money is fungible, one cannot determine which dollar received is used for which purpose. A more rational inquiry, therefore, would be whether the portion that counties may retain is reasonable. The "property" that escheats includes both real property (land and buildings and other structures that are permanently attached to land) and personal property (all other property). *Estate of Payne* (1932). This seems obvious, because the reference in this section is to "property," but under the common law only land escheated, and the court had to reject the common-law rule to arrive at this understanding.

The case law has also clarified some other issues about this section. The state may sue counties for the money that it thinks ought to go to the school fund, but in so doing the state is bound by statutes of limitations. *State v. Milwaukee* (1913). The state must use revenue obtained under this section for the purposes that this section specifies. In other words, the school fund is a trust fund and thus must be administered for the purposes for which it was established. *Id.* For example, spending that revenue for a state park is unconstitutional. *State ex rel. Sweet and another v. Cunningham and others* (1894). A statute specifying that property acquired by escheat in Milwaukee County is to be given to the Milwaukee County Orphans' Board is also unconstitutional. *Estate of Payne.*

Section 3
District schools; tuition; sectarian instruction; released time.

The legislature shall provide by law for the establishment of district schools, which shall be as nearly uniform as practicable; and such schools shall be free and without charge for tuition to all children between the ages of 4 and 20 years; and no sectarian instruction shall be allowed therein; but the legislature by law may, for religious instruction outside the district schools, authorize the release of students during regular school hours.

Public education is so fundamental to state government that all fifty state constitutions require the legislature to provide free public schools. This section, which imposes requirements on the public schools, was amended in 1972 to allow released time from those schools for religious instruction. Although this section directs the legislature to provide for the establishment of schools, the legislature may also provide for the establishment of school districts, which are units of government, and some of which, especially in rural areas, are territorially distinct from municipalities and in other instances are coterminous with municipalities. *State ex rel. Board of Education v. Racine* (1931). Now, school districts are distinct entities and each, except the Milwaukee Public Schools, which notifies the City of Milwaukee of the property taxes it requires so that the city may levy them, has taxing authority. Related sections are Article I, Section 18 (on the freedom of religion and the establishment of religion) and Article I, Section 23 (on transportation of schoolchildren to and from parochial schools).

This section's prohibition against sectarian instruction in the schools has considerable force: "Wisconsin, as one of the later states admitted into the Union, having before it the experience of others, and probably in view of its heterogeneous population, . . . has, in her organic law, probably furnished a more-complete bar to any preference for, or discrimination against, any religious sect, organization, or society than any other state in the Union." *State ex rel. Weiss and others v. District Board, etc.* (1890).

This section makes the schools responsible for children between the ages of four and twenty. During the debates at the constitutional convention, delegates justified the maximum age because some children would have to alternate between working and attending school and therefore would require a longer time to graduate. Now, however, the low minimum age and the high maximum age make the schools responsible for providing services to disabled children and youths for a considerable time.

Specifying that schools must be provided for pupils between the ages of four and twenty does not preclude creating a system of vocational schools that would be open to persons who are older than twenty. *Manitowoc v. Manitowoc Rapids* (1939). This specification of age limits also does not imply that schools must admit all children between those ages; the right to attend school is subject to the general welfare, so school officials may deny admission and expel pupils. *State ex rel. Beattie v. Board of Education* (1919). Establishing the lower limit for education at four years of age guarantees only the right of a child of that age to apply for admission; it does not guarantee admission. *Zweifel v. Joint Dist. No. 1, Belleville* (1977). However, if a child cannot complete kindergarten before attaining the age at which he or she, according to statute, is to be admitted to the first grade— a situation that pertained to children who were born between September 1 and December 1—a school must admit a four-year-old child, pursuant to the requirement of uniform education. *Pacyna v. Board of Education* (1973).

Schools may not charge tuition, so a will donating funds for a school and requiring tuition payments to it will be interpreted to mean that only nonresidents and persons who are older than twenty may be required to pay tuition. *Maxcy v. Oshkosh* (1910). However, requiring a school district that does not have a high school to pay tuition for students who live in the district and attend high school in another district does not violate the requirement that the schools be free and without charge for tuition. *State ex rel. Comstock v. Joint School District, etc.* (1886). School districts may require nonresident pupils to pay tuition because this section establishes *district* schools. *Id.* "Free" means without cost for the use of the physical facilities, and "without charge for tuition" means without charge for instruction, so a school district may charge for supplies, gym suits, and renting books and musical instruments, and these constitutional requirements apply only to classes that count toward graduation. *Board of Education v. Sinclair* (1974). The latter qualification allows schools to charge fees for such things as driver's training courses.

"Sectarian instruction" means instruction in religious doctrines as opposed to instruction in beliefs common to all religions; accordingly, allowing teachers to read, without restriction, the Bible to pupils violates this section, because different Christian sects prefer different versions of the Bible. *State ex rel. Weiss and others v. District Board, etc.* (1890). Sectarian instruction may be enjoined, but public school may be held in part of a parochial school. *Dorner v. School District* (1908). Neither holding graduation at a church nor offering nonsectarian prayers at that ceremony violates this section. *State ex rel. Conway v. District Board* (1916).

The requirement of uniformity of schools has been an issue regarding the establishment of school boundaries more frequently than it has regarding any other issue. The uniformity requirement does not apply to the method of establishing boundaries and other organizational issues, only to the attributes of the schools that exist after their district boundaries have been established and the district organized or reorganized. *T. B. Scott Lumber Co. v. Oneida County and another* (1888); *West Milwaukee v. Area Bd. Vocational, T. & A.* (1971); *State ex rel. Zilisch v. Auer* (1928); *Joint School Dist. v. Sosalla* (1958); *Larson v. State Appeal Board* (1973).

Two other minor issues have been litigated under this section. Requiring negotiation with a union about a school's calendar does not violate this section. *Joint School Dist. No. 8 v. Wis. E. R. Board* (1967). School districts need not offer early admission to kindergarten because other school districts offer it. *Zweifel v. Joint Dist. No. 1, Belleville* (1977). However, districts must adhere to a uniform age of admission to kindergarten. *Pacyna v. Board of Education* (1973).

School finance cases are the most important cases about uniformity, because of the large sums of money at stake. Understanding these cases requires understanding Wisconsin's method of financing the schools. The two major sources of revenue are the property tax and state aid. School districts vary considerably regarding the ratio of their property tax base to the number of their pupils. Accordingly, if the property tax were the only source of revenue for schools, some districts would require vastly higher property tax rates—and thus would substantially burden their taxpayers—to generate the same amount of revenue per pupil that districts that have strong property tax bases can easily generate. The most fundamental concept in the formula by which state aid is allocated to school districts reflects that fact. The formula begins with the premise that the weaker a district's property tax base per pupil is, the more state aid the district will receive. However, the formula does not apply to categorical aid—aid that is based on expenditures for particular purposes. Also, the formula has included factors that dilute its basic purpose. For example, at times it provided for minimum aid so that districts that otherwise would not qualify for aid under the formula, because of their strong property tax bases, would receive aid anyway. Now the formula has three "tiers" of aid, which are based upon expenditures per pupil compared to property value per pupil. The formula also includes a guaranteed payment, so that every district, including property-rich, high-spending districts, receives aid. Less important factors, such as the date on which pupils are counted, also distort the formula's operation and cause it fall short of achieving its purpose.

A school district's fiscal robustness certainly affects the "character of instruction" that it offers, and several cases have established that "character of instruction" is subject to the uniformity requirement. E.g., *State ex rel. Zilisch v. Auer* (1928). In *State ex rel. Joint School Dist. v. Becker* (1928), the court held that the uniformity requirement applies to the establishment of districts and to the districts themselves (apparently, the geographical area of the district) but not to the apportionment of utility taxes to them. In *Buse v. Smith* (1976), the court held a school financing plan that would require districts that had strong property tax bases in relation to the number of pupils to collect property taxes that would be placed in a pool and distributed to districts that had weak property tax bases compared to the number of pupils was not justified by this section, because, although "equal opportunity for education is a fundamental right," absolute uniformity is not required, so equality of funding (presumably on a per-pupil basis) is also not required. Providing additional revenue to districts that have a high percentage of children from poor families is not required because the school aid formula reflects only districts' property tax bases, not their needs; spending disparities do not indicate nonuniformity and providing extra funds for such districts would violate the principle of local control of the schools. *Kukor v. Grover* (1989). Because private, nonsectarian schools are not district schools, this section does not apply to them and paying to them the state aid that would be paid to public schools in respect to the private school's pupils does not violate this section. *Davis v. Grover* (1992).

The statute creating the Milwaukee Parental Choice Program, by which the state defrays the cost for certain students to attend private schools, does not violate this section. *Jackson v. Benson* (1998).

As the twentieth century came to a close, the supreme court heard one more equal funding challenge to the state's school finance formula, *Vincent v. Voight* (2000). As it had in *Kukor*, the court held that the state's funding scheme did not violate this section, and noted that the equalization formula better equalized the tax base than it had in the past. However, the court held that the constitution does not require equality in expenditures, but equality in outcomes. Thus, the court signaled a change in direction for educational funding challenges.

While rejecting the constitutional challenge based upon an equal funding argument, a 4–3 majority laid out the kind of evidence that would be required to prove that the funding formula violates this section. The court noted that recent challenges to educational funding in other states had relied upon a theory of educational adequacy rather than equal funding. Equal funding arguments do not apply because districts face varying costs for educating disabled students, economically disadvantaged students, and students with limited English language skills. The constitutional question is whether each district provides a quality education. The equalization formula will remain constitutional as long as the legislature provides adequate funding to enable each school district to provide students with a sound basic education. *Vincent*.

Under this section, the state has no responsibility for educating expelled students. The state may only expel a student for good cause and in conformity with due process. The state may not expel a student without giving notice of the charges against him, as well as an expulsion hearing that provides a meaningful opportunity for the student to be heard before an unbiased tribunal. There is no requirement that the student actually attend the hearing. *Remer v. Burlington Area School District* (2001) involved a student's plot to bring guns to school and shoot certain administrators and students. The court concluded that, regardless of whether the expulsion decision lacked wisdom or compassion, all it could do was to determine if the school district had acted in conformity with the Fourteenth Amendment.

This section also allows public schools to assign homework over the summer vacation. Parents have certain rights, but they do not have a right to direct the manner in which a public school teaches their child. The court of appeals refused to apply strict scrutiny because "[t]he U.S. Supreme Court has not extended substantive due process to [the right to a] summer vacation." As the trial court stated, ". . . the people of our state granted to the legislature in Art. X, §1 of the state constitution the power to establish school boards and the state superintendent and to confer upon them the powers and duties the legislature saw fit. [Statutes] which broadly authorize a math teacher to prescribe homework over the summer to help kids learn pre-calculus, fit comfortably within this constitutional grant of power to the government." *Larson v. Burmaster* (2006).

Section 4
Annual school tax.

Each town and city shall be required to raise by tax, annually, for the support of common schools therein, a sum not less than one-half the amount received by such town or city respectively for school purposes from the income of the school fund.

This section has not been amended. In the state's early years, when the income from the school fund was substantial compared to the schools' need for revenue, this section had some significance. Now, when that income accounts for only a minuscule portion of the schools' budgets, the section is not significant. This section, along with others, does not make a town an interested party, nor does it allow a town to determine a school district's financial needs. *Greenfield v. Joint County School Comm.* (1955). One town had tried to litigate a school district reorganization and pointed out that the reorganization placed some of its residents in a school district that had a weak property tax base, but the court responded that that was a problem of only certain taxpayers, not of the town. In contrast, this section, along with others, provided the basis for a group of taxpayers to challenge the statutory method of financing the Milwaukee Public Schools. *Tooley v. O'Connell* (1977).

Section 5
Income of school fund.

Provision shall be made by law for the distribution of the income of the school fund among the several towns and cities of the state for the support of common schools therein, in some just proportion to the number of children and youth resident therein between the ages of four and twenty years, and no appropriation shall be made from the school fund to any city or town for the year in which said city or town shall fail to raise such tax; nor to any school district for the year in which a school shall not be maintained at least three months.

This section has not been amended. It is anachronistic to the extent it refers to towns and cities, but not to villages. In the only case concerning this section, the court interpreted it to include towns, cities, and villages. *State ex rel. Board of Education v. Hunter* (1903). Moreover, now school districts impose their own property taxes (except for the Milwaukee Public Schools, which certify to the City of Milwaukee the amount of money that they need from the property tax, so that the city can levy that amount for the school district). Moreover, school districts now impose property taxes in amounts that far exceed the amount of money that they receive from the school fund.

Section 6
State university; support.

Provision shall be made by law for the establishment of a state university at or near the seat of state government, and for connecting with the same, from time to time, such colleges in different parts of the state as the interests of education may require. The proceeds of all lands that have been or may hereafter be granted by the United States to the state for the support of a university shall be and remain a perpetual fund to be called "the university fund," the interest of which shall be appropriated to the support of the state university, and no sectarian instruction shall be allowed in such university.

The requirement that a state university be at or near the capital facilitated the Wisconsin Idea: the University of Wisconsin's provision of services to the state government and to the state's people. Wisconsin is one of only nine states to have established their capital and major state university in the same city. The largest federal grant of land, made by means of the Morrill Act, occurred in 1862, fourteen years after this section established a fund in which to place such grants' proceeds. The University of Wisconsin did not make particularly wise use of the land grant, but the grant itself indicated to the university that the federal government expected it to make practical contributions to the state, especially to the state's farmers. The university responded with a wealth of useful inventions, such as the Babcock test for the butterfat content of milk, and many practical applications of its knowledge, such as the work of its plant pathologists on the diseases that attacked crops in the state.

The direction to establish a state university is not exclusive in the sense that it precludes granting aid to a private university if the grant fulfills a public purpose. *State ex rel. Warren v. Reuter* (1969). This section also does not make vocational education a concern exclusively of the state to prevent financing a system of vocational, technical, and adult education institutions, which are now called technical colleges, partly by means of taxes levied only within each of the vocational, technical, and adult education districts, which are now called technical college districts. *West Milwaukee v. Area Bd. Vocational, T. & A. Ed.* (1971).

Section 7
Commissioners of public lands.

The secretary of state, treasurer and attorney general, shall constitute a board of commissioners for the sale of the school and university lands and for the investment of the funds arising therefrom. Any two of said commissioners shall be a quorum for the transaction of all business pertaining to the duties of their office.

This section has not been amended. The lands mentioned are those under Sections 2 and 6 of this article. For example, the university lands are not all of that institution's lands but only the lands that the federal government granted. *Loomis v. Callahan* (1928). Only the commissioners that this section enumerates may perform the duties that this section prescribes. *McCabe et al. v. Mazzuchelli* (1861); *State ex rel. Owen v. Donald* (1915). The lands are held in trust, so they may be used only as this section provides. *Donald.*

Section 8
Sale of public lands.

Provision shall be made by law for the sale of all school and university lands after they shall have been appraised; and when any portion of such lands shall be sold and the purchase money shall not be paid at the time of the sale, the commissioners shall take security by mortgage upon the lands sold for the sum remaining unpaid, with seven percent interest thereon, payable annually at the office of the treasurer. The commissioners shall be authorized to execute a good and sufficient conveyance to all purchasers of such lands, and to discharge any mortgages taken as security, when the sum due thereon shall have been paid. The commissioners shall have power to withhold from sale any portion of such lands when they shall deem it expedient, and shall invest all moneys arising from the sale of such lands, as well as all other university and school funds, in such manner as the legislature shall provide, and shall give such security for the faithful performance of their duties as may be required by law.

This section has not been amended. As the first clause indicates, the legislature and governor may, by statute, direct the way sales are to be made. *State ex rel. Sweet and another v. Cunningham and others* (1894). However, statutes may not be enacted to divert funds for purposes, such as setting aside land for forestry purposes, other than those that the constitution specifies. *State ex rel. Owen v. Donald* (1915). The requirement that the state take a mortgage is intended to protect the school fund; accordingly, it is mandatory if title to land passes from the state, but it is not mandatory if title does not pass. *Smith v. Mariner* (1856).

Article XI

Corporations

Section 1
Corporations; how formed.

Corporations without banking powers or privileges may be formed under general laws, but shall not be created by special act, except for municipal purposes. All general laws or special acts enacted under the provisions of this section may be altered or repealed by the legislature at any time after their passage.

This section's original version provided, in addition to the exception for municipal corporations, an exception for instances in which, in the legislature's judgment, a corporation could not fulfill its purposes under general laws. The exception swallowed the rule, and a 1981 amendment eliminated it. Article IV, Section 31(9) also prohibits incorporating; and amending the charters of cities, towns, and villages by special or private law. Those units of government are corporations ("bodies corporate and politic"), and until Article XI, Section 3 was amended in 1924 to grant home rule powers to cities and villages, they had only the powers that were granted, under this section, in their charters and by laws that in effect amended those charters. For that reason, an attempt at that time to grant home rule power to cities and villages by statute was unconstitutional. *State ex rel. Mueller v. Thompson* (1912).

A famous federal case, *Dartmouth College v. Woodward* (1819), led to this section. *Attorney General v. Railroad Companies* (1874); *West Wis. R. R. Co.*

v. Trempealeau (1874). In *Dartmouth College*, the U.S. Supreme Court held that a college's charter was a contract and that changes to it violated the U.S. Constitution's prohibition against the impairment of contracts, Article I, Section 10. Wisconsin's constitution includes a similar prohibition in Article I, Section 12. However, this section makes it clear that statutes governing corporations are not integrated into corporate charters, and those statutes are therefore outside the scope of the U.S. Constitution's Contracts Clause. *Albert Trostel & Sons v. Notz* (2012).

The state supreme court has broadly understood "charter" to include all rights granted to, and all duties imposed upon, corporations. In other words, this section makes it possible for the state to regulate corporations. Its purpose is to "retain and secure to the state full power and control over corporate franchises, rights and privileges which it might grant." *West. Wis. R. R. Co. v. Trempealeau* (1874). The state's power and control over franchises, rights, and privileges extends to those granted by municipalities, because municipalities acting for those purposes are the state's agents. *Superior W., L. & P. Co. v. Superior* (1921).

This section applies to corporations in the common meaning of the term: business corporations. E.g., *Wisconsin Telephone Co. v. Public Service Comm.* (1932). The reference to "municipal purposes" suggests that it also applies to municipalities. In fact, that expression does not limit the kind of purposes for which special laws dealing with corporations may be enacted, but identifies one kind of corporation that special laws may affect. *Clark v. City of Janesville* (1860). It was necessary to allow special laws about municipalities because during the nineteenth century they were formed by special charter, so their powers and duties could be changed only by special laws. "Municipal" has a broad meaning and probably includes all local units of government. The term, however, does not include such quasi-governmental entities as authorities, even if the authority is designated a "public body corporate and politic." *Wisconsin Solid Waste Recycling Auth. v. Earl* (1975).

This section's grant of authority to alter or repeal charters, which is sometimes referred to as the reserved power, is the power to regulate corporations. Laws that do so in effect alter the charters of the corporations to which they apply. *Attorney General v. Railroad Companies* (1874). This section does not prohibit many kinds of regulation, such as granting the authority to examine a corporation's books and to control the rates that it charges, *id.*; charging an industry for the costs incurred to regulate it, *Wisconsin Telephone Co. v. Public Service Comm.* (1932): changing railroad lines, *Kenosha R. & R. I. R. R. Co. v. Marsh* (1863); imposing taxes, *West. Wis. R. R. Co. v. Trempealeau* (1874); subjecting corporations to the state's public utility laws, *Superior W., L. & P. Co. v. Superior* (1921); changing the tolls or rates that a corporation may charge, *Madison W. & M. P. Co. v. Reynolds* (1854), *Manitowoc v. Manitowoc & Northern T. Co.* (1911), *State ex rel. Cream City R. Co. v. Hilbert* (1888), *Duluth St. R. Co. v. Railroad Commission* (1915); divesting a corporation of a franchise for operating a dam,

Pratt v. Brown (1854); and changing the fees or taxes imposed on a corporation, *State v. Railway Cos.* (1906).

Several limits apply to the authority to regulate under this section. Alteration that is so extensive that it amounts to total change violates this section. *Kenosha R. & R. I. R. R. Co.* Because of the prohibition against taking property without providing just compensation in Article I, Section 13, that kind of alteration of a charter, as well as destruction of property, violates this section. *Water Power Cases* (1912); *State ex rel. Northern Pac. R. Co. v. Railroad Commission* (1909). Regulation under this section is limited to that which is based upon the state's police power. *Chicago, Milwaukee & St. Paul R. Co. v. City of Milwaukee* (1897).

Over time, there have developed two lines of cases concerning this section. One line interprets this section restrictively; it is pro-corporation and anti-regulation. This line applies to business corporations; no one seems to think that the state's power to regulate its units of government (municipal corporations) has limits. The other line of cases takes an expansive view and allows virtually any regulation. Two forceful and well-argued cases, the first of which meticulously explains the need for an expansive view and the second of which carefully and exhaustively reviews the prior cases and implicitly overrules or blunts the effect of the restrictive cases, make clear that the weight of opinion favors the expansive view. *Attorney General v. Railroad Companies* (1874); *Superior W., L. & P. Co. v. Superior* (1921).

Section 2
Property taken by municipality.

No municipal corporation shall take private property for public use, against the consent of the owner, without the necessity thereof being first established in the manner prescribed by the legislature.

This section's original version provided that a municipality may not take (for public use) private property unless a jury has found the taking necessary. This section was amended in 1961 to allow the legislature to establish the procedures by which it is determined whether a taking is needed. Article I, Section 13 is a broader section on taking property, and Section 3A of this article covers condemnation as well as other means of acquiring property.

This section does not apply to counties, which are created to administer state functions and are therefore political subdivisions of the state. *State ex rel. Base v. Schinz* (1927). It also does not apply to towns. *Norton v. Peck* (1854). Interference with the passage of someone to and from his or her property is not a taking for purposes of this section. *Randall v. City of Milwaukee* (1933). Moreover, dedication—transfer of private property for public use—is not a taking for purposes of this section. *Barteau v. West et al.* (1868). Whereas, Article I, Section 13 is a general provision, this section addresses procedure. Many of the cases involve the requirement of a jury verdict and are therefore irrelevant today.

The City of Milwaukee condemns property under the Kline Law (Chapter 275, Laws of 1931). The procedures under that law have been attacked under this section. That law's establishment of a Board of Assessment, which determines the property to be taken, the purposes for which it is to be used and other details of the project, is not unconstitutional, because the city appoints and finances the board. *Bolles v. Milwaukee* (1951). That law's grant of power to a jury is constitutional because the Common Council, and therefore the municipality, makes the final determination. *Milwaukee v. Taylor* (1938).

Section 3
Municipal home rule; debt limit; tax to pay debt.

(1) Cities and villages organized pursuant to state law may determine their local affairs and government, subject only to this constitution and to such enactments of the legislature of statewide concern as with uniformity shall affect every city or every village. The method of such determination shall be prescribed by the legislature.

(2) No county, city, town, village, school district, sewerage district or other municipal corporation may become indebted in an amount that exceeds an allowable percentage of the taxable property located therein equalized for state purposes as provided by the legislature. In all cases the allowable percentage shall be 5 percent except as specified in pars. (a) and (b):

(a) For any city authorized to issue bonds for school purposes, an additional 10 percent shall be permitted for school purposes only, and in such cases the territory attached to the city for school purposes shall be included in the total taxable property supporting the bonds issued for school purposes.

(b) For any school district which offers no less than grades one to 12 and which at the time of incurring such debt is eligible for the highest level of school aids, 10 percent shall be permitted.

(3) Any county, city, town, village, school district, sewerage district or other municipal corporation incurring any indebtedness under sub. (2) shall, before or at the time of doing so, provide for the collection of a direct annual tax sufficient to pay the interest on such debt as it falls due, and also to pay and discharge the principal thereof within 20 years from the time of contracting the same.

(4) When indebtedness under sub. (2) is incurred in the acquisition of lands by cities, or by counties or sewerage districts having a population of 150,000 or over, for public, municipal purposes, or for the permanent improvement thereof, or to purchase, acquire, construct, extend, add to or improve a sewage collection or treatment system which services all or a part of such city or county, the city, county or sewerage district incurring the indebtedness shall, before or at the time of so doing, provide for the collection of a direct annual tax sufficient to pay the interest on such debt as it falls due, and also to pay and discharge the principal thereof within a period not exceeding 50 years from the time of contracting the same.

(5) An indebtedness created for the purpose of purchasing, acquiring, leasing, constructing, extending, adding to, improving, conducting, controlling, operating or managing a public utility of a town, village, city or special district, and

secured solely by the property or income of such public utility, and whereby no municipal liability is created, shall not be considered an indebtedness of such town, village, city or special district, and shall not be included in arriving at the debt limitation under sub. (2).

This section, because it both grants important powers to, and imposes important restrictions on, municipalities, is one of the more important in the constitution. It has been amended eleven times, more than any other section. The increasing fiscal strength and responsibility of local units of government and their desire to borrow for particular projects have increased the pressure to make this section less restrictive, leading to its relatively frequent amendment. The original version required the legislature to provide for the organization of cities and incorporated villages and to restrict their power to tax and borrow. In 1874, this section was amended to impose on counties, cities, towns, villages, school districts, and other municipal corporations a debt limit of 5 percent of the assessed value of the taxable property in the governmental unit and to require a direct annual tax (a property tax) sufficient to pay the interest on the debt and to pay the principal within twenty years. A 1912 amendment extended the time within which debt must be paid to fifty years for the acquisition of land by cities and by counties that had a population of at least 150,000. In 1924, this section was amended to allow cities and villages to determine their own affairs subject to the constitution and to statutes of statewide concern that uniformly affect every city and village. The exception to the debt limit for expenses incurred by a town, village, or city and related to a utility was added in 1932. In 1951, the debt limit for cities that were authorized to issue bonds for school purposes (only the City of Milwaukee) was increased to 8 percent of the value of the taxable property in the city. A 1955 amendment changed the base used to calculate the debt limit of school districts from the assessed value (the value that local assessors determine) of the taxable property in them to the equalized value (the value that the Department of Revenue determines) of the taxable property in them. A 1960 amendment extended the use of equalized value to determine the property base to counties that have a population of at least 500,000 (only Milwaukee County). In 1961, the debt limit for school districts that received the highest level of state aid was increased to 10 percent of the equalized value of the taxable property in them. In 1963, the basis for calculating the debt limit of all governmental units that were subject to that limit was changed to the equalized value of the taxable property in them, and the debt limit for cities that were authorized to issue bonds for school purposes (the City of Milwaukee) was increased from 8 to 10 percent (plus the city's own 5 percent). A 1966 amendment extended the public utility exception to special districts (governmental units that perform only one or a few purposes, such as preserving lakes). A 1981 amendment applied the debt limit to sewerage districts and gave those districts fifty years to pay off their debts.

One of the three main topics in the case law on this section is home rule. The case law on the subject is voluminous; the more important terms, "local affairs" and "statewide concern," are vague, as courts have remarked since the first case addressing this part of this section, *State ex rel. Ekern v. Milwaukee* (1926), and the cases turn on courts' reactions to the relevant facts.

This section's purposes regarding home rule are to grant legislative power to cities and villages and to limit the power that the legislature would have under Article IV, Section 1 over them. *Ekern*. In home rule cases, the first inquiry is whether the subject at issue is statewide or local. In some cases the answer is clear, but in most, it is a mixture of statewide and local, which requires a court to determine the primary purpose. *Gloudeman v. City of St. Francis* (1988). Public policy falls into three categories: matters exclusively of statewide concern, matters entirely of local character, and matters that do not fit exclusively into the first two groups. *Ekern*. The court has come to refer to the third category as a "mixed bag." *State ex rel. Michalek v. LeGrand* (1977). A legislative statement that a particular statute addresses a matter of statewide concern creates a presumption that the statute does so, but such a statement does not dispose of that issue. *Van Gilder v. Madison* (1936).

A few examples will give some sense of the sort of matters that are, on the one hand, local or primarily local and, on the other hand, statewide or primarily statewide. Authorizing tenants to withhold rent because of their landlords' violation of the building code or of the zoning code and placing limits on the height of buildings are matters of primarily local concern. *Michalek*. Conversely, crime control, even down to the details of setting the compensation of police officers, *Van Gilder*, and the notice requirements for a change in zoning, because they involve due process rights, *Gloudeman*, are matters of statewide concern or primarily of statewide concern.

Because state statutes and regulations address solid waste landfill facilities in detail and expressly withdraw the power of municipalities to address the matter, a city's regulation of a landfill that violates the letter, spirit, and purpose of a statute regulating a matter of statewide concern must fail. *DeRosso Land Fill Co. v. City of Oak Creek* (1996). Livestock facilities siting is a "mixed bag." It is both a matter of statewide concern and local affairs. But in a case where the legislature has clearly withdrawn the power to act from cities and towns, state statutes preempt the field. *Adams v. Livestock Facilities Siting Review Board* (2012). The court of appeals found that an ordinance forbidding convicted sex offenders from living near schools does not conflict with the spirit or the purpose of the state's comprehensive regulations on assimilating sex offenders into society. *City of South Milwaukee v. Kester* (2013).

Van Gilder set the tone for home rule cases. The *Van Gilder* court declared that, in adopting the home rule amendment, the people had no intent to create a state within a state, an *imperium in imperio*. If an ordinance conflicts with a statute, it must pass all of the tests derived from *Anchor Sav. & Loan v. Equal*

Opport. Com'n (1984), or the court will consider it to be preempted and void. These tests open the door to implied preemption.

(1) Has the legislature expressly withdrawn the power of municipalities to act?
(2) Does the ordinance logically conflict with state legislation?
(3) Does the ordinance defeat the purpose of state legislation? or
(4) Does the ordinance violate the spirit of state legislation?

If the ordinance fails any of these tests it is void.

If a matter is of local or primarily local concern, the state may still legislate on it. If the state does legislate, a city or village may acquiesce or it may override the state's statute. *State ex rel. Sleeman v. Baxter* (1928). If a city or village wishes to override a state statute, it must do so by ordinance. *Save our Fire Dep't v. City of Appleton* (1986). An ordinance that performs that function is called a charter ordinance. *Van Gilder.* Regarding matters of local or primarily local concern, the uniformity requirement in subsection (1) precludes classification, but regarding matters of statewide concern or primarily statewide concern cities and villages may be classified. *Id.*

If the case involves a "mixed bag" of state and local concerns, the court will apply the "paramountcy test" to determine if the underlying issue is primarily a question of state or local concern. The court in *Madison Teachers, Inc. v. Walker* (2014) took an expansive view of what "statewide concern" means, holding that contributions made by the City of Milwaukee to the city employees' pension system pursuant to a city charter ordinance was primarily a matter of statewide concern and therefore a statute forbidding such payments does not violate this section. Similarly, the court in *Black v. City of Milwaukee* (2016) found that another Milwaukee charter ordinance that required city employees to live within the city limits was preempted by a statute, because the location of city employees' homes is a matter of statewide concern and not only a local affair. The court further held that, although the statute as written applies only to Milwaukee as the state's only first-class city, this section's uniformity clause is satisfied if the statute "on its face" applies to every city or village.

The second main topic in the case law concerning this section is the requirement that a "direct annual tax" (a property tax) be levied to pay the interest on municipal debt as it becomes due and to pay the principal within twenty years (fifty years for counties or sewerage districts that have a population of at least 150,000 and for cities). This section does not require a unit of government to levy a tax for operating expenses or for debts that are to be paid within one year: "the indebtedness against which a tax must be levied is one bearing interest, the time of payment of which has been extended over a series of years." *Herman v. The City of Oconto* (1901). If there clearly is no tax levied in respect to the debt, that debt violates this section. *First Wisconsin Nat. Bank v. Catawba* (1924). The levy must be definite; a statement that "there shall be annually levied" is a mere promise, not a levy of a tax, and the interest payments due on the bonds supported by that promise are a debt that violates this section. *Kyes v. St. Croix Co.* (1900). However, levying a lump sum, rather than distinguishing between levies for principal and interest, as this section does, is constitutionally valid. *Borner v. Prescott* (1912). If a debt is unconstitutional, the unit of government must still pay it. *First Wisconsin Nat. Bank v. Catawba* (1924). Because the tax must exist when the debt is incurred, timing is occasionally an issue. A tax exists when it is levied—when it is placed on the tax rolls and property owners become obligated to pay it. *Herman v. The City of Oconto* (1901); *Balch v. Beach* (1903).

The third main topic in the case law concerning this subject is debt limits. In the constitution "debt" includes all absolute obligations to pay money, or its equivalent, from funds to be provided, as distinguished from money currently available or in the process of collection and so treatable as in hand. *Earles v. Wells and others* (1896). This definition applies to this section. E.g., *City of Hartford v. Kirley* (1992). A debt exists only if the amount owed is ascertainable, *Janes v. Racine* (1913), and if there is an absolute obligation to pay, *Milwaukee Elec. Rwy. & Light Co. v. City of Milwaukee* (1921); *Connor v. City of Marshfield* (1906). Debt includes special improvement bonds that are unconditionally pledged, even if they are to be paid from special assessments. *Fowler v. City of Superior* (1893).

The requirement that there be an obligation to pay has led the court to hold several financial arrangements to not be debt, even if the facts of the case made it clear that the obligation would be paid. *State ex rel. Thomson v. Giessel* (1955). The cash in hand portion of the general definition has also prevented some financial arrangements from being debt. *Crogster v. Bayfield County and others* (1898) (assets readily liquidated were included in "cash in hand"). Other obligations that are not debt include amounts owed to a sinking fund to redeem bonds, *Eau Claire v. Eau Claire Water Co.* (1909); obligations that statutes impose, *Columbia County v. Wisconsin Retirement Fund* (1962); contractual obligations that become due after the current year, *Stedman v. City of Berlin* (1897); debts owed to the state, *State ex rel. Marinette, T. & W. R. Co. v. Tomahawk Common Council* (1897); and short-term notes for operating expenses, *School Dist. v. Marine Nat. Exchange Bank* (1960). Most revenue bonds—bonds that are funded by the proceeds of the facility that they are issued to finance—are not debt. *State ex rel. Morgan v. City of Portage* (1921); *State ex rel. Hammermill Paper Co. v. LaPlante* (1973). However, revenue bonds used to replenish a municipality's general fund, from which the money that was used to finance the project was drawn, are debt. *Roberts v. City of Madison* (1947). Most contractual obligations are not debt. *Columbia County v. Wisconsin Retirement Fund* (1962); *Herman v. The City of Oconto* (1901). However, a contractual obligation to redeem bonds is debt. *Crogster v. Bayfield County and others* (1898).

If a municipality is obligated to pay, there generally is a debt. *Burnham v. City of Milwaukee* (1897). This is true even if a creative financing plan obscures the obligation. Examples of creative financing are redemption of bonds from a fund created to stimulate economic development, by the diversion of some property tax revenues and payments by other taxpayers, *City of Hartford v. Kirley* (1992), and an arrangement with a shell corporation for a lease at the end of which the municipality would own the facility that was being indirectly financed. *Earles v. Wells and others* (1896). Special assessments owed by a municipality are debt. *Riesen v. School District* (1926). A pledge of general tax revenue is debt. *City of Hartford*. Although an obligation secured by the revenue of an asset that is to be built by means of the financial arrangement is not debt, an obligation that is secured by an asset that exists at the time the obligation is incurred is debt; this rule is called the "preexisting asset doctrine." *State ex rel. Morgan v. City of Portage.*

In calculating the limit under this section, certain assets and obligations are subtracted from the debt. They may be offset only if the municipality has a legal right to enforce them. *Rice v. The City of Milwaukee and others* (1893). They do not include the value of real estate owned. *Riesen.* Money in a special fund and anticipated revenues that are not in the process of collection do not create offsets. *Id.* The offsets reflect the distinction in the definition of debt between debts and cash in hand or in the process of collection. In determining the net debt, the time when the debt accrues is occasionally an issue. A contractual debt arises when the contract is performed. *Marinette, T. & W. R. Co.*, and obligations to pay interest arise when the interest becomes due. *Herman.*

The exemption for public utilities in subsection (5) prevents some financial obligations from being debt. The subsection limits the uses to which the borrowed revenue may be put, and it requires that the debt be secured solely by the utility's property or income. "Utility" includes "all plants or activities which the legislature can reasonably classify as public utilities in the ordinary meaning of the term." *Payne v. Racine* (1935). In other words, there are two requirements: reasonable classification and conformity to the ordinary meaning of the term "utility." Facilities that are utilities include sewage treatment plants, *Payne*, and hospitals, *Meier v. Madison* (1950). A hospital stretches the ordinary meaning of "utility," but it performs a basic governmental function: attending to the citizens' health. This exception does not apply unless revenue from the utility directly funds the obligation. *City of Hartford*. To fit within this exception the obligation must fund a new, not an existing, facility. *Morgan.*

As it does with Article VIII, Section 10 (on internal improvements), the decision in *Libertarian Party v. State* (1996) scrambles the case law concerning this section. The court offers four reasons why bonds that a special district—a governmental unit that serves one function or only a few functions—issues to generate the bulk of the revenue needed to build a professional baseball stadium are not debt. The first is that the bonds will not be funded with property tax revenue, so they resemble the bonds that were funded with special assessments and were approved in *Fowler v. City of Superior* (1893). However, this section states that if there is debt, there must be a property tax, not if there is no property tax, there is no debt. Second, the court uses cases from other states to establish for the first time in Wisconsin the rule that, if the bonds are paid from a special fund, there is no debt. However, in *City of Hartford v. Kirley* (1992), a case decided four years prior to *Libertarian Party v. State*, the court noted that the bonds at issue were paid from a special fund and proceeded to hold that financing arrangement unconstitutional. Third, the court claims that the bonds are revenue bonds, so that they do not create debt. However, revenue bonds are secured by the revenue from the project that they are used to build, which is not true of the bonds in this case. Fourth, the court argues that the baseball stadium is a public utility, so that the exception for that kind of structure applies. However, a baseball stadium cannot be a public utility if that expression is given its ordinary meaning, and if a reasonable classification is made, both of which are required by *Payne v. Racine* (1935). Moreover, even if a stadium is a public utility, the exception applies only if the obligation is secured solely by the utility's property or income, which the obligations in question are not. Either this case is an anomaly or the legislature can circumvent this section by calling anything it likes a public utility, and a unit of government can probably circumvent it by establishing a special fund. In other words, if this case is not an anomaly, the debt limit provision in this section is diminished.

Section 3A
Acquisition of lands by state and subdivisions; sale of excess.

The state or any of its counties, cities, towns or villages may acquire by gift, dedication, purchase, or condemnation lands for establishing, laying out, widening, enlarging, extending, and maintaining memorial grounds, streets, highways, squares, parkways, boulevards, parks, playgrounds, sites for public buildings, and reservations in and about and along and leading to any or all of the same; and after the establishment, layout, and completion of such improvements, with reservations concerning the future use and occupation of such real estate, so as to protect such public works and improvements, and their environs, and to preserve the view, appearance, light, air and usefulness of such public works. If the governing body of a county, city, town or village elects to accept a gift or dedication of land made on condition that the land be devoted to a special purpose and the condition subsequently becomes impossible or impracticable, such governing body may by resolution or ordinance enacted by a two-thirds vote of its members elect either to grant the land back to the donor or dedicator or his heirs or accept from the donor or dedicator or his heirs a grant relieving the county, city, town or village of the condition; however, if the donor or dedicator or his heirs are unknown or cannot be found, such resolution or ordinance may provide for the commencement of proceedings in the manner and in the courts as the legislature shall designate for the purpose of relieving the county, city, town or village from the condition of the gift or dedication.

This section, which was added to the constitution in 1912 and amended in 1956 to make it apply not only to the state and cities, but to counties, towns, and villages, and to add the second sentence. Except for a single case, one can divide the cases concerning this section into two categories: those on acquiring property and those on disposing of property. The odd case makes it clear that the section does not convert an easement—a grant of a right regarding property, such as the right to run a utility line over it—into ownership. *Mueller v. Schier* (1926).

As to acquiring property, a wildlife refuge is a park, because it exists for the benefit of the public and provides opportunities for recreation and viewing scenic beauty. *State ex rel. Hammann v. Levitan* (1929). Although they are not included in the list of purposes for which property may be condemned, airports qualify because the eminent domain power is plenary *Ferguson v. Kenosha* (1958). It would have been much more logical to arrive at the result in both cases by resorting to the broader, but still less than plenary, eminent domain powers in Article I, Section 13.

As to the disposal of property, the court had to stretch to approve certain dispositions. Sale of state buildings to a shell corporation was approved because this section did not include a limitation on the sale of state land and because the court was "obliged to determine that the provision is a grant of power which broadened the authority of the state and cities in the matter of excess condemnation." *State ex rel. Thomson v. Giessel* (1955). In 1954, the court had held that a city may lease part of a park to a business, because cities have the same right to sell property that they have to acquire it. *Kranjec v. West Allis* (1954). This section does not apply to transferring possession of property from one state agency to another. *Cutts v. Department of Public Welfare* (1957). Two other courts cited to the passage quoted above about the section's purpose, and approved the sale of a portion of a park to a college, even though the sale made public access to the park exceedingly difficult, *Newell v. Kenosha* (1959); and the lease of park land to a television station for a tower, because another tower was already on the site, the park's beauty was not diminished and the plot sold was tiny and not needed for the park. *State ex rel. Evjue v. Seybeth* (1960).

Section 4
General banking law.

The legislature may enact a general banking law for the creation of banks, and for the regulation and supervision of the banking business.

The sentiment that led to the prohibition against banking in the 1846 constitution, which the voters failed to ratify, affected this section for decades. This section originally prohibited the legislature from authorizing any bank except as provided in this article. At that time a Section 5 followed, requiring a referendum that would offer the voters two straightforward choices: "bank" or "no bank." If the voters approved the first alternative, the legislature could either grant individual charters to banks or pass a general banking law, but in either case, the legislation would not take effect without the voters' approval. Throughout the nineteenth century, many citizens were skeptical about banking's value and about the legislature's actions on the subject, although not skeptical enough, or politically powerful enough, to insert a prohibition against banking into the constitution. The voters, in 1902, repealed Section 5 and amended Section 4 to allow a general banking law. Uneasiness about banking had abated, but it had not disappeared. Discontinuing the option of granting individual charters is evidence of suspicion that the legislature would show favoritism. In addition, the new version required a two-thirds vote in each house of the legislature to pass any banking bill. That requirement was not deleted until 1981.

An early case, no longer relevant but of historical interest, is *State ex rel. Reedsburg Bank v. Hastings* (1860.). In 1860, at a time when Section 5 required approval by the voters of all banking legislation and before the case law on Article VIII, Section 1 had made it clear that this section applied only to the property tax, the court held that, because banking statutes were the product of a legislative act of the people, a tax on the capital stock of banks was unique and not subject to the latter section's requirement of uniformity.

Regulation of banking includes providing for the operation of the state banking department, which is now part of the Department of Financial Institutions, and specifying that some of its employees are not to be in the civil service. *State ex rel. Bergh v. Sparling* (1906). Although this section authorizes regulation of banking, it does not authorize prohibition of it masking as regulation. Requiring all banks to be either national, state, mutual savings, or trust company banks is permissible regulation. *Weed v. Bergh* (1910). The authority to regulate banking extends to banking activities, including receiving deposits, paying checks, and making loans, even when a company, the primary business of which is not banking, carries on those activities. *MacLaren v. State* (1910).

Article XII

Amendments

Section 1
Constitutional amendments.

Any amendment or amendments to this constitution may be proposed in either house of the legislature, and if the same shall be agreed to by a majority of the members elected to each of the two houses, such proposed amendment or amendments shall be entered on their journals, with the yeas and nays taken thereon, and referred to the legislature to be chosen at the next general election, and shall be published for three months previous to the time of holding such election; and if, in the legislature so next chosen, such proposed amendment or amendments shall be agreed to by a majority of all the members elected to each house, then it shall be the duty of the legislature to submit such proposed amendment or amendments to the people in such manner and at such time as the legislature shall prescribe; and if the people shall approve and ratify such amendment or amendments by a majority of the electors voting thereon, such amendment or amendments shall become part of the constitution; provided, that if more than one amendment be submitted, they shall be submitted in such manner that the people may vote for or against such amendments separately.

This section has not been amended, but it has been litigated. Because it states that only the legislature, not the governor, plays a role in the first two steps in amending the constitution, the legislature takes these steps by joint resolutions, which do not require the governor's approval, rather than by bills, which must be presented to the governor under Article V, Section 10. Requiring publication of proposed constitutional amendments for three months (the practice is to pub-lish them once a month for three months) before a general election allows voters to ask candidates whether they would support the proposed amendment. That requirement applies even if the proposed amendment is to be considered by the voters at a spring election rather than at a general (November of even-numbered years) election. This section contains two kinds of requirements that have been the subject of litigation: those related to the legislature's procedures and those related to the submission of the question to the electors for a vote on ratification. Courts have invalidated two constitutional amendments because of deviations from the directions on legislative procedure and one amendment because of deviations from the directions on submission to the electors.

Courts have varied in the degree of rigor with which they have enforced the directions that this section gives to the legislature. Although the part of this sec-tion that describes the procedures for "first consideration" refers to entering the proposed amendment on "their" journals, which suggests that entries must be made on the journals of both houses, the court held that accurately referring to the joint resolution by number and title, thus notifying the members of the other house about the matter on which they were voting, sufficed. *State ex rel. Postel v. Marcus* (1915). However, in the same term, the supreme court held that failure to enter a joint resolution on the journals is grounds for invalidating a constitu-tional amendment. *State ex rel. Owen v. Donald* (1915). There, misleading legis-lative journal entries made it impossible for anyone, including legislators, merely by reading those journals, to determine the phrasing of the joint resolution upon which the legislature voted. That result made the violation of the required pro-cedure more serious than the violation at issue in *Postel*. A few years later the court refused to allow considerably more flexibility; in *State ex rel. Bentley v. Hall* (1922), the legislature had inadvertently neglected to vote on a proposed con-stitutional amendment, although it had filed the amendment with the secretary of state preparatory to a referendum. The court would not accept that procedure in lieu of a vote.

Similarly, the court has allowed some flexibility about submission of proposed constitutional amendments to the electors but has drawn a line beyond which it will not go. This section does not require an explanation of the proposed amend-ment to be published. One court held that an inaccurate summary did not in-validate an amendment. *State ex rel. Thomson v. Peoples State Bank* (1955), but another disagreed, *State ex rel. Thomson v. Zimmerman* (1953). However, the sec-tion does require allowing the electors to vote separately on separate proposed amendments. Requiring separate votes on each detail of a proposed amendment would make it difficult for voters to understand the issues and would occasion-ally result in incomplete or incoherent amendments. Accordingly, allowing some flexibility regarding that requirement makes sense.

The court in *The State ex rel. Hudd v. Timme, Secretary of State* (1882) rejected the plaintiff's argument that a proposed amendment that would result in biennial legislatures consisted of four changes to the constitution that should have been submitted separately to the voters. Three of the allegedly separate changes intertwined, but the fourth increased legislators' salaries. Arguably, that was a separate issue, but the court held that the increase reflected the added duties that the rest of the proposed amendment created and that the proposed amendment therefore was unitary. Much later the court approved a proposed amendment that combined several changes to the constitution. One authorized conditional release of persons who had been charged with a crime, and another allowed legislation that would authorize courts to detain, within certain time limits, persons who are accused of certain crimes. *Milwaukee Alliance v. Elections Board* (1982). The court held the first issue subsumed the second. In contrast, an earlier court had invalidated a constitutional amendment because only one question was submitted to the electors but it included separate issues: redrawing state senate districts on the basis of both area and population, allowing untaxed Indians and persons in military service to be counted in calculating the population of legislative districts and changing the requirement that legislative districts be bounded by county, precinct, town, or ward lines to a requirement that they be bounded by town, village, or ward lines. *State ex rel. Thomson v. Zimmerman.*

A constitutional amendment submitted to the people may state its effective date. If it does not, this section authorizes the legislature to establish the general effective date for amendments. In 1955, the legislature set the effective date of amendments as the date the board of canvassers certifies the election results. *State v. Gonzales* (2002).

In 2006, the people added Article XIII, Section 13 to the constitution, consisting of two sentences: "Only a marriage between one man and one woman shall be valid or recognized as a marriage in this state. A legal status identical or substantially similar to that of marriage for unmarried individuals shall not be valid or recognized in this state." This language was challenged as comprising two separate amendments. However, the court held that the two sentences both relate to marriage and tend to further the same purpose, of preserving the status of marriage as between only one man and one woman, and therefore constitute just one amendment. *McConkey v. Van Hollen* (2010). A federal court later held the new section violated the Fourteenth Amendment of the U.S. Constitution, and was therefore void. *Wolf v. Walker* (2014).

Section 2
Constitutional conventions.

If at any time a majority of the senate and assembly shall deem it necessary to call a convention to revise or change this constitution, they shall recommend to the electors to vote for or against a convention at the next election for members of the legislature. And if it shall appear that a majority of the electors voting thereon have voted for a convention, the legislature shall, at its next session, provide for calling such convention.

This section has not been amended or litigated, and no constitutional convention has met since the one that drafted the 1848 constitution—Wisconsin still has its original constitution, although that document has of course been amended. In 1950, the state attorney general and a colleague wrote a law review article advocating that a convention be called and pointing out several changes that they thought should be made to the constitution.[1] They thought that so many changes were needed that piecemeal amendments would not work.

This article contains the two exclusive mechanisms for amending the constitution. The legislature cannot amend the constitution by passing a bill. *State ex rel. Ozanne v. Fitzgerald* (2011).

---

[1] Thomas E. Fairchild and Charles P. Seibold. "Constitutional Revision in Wisconsin," *Wisconsin Law Review* (1950): 201.

Article XIII

Miscellaneous Provisions

Section 1
Political year; elections.

The political year for this state shall commence on the first Monday of January in each year, and the general election shall be held on the Tuesday next succeeding the first Monday of November in even-numbered years.

This section's original version required annual general elections. An 1884 amendment made elections biennial and stated rules for a transition to the new system. A 1986 amendment removed the transitional material. The beginning of the political year marks the time when successful candidates first have the right to take office and the time by which the procedures that are needed to certify the winning candidates, such as canvassing the votes, recounting the votes and appealing the results, must be completed. *State ex rel. Husting v. Board of State Canvassers* (1914).

Section 3
Eligibility to office.

(1) No member of congress and no person holding any office of profit or trust under the United States except postmaster, or under any foreign power, shall be eligible to any office of trust, profit or honor is this state.

(2) No person convicted of a felony, in any court within the United States, no person convicted in federal court of a crime designated, at the time of commission, under federal law as a misdemeanor involving a violation of public trust and no person convicted, in a court of a state, of a crime designated, at the time of commission, under the law of the state as a misdemeanor involving a violation of public trust shall be eligible to any office of trust, profit or honor in this state unless pardoned of the conviction.

(3) No person may seek to have placed on any ballot for a state or local elective office in this state the name of a person convicted of a felony, in any court within the United States, the name of a person convicted in federal court of a crime designated, at the time of commission, under federal law as a misdemeanor involving a violation of public trust or the name of a person convicted, in a court of a state, of a crime designated, at the time of commission, under the law of the state as a misdemeanor involving a violation of public trust, unless the person named for the ballot has been pardoned of the conviction.

This section was amended in 1996. Its original version forbade federal officers, persons who had been convicted of "infamous crimes" and persons who were defaulters from holding office in the state. The changes made irrelevant a few cases in which the meaning of "infamous crimes" and "defaulter" were at issue. Article VII, Section 10 prohibits judges from holding nonjudicial offices.

Courts have stated this section's purposes in two ways. One view is that it is designed to protect the state's sovereignty, which fits well with the court's definition of "office": "[a]n office is where, for the time being, a portion of the sovereignty, legislative, executive or judicial, attaches, to be exercised for the public benefit," and its statement that an office means a public office. *Martin v. Smith* (1941). The other view is that the section's purposes are to preserve confidence in government, to prevent dishonesty involving the public resources, and to prevent use of public office for private gain. *Wis. Law Enforce. Stds. Bd. v. Lyndon Station Vil.* (1980, 1981). This view fits with the part of the section that was deleted by the 1996 amendment and that prohibited defaulters from holding office and with both the original and the current statements that certain kinds of criminals may not hold office.

The 1996 amendment shifted the focus of subsection (2) from "infamous crime" to "crime . . . involving a violation of public trust." In a case decided after the 1996 amendment, the court of appeals held that the amendment is not punitive but is intended to maintain confidence in public officers and, therefore, the amendment is not an ex post facto law. *Swan v. Lafollette* (1999).

For purposes of this section, the following individuals are officers: county court commissioners, *State ex rel. Hazelton v. Turner* (1918); town treasurers, *State ex rel. Shea v. Evenson* (1915); circuit court judges, *In Matter of Complaint Against Raineri* (1981); municipal police chiefs, *Wis. Law Enforce. Stds. Bd.*; and county judges, *Becker v. Green County* (1922). However, the president of the University of Wisconsin is not an officer; although the president has substantial authority, that authority is subject to the will of the Board of Regents, which makes policy decisions for the university. *Martin v. Smith* (1941).

Section 4
Great seal.

It shall be the duty of the legislature to provide a great seal for the state, which shall be kept by the secretary of state, and all official acts of the governor, his approbation of the laws excepted, shall be thereby authenticated.

This section has not been amended or litigated. A statute, Wis. Stat. § 14.38(2), directs the secretary of state to affix the great seal to all the governor's official acts except the approbation of the laws, and to keep all enrolled bills and publish notice of them.

Section 6
Legislative officers.

The elective officers of the legislature, other than the presiding officers, shall be a chief clerk and a sergeant at arms, to be elected by each house.

This section has not been amended or litigated.

Section 7
Division of counties.

No county with an area of nine hundred square miles or less shall be divided or have any part stricken therefrom, without submitting the question to a vote of the people of the county, nor unless a majority of all the legal voters of the county voting on the question shall vote for the same.

This section has not been amended. As one would expect, all the cases concerning it date from the early decades of statehood. In determining the area of a county for this section, bodies of water that lie within the county's borders are included. *State of Wisconsin v. Larrabee* (1853). For that determination, the U.S. government survey is presumed to be correct, but it may be rebutted. *Attorney General ex rel. Brayton and Waldo v. Merriman* (1859). If a law is enacted that adds enough land to a small county to make its area more than 900 square miles and another law is enacted later (three days later) that detaches land from that county, the question of detachment need not be submitted to the voters because at the time of the detachment the county had more than 900 square miles. *The State ex rel. Haswell v. Cram* (1863). Slight irregularities in the question submitted to the voters (for example, asking whether the act detaching the land should be effective, not whether the land should be detached) do not invalidate the vote. *State ex rel. Spaulding v. Elwood* (1860).

Section 8
Removal of county seats.

No county seat shall be removed until the point to which it is proposed to be removed shall be fixed by law, and a majority of the voters of the county voting on the question shall have voted in favor of its removal to such point.

This section has not been amended. Although it appears to be straightforward, it has generated some bizarre opinions. In *The State ex rel. Lord v. Board of Supervisors of Washington County* (1850), a sensible literal reading of the section led to a strange result. A law established a county seat for five years but did not specify that seat's location after that period expired. The court held that, if a new seat was not fixed by the end of that period, the county seat would be nowhere. Consider as well the decision in *County Seat of La Fayette County ex rel. James H. Knowlton* (1850):

> This is a most extraordinary proceeding, and one which, in my opinion, we ought never to have entertained. The question, in the shape in which it has been presented, is not properly before us, and even if it were, it does not appear to me to be a case of which this court has original jurisdiction. The legislature having, however, in its wisdom, sent the matter to us, and we (whether as judges, commissioners, or arbitrators, it would be difficult to determine) having consented to entertain it, the parties interested are entitled to a decision, or, at least, to an expression of opinion from us.

It is also strange that in some cases this section ought to have been, but was not, an issue. In three cases, stretching over ninety years, the court decided cases about a statute that provided that if 40 percent of the voters in a county petitioned the county board for an election about whether to remove a county seat the board had to call such an election. *La Londe v. The Board of Supervisors of Barron County and others* (1891); *State ex rel. Hawley v. Board of Sup'rs of Polk County and another* (1894); *McNally v. Tollander* (1981). None of the parties argued that the statute at issue violated this section.

Other cases on this section are more ordinary, although two of them leave some confusion. Counties that do not have seats, because of a division of a county under Article XIII, Section 7, may be fixed by law, without voter approval, because a seat is being created, not removed. *Attorney General ex rel. Turner v. Fitzpatrick* (1853). The law by which the seat is fixed must be procedurally correct; for example, it must be published in the proper manner. *State ex rel. Cothren v. Lean* (1859). The act authorizing the referendum may include contingencies, such as the new county seat providing money to the county for buildings, in addition to a positive vote. *State ex rel. Park v. Portage County Sup'rs* (1869). The statutory procedures for voting on the removal may include certain conditions that voters must fulfill, such as answering questions about their residence, in addition to the ones under Article III, Section 1. *Cothren*. However, such procedures may not add residency requirements beyond those in Article II, Section 1. *State v. Williams* (1856). The last two cases cited do not, together, draw a clear boundary between acceptable additions and unacceptable additions.

Section 9
Election or appointment of statutory officers.

All county officers whose election or appointment is not provided for by this constitution shall be elected by the electors of the respective counties, or appointed by the boards of supervisors, or other county authorities, as the legislature shall direct. All city, town and village officers whose election or appointment is not provided for by this constitution shall be elected by the electors of such cities, towns and villages, or of some division thereof, or appointed by such authorities thereof as the legislature shall designate for that purpose. All other officers whose election or appointment is not provided for by this constitution, and all officers whose offices may hereafter be created by law, shall be elected by the people or appointed, as the legislature may direct.

This section has not been amended. The reference to city, village, and town officers whose election or appointment is not provided for by the constitution is now misleading. Article VII, Section 23 provided for the election of justices of the peace for cities (except first-class cities—i.e., Milwaukee), villages, and towns. After it was repealed, the appointment or election of city, town, or village officials was not provided for in the constitution. Article VI, Section 4 refers to the election of certain county officials.

The threshold issue under this section is identifying the officers to whom it applies. Several tests have been proposed. One is whether an officer holds a municipal office, whether the office existed at the time the constitution was ratified and whether the office is essential to the municipality's existence or efficiency (presumably, "municipality" in this instance includes county). *Income Tax Cases* (1912). Another test is whether the office existed at the time the constitution was ratified, because the framers of the constitution "intended that all local officers, according to the then known schemes for local self-government, should be chosen by the people of the localities affected." *O'Connor v. City of Fond du Lac* (1901). A third test is whether the officers are "sheriffs, coroners, registers of deeds, and the like"; not minor officials. *State ex rel. Williams v. Samuelson* (1907). In fact, these tests amount to virtually the same thing. The county offices named in the third test existed at the time the constitution was ratified and, clearly, they are essential to the municipality's efficiency. Therefore, the tests can be combined, and allowance made for county officials, by defining "officer" in this section as the holder of a municipal or county office that existed at the time the constitution was ratified.

These tests have not always been applied, so it is useful to determine the scope of this section as it appears from the cases. Members of the board of school directors are officers, *State ex rel. Harley v. Lindemann* (1907)—a surprising result, not only because that office probably did not exist at the time the constitution was ratified, but because they are not county, city, village, or town officials. The city (Milwaukee) and the school district (the Milwaukee Public Schools) that were pertinent to this case have the same boundaries, so it is difficult to understand why this section applies to them. Members of a county board of administration, which also did not exist at ratification, are also "officials." *State ex rel. Langland v. Manegold* (1916). The Milwaukee City Attorney is an official because the job existed under the charter that the territorial government had issued to that city and therefore it existed at the time that the constitution was ratified. Persons who are not "officials" include temporary property tax assessors and temporary members of boards of review. *State ex rel. Hessey v. Daniels* (1910); local assessors of income, *Income Tax Cases* (1912); and persons who are appointed to review the equalization of values for the property tax, *State of Wisconsin ex rel. Brown County v. Myers, Judge, etc.* (1881).

The other important issue regarding this section is the scope of the legislature's authority to control the selection of local officials. The legislature may only direct that officials be elected or direct that they be appointed by an authority of the city, village, town, or county that they are to serve, and in the latter instance it may specify the appointing authority. *Cole v. The President and Trustees of the Village of Black River Falls* (1883). The legislature may not appoint local city, village, town, or county officials. It may, however, delegate to a municipality or county the choice of whether an official is to be elected or appointed. *Thompson v. Whitefish Bay* (1950). The legislature may not in effect appoint a municipal or county official by extending the office's term or by setting a term of office so that the incumbent remains in office. *State ex rel. Dithmar v. Bunnell* (1907).

The courts have also resolved several minor issues related to this section. The "electors" to whom the section refers are residents qualified to be electors under Article III, so the legislature may not impose additional qualifications for voting in municipal and county elections. *The State ex rel. Cornish v. Tuttle* (1881). A statute allowing leaves of absence may not be read to allow leaves to be granted after an official abandons a position so that, by having gone on leave, the person preserves his or her civil service status; such an interpretation would allow the person who grants the leave of absence in effect to make an appointment and thus to violate this section. *Becker v. Spieker* (1954). A county board's appointment of a county assessor is not an appointment of a municipal official even though the assessor will operate throughout the county and replace the local assessors. *Thompson v. Kenosha County* (1974). The power to appoint under this section is important for another reason: if an official has been appointed for an indefinite term and no statute provides for the removal of officials from that office, the person or group that appointed him or her has the power, as an incident of the power to appoint, to remove that official. *State ex rel. Wagner v. Dahl* (1909).

Section 10
Vacancies in office.

(1) The legislature may declare the cases in which any office shall be deemed vacant, and also the manner of filling the vacancy, where no provision is made for that purpose in this constitution.

(2) Whenever there is a vacancy in the office of lieutenant governor, the governor shall nominate a successor to serve for the balance of the unexpired term, who shall take office after confirmation by the senate and by the assembly.

This section originally consisted of the current subsection (1). In 1937 the lieutenant governor resigned, and the governor appointed someone else to the position. At the time, the legislature, in a very general way, had specified the method of filling that position in the event of a vacancy: a statute specified that if no other provision was made for filling a vacancy in a state office, the governor must appoint someone to it. Based upon that statute, the court held the appointment did not violate this section. *State ex rel. Martin v. Ekern* (1938). Almost forty years later, in 1979, the second subsection was added, validating the act that was the subject of that litigation and codifying the court's decision.

Section 11
Passes, franks and privileges.

No person, association, copartnership, or corporation, shall promise, offer or give, for any purpose, to any political committee, or any member or employee thereof, to any candidate for, or incumbent of any office or position under the constitution or laws, or under any ordinance of any town or municipality, of this state, or to any person at the request or for the advantage of all or any of them, any free pass or frank, or any privilege withheld from any person, for the traveling accommodation or transportation of any person or property, or the transmission of any message or communication.

No political committee, and no member or employee thereof, no candidate for and no incumbent of any office or position under the constitution or laws, or under any ordinance of any town or municipality of this state, shall ask for, or accept, from any person, association, copartnership, or corporation, or use, in any manner, or for any purpose, any free pass or frank, or any privilege withheld from any person, for the traveling accommodation or transportation of any person or property, or the transmission of any message or communication.

Any violation of any of the above provisions shall be bribery and punished as provided by law, and if any officer or any member of the legislature be guilty thereof, his office shall become vacant.

No person within the purview of this act shall be privileged from testifying in relation to anything therein prohibited; and no person having so testified shall be liable to any prosecution or punishment for any offense concerning which he was required to give his testimony or produce any documentary evidence.

Notaries public and regular employees of a railroad or other public utilities who are candidates for or hold public offices for which the annual compensation is not more than three hundred dollars to whom no passes or privileges are extended beyond those which are extended to other regular employees of such corporations are excepted from the provisions of this section.

This section was adopted in 1902. One would expect Robert M. La Follette, because of his desire to reduce the power and influence of railroads, to have initiated it. However, the first joint resolution on the section was passed during the tenure of La Follette's predecessor, Edward Scofield, although La Follette was probably pleased to support it in its second consideration and the vote on its ratification. The original version included an exemption for the railroad commissioner and deputy commissioner in the exercise of their duties. The section was amended in 1936 to remove that exemption and to add the exemption in the last paragraph. Because the section's purpose is to forbid businesses, especially railroads, from trading favors for influence, it does not prevent a county from providing free parking to its employees. *Dane County v. McManus* (1972).

Section 12
Recall of elective officers.

The qualified electors of the state, of any congressional, judicial or legislative district or of any county may petition for the recall of any incumbent elective officer after the first year of the term for which the incumbent was elected, by filing a petition with the filing officer with whom the nomination petition to the office in the primary is filed, demanding the recall of the incumbent.

(1) The recall petition shall be signed by electors equalling at least twenty-five percent of the vote cast for the office of governor at the last preceding election, in the state, county or district which the incumbent represents.

(2) The filing officer with whom the recall petition is filed shall call a recall election for the Tuesday of the 6th week after the date of filing the petition or, if that Tuesday is a legal holiday, on the first day after that Tuesday which is not a legal holiday.

(3) The incumbent shall continue to perform the duties of the office until the recall election results are officially declared.

(4) Unless the incumbent declines within 10 days after the filing of the petition, the incumbent shall without filing be deemed to have filed for the recall election. Other candidates may file for the office in the manner provided by law for special elections. For the purpose of conducting elections under this section:

(a) When more than 2 persons compete for a nonpartisan office, a recall primary shall be held. The 2 persons receiving the highest number of votes in the recall primary shall be the 2 candidates in the recall election, except that if any candidate receives a majority of the total number of votes cast in the recall primary, that candidate shall assume the office for the remainder of the term and a recall election shall not be held.

(b) For any partisan office, a recall primary shall be held for each political party which is by law entitled to a separate ballot and from which more than one candidate competes for the party's nomination in the recall election. The person receiving the highest number of votes in the recall primary for each political party shall be that party's candidate in the recall election. Independent candidates and candidates representing political parties not entitled by law to a separate ballot shall be shown on the ballot for the recall election only.

(c) When a recall primary is required, the date specified under sub. (2) shall be the date of the recall primary and the recall election shall be held on the Tuesday of the 4th week after the recall primary or, if that Tuesday is a legal holiday, on the first day after that Tuesday which is not a legal holiday.

(5) The person who receives the highest number of votes in the recall election shall be elected for the remainder of the term.

(6) After one such petition and recall election, no further recall petition shall be filed against the same officer in the term for which he was elected.

(7) This section shall be self-executing and mandatory. Laws may be enacted to facilitate its operation but no law shall be enacted to hamper, restrict or impair the right of recall.

This section was adopted in 1926. Subsection (7) makes it explicitly self-executing, which ensured that the legislature, in case its members would prefer not to provide for recall elections (including those applying to themselves) could not prevent it from taking effect. Its purpose is to allow the voters immediate recourse, rather than waiting to the next scheduled election, if they believe that they must remove one of their representatives. The first version required that, if the official who was the subject of the recall wished to prevent his or her name from appearing on the ballot, he or she must resign; whereas, the current version, ratified in 1981, requires only that the official decline to run. The original version also required an election to be held between forty and forty-five days after the filing of the petition and did not provide for a primary. This section does not authorize the recall of city, village, or town officials, although a statute, Wis. Stat. § 9.10, does so. Article IV, Section 8 authorizes the expulsion of legislators; Article VI, Section 4(4) authorizes the governor to remove county officers; Article VII, Section 1 authorizes the impeachment of all civil offices; Article VII, Section 11 authorizes the removal of judges and justices; and Article VII, Section 13 authorizes the removal of justices and judges. This article has been mentioned in a few decisions, but none is directly relevant to this section.

Section 13
Marriage.

Only a marriage between one man and one woman shall be valid or recognized as a marriage in this state. A legal status identical or substantially similar to that of marriage for unmarried individuals shall not be valid or recognized in this state.

The people adopted Section 13, the "marriage" amendment, in 2006. This section was held to violate the Due Process and Equal Protection Clauses of the Fourteenth Amendment of the U.S. Constitution. *Wolf v. Walker* (2014).

Article XIV

Schedule

Section 1
Effect of change from territory to state.

That no inconvenience may arise by reason of a change from a territorial to a permanent state government, it is declared that all rights, actions, prosecutions, judgments, claims and contracts, as well of individuals as of bodies corporate, shall continue as if no such change had taken place; and all process which may be issued under the authority of the territory of Wisconsin previous to its admission into the union of the United States shall be as valid as if issued in the name of the state.

This section facilitated Wisconsin's transition from territory to state; it has not been amended. In this section "process" means a way for a court to acquire or assert its jurisdiction. The most common kind of process is one by which a court compels a defendant to appear before it. Only one case bears directly on this section. A builder had entered a contract with the territory for work on the capitol but had not been paid. The territorial legislature approved the claim and made partial payment, but the new state government refused to pay the remaining debt. The court in *Baxter v. The State* (1859) held that, under this section, valid claims against the territory must be paid by the state.

Section 2
Territorial laws continued.

All laws now in force in the territory of Wisconsin which are not repugnant to this constitution shall remain in force until they expire by their own limitation or be altered or repealed by the legislature.

This is another transitional section that has not been amended. The court addressed it in *State ex rel. Dunning v. Giles* (1849). Under territorial law, sheriffs could not serve two consecutive terms. One of them, who had been elected when Wisconsin was a territory, received the highest number of votes in the first election after Wisconsin achieved statehood. However, citing this section, the candidate who received the second highest number of votes asked for a writ of mandamus to ensure that he received a certificate of election. The court refused, claiming that the territorial law did not remain in force because it was repugnant to the state constitution: keeping the law in effect would deprive the sheriffs who were in office at the transition from territory to state of right that everyone else in the state enjoyed.

Section 13
Common law continued in force.

Such parts of the common law as are now in force in the territory of Wisconsin, not inconsistent with this constitution, shall be and continue part of the law of this state until altered or suspended by the legislature.

This section has not been amended. Because its key term, common law, is ambiguous and because even if its meaning regarding a detail is clear, it might not be clear whether the legislature has altered or suspended that part of the common law, one would expect some litigation on this section. That expectation has been fulfilled.

In general, the common law is a body of law that developed in England. At one time England had several different courts: the King's Bench, Courts of Equity, and so forth. Moreover, courts in different parts of the country acted with considerable independence, following local precedents. Gradually, courts began to develop a body of precedents that became accepted throughout the country. That courts, rather than Parliament, accomplished this uniformity has led to another use of the term common law: to refer to judge-made law as opposed to statutory law. Some Englishmen considered this development to be a salutary departure from the chaos and potential for tyranny that a welter of virtually independent courts created. Others considered this development to be a tyrannical centralization of power. In any event, the system continued to grow until it supplied a considerable amount of English law, and the colonists brought it to this country. English common law was part of the law of the Wisconsin Territory.

Two motives probably induced the framers of the constitution to include this provision. One is that the state, when it entered the union, had very little law: no state legislature had met to consider bills, although there had been a territorial legislature. Accordingly, adopting the common law gave the new state a body of law. Second, residents of the territory had relied upon the common law, so maintaining it created some degree of certainty about the law, which is a virtue for a legal system. As litigation concerning this section began to occur, however, the section's meaning and effect became less certain.

Although one would expect general agreement on the content of the common law, litigants have argued about whether certain elements of the law belonged to it. The court even held that English statutes, if they were intimately enough related to judge-made law, were included. *Coburn v. Harvey and another* (1864). In a later case, the court held that customs, usages, and legal maxims and principles were part of the common law. *Menne v. City of Fond du Lac* (1956). In contrast, common-law pleading and practice are not part of the common law for this section. *Caveney v. Caveney* (1940), a fortunate exclusion, given that the common-law violations of the elaborate rules about pleadings often spelled defeat for the party who had the better case on the merits.

Because the section explicitly refers to "such parts of the common law as are now in force in the territory of Wisconsin," one would not expect the cutoff date to be an issue. Frequently courts have read that statement literally and looked at the common law as it existed at the time of ratification. *Huber v. Merkel* (1903); *Metropolitan Casualty Insurance Co. v. Clark* (1911); *Schwanke v. Garlt* (1935); *Menne*. However, another line of cases sets the cutoff at the Revolutionary War. *Coburn v. Harvey and another* (1864); *In re Budd's Estate* (1960); *Davison v. St. Paul Fire and Marine Ins. Co.* (1976). In the first of that latter line of cases, the court ignored the section's phrasing and based its decision upon cases from other jurisdictions.

Although the section also clearly authorizes only the legislature to modify common-law rules, the court has ascribed that power to itself. Some examples occurred in tort cases, *Bielski v. Schulze* (1962), *Dippel v. Sciano* (1967), *Moran v. Quality Aluminum Casting Co.* (1967); and in a probate case, *Will of Wehr* (1945). The doctrine of assumption of risk, a common-law principle, is no longer valid, although the cases in which it was invalidated did not allude to this section. *McConville v. State Farm Mut. Auto Ins. Co.* (1962); *Colson v. Rule* (1962); *State v. Picotte* (2003).

One particular case, *Holytz v. Milwaukee* (1962), bears analysis because it exemplifies the court's attitude toward the limits that this section places on it and because of its consequences for municipal finance. The common law included a grant to local units of government of immunity from liability. This rule originated in the concept of the divine right of kings, and it somehow became applicable to local units of government. The court in *Holytz* presented a capsule history of the principle in English common law and in the law of this country, as well as indicating some cases in which Wisconsin courts had made exceptions to the general rule. The court, citing a number of commentators and judges, stated that the principle no longer made sense. It also held that, despite the wording of Article XIV, Section 13, the court had the power to alter this common-law principle because it had judicial origins (an argument that might be applied to all common-law principles). It then abrogated the doctrine, effective forty days after the decision, except that the abrogation also applied to the case being decided. The delay allowed time for local units of government to obtain additional insurance. When the court changes the common law but does not apply the change to the case under consideration, it sometimes refers to this as "sunbursting," in reference to the U.S. Supreme Court's decision in *Great Northern Railway Company v. Sunburst Oil & Refining Company* (1932).

At the time that the constitution was adopted, the common law in Wisconsin included the M'Naghten Rules—the standards by which a jury should evaluate a defendant's plea of not guilty by reason of insanity. In a murder case in 1961, the circuit court gave a jury instruction on insanity less rigorous than the common-law rule, and the jury found for the defendant. The state appealed, arguing that the constitution, having adopted the common law, prohibits the courts from changing it. The court rejected that argument, holding that courts' judicial powers includes the power to develop the common law. *State v. Esser* (1962).

The common law, although disappearing slowly, lives on. In a relatively recent obstruction of justice case, where the defendant had changed his name and told a police detective his new name, in effect misleading the detective, the court held he was entitled to a jury instruction that he had the common-law right to change his name through consistent and continuous use as long as he had not done so for a fraudulent purpose. Apparently the court found that he had not intentionally misled the detective. *State v. Hansford* (1998).

The legislature may discontinue causes of action and remedies that were available at common law. *Guzman v. St. Francis Hosp. Inc.* (2000). Recent examples of abrogation of the common law have centered on updating the criminal law. In a case involving an illegal arrest where the defendant fought with three police officers, the court prospectively abrogated the common-law right to resist an *illegal* arrest on public policy grounds, stating that the common-law right endangered the police and citing improvements in the circumstances surrounding arrests and detention. *State v. Hobson* (1998).

In a 2003 case, *State v. Picotte* (2003), the supreme court prospectively overruled the common-law "year and a day rule." Under the common law, a person could only be prosecuted for homicide if the victim died within one year and one day of the act causing the injury. In this case, the defendant struck the victim against a brick wall, causing him to fall into a coma. Two years later, the victim died. Meanwhile, the defendant pleaded guilty to assault and was serving a fifteen-year prison term. When the victim died, the state began a prosecution for murder. The court held that the common-law doctrine was obsolete because, unlike in ancient times, medical science had advanced to the point that a cause of death can be established, even if the death occurs years after the injury. The court gave two other reasons why the common-law rule should no longer apply: expert testimony is now allowed, so juries do not have to rely solely on their own medical theories, and the death penalty is outlawed in Wisconsin. In this case, the court made the abrogation prospective only.

Section 16
Implementing revised structure of judicial branch.

(4) The terms of office of justices of the supreme court serving on August 1, 1978, shall expire on the July 31 next preceding the first Monday in January on which such terms would otherwise have expired, but such advancement of the date of term expiration shall not impair any retirement rights vested in any such justice if the term had expired on the first Monday in January.

The original version of this section, which was adopted in 1977 to implement the reorganization of the state courts, had five subsections. A 1982 amendment deleted the other four. Supreme court justices have ten-year terms, so, at least in 1982, the reference to their tenure was still relevant. The portion of this section about retirement rights continues to be relevant. This section has not been litigated.

■ BIBLIOGRAPHICAL ESSAY

I. TEXTS OF THE CONSTITUTION

The *Wisconsin Statutes*, published biennially, contain the current version of the constitution. This is the most easily obtainable version of the constitution as it now exists.

Two volumes of West Publishing Company's *Wisconsin Statutes Annotated* are devoted to the constitution. Because the hardbound copy of that book is rarely updated, one needs to merge the text of the constitution printed there and the changes to the text printed in the soft-bound supplement to recreate the current text. Its annotations extend back much further in time than do those in the *Wisconsin Statutes*. One needs to use those annotations skeptically, because some of the summaries of cases are inaccurate, a few relevant cases are missing, some cases that purportedly are on particular sections of the constitution actually are not, and a few of the citations are inaccurate.

The State of Wisconsin Blue Book, also published biennially, contains a chronological list of the amendments that were submitted to the voters for ratification, which includes the numbers of the article and section, the subject matter of the amendment, the year and number of each joint resolution, the month and year of the ratification vote, and the results of the vote.

II. HISTORIES OF WISCONSIN

Because the constitution does not exist in a vacuum but interrelates with the history of the state, a serious student of the document should know something of Wisconsin history. Wisconsin is blessed with several first-rate histories. Robert C. Nesbit's *Wisconsin: A History* (Madison: University of Wisconsin Press, 1973, updated by William F. Thompson, 1989) is a lively but scholarly one-volume account. Annotated (often witty) bibliographies follow each chapter. Nesbit describes the two constitutional conventions and occasionally refers to the constitution. The State Historical Society of Wisconsin has published a six-volume history of Wisconsin. Each volume is long, scholarly, and well done. The first volume includes an account of the two constitutional conventions that is longer than Nesbit's. The six volumes are Alice E. Smith, *From Exploration to Statehood* (1973); Richard N. Current, *The Civil War Era, 1848–1873* (1976); Robert C. Nesbit, *Urbanization and Industrialization, 1873–1893* (1985); Paul Glad, *War, A New Era and Depression, 1914–1940* (1990); William F. Thompson, *C ontinuity and Change, 1940–1965* (1988); and John D. Buenker, *The Progressive Era, 1893–1914* (1998).

Other interesting books include: Frederic C. Howe, *Wisconsin: An Experiment in Democracy* (New York: Charles Scribner's Sons, 1912), a nearly breathless account of the accomplishments of the 1911 legislative session; and Bethel Saler, *The Settler's Empire: Colonialism and State Formation in America's Old Northwest* (Philadelphia: University of Pennsylvania Press, 2015), a study in state-building that details the pre-statehood period and the various multicultural forces that influenced the Wisconsin constitutions of 1846 and 1848.

III. ACCOUNTS OF THE MAKING OF THE CONSTITUTION

Each of the constitutional conventions published a *Journal of the Convention to Form a Constitution for the State of Wisconsin* (Madison, 1847 and 1848). Milo M. Quaife edited three volumes on the state's constitution making: *The Conventi on of 1846* (Madison: State Historical Society of Wisconsin, 1919), *The Struggle over Ratification: 1846–1847* (Madison: State Historical Society of Wisconsin, 1920), and *The Attainment of Statehood* (Madison: State Historical Society of Wisconsin, 1920). In the first and third of those volumes he compiled summaries of the conventions' debates (except for the remarks of a few delegates who declined to have them published) and contemporary newspaper accounts. These are invaluable volumes for historians as well as for attorneys and judges who are looking for statements of intent about constitutional provisions. Ray A. Brown published two fine articles on the subject: "The Making of the Wisconsin Constitution: Part I," *Wisconsin Law Review* (1949): 648, and "The Making of the Wisconsin Constitution: Part II," *Wisconsin Law Review* (1952): 23.

IV. LEGAL HISTORIES AND BIOGRAPHIES

Alfons J. Beitzinger's *Edward G. Ryan: Lion of the Law* (Madison: State Historical Society of Wisconsin, 1960) is the most readable and interesting of the books on Wisconsin legal history. Because Ryan was a central figure in that history for many decades, Beitzinger's book is also an excellent beginning point for a general reader who wishes to study that topic.

Other books on Wisconsin legal history are specialized and many are aimed at an academic audience. Some of them are:

John R. Berryman, ed., *History of the Bench and Bar of Wisconsin* (Chicago: H. C. Cooper, Jr., 1898).
Stanley P. Caine, *The Myth of a Progressive Reform: Railroad Regulation in Wisconsin 1903–1910* (Madison: State Historical Society of Wisconsin, 1970).
James I. Clark, *Wisconsin Defies the Fugitive Slave Law: The Case of Sherman M. Booth* (Madison: State Historical Society of Wisconsin, 1955).

Gordon M. Haferbecker, *Wisconsin Labor Laws* (Madison: University of Wisconsin Press, 1958).

Robert S. Hunt, *Law and Locomotives: The Impact of the Railroad on Wisconsin Law in the Nineteenth Century* (Madison: State Historical Society of Wisconsin, 1958).

J. Willard Hurst, *Law and Economic Growth: The Legal History of the Lumber Industry in Wisconsin, 1836–1915* (Cambridge: Belknap Press of Harvard University, 1964).

Roujet Marshall, *Autobiography of Roujet D. Marshall: Justice of the Supreme Court of the State of Wisconsin 1895–1918*, 2 vols. (Madison, 1923, 1931).

Samuel Mermin, *Jurisprudence and Statecraft: The Wisconsin Development Authority and Its Implications* (Madison: University of Wisconsin Press, 1964).

Joseph A. Ranney, *Trusting Nothing to Providence: A History of Wisconsin's Legal System* (Madison: University of Wisconsin Law School, Continuing Education and Outreach, 1999).

Joseph A. Ranney, *Wisconsin and the Shaping of American Law* (Madison: University of Wisconsin Press, 2017).

Parker M. Reed, *The Bench and Bar of Wisconsin* (Milwaukee: P. M. Reed, 1882).

Erling D. Solberg, *New Laws for New Forests: Wisconsin's Forest-Fire, Tax, Zoning, and County Forest Laws in Operation* (Madison: University of Wisconsin Press, 1961).

John Bradley Winslow, *The Story of a Great Court* (Chicago: T. H. Flood and Company, 1912).

V. GENERAL TOPICS

BOOKS

As mentioned at the beginning of Part One of the book, the two phenomena that did the most to make Wisconsin politics and law unique are the Progressive movement and the Wisconsin Idea. Herbert F. Marguiles' *The Decline of the Progressive Movement in Wisconsin, 1899–1920* (Madison: State Historical Society of Wisconsin, 1968), Robert S. Maxwell's *La Follette and the Rise of the Progressives in Wisconsin* (Madison: State Historical Society of Wisconsin, 1956), and David B. Thelen's *The New Citizenship: Origins of Progressivism in Wisconsin 1885–1900* (Columbia: University of Missouri Press, 1971) and *Robert M. La Follette and the Insurgent Spirit* (Madison: University of Wisconsin Press, 1985) are solid, scholarly treatments of the Progressives. For a view from one perspective, that of the driving force of the movement, see Robert M. La Follette, *La Follette's Autobiography: A Personal Narrative of Political Experience* (Madison: University of Wisconsin Press, [1913] 1960). For a view from the opposite perspective, that of the conservative wing of the Republican Party, see Emanuel Philipp's *Political Reform in Wisconsin:*

A Historical Review of the Subjects of Primary Election, Taxation and Railroad Regulation (Madison: State Historical Society of Wisconsin, [1910] 1973 abridged). The only lengthy history of the Wisconsin Idea is Jack Stark's "The Wisconsin Idea: The University's Service to the State," *State of Wisconsin Blue Book, 1995–1996* (Madison: State of Wisconsin, 1995): 101–179.James K. Conant, *Wisconsin Politics and Government, America's Laboratory of Democracy* (Lincoln: University of Nebraska Press, 2006). Reviews the factors that made Wisconsin one of the foremost "laboratories of democracy" in the twentieth century.

Katherine J. Cramer, *The Politics of Resentment: Rural Consciousness in Wisconsin and the Rise of Scott Walker* (Chicago: The University of Chicago Press, 2016). Clearly demonstrates the rural resentment toward Wisconsin's metropolitan areas and state government generally that is a major factor in Wisconsin's ideological divide.

Mark W. Denniston, *Dialog Among State Supreme Courts: Advancing State Constitutionalism* (El Paso: LFB Scholarly Publishing, 2014). The Wisconsin Supreme Court traditionally gets high ratings as a "prestigious" state court— it's generally rated in the top ten. This is an interesting statistical study of the degree to which other states' courts cite to and rely upon each others' holdings in state constitutional cases. The research for this book ended in 2012 so it does not address the more recent changes in Wisconsin politics.

G. Alan Tarr, *Understanding State Constitutions* (Princeton: Princeton University Press, 1998). Explores the historical and political importance of state constitutions.

Robert F. Williams, *The Law of American State Constitutions* (New York: Oxford University Press, 2009). Provides a thorough national overview of state constitutional jurisprudence.

ARTICLES

Shirley S. Abrahamson, "State Constitutional Law, New Judicial Federalism, and the Rehnquist Court," 51 *Cleveland State Law Review* (2004): 339.

Lynn Adelman and Shelley Fite, "Exercising Judicial Power: A Response to the Wisconsin Supreme Court's Critics," 91 *Marquette Law Review* (2007): 425.

William J. Brennan, Jr., "State Constitutions and the Protection of Individual Rights," 90 *Harvard Law Review* (1977): 489.

Neal Devins, "How State Supreme Courts Take Consequences into Account: Toward a State-Centered Understanding of State Constitutionalism," 62 *Stanford Law Review* (2010): 1629. Examines the effects of future judicial elections and campaign contributions upon judicial decision-making.

Jack Stark, "Enigmatic Grants of Law-Making Rights and Responsibilities in the Wisconsin Constitution," 81 *Marquette Law Review* (1998): 961.

Jack Stark, "A History of the Internal Improvements Section of the Wisconsin Constitution," *Wisconsin Law Review* (1998): 829. Traces the history of the court's decisions modifying this section's effect.

Diane S. Sykes, "Reflections on the Wisconsin Supreme Court," 89 *Marquette Law Review* (2006): 723. This is the most prominent dissection of recent Wisconsin opinions that the conservatives disliked most.

G. Alan Tarr, "Models and Fashions in State Constitutionalism," *Wisconsin Law Review* (1998): 729.

Robert F. Williams, "Is the Wisconsin Constitution Obsolete?" 90 *Marquette Law Review* (2007): 425.

VI. PARTICULAR CONSTITUTIONAL ISSUES

BOOKS

Robert F. Williams, *The New Judicial Federalism* (New York: Oxford University Press, 2009). As the progressivism of the Warren Court faded and Burger Court ascended, reducing the civil liberties in the Bill of Rights, the idea of judicial federalism arose.

ARTICLES

Shirley S. Abrahamson, "Criminal Law and State Constitutions: The Emergence of State Constitutional Law," *Texas Law Review* 63 (1985): 1141–1183. [Preamble]

Robert M. Andalman, "Ineffective Assistance of Counsel Claims Under the Wisconsin Constitution," *Wisconsin Lawyer* 67, no. 2 (February 1994): 14–17, 55. [Art. I, § 7]

Rex R. Anderegg, "OWI Blood Draws: An Uncertain Road Ahead," 90 *Wisconsin Lawyer* Vol. 10, p. 22 (2017). [Art. I, § 11]

Jeanne Marie Armstrong, "*State v. Seibel*: Wisconsin Police Now Need Only a Reasonable Suspicion to Search a Suspect's Blood Incident to an Arrest," *Wisconsin Law Review* (1993): 523–561. [Art I, § 11]

William W. Boyer, Jr., "Public Transportation of Parochial School Pupils," *Wisconsin Law Review* (1952): 64–90. [Art. I, § 18]

Sam Brugger, "Municipal Corporations—Home Rule in Wisconsin," *Wisconsin Law Review* (1955): 145–153. [Art. XI, § 3]

Kenneth J. Bukowski, "'Inherent Power' of the Court—A New Direction?" *Wisconsin Bar Bulletin* 54 (1981): 22–26. [Art. VII]

John H. Burlingame, "Criminal Law—Search and Arrest Standards in Wisconsin—An Anomaly," *Wisconsin Law Review* (1963): 153–158. [Art. I, § 11]

Junaid H. Chida, "Rediscovering the Wisconsin Constitution: Presentation of Constitutional Questions in State Courts," *Wisconsin Law Review* (1983): 483–511. [Preamble, Art. I]

Arlen Christenson, "The State Attorney General," *Wisconsin Law Review* (1970): 298–340. [Art. VI, § 3]

Thomas K. Clancy et al., "Independent State Grounds: Should State Courts Depart from the Fourth Amendment in Construing Their Own Constitutions, and If So, on What Basis Beyond Simple Disagreement with the United States Supreme Court's Result?" 77 *Mississippi Law Journal* (2007): 1–464. Four state appellate judges and three law professors explore the independent state grounds concept. Primarily focused on search-and-seizure cases and explores the concept of "lock-stepping."

George R. Currie, "The Wisconsin Supreme Court and the Common Law Tradition," *Wisconsin Law Review* (1971): 818–831. [Art. XIV, § 13]

Richard W. Cutler, "Chaos or Uniformity in Boating Regulations? The State as Trustee of Navigable Waters," *Wisconsin Law Review* (1965): 311–321. [Art. IX, § 1]

William F. Eich, "A New Look at the Internal Improvements and Public Purpose Rules," *Wisconsin Law Review* (1970): 1113–1132. [Art. VIII, § 10]

"Eminent Domain—Compensation for Lost Rents," *Wisconsin Law Review* (1971): 657–665. [Art. I, § 13]

Douglass Charles Ellerbe Farnsley, "Gambling and the Law: The Wisconsin Experience, 1848–1980," *Wisconsin Law Review* (1980): 811–878. [Art. IV, § 24]

Lawrence Friedman, "Reconsidering Rational Basis: Equal Protection Review Under the Wisconsin Constitution," 38 *Rutgers Law Journal* (2007): 1071. [Art. I, § 1]

Alemante Gebre-Selassie, "Inverse Liability of the State of Wisconsin for a *De Facto* 'Temporary Taking' as a Result of An Erroneous Administrative Decision: *Zinn v. State*," *Wisconsin Law Review* (1984): 1431–1468. [Art. I, § 13]

Robert L. Gordon, "How Vast Is *King's* Realm: Constitutional Challenge to the Church-State Clause," *Wisconsin Lawyer* 68 (1995): 18–21, 65. [Art. I, § 18]

Marilyn Grant, "Judge Levi Hubbell: A Man Impeached," *Wisconsin Magazine of History* 64 (1980): 28–39. [Art. VII, § 1]

Arthur J. Harrington, "The 'Invisible Lien': Public Trust Doctrine Impact on Real Estate Development in Wisconsin," *Wisconsin Lawyer* 69 (1996): 10–12, 69–70. [Art. IX, § 1]

David M. Hecht and Frank L. Mallare, "Wisconsin Internal Improvements Prohibition: Obsolete in Modern Times?" *Wisconsin Law Review* (1961): 294–309. [Art. VIII, § 10]

Michael S. Kenitz, "Wisconsin's Caps on Noneconomic Damages in Medical Malpractice Cases: Where Wisconsin Stands (and Should Stand) on Tort Reform," 89 *Marquette Law Review* (2006): 601. [Art. I, § 1]

William J. Kiernan, "Wisconsin Municipal Indebtedness, Part I: The Power to Become Indebted and Its Limits," *Wisconsin Law Review* (1964): 173–251. [Art. XI, §3]

Bernard S. Kubale, "Wisconsin Municipal Indebtedness, Part II: Procedures for Issuance of General Obligation Bonds," *Wisconsin Law Review* (1964): 406–425. [Art. XI, § 3]

Erik LeRoy, "The Egalitarian Roots of the Education Article of the Wisconsin Constitution: Old History, New Interpretation, *Buse v. Smith* Criticized," *Wisconsin Law Review* (1981): 1325–1360. [Art. X]

Lena London, "Homestead Exemption in the Wisconsin Constitution," *Wisconsin Magazine of History* 32 (1948), 176–184. [Art. I, § 17]

Joel L. Massie, "Constitutional Law—Criminal Procedure—The Fourth Amendment and the Wisconsin Constitutional Provision Against Unreasonable Searches and Seizures: *State v. Starke*," *Marquette Law Review* 62 (1978): 622–630. [Art. I, § 11]

Lewis R. Mills, "The Public Purpose Doctrine in Wisconsin, Part I," *Wisconsin Law Review* (1957): 40–58.

Lewis R. Mills, "The Public Purpose Doctrine in Wisconsin, Part II," *Wisconsin Law Review* (1957): 282–308.

Glen E. Mundschau, "Wisconsin Lotteries—Are They Legal?" *Wisconsin Law Review* (1967): 556–566. [Art. IV, § 24]

Milton Orman, "The Constitutional Right of Wisconsin to Do Its Own Printing," *Wisconsin Law Review* (1951): 556–567. [Art. IV, § 25]

Daniel S. Schneider, "The Future of the Exclusionary Rule and the Development of State Constitutional Law," *Wisconsin Law Review* (1987): 377–402. [Art. I, § 11]

Claire Silverman, "Municipal Home Rule in Wisconsin," *The Municipality*, June 2016 pp. 16–19. [Art. XI, § 3]

Jack Stark, "The Authority to Tax in Wisconsin," *Marquette Law Review* 77 (1994): 457–473. [Art. VIII, § 1; Art. XI, § 3]

Jack Stark, "The Uniformity Clause of the Wisconsin Constitution," *Marquette Law Review* 76 (1993): 577–621. [Art. VIII, § 1]

John Sundquist, "Construction of the Wisconsin Constitution—Recurrence to Fundamental Principles," *Marquette Law Review* 62 (1979): 531–563. [Preamble; Art. I]

Joanne R. Whiting, "When Probable Cause Is Constitutionally Suspect: The Status of Pretext Arrests and Searches in Wisconsin," *Wisconsin Law Review* (1991): 345–374. [Art. I, § 11]

A

B

C

D

E

F

H

I

J

K

L

S

T

U

X

Z

■ INDEX

About the Authors

JACK STARK was Assistant Chief Counsel in the Legislative Reference Bureau for the State of Wisconsin. He is the author of numerous books, monographs, and articles, among which is "The Uniformity Clause of the Wisconsin Constitution" (*Marquette Law Review*), the only exhaustive study of that section of the Wisconsin constitution.

STEVE MILLER served as chief of the Wisconsin Legislative Reference Bureau and as general counsel for the Mississippi legislature's Performance Evaluation and Expenditure Review Committee.

Printed in the USA/Agawam, MA
August 9, 2019

709044.001